Human Ecology

PROBLEMS AND SOLUTIONS

A Series of Books in Biology

EDITORS: *Donald Kennedy*
Roderic B. Park

Human Ecology

PROBLEMS AND SOLUTIONS

Paul R. Ehrlich
Stanford University

Anne H. Ehrlich
Stanford University

John P. Holdren
California Institute of Technology

W. H. FREEMAN AND COMPANY / San Francisco

Cover Photograph: George Gerster, *Photofind-Rapho*

Printed in the United States of America
International Standard Book Number: 0–7167–0595–8

5   6   7   8   9

Library of Congress Cataloging in Publication Data

Ehrlich, Paul R.
Human ecology.

Bibliography: p.
1. Human ecology. 2. Environmental policy.
I. Ehrlich, Anne H., joint author. II. Holdren,
John P., joint author. III. Title. [DNLM: 1.
Ecology. 2. Environmental health. 3. Population
control. 4. Population growth. HB 875 E33h 1973]
GF41.E37   301.31   72-12828
ISBN 0–7167–0595–8

Preface

In the three years since *Population, Resources, Environment* was first published, a need for a less detailed and comprehensive introduction to human ecology has become apparent. A survey of potential users indicates that a short treatment of the subject, focusing on the biological and physical aspects of man's present problems and on the ways that they can be solved, would be useful in many courses and for many readers.

In the first part of this book we attempt to present the essence of demography, man's utilization of resources, the world food problem, and man's assaults on his own health and on the health of the ecological systems upon which his existence depends. Our discussion of problems ends with an analysis of the interrelationships of population growth, "affluence" (or standard of living), and technological errors as causes of what is coming to be recognized as the most serious crisis ever faced by *Homo sapiens*.

In the second part we look to solutions. Having established the need to halt population growth, we turn to what is now being done in this area, and to what needs to be done. Then, after discussing possible means to control the numbers of people, we examine what must be done about other aspects of human behavior. How can the demands of individuals on resources be reduced? How can each individual's deleterious impact on his or her environment be minimized? How can people be made aware that man's many problems are inextricably intertwined and that, therefore, ecological problems will not

Canals of the California Water Project, which brings water from sparsely
populated Northern California to heavily populated Southern California.
(Tom Tracy, Photofind, San Francisco)

be solved unless racism, poverty, exploitation, and war are tackled at the
same time?

Needless to say, these problems are not new (although their present scale
and increasingly complex interactions sometimes make them seem so). Actually, some of the most serious problems of the ecological variety began with
the invention of agriculture, some 10,000 years ago. Many civilizations in
the past suffered ecocatastrophes as rising population densities led to agricultural practices which overstressed natural systems. The ruins of Angkor

Ruins of Mayan temples in Tikal, Guatemala. (Larry Keenan, Jr., Photofind, San Francisco).

Wat and Mayan temples and the deserts of the once rich Tigris and Euphrates valleys are among many testaments to the folly of man's attempts to dominate nature. Today that folly continues: in tropical forests, where "slash and burn" agriculture is being practiced too intensively; in California, where gigantic public works are being used to transport water to the Los Angeles basin where *air* is in short supply; in Europe, where the Rhine River has been turned into a vast sewer; in the Soviet Union, where supersonic transports are under construction; indeed, all over the world.

If man changes his ways in time, turning away from folly and toward survival, civilization may endure the critical decades ahead. Even achieving the necessary transition to stable population size and stable resource consumption will not mean the end of ecological problems, however. Supporting a constant world population smaller than today's at a material standard of living lower than that now enjoyed in the United States would still require constant vigilance if the quality of the Earth's life support systems were to be maintained. Human ecology — the study of human relationships with the environment — will persist as a discipline for a long time, if civilization is to persist for a long time.

Acknowledgments

So many people have made contributions to this book, either directly or indirectly, that it is virtually impossible to thank them all individually. Because this book essentially grew out of *Population, Resources, Environment*, we are first of all indebted to all of the many people who assisted us with either or both editions. Moreover, some fifty college and university teachers who have used *Population, Resources, Environment* in courses answered questionnaires about the development of this book. We hope that they will be pleased with the results.

We particularly wish to thank Gary I. Anderson, Department of Environmental Science, Santa Rosa Junior College, Santa Rosa, California, and Robert L. Ellison, Department of Environmental Sciences, University of Virginia, Charlottesville, Virginia, for their detailed critical readings of the manuscript and valuable recommendations. Cheri Holdren has also reviewed portions of the manuscript and made many helpful comments.

We would also like to express our appreciation to Carl May, whose contributions extended far beyond the usual scope of editorial assistance. In addition to critically reviewing the manuscript and making numerous helpful suggestions, he was responsible for obtaining nearly all of the photographic illustrations. We are also grateful to William A. Garnett, who not only provided many of these photos, but who went out of his way to locate others for us through his photographic connections.

We are again indebted to the staff of the Falconer Library for their assistance in finding materials and information and in making seemingly endless Xerox copies of manuscript. We also are grateful to the typists, without whose efforts this book could never have been finished: Barbara Baxter, Catherine Chinn, Ann Duffield, Frances Duignan, Claudia McMahon, and Patricia Mersman. Jane Lawson Bavelas made an important contribution coordinating the clerical operations. We are grateful to her, and to Page Kennedy for the long hours they spent proofreading. Finally, we especially want to thank Jeanne Kennedy, whose polished index is an invaluable addition to this book.

Paul R. Ehrlich
Anne H. Ehrlich
John P. Holdren

October 1972

Contents

Part One   PROBLEMS   1

ONE   Population, Resources, Environment — Is Mankind Really In Trouble?   3

    Man and Environment   4
    Exponential Growth   8
    Momentum, Time Lags and Irreversibility   10
    Interlocking Crises, Interlocking Causes   12
    Limitations of the Technological "Fix"   13
    The Outlook   15

TWO   The Human Population   19

    Birth and Death Rates   21
    Growth Rates   21
    History of Population Growth   22
    Population Structure   29
    Distribution and Dispersion   37
    Urbanization   40
    Demographic Projections   46

THREE   Carrying Capacity: Land, Energy, and Mineral Resources   51

Land   51
Energy   54
Mineral Resources other than Fuels   62

FOUR   Carrying Capacity: Food and Other Renewable Resources   69

A Hungry World   70
The Biology of Food Production   77
The Practice of Agriculture   80
Increasing Food Production   89
Food from the Sea   97
Other Renewable Resources   106

FIVE   Pollution: Direct Effects on Society   115

Air Pollution   116
Water Pollution   127
Solid Wastes   130
Pesticides and Related Compounds   132
Pollution by Heavy Metals   135
Radiation   139
Chemical Mutagens   143
Noise Pollution   144
The Urban Environment   145

SIX   Disruption of Ecological Systems   151

Biochemical Cycles   152
Food Webs: Ecological Complexity and Stability   156
Modifying Ecosystems   159
Types of Pollutants   165
Insecticides and Ecosystems   166
Pollutants in the Soil   178
Herbicides and Ecosystems   181
Nitrogen and Phosphates   184
Pollutants and Oceanic Ecosystems   189
Pollutants and the Atmosphere   193
Ecological Accounting   200

SEVEN   Understanding the Web of Blame: The First Step to Solutions   205

Multiplicative Factors   *206*
The United States since World War II   *213*
Cause-and-Effect Relations   *215*
Perfect Technologies and Shifting Impact   *219*
The Prospects   *221*

Part Two   SOLUTIONS   **223**

EIGHT   Population Limitation   225

The Optimum Population   *226*
Birth Control   *230*
Family Planning   *239*
Attitudes and Birth Rates   *245*
Population Growth and Policies in the United States   *246*
Population Control   *253*

NINE   Changing Human Behavior: Toward the Environment
and Toward Our Fellow Man   259

Economics, Resources, and the Environment   *260*
The Social System   *266*
The Political System   *268*
The International Scene   *271*

TEN   Synthesis and Recommendations   277

Summary   *277*
Recommendations: A Positive Program   *278*

Appendix   281

Index   289

Human Ecology

PROBLEMS AND SOLUTIONS

Part One
PROBLEMS

Examples of simple and complex natural ecosystems. Above, polar desert on Cornwallis Island, Northwest Territories, Canada. Vegetation consists mainly of two species in scattered clumps. (Courtesy of W. D. Billings.) Below, tropical forest on the Isthmus of Panama. Foliage at left has been cleared by a colony of leaf-cutting ants (Atta colombica tonsipes); the refuse dump of the colony may be seen on the right amid less disturbed foliage. (Courtesy of Bruce Haines.)

ONE

Population, Resources, Environment — Is Mankind Really In Trouble?

Human values and institutions have set mankind on a collision course with the laws of nature. Human beings cling jealously to their prerogative to reproduce as they please — and they please to make each new generation larger than the last — yet endless multiplication on a finite planet is impossible. Most humans aspire to greater material prosperity, but the number of people that can be supported on Earth if everyone is rich is even smaller than if everyone is poor. We are told that only economic growth can ease the pain of poverty — of the inequitable distribution of wealth — but we know that the quantity of physical goods, like the human population, cannot grow forever. It is not yet clear precisely when and in what form the collision between the growth ethic and natural limits will occur, but there can be no doubt as to the outcome. Human values and institutions will bend or be crushed by biological and physical realities.

Is there any reason to believe, though, that the collision will be sooner rather than later? What is fundamentally different about the 1970s compared with, say, the 1920s or the 1870s? Haven't science and technology always pushed back the natural barriers? Are today's environmental problems the early symptoms of a fundamental disorder or are they merely bothersome side effects of the orderly progress of technology? What would be gained and what would be lost by deferring action until the evidence of impending disaster is more conclusive?

The answers to these questions emerge from the study of several pivotal issues: (1) the extent of human dependence on the natural environment and the fundamental character of our disruption of it; (2) the exponential properties of growth both of the human population and of its impact on the environment; (3) the importance of time lags and irreversibility in the man-environment system; (4) the interlocking nature of present problems of environmental deterioration, of resource consumption, and of social organization; and (5) the limitations of the technological "fix." The details of the human dilemma will unfold in the chapters that follow, but it may be helpful to set forth some of the basic elements at the outset.

Man and Environment

For our purposes, the environment is the unique skin of soil, water, gaseous atmosphere, mineral nutrients, and organisms that covers this otherwise undistinguished planet. The conditions that make Earth hospitable to human life result from complex and perhaps fragile balances among the great chemical cycles—water, nitrogen, carbon, oxygen, phosphorus, sulfur—all powered by the energy of the sun. Deadly ultraviolet radiation from that same lifegiving star is kept out by the tiny trace of ozone in the atmosphere; the trace of carbon dioxide maintains the Earth's surface at tolerably warm temperatures by preventing heat from escaping into space. Organisms regulate the environmental concentrations of nitrites, ammonia, and hydrogen sulfide—all poisonous—and, in the much longer term, the concentrations of atmospheric nitrogen and oxygen as well (Chapter 6).

In his tenure of some thousands of centuries on this planet, man has learned to modify and to exploit the environment to his advantage in many ways: to clear, to plant, to mine, to dam, to dredge; to domesticate animals, to breed varieties of plants and animals more suitable to his needs, to increase the yields of crops, fish, and fiber he extracts from the natural systems of the planet. Yet, in the last third of the twentieth century, man still cannot claim either full understanding or control of the environmental systems that support his growing population. This is the central truth of the man-environment relation today: man is still part of nature, not master of it. He is exploiting 40 percent of the Earth's land area; he has reduced the mass of land vegetation by one third;[1] he has power beyond precedent to influence natural environmental systems. But power is not control.

This is the point missed by those who regard environmental concerns as no more than a fad or a rich man's crusade to preserve some scenic places in which to hike or hunt. Such people presumably believe that mankind can

---

[1]*Man's Impact on the Global Environment*, Report of the Study of Critical Environmental Problems, M.I.T. Press, 1970, p. 22.

Figure 1-1 An example of how mankind has altered the natural environment in southern Illinois. Perhaps only the isolated clumps of trees along the creeks and the creeks themselves can be considered "undisturbed," in comparison to the carefully cultivated fields and farmyards. (Photo by William A. Garnett.)

support ever-increasing billions forever in the same way that a handful of men have been supported for two weeks at a time in an Apollo capsule—that is, with life-support systems of our own devising. Unfortunately, that presumption is the sheerest naiveté. The fact is that we are utterly dependent on natural processes for the bulk of our waste disposal; for most of the cycling of chemical nutrients that sustain our food production; and for maintaining a library of genetic information from which new food crops, biological pest controls, and antibiotics (among other indispensables) will come. Further, almost all potential crop pests are controlled by nature, not by man, and almost all commercial fish—the source of perhaps 10 to 20 percent of the animal protein consumed by mankind—are produced in natural ecosystems (see Box

1–1). Natural vegetation reduces floods and helps prevent erosion, and soil itself is produced from organic matter and weathered rock by fungi and soil organisms.

As incomplete as our knowledge may be concerning the operation of the natural systems that support human life, one cardinal principle now seems clear: the ability of ecological systems (ecosystems) to persist and perform their functions in the face of inevitable environmental change is related to the complexity of those ecosystems. The more species that flourish and share substantially in the energy that flows through an ecosystem, the more stable the system is likely to be—in other words, the less likely it is that small changes in conditions will cause major disruptions (Chapter 6).

Box 1–1   Some Ecological Terminology

Biologists often divide the world of life into several "levels of organization" for purposes of description and analysis. The simplest level is the molecular, or that concerned with the chemistry of life. Next in increasing order of complexity are the cell and organism levels, dealing respectively with the structure and functioning of the basic building blocks of individual organisms and of the individual organisms themselves (plants, animals, and microorganisms). Most of the concerns in this book will be with the highest levels of biological organization: those of the *population*, *community*, and *ecosystem*.

A *population* is a group of individuals of the same *species* (kind) of organism; for instance, a flock of ducks or all the human beings on Manhattan Island. It is always important to define the population under discussion. The rainbow trout in a single lake make up a population; all the rainbow trout in the world make up another population (which happens to include the first one).

All the individuals of different populations living in a given area make up a *community*. A community, taken together with its nonliving physical environment, is known as an ecological system, or an *ecosystem*. One refers to an ecosystem when it seems desirable to emphasize the physical, chemical, and biological relationships that bind communities and their physical surroundings into more or less functional units. The ecosystems of the world are linked by movements of energy, chemicals, and organisms into one global ecosystem, often called the *biosphere* or *ecosphere*.

Ecology is the subdiscipline of biology that deals with interactions between organisms and their environment on the population, community and ecosystem levels of organization. Terms such as *population dynamics, systems ecology,* and *animal ecology* indicate special areas of ecological research. *Human ecology* focuses specifically on the relationships of human populations to the ecosystems of which they are a part.

The flow of energy and mineral nutrients through ecosystems is one of the principal interests of ecologists. The flow processes are described in terms of *food chains*, in which light energy from the sun is captured and converted to chemical energy via *photosynthesis* in green plants and is then passed on in succession to *herbivores* (plant eaters), *primary carnivores* (eaters of herbivores), *secondary carnivores* (eaters of primary carnivores), and so on. Each stage in such a food chain is called a *trophic level* (from *trophē*, the Greek word for food). Organisms known as *decomposers* use the energy stored in dead plant and animal matter from all trophic levels and return mineral nutrients to the biosphere in forms usable by other organisms. Often the term *food web* is used in place of food chain, since there are

Mankind has been an enemy of complexity in ecological systems — and hence a destabilizing force — at least since the agricultural revolution (his hunting activities may have been a factor in the extinction of many large mammals even earlier). Agriculture itself is the practice of replacing complex natural ecosystems with simpler artificial ones based on a few strains of highly productive crops. These croplands ordinarily require constant vigilance and inputs of energy (in the form of cultivation, fertilizers, pesticides, and so forth) to stave off the collapse to which their biological simplicity makes them susceptible. Even with prodigious effort, however, it is unlikely that man could maintain this perilous enterprise unaided. Many ecologists now believe that an essential accompaniment to man's intensely exploitive

usually many species on each trophic level, and the food chains are interlaced — that is, each plant species is eaten by more than one species of herbivore, and each herbivore eats more than one species of plant. Each transfer of energy in the food web entails the loss, as heat, of a substantial fraction of the energy involved. Thus the available energy diminishes at each higher trophic level. For this reason, populations of carnivores tend to be smaller (have fewer individuals) than those of herbivores.

Any population of organisms that multiplied as rapidly as the organism's own reproductive biology permitted would soon cover the Earth. This is prevented from occurring by deaths caused by such factors as predators, disease, scarcity of resources (such as food, water, breeding sites), and many others. What factor or combination of factors determines the size limit on a population varies from species to species, from place to place, and from time to time. The maximum size of a population that can be sustained at a given time (under a given set of environmental conditions) is referred to as the *carrying capacity* of the environment for that organism.

A critical ecological question is the relation between complexity and stability in ecosystems. *Stability* is usually defined as the ability of an ecosystem that has been disrupted to return to the conditions that preceded the disruption. A closely related meaning is that a stable eco-

system resists large, rapid changes in the sizes of its various populations. When such changes (called *fluctuations* or *instabilities*, depending on the circumstances) occur, the flow of energy and nutrients in the ecosystem is altered. These changes may affect the human population, whether or not extinctions of other species are involved. *Complexity* takes many forms — diversity of the physical environment, variety and spatial distribution of species, size and genetic diversity of populations within a given species, and others. On the basis of theoretical arguments, general observations, and limited experimentation, many ecologists believe that complexity tends to impart stability.

Ecological change also takes place over much longer time spans than the month-to-month or year-to-year time scale of fluctuations and instabilities. Ecological *succession* refers to the orderly replacement of one community in an area with other communities over periods often measured in decades, culminating in a relatively persistent *climax community*, the nature of which is determined largely by climate and soil type. *Evolution* refers to changes in the genetic characteristics of species, brought about by natural selection over time periods ranging from a few generations to hundreds of millions of years.

activities on land and, increasingly, in the oceans is the preservation of extensive lightly exploited natural communities, which serve as ecological buffers and reservoirs of species diversity.

The central problem, then, of which many specific environmental difficulties are but symptoms, is this: mankind is systematically diminishing the capacity of the natural environment to perform its waste disposal, nutrient cycling, and other vital roles at the same time that the growing human population and rising affluence are creating larger demands for these natural services. Cornfields are replacing forests, while huge monocultures of new high-yielding grains replace a broad assortment of traditional crop varieties. These far-flung simplifying effects of agriculture are reinforced by additional assaults on natural complexity in the form of urban sprawl, highway systems, and the release of toxic industrial chemicals. Whole species of plants and animals are being decimated or exterminated by intentional or inadvertent poisoning, by too intensive harvesting and, especially, by destruction of habitat.

These are not trivial losses to be mourned only by nature lovers and bird watchers; they represent dangerous and irreversible tinkering with the natural systems on which the planet's carrying capacity for human beings is dependent. Ecology is not a fad but a scientific discipline whose practitioners attempt to decipher the complex relationships among organisms and their physical environment. Slowly, painstakingly, but steadily, ecologists are providing scientific substance to notions once held by conservationists largely on aesthetic grounds: that one does not exterminate any population or species lightly; that man's fate is inextricably tied to nature; that all human beings, including those billions who may never set foot in the wilderness, have a stake in unexploited land.

Exponential Growth

The human population, its consumption of resources, and its adverse impact on the environment are all growing *exponentially*, in other words, at compound interest. Anything growing in this way increases in any given time period by a fixed percentage of its size at the beginning of the period. (When interest is compounded in a savings account, the interest becomes part of the balance and in turn earns more interest. As time goes on, the balance gets bigger and the additions in the form of interest get bigger in proportion.) When growth is exponential, as it is now in the human population, each addition becomes a contributor of new additions. If the *percentage* growth in two successive periods is the same, the *absolute* growth in the second period is larger. Between 1960 and 1970, growing at about 2 percent per year, world population increased by 650 million people; if the 2 percent annual rate of growth persists through the 1970s, the population increase for that decade will be 800 million people (Chapter 2).

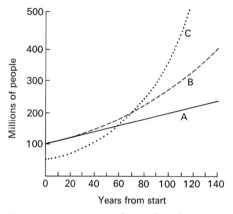

Figure 1–2 Exponential growth and arithmetic growth. A. Initial population of 100 million growing arithmetically at 1 million per year. B. Initial population of 100 million growing exponentially at 1 percent per year. C. Initial population of 50 million growing exponentially at 2 percent per year. Compare A and B: the difference is negligible at first, then grows dramatically. This is the effect of "compound interest." Compare B and C: a higher exponential growth rate soon compensates for a smaller initial population.

Exponential growth at a constant annual percentage increase can be characterized by the time it takes for any given quantity to double. The doubling time for a population growing at 2 percent per year is about 35 years. Consumption of energy — a useful index both of resource consumption and of impact on the environment — is growing worldwide at 5 percent per year, corresponding to a doubling time of only 14 years. (The general relation is: doubling time equals 70 years divided by annual percentage increase.)

Use of the concept of doubling time emphasizes what for our purposes is the most important property of exponential growth: the rapidity with which such growth can exceed a given limit after seeming safely small for a long time. To understand this phenomenon, imagine a large aquarium with filter and aeration systems adequate to the needs of 1,000 guppies. Suppose we start with two guppies in the tank and that the number grows exponentially with a doubling time of one month. It takes eight doublings, or eight months, for the guppy population to reach half the carrying capacity of the tank ($2 \rightarrow 4 \rightarrow 8 \rightarrow 16 \rightarrow 32 \rightarrow 64 \rightarrow 128 \rightarrow 256 \rightarrow 512$). For this entire period, the population seems safely small; no crisis seems imminent.

Symptoms of impending disaster are unlikely to appear until the population is well over half the tank's capacity. The critical phase of the growth, when the population zooms from 512 to over 1,000, occurs within the ninth month, and the last 100 guppies are added in less than five days. After 265 days of apparent prosperity, exponential growth carries the population from 90 percent of capacity to a disastrous excess in well under a week.

If we talk of human beings instead of aquarium fish, the limits are not so obvious, but the treacherous properties of exponential growth are just as relevant. *A long history of growth does not imply a long future.* Limits do exist, and exponential growth is carrying mankind toward them at an accelerating rate. It is probably no accident that certain environmental problems have seemed to materialize so suddenly in the last two decades; more likely, the abruptness with which these problems have appeared is the usual manifestation of an exponential growth process approaching a threshold. Whether the ultimate limits on human population growth or impact on the Earth's ecological systems assert themselves through crop failures, collapse of ocean fisheries, disease, rising political tensions, or whatever, the time between the appearance of unmistakable symptoms and real disaster is likely to be but an instant in human history.

Momentum, Time Lags, and Irreversibility

As we have seen in the instance of the guppies, the nature of exponential growth is such that limits can be approached with surprising suddenness. The likelihood of overshooting such a limit, with catastrophic results, is made even greater by (a) the momentum of human population growth, (b) by the delays between cause and effect in many environmental systems, and (c) by the fact that some kinds of damage are irreversible by the time they are visible.

Momentum can be defined as the tendency of a system to continue in the direction it is already moving. The momentum of human population growth has two origins. First, attitudes toward childbearing have deep biological and cultural roots, and therefore resist change. Second, today's population is heavily weighted with young people; 37 percent of the world's population is under 15 years of age. This means there are far more young people who will soon be reproducing—adding to the population—than there are old people who will soon be dying—subtracting from it. Thus, even if the resistance to new attitudes could miraculously be overcome overnight, so that every pair of parents in the world henceforth had only enough children to replace themselves, the imbalance between young and old would cause the population to grow for another 50 to 70 years before leveling off (Chapter 2). Of course, the *exponential* phase of growth would stop when "replacement fertility" (an average of two children per family if everyone marries and all children survive to reproductive age) became a universal reality. But the population would

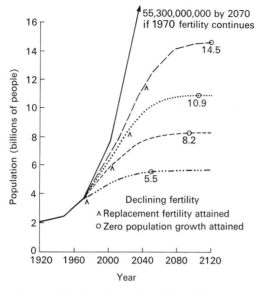

Figure 1–3 Momentum of world population
growth. If replacement fertility is not attained
until the year 2000, the world population will
not stabilize at less than 8 billion people.

still increase by some 30 percent before it stabilized (Figure 1–3). Even making
extremely optimistic assumptions about when the two-child family might
really become the worldwide norm (say, in 30 years), one must conclude that
the world population will not stabilize below 8 billion people. To be complacent about population growth, therefore, one must not only be unworried by
the condition of today's world with its 3.8 billion human inhabitants; one
must also be confident that there are no pitfalls in the additional doubling
and more to which mankind now seems committed.

The momentum of population growth thus will manifest itself as a delay
between the time when the need to halt population growth is universally
perceived and the time when stabilization is actually accomplished. Forces
perhaps even more firmly entrenched than those affecting population growth
lend momentum to economic growth and to the misuse of technology, which
are partners with population growth in generating pressure on resources and
the environment. These forces will cause similar time lags to those involved
in halting population growth before the consumption of resources per person
can be leveled off and ecologically hazardous technologies can be corrected.

Time lags between the initiation of environmental insults and the appearance of the consequent effects further compound the predicament, because
they postpone recognition of the need for any corrective action at all. Such
environmental time lags come about in a variety of ways, depending both on

the ability of some pollutants to persist in dangerous forms for long periods and on the ways in which such pollutants move, accumulate in and damage biological systems (Chapter 6). Unfortunately, time lags between cause and effect often mean that corrective action is ineffective or impossible by the time the symptoms finally appear. Species that have been eradicated cannot be restored; the radioactive debris of atmospheric bomb tests cannot be reconcentrated and isolated from the environment, nor can radiation exposure be undone. If *all* use of persistent pesticides like DDT and related chemicals were stopped tomorrow, the concentrations of these substances in some organisms might continue to increase for years to come.

Thus the momentum of growth, the delays between causes and effects, and the irreversibility of many kinds of damage combine to make overshooting some natural limit a likely outcome of mankind's present course. Indeed, one cannot be sure that we have not already overshot; the practices that support today's world population at the present level of affluence may be unsustainable in the long term, or already may have done enormous irreversible damage that has yet to manifest itself. As zoologists are well aware, animal populations often overshoot the carrying capacity of their environment—a phenomenon invariably followed by a population crash.

Interlocking Crises, Interlocking Causes

Environmental degradation is not the sum of independent causes, it is the multiplicative product of interconnected ones. The relation can be written as a mathematical equation: total environmental damage equals population, times the level of material affluence per person, times the environmental damage done by the technology we use to supply each bit of affluence. These factors are related to each other and to the economic and social framework in which choices are made. A high rate of population growth may depress the rate of growth of affluence per person, for income that would provide for amenities or savings in a small family must be spent entirely on necessities in a larger family. Also, the sorts of technologies required to support a large affluent population may be more damaging *per capita* than those that supported a small poor one. This occurs, for instance, when aluminum and plastic are used to supplement wood, or when large increases in fertilizers and pesticides are needed to provide small increases in agricultural production—an example of the law of diminishing returns (Chapter 7). A socioeconomic system that discourages long-term planning or that levies no fees for the consumption of public goods such as clean air and water encourages careless and wasteful technology.

These complexities mean there are no simple, single-faceted ways to stop the escalation of environmental problems. Halting population growth must be done, but that alone would not be enough. Stabilizing or reducing the per capita consumption of resources in the United States is necessary, but not sufficient. Attempts to reduce technology's impact on the environment are essential, but ultimately will be futile if population and affluence grow unchecked. Clearly, if there is to be any chance of success, simultaneous attacks must be mounted on *all* the components of the problem. Such a coordinated effort may be unlikely, but nothing less will do the job.

Just as the causes of environmental degradation cannot be completely disentangled and tackled separately, neither can environmental problems and their causes be considered in isolation from the other grave difficulties that plague mankind: widespread poverty and the overconcentration of wealth, rapid consumption of the world's readily available supplies of mineral resources by the affluent nations, domestic and international tensions of racial, religious, and ideological origin. Population growth in the poor countries (often called "the underdeveloped countries" or "UDCs") eats up much of the gain from economic growth, and whatever per capita growth remains is unevenly distributed; so poverty persists. The rapid conversion of resources into waste in the rich countries (often called "the developed countries" or "DCs") generates some of the world's most serious environmental problems at the same time that it further compromises the aspirations of the poor countries to a decent standard of living; the rich perhaps will be able to afford to use poorer quality ores after the cream has been skimmed from the world's supplies, but the poor will not (Chapter 3).

In the meantime, the politics of access to the best mineral deposits continues to be a potential source of international conflict. Indisputably, these considerations partly account for the intense interest of the U.S. in both the Middle East (oil) and Southeast Asia (oil, nickel, tin). The widening prosperity gap between rich and poor countries is also a probable source of political instability, as is the sheer pressure of too many people on land in some parts of the world. The race to loot the sea of its fishes in a protein-hungry world is another international powder keg. The oceans may be the ecosystem most vulnerable of all to human disruption. Japan is dependent on the sea for more than half her protein; what would she do if pollution, overexploitation, and destruction of estuaries and wetlands drove oceanic fisheries to collapse?

In these circumstances, the continued worldwide increase in military expenditures (even more rapid in the UDCs than in the DCs) is ominous and tragic. The billions of dollars going into weaponry are desperately needed to support rational programs to alleviate the very tensions and inequities that are increasing the odds that the weaponry will be used.

Limitations of the Technological "Fix"

One might argue that technology has always pushed aside apparent limits to the growth of population and wealth in the past, and that it will continue to do so far into the future. This view holds, in essence, that the cheap, abundant energy "sure" to be available from nuclear-fission breeder reactors and controlled thermonuclear fusion will enable human society to feed, clothe, and house a world population several times today's and still maintain the environment in tolerable condition. One of the defects in this view is the fact that we are failing to feed, clothe and house decently the 3.8 billion people who exist today (Chapter 4). Technology cannot *stay ahead* of population growth unless it can first *catch up*, and today there is little sign of even the latter. The difference between the per capita gross national products of the rich countries and the poor countries of the world actually *widened* throughout the 1950s and 1960s.[2]

By ignoring environmental and social problems, one might possibly conclude that a constant population of 8 or 10 billion people could be supported for some time by means of advanced technologies for desalting sea water, increasing agricultural yields, and extracting metals from common rock. However, this is a mere hypothetical exercise; man cannot get there from here. New technologies of the sorts envisioned would take decades to develop and thousands of billions of dollars to deploy on the scale that is required. If present population trends persist, we will have 8 billion people long before this hypothetical technology is ready for them, just as today's technologies are inadequate to support today's population.

Of course, environmental and social problems cannot be ignored, and new technologies aggravate them as often as not. For example, schemes specifically intended to increase food production can engender ecological liabilities that decrease it in the long term. Thus, dams for irrigation may flood good land, decrease productivity in previously fertile delta regions, and lead to salt accumulation and waterlogging of the newly irrigated land. Indiscriminate use of pesticides wipes out the natural enemies of pests and encourages the development of resistant strains of the pests (Chapter 6).

Pollution control itself has liabilities. Many "solutions" simply shift environmental impact rather than removing it: removal of lead from gasoline is associated with an increase in certain dangerous hydrocarbon compounds; incinerating solid waste pollutes the air; and removing ash and sulfur dioxide from power-plant effluent produces more solid waste. Zero emission of any pollutant is an impossible goal; the larger the population, however, the more closely we must approach that goal if total environmental impact is to be held constant. This ultimately means very large expenditures of energy in pollution control; but energy use itself is responsible for some of the most serious environmental problems.

[2]*Statistical Yearbook of the United Nations, 1970.* Statistical Office of the U.N., New York, 1971.

On the social side, the introduction of mechanized agriculture in some parts of the world has aggravated unemployment problems that were already very serious. The Green Revolution (consisting partly of new high-yield crops and heavy fertilizer use) has increased disparities in income among farmers in the poor countries by favoring those who have the money to buy seed, fertilizer, and equipment.

In general, a high rate of growth of population or consumption leads to the hasty application of new technologies in the attempt to meet increasing demands, but haste breeds mistakes. The larger the absolute size of the population and its level of consumption, the larger the scale of the technology must be, and, hence, the more serious are the mistakes that are made.

The Outlook

Some people protest that these same arguments could as easily have been made 50 or 100 years ago, that the case against growth was wrong then and is wrong now. But there are fundamental differences between the 1970s and the 1920s or 1870s. The absolute number of people added to the world population each year now is about twice what it was in the 1920s, and the annual increase in human impact on the environment (in absolute magnitude) is between five and ten times larger now than then.[3]

As a global geological and biological force, mankind is today becoming comparable to and even exceeding many natural processes. Human input of oil to the oceans exceeds natural seepage by perhaps twentyfold. Human activities have increased the atmospheric concentration of carbon dioxide by 10 percent since the turn of the century. Roughly 5 percent of the energy captured by photosynthesis on Earth now flows through agricultural ecosystems supporting the metabolic consumption of humans and their domestic animals—which comprise but a few of some millions of species on Earth. The flows of many metals and chemicals through industrial society exceed the natural flows of these materials through the biosphere.[4] Heat released by human activities in urban regions of thousands of square miles is equivalent

[3]The figure of 10 times the annual increase in environmental impact, compared to the 1920s, comes from using energy consumption as a rough index of environmental impact. Historical statistics for world energy consumption are given in *Energy in the World Economy*, Joel Darmstadter, Johns Hopkins Press, 1971.

[4]The figures for oil, carbon dioxide, flow of metals and chemicals, and heat are from *Man's Impact on the Global Environment*. The photosynthesis figure is from "The Energy Cycle of the Biosphere," George M. Woodwell, *Scientific American*, September 1970. Also in *The Biosphere*, W. H. Freeman and Company, San Francisco, 1971, and available as Offprint No. 1190.

to 5 percent or more of the incident solar energy falling upon these regions. Such figures do not prove that disaster is upon us, but they are cause for concern. In terms of the scale of its disruptions, mankind in the second half of the 20th century is for the first time operating on a level at which global balances could hinge on its mistakes. Human knowledge of the thresholds by no means matches the human capacity for rushing toward them.

The predicament is deepened by two contrary properties of growth. On the one hand, the growth of population accelerates the rate at which new problems appear and grow to large proportions. This means that population growth increases the need for society to be able to respond quickly and rationally to new situations. But while it increases the need, population growth diminishes the ability. The difficulties of government and management increase with size; bureaucratic structures and regulations become more complex, less flexible, less responsive; the governors become more remote from the governed. Other things being equal, the time lag between perception of an impending problem and implementation of a corrective change in society almost inevitably grows larger with the population.

The present situation, then, is somewhat like driving an automobile with failing brakes down a treacherous road at an accelerating speed. So far we have managed to stay on the road, but the task becomes more and more difficult because our brakes become less effective as our speed increases. To take the analogy further, mankind's ignorance of the exact carrying capacity of social institutions and the physical environment makes the whole enterprise akin to driving our defective, accelerating automobile down that treacherous road in a heavy fog. In this situation, certain politicians, economists, and technologists who offer us glib reassurances that no crisis is evident are like blind backseat drivers who urge us to keep our foot on the gas.

But what if some time remains before an unavoidable obstacle looms up out of the fog? What if 30 or even 50 years are left? What is gained and what is lost by waiting until the evidence of impending collision is absolutely unambiguous? By waiting, we leave to our children or grandchildren the inevitable confrontation with reality that we haven't the nerve to face today. We leave to them the tough issues of stabilizing growth and sharing wealth, of devising a human society that can endure. And we surely leave them less time in which to do it, a more crowded and ravaged world in which to try, a more structured and less flexible existence in a system in which more people are competing for less wealth. Our chances are not encouraging, but theirs will be even smaller. What benefits can the continuation of present trends offer to balance these costs?

There is no lack of defenders of the status quo, so we leave it to them to enumerate the benefits of trends that promise only more of the same. In the remainder of the first part of this book (Chapters 2 through 7), we will amplify and document the arguments just summarized — the case for action, as we see it. In Chapters 8 through 10, we will discuss some of the specific social, political, economic, and technological changes necessary to halt the destructive and demoralizing course of events that seems the most probable — although still not inevitable — future.

(Photo by Walt Mancini.)

TWO

The Human
Population

The first small population of human beings appeared on Earth between 1 and
2 million years ago, probably on the continent of Africa. Since then, the
human population has spread out to occupy virtually the entire land surface
of the planet, and in the last century or two has exploded in numbers to almost 4 billion. Since there are no substantial historical data on which to
base estimates of human population size before 1650, estimates must be based
on circumstantial evidence. For instance, agriculture was unknown before
about 8000 B.C.; prior to that time all human groups made their living by
hunting and gathering food. No more than 20 million square miles of the
Earth's total land area of some 58 million square miles could successfully
have supported our early ancestors. From the population densities of the hunting and gathering tribes of today, we can estimate that the total human population of 8000 B.C. was about 5 million people.

Population sizes at various times, from the onset of the agricultural revolution until census data first were kept in the seventeenth century, have also
been estimated. This was done by extrapolation from census figures that
exist for agricultural societies, and by examination of archaeological remains.
It is thought that the total human population at the time of Christ was around
200 to 300 million people, and that it increased to about 500 million ($\frac{1}{2}$ billion)
by 1650. It then doubled to 1,000 million (1 billion) around 1850, and doubled again to 2 billion by 1930. The course of human population growth can
be seen in Figure 2–1. Note that the size of the population has, with minor

irregularities, increased continuously, and that *the rate of increase has also increased.*

Perhaps the best way to describe the growth rate is in terms of "doubling time"—the time required for the population to double in size. To go from 5 million in 8000 B.C. to 500 million in 1650 meant that the population increased a hundredfold. This required between six and seven doublings in a period of 9,000 to 10,000 years:

Population: 5 million → 10 → 20 → 40 → 80 → 160 → 320 → 640 milli
Doublings: 1   2   3   4   5   6   7

Thus, on the average, the population doubled about once every 1,500 years during that period. The next doubling, from 500 million to a billion, took 200 years, and the doubling from a billion to 2 billion took only 80 years. Barring a catastrophic increase in the death rate, the population will reach 4 billion around 1975, having doubled again in 45 years. The rate of growth around 1972 would, if continued, double the population in about 35 years. Table 2–1 summarizes past human population growth in these terms.

The reasons for this pattern of growth are quite well known, but before these reasons are examined, some details of population dynamics—the ways in which populations change size—must be considered. The size of a population is essentially the result of additions and subtractions. Additions to local human populations consist of births and immigrations; subtractions consist of deaths and emigrations. Demographers (scientists concerned with the statistical study of human populations) who are interested in the total population of the planet work primarily with birth and death rates, since there has been no migration to or from the Earth.

Figure 2–1 Growth of human numbers for the past one-half million years. If Old Stone Age were in scale, its base line would extend about 18 feet to the left. (After *Population Bulletin*, vol. 18, no. 1.)

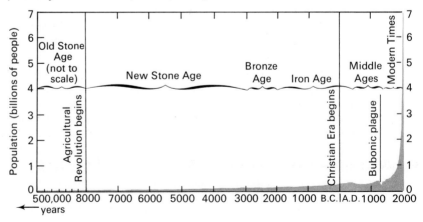

Table 2–1   Doubling Times

Date	Estimated World Population	Time Required for Population to Double
8000 B.C.	5 million	1,500 years
1650 A.D.	500 million	200 years
1850 A.D.	1,000 million (1 billion)	80 years
1930 A.D.	2,000 million (2 billion)	45 years
1975 A.D.	4,000 million (4 billion)	35 years*

*Computed doubling time around 1972.

Birth and Death Rates

The birth rate is usually expressed as the number of babies born per thousand people per year. The total number of births during the year is divided by the estimated population at the midpoint of the period. For instance, if in a population of 10,000 people there were 250 births in a given year, the birth rate would be 25 per thousand. If 150 people died in the same year, the death rate would be 15 per thousand. To take an actual example, in the United States there were 3,729,000 live births during the 12 months ending April 30, 1971. The population on October 31, 1970 (the midpoint of that period) was estimated to be 205,200,000. The birth rate for that period was therefore 3,729,000/205,200,000 = 0.0182. There were 0.0182 births per person, or 0.0182 × 1,000 = 18.2 births per thousand people. Similarly, there were 1,919,000 deaths during the period, giving a death rate of 1,919,000/205,200,000 = 0.094 × 1,000 = 9.4 deaths per thousand people in the year from May 1, 1970 to April 30, 1971.[1]

Growth Rates

Since birth rate represents additions and death rate represents subtractions, we can calculate the rate of natural increase (or decrease) of the population by subtracting the death rate from the birth rate. The *total* rate of growth would include net immigration, if any. During the year ending April 30, 1971, the rate of natural increase for the United States was 18.2 minus 9.4 or 8.8 per thousand.[1] That is, in the period from May 1, 1970, to April 30, 1971, the excess of births over deaths added 8.8 people to each 1,000 people in the American population. Net immigration into the United States added another 2 people per thousand. Demographers express growth rates as annual percentage increases—that is, not as a rate per thousand but as a rate per hundred. In the example cited above, the annual natural increase would be 0.88 percent, a

[1]Data from the *Monthly Vital Statistics Report*, published by the U.S. Public Health Service, National Center for Health Statistics. These provide current statistics on live births, deaths, marriages, divorces, and infant deaths.

Table 2–2

Annual percent Increase	Doubling Time (Years)
0.5	139
0.8	87
1.0	70
2.0	35
3.0	23
4.0	17

typical rate for an industrialized nation. In 1972 the estimated world birth rate was 33 per thousand and the death rate 13 per thousand. The population growth rate was thus 33 minus 13 equals 20 per thousand, or 2 percent.

If the world rate of increase is 2 percent and remains constant, then the population will double in 35 years. A 2 percent rate of increase means that 20 persons per thousand are added to the population each year. Note that if you simply *add* 20 persons per year to a population of 1,000 people, it will take 50 years to double that population (20 × 50 = 1,000). But the doubling time is actually much less, because populations grow exponentially, the way that money grows when interest is compounded. Just as the interest dollars themselves earn interest, so people added to populations produce more people. It is exponential growth that makes populations double so much more rapidly than seems possible. The relationship between the annual percentage increase (interest rate) and the doubling time is shown in Table 2–2.

History of Population Growth

The story of human population growth is not primarily a story of changes in birth rate, but of changes in death rate. The sustained and dramatic increases in population that have occurred in different periods of human history have invariably been caused by forces that favored lower death rates, and the intermittent slowdowns in growth have most often been caused by factors that increased death rates. Large, sustained changes in birth rates have been important only in the last 100 years or so.

Cultural Change and the Agricultural Revolution. The populations of our ancestors a few million years ago (Australopithecus and relatives) were confined to Africa and numbered perhaps 125,000 individuals. These ancestors of ours had already "invented" culture, the body of nongenetic information passed from generation to generation. The possession of a substantial body of culture is what differentiates man from the other animals. During man's evolutionary history, the possession of culture has been responsible for a great increase in human brain size (the australopithecines had small brains, with an average volume less than half of ours—only about 500 cubic centimeters). Early men added to the store of cultural information, developing and learning techniques of social organization and group and individual survival. This gave an evolutionary advantage to individuals with the large brain capacity necessary to take full advantage of the culture. Larger brains in turn increased the potential store of cultural information, and a self-reinforcing coupling of the growth of culture and brain size resulted. This trend continued until perhaps 200,000 years ago, when growth of brain size leveled off at an average of some 1,350 cubic centimeters, and men considered to belong to the same species as modern man, *Homo sapiens*, appeared.

The evolution of culture had an important side effect. Although the human birth rate remained around 40 to 50 per 1,000, cultural advances caused a slight decline in the average death rate. But until the agricultural revolution the average death rate could not have been much less than .02 per thousand below the birth rate. In prehistoric times there unquestionably were sizable fluctuations in birth rates and especially in death rates, particularly during the difficult times associated with glacial advance. The end result, however, was a population of about 5 million around 8000 B.C. Mankind had by that time spread from Africa to occupy the entire planet, probably first entering the Western Hemisphere around 30,000 B.C.

The consequences of cultural evolution for human population size and for the environment were minor compared with those that were to follow in the agricultural revolution. It is not certain when the first group of *Homo sapiens* started to supplement their hunting and food gathering with primitive farming. On the basis of studies of archaeological sites in the Middle East, there is firm evidence that established village-farming communities functioned between 7000 and 5500 B.C., and archaeologists estimate that agriculture began there around 9000–7000 B.C. Recent evidence indicates that an independent development of agriculture took place, perhaps even earlier, in Southeast Asia. Like modern Eskimos, these preagricultural people practiced intensive food collection and were presumably intimately familiar with the local flora and fauna. It was a natural step from gathering foodplants to cultivating them. This step, accompanied by the development of relatively permanent settlements and food-storage facilities, freed men from the constant search for food. As a result some members of early agricultural communities were able to turn entirely to other activities, all of which helped to raise the general standard of life. Wheeled vehicles appeared; copper, tin, and then iron were utilized; and dramatic sociopolitical changes occurred along with urbanization. Life expectancy began to creep upward from its primitive level of perhaps 25–30 years.

However, the more rapid growth of human populations after the agricultural revolution was not continuous. Civilizations grew, flourished, and disintegrated; periods of good and bad weather occurred; and pestilence, famine, and war took their toll. Of course, there has been no accurate record of human population sizes until quite recently, and, even today, demographic statistics for many areas are unreliable. Even so, a general picture, quite adequate for the purposes of this discussion, can be reconstructed. Population growth was still relatively slow until the mid-seventeenth century. Then innovations in agriculture and, in all probability, the opening of the frontiers of the Western Hemisphere to exploitation (but not yet to substantial emigration), led to a burst of growth in the European population.

The World Since 1650.   Although we can speculate with ease about the causes of Europe's population boom between 1650 and 1750, it is somewhat more difficult to explain a similar boom in Asia. The population there increased by some 50–75 percent in this period. In China, after the collapse of the Ming Dynasty in 1644, political stability and the new agricultural policies of the Manchu emperors doubtless led to a depression of death rates. Much of the Asiatic population growth during this period probably took place in China, since India was in a period of economic and political instability caused by the disintegration of the Mogul Empire.

World population seems to have grown at a rate of about 0.3 percent per year between 1650 and 1750. The growth rate increased to approximately 0.5 percent between 1750 and 1850. During this latter period the population of Europe doubled in response to a number of favorable changes: agricultural techniques advanced fairly rapidly, sanitation improved, and, at the end of the period, the introduction of smallpox vaccination signalled improvements in public health. Furthermore, this growth was achieved in the face of heavy emigration to the New World, where the population jumped from some 12 million to about 60 million in the same period. Growth in Asia between 1750 and 1850 was slower than in Europe, amounting to an increase of about 50 percent. Most of the developments that favored rapid increase in Europe's population were to appear in Asia only much later, if at all.

Little is known about the past population size of Africa, a continent that remained virtually unknown to Europeans until well past the middle of the nineteenth century. It is generally accepted that the population remained more or less constant at around 100 million, plus or minus 5–10 million, between 1650 and 1850. Then European technology and medicine began to take effect in Africa, death rates started to drop, and the population increased some 20–40 percent between 1850 and 1900, doubling to 200 million by 1950.

The average growth rate of the world population between 1850 and 1950 was about 0.8 percent per year. Population increased in that time from slightly more than 1 billion to almost 2.5 billion. The estimated populations shown in Table 2–3 indicate that between 1850 and 1950 the population of Asia did not quite double, but population more than doubled in Europe and Africa, multiplied about fivefold in Latin America, and increased more than sixfold in North America.

Table 2–3   Populations in Millions

Date	World	Africa	North America	Latin America	Asia (except USSR)	Europe and Asiatic USSR	Oceania
1850	1,131	97	26	33	700	274	2
1950	2,495	200	167	163	1,376	576	13

SOURCE: United Nations (1963) and estimates (somewhat modified) by Willcox, *Studies in American Demography* (1940) and Carr-Saunders, *World Population* (1936).

The death rate continued to decline during the period 1850–1900 as a result of the industrial revolution and the accompanying advances in agriculture and medicine. Although the horrible conditions that prevailed in the mines and factories during the early stages of the rise of industry are well known to all who have read the literature of the period, the overall conditions in areas undergoing industrialization actually improved. Life in the rat-infested cities and rural slums of pre-industrial Europe had been grim almost beyond description. Progress in agriculture, industry, and transportation had, by 1850, substantially bettered the lot of Western man. Improved agriculture reduced the chances of crop failures and famine. Mechanized land and sea transport made local famines less disastrous when they occurred, and provided access to more distant resources. Great improvements in sanitation around the beginning of the twentieth century helped to reduce death rates further, as did knowledge of the role of bacteria in infection, which transformed medical practice and saved many lives. European death rates, which had been in the vicinity of 22–24 per thousand in 1850, decreased to around 18–20 per thousand and went as low as 16 per thousand in some countries. For instance, combined rates for Denmark, Norway, and Sweden dropped from about 20 per thousand in 1850 to 16 in 1900.

In Western Europe in the latter half of the nineteenth century low death rates (and the resultant high rate of population increase) contributed to a massive emigration. And, as the industrial revolution progressed, another significant trend appeared. Birth rates in Western countries began to decline. In Denmark, Norway, and Sweden the combined birth rate was around 32 per thousand in 1850; by 1900 it had decreased to 28. Similar declines occurred elsewhere. This was the start of the so-called "demographic transition"—a falling of birth rates that followed the industrialization of the Western nations.[2]

The demographic transition carried on into the first half of the twentieth century. By the 1930s decreases in birth rates in some countries had outpaced decreases in the death rate. By then the combined death rate of Denmark, Norway, and Sweden had fallen to 12 per thousand, but the birth rate had dropped

[2]Details on the demographic transition can be found in *Principles of Demography*, D. J. Bogue (Wiley, New York, 1969).

precipitously to about 16. If these low birth rates in the industrial countries of Europe in the 1930s had continued, they would *eventually* have led to population declines as the average age of the populations increased followed by rising death rates. However, stimulated by improving economic conditions and World War II, birth rates rose again during the 1940s and 1950s. European growth rates have generally averaged between 0.5 and 1.0 percent since the war.

What is the cause of the lowered birth rates in industrialized countries? No one knows for certain, but some rather good guesses can be made. In agrarian societies, children are often viewed as economic assets. They serve as extra hands on the farm and as old-age insurance for the parents. In an industrial society, children are not potential producers; they are consumers. They require expensive feeding and education. Large families, which become more likely with lowered death rates, tend to reduce mobility and to make the accumulation of capital more difficult. The result of this in Europe was a trend toward later marriage (which reduces birth rates largely by reducing each woman's years of reproductive activity) and toward control of the number of births within marriage.

The demographic transition was not, however, limited to urban areas in Europe. Population increase created a squeeze in rural areas as well, a squeeze that was compounded by the modernization of farms. A finite amount of land had to supply a livelihood for more and more people. At the same time, mechanization, which reduced the need for farm labor, made it more and more difficult for a young couple to establish themselves on a farm of their own. As a result, rural birth rates dropped and many people moved to the cities.

There was, of course, no demographic transition outside the industrialized countries. For instance, the birth rate of India in 1891 was estimated to be 49 per thousand per year, but in 1931 it was still 46 per thousand. In the decade 1930–1940 the rate of population growth in North America and Europe was 0.7 percent, whereas that of Asia was 1.1 percent, Africa 1.5 percent, and Latin America 2.0 percent; even though the death rates were considerably higher in the last three areas. The world growth rate for the decade was 1.1 percent.

Thus far, two principal demographic trends in the modern world have been discussed. The first was a decline in the death rate in countries undergoing industrialization, and the second was a decline in the birth rate following industrialization. The first of these trends resulted in a relatively rapid growth rate in Western countries, a growth rate above the world average. The second trend moved the growth rate of these countries below the world average, Europe making the demographic transition around the turn of the twentieth century, and the United States and Canada more recently.

Population Growth Since World War II.   A third major demographic trend began around the time of World War II. A dramatic decline in death rates occurred in the underdeveloped countries. In some areas, such as Mexico, the decline started before the war. In others, such as Ceylon, it did not start

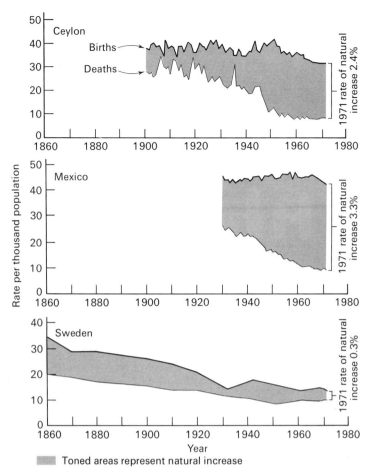

Figure 2–2 Different patterns of change in birth and death rates and rate of natural increase. Death rates dropped gradually in western industrial countries such as Sweden and precipitously in UDCs such as Ceylon and Mexico. (Courtesy of the Population Reference Bureau.)

until the end of the war. Compare, for instance, the trend in Sweden since 1860 with that in Mexico since 1930 (Figure 2–2). This decline was caused primarily by the rapid export of modern drugs and public health measures from the developed countries (DCs) to the underdeveloped countries (UDCs). The consequent "death control" produced the most rapid, widespread change known in the history of human population dynamics.

The power of exported death control can be seen by examining the classic case of Ceylon's assault on malaria after World War II. The death rate in Ceylon in 1945 was 22 per thousand. The introduction of DDT in 1946 brought rapid control over the mosquitoes that carry malaria. As a result, the death rate on the island was reduced by about one-half in less than a decade. It dropped to 10 per thousand in 1954 and has continued to decline since then. In 1972 it was 8 per thousand. Although part of the drop is due to the killing of insects that carry nonmalarial diseases and to other public health measures, most of it can be accounted for by the control of malaria.

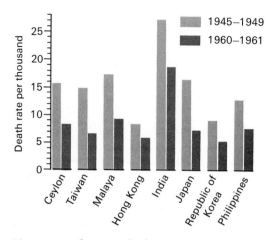

Figure 2–3 Change in death rates in selected
Asian nations. The average rates of 1945–1949
are compared with those of 1960–1961. (After
Population Bulletin, vol. 20, no. 2.)

Victory over malaria, yellow fever, smallpox, cholera, and other infectious
diseases has been responsible for similar decreases in death rates throughout
most of the UDCs, a decline that has been most pronounced among children
and young adults.[3]

In the decade 1940–1950, death rates declined 46 percent in Puerto Rico,
43 percent in Formosa, and 23 percent in Jamaica. In a sample of 18 underdeveloped areas, the average decline in death rate between 1945 and 1950
was 24 percent. Figure 2–3 shows the dramatic change in death rates from
the 1945–1949 average to 1960–1961 in selected Asian nations.

A critical point to remember is that this decline in death rate is different in
kind from the long-term slow decline that occurred throughout most of the
world following the agricultural revolution. It is also different in kind from
the comparatively more rapid decline in death rates in the Western World
over the past century. The difference is that it is a response to a spectacular
environmental change in the UDCs, largely through control of infectious
diseases, not a fundamental change in their institutions or general way of life.
Furthermore, the change did not originate within these countries, but was
brought about from the outside. The factors that led to a demographic transition (to low birth rates) in the DCs were not and are not present in the UDCs.
Instead, a large proportion of the world's population has moved rapidly from
a situation of high birth and death rates to one of high birth rates and low
death rates. As a result, the annual rates of increase have risen sharply. Egypt,
for instance, moved from a growth rate of slightly more than 1.5 percent before 1945 (birth rate 40–45; death rate about 28) to 2.5–3.0 percent after 1945

[3]"The Amazing Decline of Mortality in Underdeveloped Areas," Kingsley Davis,
in the *American Economic Review*, vol. 46, pp. 305–318, 1956.

(1972 birth rate 44; death rate 16, growth rate 2.8 percent). Most UDCs are growing at rates considerably higher than the world average, ranging between 2.5 and 3.5. The fastest growing region is Latin America, where many countries are growing at a rate that will double their populations in 20 to 25 years. (Figure 2–4).

Because of the reduction of death rates in the UDCs, the world growth rate moved from 0.9 percent (doubling time 77 years) in the decade 1940–1950 to a rate of 1.8 percent (doubling time 39 years) in the decade 1950–1960. The world's population grew from a total of about 2.3 billion in 1940 to 2.5 billion in 1950, 3.0 billion in 1960, and 3.6 billion in 1970. According to the Population Reference Bureau's *1972 World Population Data Sheet* (reproduced here in the Appendix), the total human population size in mid-1972 was estimated to be 3.78 billion, the growth rate to be 2.0 percent, and the doubling time to be 35 years. During the 1960s the world growth rate fluctuated between 1.8 and 2.0 percent. Of course, these figures are only approximations because census data from many countries are inadequate, but they are more than sufficient for the purposes of the discussion in this book. If there were actually only 3.6 billion people or as many as 4 billion people in the world as of mid-1972, or if the world growth rate were actually 1.7 or 2.2 percent, our analysis of the future and our basic conclusions would be the same.

Population Structure

The discussion of population so far has dealt mainly with population sizes and growth rates, but there is much more to demography. Populations have structure: age composition, sex ratio, as well as distribution and dispersion

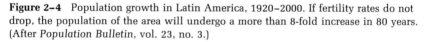

Figure 2–4   Population growth in Latin America, 1920–2000. If fertility rates do not drop, the population of the area will undergo a more than 8-fold increase in 80 years. (After *Population Bulletin*, vol. 23, no. 3.)

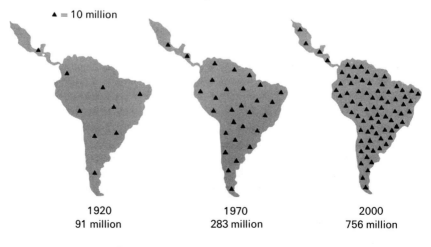

▲ = 10 million

1920	1970	2000
91 million	283 million	756 million

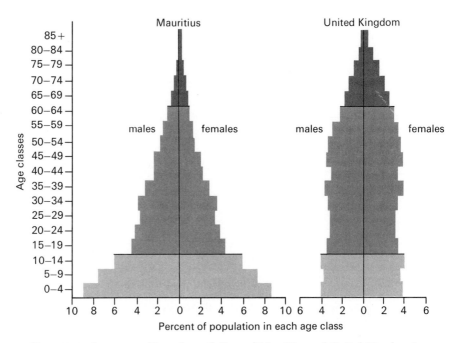

Figure 2-5   Age composition of populations of Mauritius and United Kingdom in 1959. These age profiles contrast the age distribution in a rapidly growing UDC with a very slowly growing DC. In Mauritius young people predominate; in the United Kingdom the population is more evenly distributed over the age spectrum. Note that in each profile the percentage of males of each age class in the population is shown to the left of the center line and that of females to the right. In Figures 2-5 and 2-6 the working ages (15-64) are shown in medium gray, the young dependents (0-14) in pale gray, and the elderly dependents (65 or over) in dark gray. (After *Population Bulletin*, vol. 18, no. 5.)

(the geographic locations and relative spacing of individuals). Age composition, distribution and dispersion, and projections of future population sizes will be considered in the last part of this chapter.

Age Composition.   During the Depression in the 1930s, an interesting demographic situation existed in some European countries. Family sizes were small and death rates were low. If the birth and death rates had held constant, the populations in these countries eventually might have stopped growing and begun to decline. But in fact these populations continued to increase, although slowly. This increase was due to the particular *age composition* of the population—the relative numbers of people in different age classes.

Contrast, for instance, the age compositions of the populations of Mauritius (an island in the Indian Ocean) and the United Kingdom in 1959 as shown by their population profiles (Figure 2-5). These profiles are a graphic means of showing the age compositions of the populations. Because the profiles are based on proportions, they both have the same area in spite of the great difference in the absolute sizes of the populations. This permits one to focus easily on their shapes, which, of course, reflect their different age compositions. Mauritius' profile exemplifies rapidly growing countries with high birth rates and declining death rates. Most of its people are young; 44 percent are under age 15. The United Kingdom, however, has had low birth and death rates for many decades. It has a much narrower population profile than Mauritius. Only 23 percent of the 1959 population of the United Kingdom was under age 15.

In Mauritius and many other UDCs, high birth rates and increasing control over infant and child mortality have greatly inflated the younger age groups in the population. There has not yet been sufficient time for individuals born in the period of "death control" to reach the older age classes, whose death rates are higher than those of the younger age classes. In most of these countries the greatest decreases in death rates among infants and children occurred in the late 1940s, and the large numbers of children born in that period will be in their peak reproductive years in the early 1970s. Their children will in turn further inflate the lower tiers of the population pyramid. Eventually, either population control will lower birth rates in these countries, or famine or other natural checks on population will once again increase mortality in the youngest age classes — or possibly in all age classes. If birth rates are lowered, there will also be a rise in the death rate as the population ages. In the absence of both birth control and natural checks, however, death rates in the extraordinarily young populations of these UDCs may temporarily fall below those of the DCs. For instance, in 1972 the death rate in the United Kingdom was 11.7 per thousand, in Belgium 12.3, and in the United States 9.3. In contrast, the death rate in Costa Rica was 7.0, Trinidad 7.0, Ceylon 8.0, Singapore 5.0, and Hong Kong 5.0.

Other types of population profiles are often found. For instance, rapid and substantial decreases in birth rate, which can be produced by the onset of a successful birth-control program, may temporarily produce a population profile that is sharply constricted at the base. Such is the shape of Japan's 1960 profile (Figure 2–6), which shows the effects of an extremely rapid postwar decline in the birth rate. Japan is a DC today, but the profile resembles that of a typical UDC from the 10–14 age class upward. However, the 0–4 and 5–9 classes are considerably smaller than in most UDCs, so only 30 percent of the population is under 15.

One of the most significant features of the age composition of a population is the proportion of people who are economically productive to those who are dependent on them. For purposes of convenience, the segment of the population in the age class 15–64 is chosen as an index of the productive portion of the population. In the population profiles (Figures 2–5 and 2–6), the working ages are shown in medium gray, the young dependents in pale gray; and older people in dark gray. Figures 2–5 and 2–6 provide a comparison of the proportion of dependents in these same populations. The proportion of dependents in UDCs is generally much higher than in the DCs, primarily because a large fraction of the population is under 15 years of age (Figure 2–7). Thus the ratio of dependents to the total population size is higher in the poor countries and lower in the rich countries, although the ratio is somewhat misleading because of the heavier utilization of child labor in UDCs. This unfortunate dependency ratio is an additional heavy burden to the UDCs as they struggle for economic development.

The birth and death rates, which are expressed in births and deaths per thousand people in the entire population, are known technically as *crude birth rates* and *crude death rates*. They are called "crude" simply because they do not allow for differences in the structure of populations. They are the most readily available (and thus most widely quoted) figures, and, although they are often useful, comparison of crude rates may be quite misleading.

An outstanding example was the highly publicized drop in the birth rate of the United States during the 1960s, which was widely misinterpreted as heralding the end of the U.S. population explosion. For instance, the birth rate in 1968 was 17.4 per thousand, a record low for the country, going below

Figure 2–6   Age composition of population of Japan in 1960. Note narrow base of profile, caused by a sharp decrease in the birth rate. (After Thompson and Lewis, *Population Problems*, 5th ed. McGraw-Hill, 1965.)

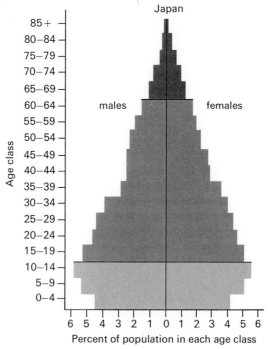

Figure 2–7 High birth rates and low death rates create burdens both for families and for nations in underdeveloped areas. These homeless children live in the streets of Bombay. (Wide World Photos.)

the previous low of the depression year 1936. The trend in birth rates between 1959 and 1968 is shown in Figure 2–8. In this period the crude birth rate declined about 25 percent. Closer examination of the data, however, shows that this decrease was caused only in part by a drop in the number of children born to the average couple. The rest of the decrease was due to a reduction in the percentage of the population in the childbearing years. The relevant demographic statistic here is the *fertility rate.*

The fertility rate—the number of births per thousand women 15–44 years of age—is a more refined indicator of birth trends because it compensates for differences in age composition. As is shown in Figure 2–9, the fertility rate in the U.S. was declining during the period 1959–1968. Thus, not only were fewer babies being born in proportion to the entire population, but fewer babies were being born in relation to the population of females in their childbearing years. The 1968 fertility rate of about 85 was still higher than the lows reached during the Depression, when the figure was well below 80. In 1970 the fertility rate rose to 87.6. However, in 1971 it fell again to 82.3, and in 1972, it dropped below 80.

Does this mean that the population explosion in the United States is coming to an end? Actually, it is impossible to say at this point whether the figures for the last decade denote the beginning of a sustained trend, or whether they are merely part of the short-term ups and downs that continually confound the demographers and economists who try to explain these things.

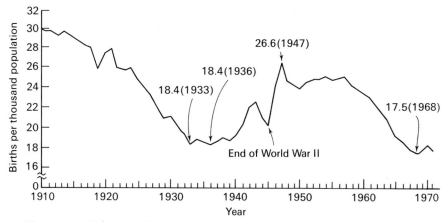

Figure 2-8   Birth rate in United States, 1910–1971. (After *Population Profile*, Population Reference Bureau, March 1967; recent data from U.S. Census Bureau.)

A continued decline and persistent low level of fertility may result from the social forces now at work in our society: rising public awareness of the consequences of overpopulation, the growth of the women's liberation movement, the extension of family-planning services to low-income groups, the liberalization of abortion laws. If, on the other hand, the fertility rate is still largely determined by economic factors, such as the unemployment rate among prospective fathers, then continuing fluctuations rather than a steady downward trend are to be expected.

We know from the statistics on births over the past two decades that the number of women in the 15–44 age class in the United States will be increasing throughout the 1970s, and that the age 20–29 subgroup, which bears most of the children, will be increasing even faster—about 33 percent between 1970 and 1980. Therefore, unless the fertility rate *stays* near its 1972 low or falls lower, the *crude birth rate* in the U.S. will be higher in the late 1970s than it

Figure 2-9   Fertility rate in United States, 1910–1971. (After *Population Profile*, Population reference Bureau, March 1967; recent data from U.S. Census Bureau.)

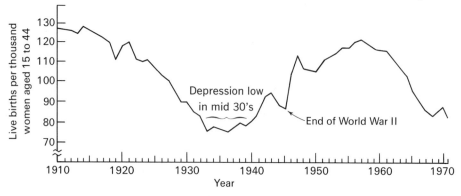

was in the 1960s. Unless the death rate also rises, this will result in a higher growth rate for the population.

The Potential for Population Growth.   Fertility and death rates (vital rates) may be separately calculated for any age class in the population. For instance, the number of babies born to each thousand women of age 25 is the *age-specific fertility rate* for 25-year olds. The number of 25-year olds who die per thousand people of that age in the population is the *age-specific death rate* for 25-year olds. At any given time a population has a schedule of age-specific fertility and death rates. Most human populations show rather high age-specific death rates in the age 0–1 and considerably lower rates in the next nine years. Infants are more likely to die than young children. After the age of 10, there is generally a slow rise in death rates until around 45 to 50, and then a rapid rise. There is, of course, considerable variation from country to country. UDCs, for instance, tend to have proportionately much higher infant and child mortality rates than do DCs.

The high percentage of people under 15 years of age is also indicative of the explosive growth potential of UDC populations. In most UDCs this percentage is 40–45; in a few as high as 50. By contrast, the percentage under age 15 in DCs is usually 20 to 30. Thus UDCs have a much greater proportion of people now in their prereproductive years than DCs have. That population of young people will soon be moving into age classes with high age-specific fertility rates, *but it will be some 50 years before they are subject to the high age-specific death rates associated with old age.* Fifty years is about two generations, which means that those youngsters will have children and grandchildren before they swell the upper part of the age pyramid and begin to make heavy contributions to the crude death rate. Therefore, even if the fertility in the population dropped precipitously to a level that would eventually result in an end to population growth, that end would not be reached for 50 years or more. That is, *assuming there is no rise in the age-specific death rates,* there will be a long "braking-time" before even very successful birth-control programs can halt growth in UDCs. The momentum inherent in the age composition means that population size will go far beyond the level at which the "brakes" are applied.

Demographer Nathan Keyfitz has calculated the magnitude of that momentum.[4] He showed what would happen if a birth-control miracle were to occur and the average number of children born to each woman in a typical UDC were to drop immediately to the replacement level. (With replacement reproduction, each married couple would on the average have just the number of children that would lead to their replacement in the next generation. Where death rates are at typical DC levels, this would be about 2.3 children per couple. The extra children beyond two would compensate for child mortality, non-

---

[4]"On the Momentum of Population Growth," Nathan Keyfitz, in *Demography*, vol. 8, no. 1, pp. 71–80, Feb. 1971.

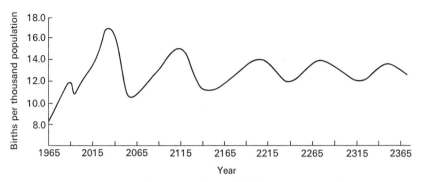

Figure 2–10   Projection of changes in the crude birth rate that would be necessary if the total population of the U.S. were to remain constant during the period from 1965 to 2365. (After Frejka, *Population Studies*, Nov. 1968.)

marriage and infertility in their generation.) If replacement reproduction were achieved overnight, a typical UDC would continue to grow until it was about 1.6 times its present size. Should the fertility rates drop to the replacement level gradually over the next 30 years, the final population size would be some 2.5 times the present size. However, even a drop to replacement level in 30 years is extremely unlikely to occur.

Demographer Tomas Frejka, using 1965 as a base year, has shown what would happen to the United States population under a variety of assumptions.[5] For instance, instant ZPG (zero population growth—a stationary or nongrowing population) could be achieved only by reducing the average family size to about 1.2 children for the years between 1965 and 1985. Thus, to bring the crude birth and death rates immediately into balance (so that the growth rate is zero), the average completed family size would have to drop *far below* the replacement level. After that, in order to hold the population size constant, the crude birth rate and average family size would have to fluctuate wildly above and below the long run equilibrium values for several centuries (Figure 2–10). The age composition, correspondingly, would change violently, undoubtedly producing a variety of severe social problems. These problems could be avoided by reducing the fertility rate less abruptly and then accepting a temporary decline in population, rather than attempting, by temporary increases and decreases, to hold the population precisely at ZPG. As will be discussed later, there are powerful arguments for reducing the size of the American population well below its present level.

Frejka also described what would happen if the average size of the American family simply declined from its 1965 level to replacement level. From that

[5]"Reflections on the Demographic Conditions Needed to Establish a U.S. Stationary Population Growth," Tomas Frejka, in *Population Studies*, vol. 22, pp. 379–397, Nov. 1968.

time until population growth actually stops would take about 65 to 75 years. Figure 2–11 shows projected population growth if replacement reproduction were reached and maintained in a series of years starting with 1975, assuming no immigration. The projections clearly show that substantial population growth will occur after a pattern of replacement reproduction is established, no matter when that may be. For instance, if it were reached in 1985, the population would not stop growing until 2055, in which case there would be an ultimate population of around 300 million.

Distribution and Dispersion

Mankind is not uniformly distributed over the face of the Earth. Figure 2–12 shows the rough pattern of population density in 1965. Population density is the number of individuals per unit of area. For human populations this figure is normally expressed as people per square mile or per square kilo-

Figure 2–11   Projections of the course of population growth in the U.S. if replacement reproduction is achieved in various years. Total population size would be slightly less than twice the size of the female population, since there are slightly fewer men than women. (After Frejka, *Population Studies*, Nov. 1968.)

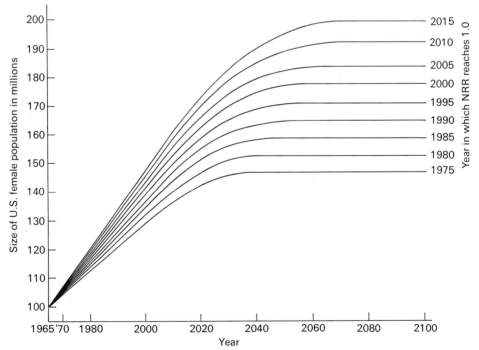

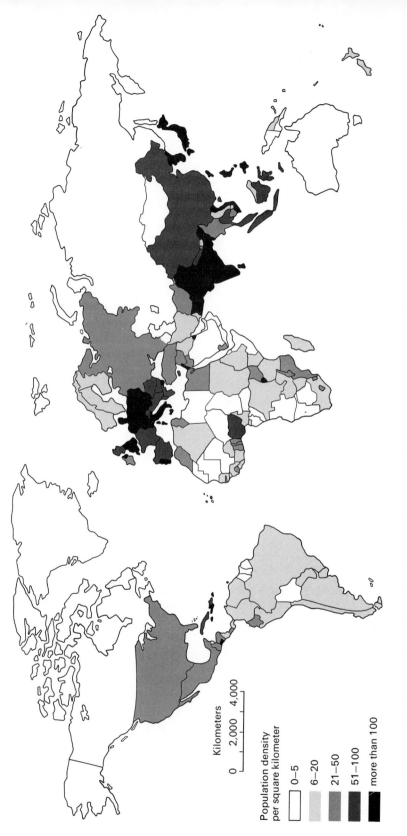

Figure 2-12 Patterns of population density, 1969. Figures are given in persons per square kilometer. A square kilometer is 0.3861 square miles. (Data from UN, *Demographic Yearbook*, 1969.)

Population density
per square kilometer

0–5
6–20
21–50
51–100
more than 100

Kilometers

0   2,000   4,000

meter. Some rough estimates (people per square mile) of population densities in the late 1960s are:

Earth (land area)	65
United States	55
Japan	700
Tokyo	20,000
New York City	25,000
Manhattan	75,000

In contrast, before the arrival of Europeans in what is now the continental United States, the population density was about 0.33 people per square mile; the density rose to 5 people per square mile by about 1800. Of course, one must be cautious in picturing densities in terms of people per square mile because of the human tendency to gather in clusters. Although the United States in 1971 had about 57 people per square mile *on the average* (67 per square mile in the 48 adjacent states), there are, of course, many square miles that have no people. Furthermore, within any given square mile people will not ordinarily be evenly distributed.

The densities and distributions of populations, especially in relation to resources, have played critical roles in many important events in human history. Densities that are perceived by the members of populations themselves as "high" generate what is generally referred to as "population pressure." Overpopulation is usually thought of in relation not to the absolute size of a population but to its density. There must have been many thousands of occasions in prehistory when individuals of one tribe or another decided that their home territory was running short of berries or game, and moved in on their neighbors. Many of the famous migrations of history, such as the barbarian invasions of Europe in the early Christian era, may have been due to such population-resource pressures. In 1095, when Pope Urban II preached the First Crusade, he referred to the advantages of gaining new lands. The crusaders were mainly second sons who were dispossessed because of the growing European trend toward primogeniture (inheritance by the first-born son only).

Considerable evidence indicates that population pressures were building up in fifteenth-century Europe. There is, for instance, evidence of attempts at land reclamation during the period. Then, the addition of the New World frontier to Europe at the end of the fifteenth century reduced the overall population density from about 27 people per square mile of Europe to less than 5 people per square mile in the West (Europe plus the Western Hemisphere). European exploitation of the spatial, mineral, and other material wealth of the New World led to the creation of a basic set of institutions attuned to frontier attitudes. The economic boom that followed lasted for 400 years. As far as land is concerned, the boom is now plainly over. The population density of today's European metropolis (Western Europe plus the Western Hemisphere) increased until it again exceeded 27 per square mile before 1930. Since all of the material things on which the boom depended came ultimately from the land, the entire boom is clearly limited. In fact, many of the institutions and attitudes that evolved in the frontier setting now constitute a major threat to the survival of mankind.

Many wars were fought by European nations as they scrambled to occupy the Western Hemisphere. They warred among themselves and against the small native populations in the New World. More recently, population pressure contributed to Nazi Germany's famous drive for "lebensraum" (literally, room for living).

Japan's expansionist moves in the 1930s and early 1940s can also be traced in part to the high population density on her small islands. The population growth of Japan in the last third of the nineteenth century and the first third of the twentieth century was unprecedented among industrialized nations. It doubled in size (from 35 to 70 million) and therefore in density during the 63 years between 1874 and 1937. When the attempt to conquer additional territory failed, and population growth continued to accelerate, Japan took drastic steps to slow down her population growth. Japan is now again feeling the pinch of population pressure and is looking toward the continent of Asia for at least economic lebensraum.

Population pressures are certainly contributing to international tensions in the world today. Russia, India, and other neighbors of grossly over-populated, still rapidly growing China guard their frontiers nervously. Chinese forces have already occupied Tibet. Population growth in China may leave her little long-range choice but to expand or starve, unless her population control policies are successful. Australians are clearly apprehensive about the Asian multitudes. This attitude is reflected in their nation's "whites only" immigration laws and western-oriented foreign policy. They have reason to be fearful, since the generally unfavorable and unreliable climate over much of Australia, together with its history of disastrous agricultural practices, mean that the entire continent lacks the resources for absorbing even a single year's increment to the Asian population. Such an increment would more than *quadruple* Australia's population from 13 million to 61 million. The number of people added *annually* to India's population alone is more than the entire population of Australia today.

Urbanization

One of the oldest of all demographic trends is the one toward urbanization. Preagricultural man, by necessity, had to be dispersed over the landscape. Hunting and gathering required perhaps a minimum of 2 square miles of territory to produce the food for one person. Under such conditions, and without even the most primitive of transportation systems, it was impossible for people to exist in large concentrations. But the agricultural revolution began to change all that. Because more food could be produced in less area, people

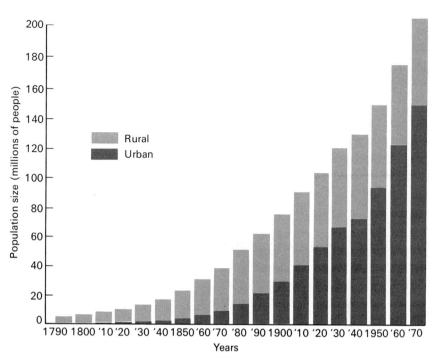

Figure 2–13 Urbanization of the United States. (After *Population Bulletin*, vol. 19, no. 2.)

began to form primitive communities. The ability of a farmer to feed more than his own family was obviously a prerequisite of urbanization. A fraction of the population first had to be freed from cultivation of the land in order to form cities. The actual impetus for the development of cities may have been to have centers for storage and distribution of food or for defense. Whatever the reason, the first cities arose along the Tigris and Euphrates rivers between 4000 and 3000 B.C.

The trend toward urbanization continues today, as it generally has since those first cities were formed. The move to the cities has at times been accelerated by agricultural advances that have made possible the establishment of larger, more efficient farms. It seems also to have been accelerated by growth in rural areas, which necessitated either the subdivision of farms among several sons, or the migration of "surplus" offspring to the cities. In the past, advances in agriculture were generally accompanied by advances in other kinds of technology, which provided new opportunities for employment in cities. Beyond providing places for those displaced from the land, cities have always been attractive in themselves to people who hoped to improve their economic condition. The movement into large urban concentrations has been especially accelerated in the last century. For instance, in the United States about 6 percent of the population lived in urban areas in 1800, 15 percent in 1850, 40 percent in 1900; today, nearly 75 percent live in cities or their suburbs (Figure 2–13).

Rapid urbanization has not been confined to industrialized countries, however. Between 1950 and 1960, the populations of cities in the DCs increased 25 percent, while those of cities in the UDCs increased 55 percent. In Latin America, especially since the end of World War II, there has been an increasing flood of impoverished peasants into urban areas. Yet employment opportunities there have not materialized. The result has been the development of characteristic huge shantytowns (Figure 2–14).

The trend in Africa has been similar, with hundreds of thousands migrating to the cities annually in search of a better life. Nairobi, the capital of Kenya,

Figure 2–14   A shantytown in the Rimac District of Lima, Peru. Many squatter houses, originally straw shacks, are being rebuilt in brick and masonry whenever the earnings of the owners permit. (Courtesy of William Mangin.)

had a 1968 population of 460,000 and was growing at a rate of 7 percent per year. That is more than double the growth rate of Los Angeles in the decade 1950–1960. Accra, the capital of Ghana, is growing at almost 8 percent per year; Abidjan, capital of the Ivory Coast, at almost 10 percent; Lusaka, capital of Zambia, and Lagos, capital of Nigeria, both at 14 percent. In both Latin America and Africa the trend to the cities seems to be caused in large part by the kind of hope for a better life that has drawn many people from rural areas of the southern United States and Puerto Rico to a slum life in New York, Chicago, and other Northern metropolises. And in the cities of underdeveloped countries where there is little industry, the opportunities are much more limited than in the United States. Yet, miserable as their condition is, nearly all the migrants evidently prefer to remain in the cities rather than return to what they left. Of course, many may also have burned their bridges behind them and have no way of successfully returning to their former homes.

The rate of urbanization in Asia in this century has also been rapid, but in many areas the increases have been from a rather low base. For instance, at the turn of the century about 11 percent of India's population was urban. Today more than 20 percent of India's people live in cities. Most of this increase has occurred since 1931, with the largest percent increase occurring in the decade 1941–1951 and the largest absolute increase in the decade 1951–1961. Data for the period since the 1961 census are not available, but the figure of 20 percent is based on the 1961 figures corrected for comparability with previous censuses and projected. Under the new, more restricted definition of "urban," the figure would be close to 20 percent today.

Urbanization in the United States in some ways differs dramatically from urbanization in most UDCs. For instance, the difference between city-dwellers and country-dwellers in the United States has become increasingly blurred, especially in recent years, with urban culture becoming dominant. Rapid transportation and mass media have exposed the country folk to the ways of the city. Furthermore, the phenomenon of suburbanization has developed. Suburbanites, who take advantage of high-speed transport and general affluence, attempt to enjoy the advantages of city and countryside simultaneously, working in the former and living close to the latter.

While urbanization in the United States has been much less rapid than in the UDCs, suburbanization has been extremely rapid since World War II and has led to some severe problems. While affluent and middle-class taxpayers have left the cities, poor and unskilled people from rural areas, squeezed out by increasingly mechanized agriculture, have flooded to them seeking jobs in industry. As tax returns to city governments have dwindled, it has become more and more difficult for cities to maintain even basic services. In an effort to restore their tax losses, many cities' urban renewal projects consist mainly of highrise office buildings, which are mostly used by commuting suburbanites, while the slum areas housing the poor become even more crowded, neglected, and crime-ridden. Thus the contemporary American city consists largely of office buildings and slums, surrounded by affluent suburbs, free-

ways, and industrial areas. It is strangled during the day by traffic, as suburbanites commute to the city and factory workers commute out of it. Nevertheless,
American and other DC cities have the resources to solve their urban problems,
difficult though they are. Their problems are largely the result of poor planning
or none at all. In UDCs, urban problems are largely the result of being over-
whelmed by massive, unanticipated immigration from the countryside.

In the UDCs communications and transportation are much less efficient
than in DCs, and the peasant culture is less influenced by the urban. According to Nathan Keyfitz,[6] the overwhelming majority of urban dwellers in
the UDCs are recent migrants from the countryside who have brought their
peasant culture with them. Unlike most DC urbanites or suburbanites, whose
specialized education, training, and skills assure them of a place in the city's
complex social web, the UDC immigrant has no such skills to offer. Unskilled
U.S. rural immigrants are definitely in the minority; although they may have
employment problems, most can be absorbed into the industrial society.
Cities in developed countries are a source of wealth and power, generated
through technology and manufacturing. The goods they produce are exchanged
for food from the countryside.

In contrast, many UDC cities subsist in times of shortage primarily on food
imported from other countries. Attracted by the opportunity to obtain a share
of the imported food, inhabitants of the countryside move into these cities
when the countryside can no longer support them. Inevitably, they find that
their limited skills render them incapable of contributing to the economy. As
a consequence, they are not much better off than they were where they came
from. In many UDC cities these unproductive squatters now make up a majority
of the population, and their number in most places is growing very rapidly.
Many migrants to the UDC city maintain contact with their home villages or
form modified village societies within the city and thus tend to transfer the
village culture to the city. This may explain why the reproductive rates and
attitudes of the inhabitants of these cities closely resemble those of their
rural relatives.

Even more interesting than the present situation are projections of trends
in urbanization. For instance, one projection leads to a population estimate for
Calcutta in the year 2000 of 66 million people, more than eight times today's
population. Needless to say, this will not be reached—but there is a realistic
expectation that the population of this teeming city (Figure 2–15), which has
several hundred thousand people living homeless in its streets today, will
increase from 7.5 million to 12 million in the next two decades. Calcutta is
already a disaster area, and the consequences of further growth at such a rate
are heart-rending to contemplate. The population of relatively prosperous
Tokyo is projected to reach 40 million in the year 2000 (as opposed to perhaps

[6]"Population Density and the Style of Social Life," Nathan Keyfitz, in *BioScience*,
vol. 16, no. 12, pp. 868–873, Dec. 1966. This interesting article includes some information on the origin of cities as well as on differences between DC and UDC cities.

Figure 2–15 A street in Calcutta. These people live in makeshift shacks built on the sidewalk. Some of the shacks also function as shops where the "owners" sell food and handmade articles. (Wide World Photos.)

16 million in 1970). In a desperate attempt to create land for expansion, Tokyo is using 7,000 tons of garbage a day to fill Tokyo Bay. Flat, empty land is at a premium in mountainous, overpopulated Japan. Middle-class apartments are already so scarce that there is a 2-year waiting list. Tokyo's incredible crowding seems destined only to get worse.

Demographer Kingsley Davis has made some extrapolations of urbanization trends and has produced some startling statistics. If the urban growth rate that has prevailed since 1950 should continue, half of the people in the world would be living in the cities by 1984. If the trend should continue to 2023 (it cannot!), everyone in the world would live in an urban area. Most striking of all, in 2020 most people would not just be in urban areas; half of the world's human beings would be in cities of over one million population, and in 2044 *everyone* would be existing in "cities" of that size. At that time the largest "city" would have a projected population of 1.4 billion people (out of a projected world population of 15 billion). The word "city" is in quotation marks because, should such a stage be reached, world living conditions would make the term meaningless in its usual sense.

Demographic Projections

Horrendous figures may be generated by projecting the present rate of human population growth worldwide into the future. After all, the doubling time for that population is now only about 35 years. If growth continued at that rate, the world population would exceed a billion billion people only 1,000 years from now. That would be some 1,700 persons per square yard of the Earth's surface, land and sea! Even more preposterous illustrations can be made. In a few thousand more years, everything in the visible universe would be converted into people, and the diameter of the ball of people would be expanding with the speed of light! Such projections should convince all but the most obtuse that growth of the human population must stop eventually.

Of primary interest and significance to us are predictions of population sizes in the next few decades. The most complete of these are the medium, low, and high population projections for the period 1965–2000 made by the

Figure 2–16   Projected growth of world population, based on the United Nations "constant fertility" projections. (After *Population Bulletin*, vol. 21, no. 4.)

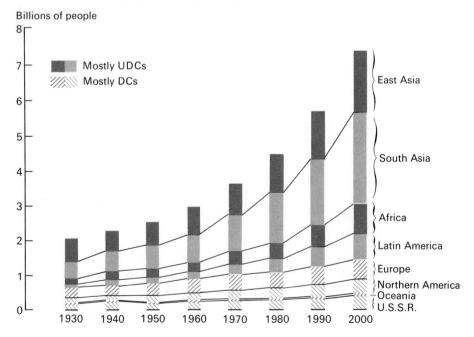

United Nations in 1963. These projections are not simple extrapolations of past trends or present rates of change in total size into the future. Instead, they take into account the many components of population growth. Specific forecasts are made of trends in age-specific fertility, death rates, migration, and so forth, based on the best available demographic data for the nations or regions of the world, and the scope of future variation in these rates is estimated on the basis of past trends in developed and underdeveloped areas. (Possible major disasters, such as thermonuclear war, are not considered.) All of these data are integrated to provide medium, low, and high projections, the last two of which the demographers hope will bracket the actual figures. The accuracy of the projections depends, of course, on the degree to which the various actual rates differ from the predicted rates. Another projection, called the "constant fertility, no migration" projection, is made on the simpler assumption that current fertility and the current trend in mortality will continue and that there will be no migration between areas. A revision of the 1963 projections was made in 1968, but only the medium variant was prepared for areas within the developed regions (Figure 2–16).

The low 1963 U.N. forecast projects a world population of about 5,449 million in the year 2000; the medium forecast, 6,130 million: the high, 6,994 million; and the constant-fertility projection is 7,522 million. The United Nations' low, medium, and high projections all rest on an assumption that fertility rates will be lowered in those areas where they are now dangerously high. Data for various regions are given in Table 2–4.

Table 2–4   Estimate of Population in the Year 2000 (in millions)

Region	1971 Population	Projection							
		Low		Medium		High		Constant Fertility, No Migration	
		1963	1968	1963	1968	1963	1968	1963	1968
World total	3,706	5,449		6,130	6,494	6,994		7,522	
East Asia	946	1,118		1,287	1,424	1,623		1,811	
South Asia	1,157	1,984	2,119	2,171	2,354	2,444	2,617	2,702	2,989
Europe	466	491		527	568	563		570	
Soviet Union	245	316		353	330	403		402	
Africa	354	684	734	768	818	864	906	860	873
Northern America	229	294		354	333	376		388	
Latin America	291	532		638	652	686		756	
Oceania	20	28		32	35	35		33	
Developed regions	1,105	1,293		1,441	1,454	1,574		1,580	
Underdeveloped regions	2,601	4,155	4,523	4,688	5,040	5,420	5,650	5,942	6,369

SOURCE: United Nations, *World Population Prospects as Assessed in 1963 and 1968.* 1971 data from World Population Data Sheet, Population Reference Bureau.

The history of population projections and forecasts in the past few decades has been that they have erred fairly consistently on the low side. For instance, in its November 8, 1948, issue, *Time* magazine quoted the opinions of unnamed experts who felt then that a prediction (by the Food and Agriculture Organization of the United Nations) of a world population of 2,250 million in 1960 was probably too high. The actual population in 1960 was about 3000 milion. In 1949 economist Colin Clark predicted a world population in 1990 of 3.5 billion, and in 1950 demographer Frank Notestein predicted that by the year 2000 there would be 3.3 billion people. Both figures were exceeded well before 1970. In 1957 the demographers of the United Nations offered the following population projections for 1970: low, 3,350 million; medium, 3,480 million; and high, 3,500 million. The population actually passed the high projection for 1970 sometime near the end of 1968. In the Depression years it was common for demographers to show great concern over the possibility of population declines in Europe and North America. Their apprehension was based on projections of trends in both the birth rate and the death rate. But Depression declines in DC birth rates were more than compensated for by the baby boom of the 1940s and 1950s. And the unprecedented effect of death control exported from DCs to UDCs was not foreseen.

The changes between the 1963 and 1968 U.N. projections are based on the findings that during the 1960s birthrates dropped only slightly, mainly in DCs, while death rates declined considerably in UDCs and remained low in DCs. The new figures are higher for most regions, but particularly for those areas in Asia and Africa where death rates have declined from previous high levels. Table 2–5 summarizes the history of United Nations projections of the population size in 1980 and indicates what a tricky business the making of such forecasts can be.

We feel that United Nations projections for the year 2000, with the possible exception of the low forecast, *are too high*. This is not, however, because we share their optimism about the future impact of family-planning programs on birth rates. Instead, for reasons explained in later chapters, we fear that a

Table 2–5 Projections of World Population in 1980 as Made by the United Nations at Several Points of Time from 1951 to 1968

Made in	Low	Medium Variant	High
1951	2,976		3,636
1954	3,295		3,990
1957	3,850	4,220	4,280
1963	4,147	4,339	4,550
1968		4,457	

Courtesy of Nathan Keyfitz

drastic rise in the death rate will either slow or end the population explosion, unless efforts to avoid such a tragic eventuality are immediately mounted.

Bibliography

Keyfitz, N., and W. Flieger, 1971. *Population: Facts and Methods of Demography.* W. H. Freeman and Company, San Francisco. Gives life tables and other calculations for most countries where birth and death statistics exist, and explains methods used in these calculations. Age distributions, sex ratios, and population increase are among its themes. Highly recommended.

Population Reference Bureau. *Population Bulletin.* This periodical is a major source of information for the educated layman on all aspects of demography. The Bureau also produces an invaluable annual "Population Data Sheet" (see Appendix). For more information write Population Reference Bureau, 1755 Massachusetts Avenue, N.W., Washington, D.C. 20036.

Thompson, W. S., and D. J. Lewis, 1965. *Population Problems*, 5th ed. McGraw-Hill, New York. An excellent, comprehensive source.

United Nations Statistical Office. *Demographic Yearbook.* This annual compilation is *the* source for world data on population.

The pressure of energy consumption upon the land. Above, strip-mining of coal in Illinois. Three million acres of land in the United States have been strip-mined. (Photo by William A. Garnett.)

THREE

Carrying Capacity: Land, Energy, and Mineral Resources

What is the capacity of the Earth to support people? There is no simple answer. Capacity may be defined in different ways, and it may change with time. Do we wish to know how many humans can be kept barely alive in a teeming, oppressive, and squalid world? Or shall we define capacity in terms of the number that might be supported with some measure of comfort and dignity? Whichever way we choose to look at carrying capacity, there are a number of different factors that might determine its limits. It is not yet clear whether physical, biological or social resources will prove to be in shortest supply, but some feeling for the question of carrying capacity can be gained by looking at where mankind stands today in relation to each of these categories. We begin with the physical resources of land, energy, and minerals.

Land

The Earth has a land area of some 58.4 million square miles, which in 1971 was occupied at an average density of about 64 people per square mile. This is not such a high density—it amounts to 10 acres per person. If acreage were all there is to evaluating land resources, there would be little reason for immediate concern. However, land area is a resource only insofar as topography,

climate, vegetation, quality of soils, availability of water, and other characteristics enable the land to serve some human need. At best, only about 30
percent of the land surface is potentially arable (farmable); 20 percent is
uncultivable mountainous terrain; 20 percent is desert or steppe; 20 percent
is under ice, snow, and permafrost (Antarctica alone accounts for 6 million
square miles); and 10 percent consists of other types of land with soils inadequate for cultivation. A third of the potentially arable land is now actually
being cultivated, amounting to an average of one acre per person, worldwide.

Needless to say, much of the land that is uncultivable is also so inhospitable
as to be nearly uninhabitable—the Arctic and Antarctic, steep slopes, swamps,
certain desert regions, and so on. For good reason, the human population is
spread very unevenly over the Earth's land surface. People have concentrated
and continue to concentrate today in the areas that are most hospitable.

Some of the most serious land problems arise from competing, mutually
exclusive uses for the same advantageously located pieces of land. Many of
our cities arose in the center of the best farmland, so that some of this valuable
resource has been lost beneath highways, suburbs, and airports as the cities
have spread. Coastlines are in demand as a desirable place to live, as a recre-

Figure 3–1   An example of development on an estuary near San Rafael, California,
on San Francisco Bay. Houses and boat docks are built right on the shore; a freeway
interchange has been built over the water. Dikes are shown at the lower left, and even
the channels are manmade. (Photo by Aero Photographers.)

Table 3–1   Land Use in the United States in 1970

Use	Millions of Acres	Percentage of Total
Cropland and pasture	445	23.4
Nonproducing farm uses	45	2.4
Grazing	700	36.8
Commercial forest	484	25.4
Recreation	60	3.2
Urban	26	1.3
Transportation	27	1.4
Military	18	0.9
Wildlife refuge	16	0.8
Reservoirs	13	0.7
Other	70	3.7
Total	1904	100.0

NOTE: These estimates are based on data from *Resources in America's Future*. They apply to the 48 adjacent states and do not include Alaska or Hawaii.

ational resource for those who do not live there, as economical sites for electric power plants, and most importantly as outlets for commerce and bases for the utilization of marine resources (Figure 3–1). Unfortunately, the coasts are also the location of relatively fragile communities of plants and animals, such as those in salt marshes and estuaries, upon which much of the productivity of the sea depends. More than 60 percent of the rich commercial fishery on the continental shelf of the eastern United States, for example, consists of species that spend part of their life cycles in estuaries.[1] Leaving essential ecological systems such as these intact may prove to be one of the most important uses of land; it may also prove to be one of the uses that is least compatible with other human activities. To assume that man should dare to exploit every bit of land that appears potentially capable of being exploited would be dangerous (although not unprecedented) arrogance.

In summary, there seems to be a good deal of available land if one does not inquire too carefully as to what kind it is; but the most useful sorts of land are already in short supply in most parts of the world. A breakdown of land use in the United States in 1970 is given in Table 3–1. One need only add that American consumers (and those in many other nations that rely heavily on imports of food or raw materials) must be considered to be "occupying" a good deal of land outside their national boundaries. In this sense, DC's "occupy" coffee plantations in Brazil and rubber plantations in Laos, land used for bauxite mines in Jamaica and copper mines in Zambia, rangeland for cattle

[1]"Management of Estuarine Fisheries," J. L. McHugh, in *A Symposium on Estuarine Fisheries*, Special Publication No. 3, American Fisheries Society, Washington, D.C., 1966.

and sheep in Argentina, lumber producing forests in Ethiopia and Indonesia, and land used for growing soybeans in Colombia and peanuts in Nigeria.

Energy

A good working definition of energy is "the capacity to do work" (Box 3–1). The use of energy, other than that derived from food, as a substitute for labor and time (and to permit activities not otherwise possible at all) is a major ingredient of material prosperity. Will the amount of available energy impose an ultimate limit on human population growth? No simple answer is possible — but the way society manages its use of energy will clearly be a major determinant of the *quality* of human life, not merely in the distant future but in the decades immediately ahead.

The situation may be summarized as follows: we are not running out of

---

Box 3–1   Energy and the Laws of Thermodynamics

The Laws of Thermodynamics are actually a set of rules formulated by scientists to describe a vast number of observations of the physical world. The First Law of Thermodynamics states simply that energy is neither created nor destroyed, although it may change form. This is the law of conservation of energy. For instance, when a gallon of gasoline is burned in an automobile, *chemical energy* is converted in complex ways into *energy of motion* of the car and of parts of its engine, and into *heat energy* emitted from the car. When the car stops, the energy of motion, too, is converted into heat. A careful accounting will show that, at any given time, the net amount of chemical energy used is equal to the amount of energy of motion and/or heat produced; that is, energy is conserved. Cases of apparent violations of this law have invariably been due to inaccurate measurements or to leaving a form of energy out of the accounting altogether.

The Second Law of Thermodynamics is much more subtle and difficult to grasp. The observations it describes that are of greatest importance to considerations in this book may be summarized in several ways. One is that changes in the physical world proceed, on the whole, in such a way as to reduce the amount of energy available to do work. (Think of work as lifting a weight, turning a crank,

and so on.) In other words, this law says the *usefulness* of energy is always being consumed, even though the energy is still present in one form or another. For this reason it is often said that the Second Law of Thermodynamics tells us that the Universe is "running down."

Energy is most useable where it is most concentrated — as it is in the chemical bonds of gasoline or at high temperature in steam. The Second Law says that there is an overall tendency *away* from concentration, *away* from high temperature. Energy that has been changed in form with an accompanying reduction in usefulness (that is, a reduction in its availability for doing work) is said to have been *degraded*. Typically this degradation of energy leads to the production of heat at relatively low, hence relatively useless, temperatures — for example the heat of a car's exhaust, the heat of the tires' friction against the road, the heat radiated by your body, the heat of a decomposing animal carcass. The Second Law of Thermodynamics tells us why energy cannot be recycled and, hence, why we need a continual input of energy to maintain ourselves; why we must eat much more than a pound of food to gain a pound of weight; and why humanity may make this planet uncomfortably warm with degraded energy long before we run out of high-grade energy to consume.

**Table 3–2   Sources of Nonfood Energy
Consumption in 1968**

Source	Percentage of World Consumption	Percentage of U.S. Consumption
Coal	36.6	22.5
Petroleum	42.7	43.0
Natural gas	18.3	33.0
Hydroelectric	2.1	1.3
Nuclear	0.3	0.2

SOURCE: *Energy in the World Economy.*
NOTE: Table excludes wood and dung burned for fuel. These
sources probably accounted for less than 10 percent of world
nonfood energy consumption in 1968, and perhaps 1 percent
of the U.S. figure.

energy, but heavy environmental costs attend both its production and consumption. Moreover, people in the DCs are using the richest and most accessible energy resources at a rate not justified by legitimate needs (Figure 3–2),
and energy consumption is doubling every 14 to 17 years in DCs and UDCs
alike. The difficulties and consequences of maintaining this rapid growth rate
raise many questions besides that of potential supplies of fuels. Can the technology to extract, transport, and process the fuels keep pace with rising
demand? Will environmental mistakes become more frequent and serious as
we attempt to deploy such technology rapidly? Will sufficient investment
capital be available to pay for expanding the energy supplies?

Fossil Fuels.   The issue of supply itself is not a simple one. The supplies
of high grade fossil fuels (coal, petroleum, and natural gas) are limited, and
even coal, the most abundant of these, will probably be consumed within a
few hundred years. This does not mean that *all* the coal, oil, and gas will be
gone, of course. Society will simply reach the point at which the quality of
the remaining supplies is so low, or the effort required to get at it so great,
that extraction is not worth the cost.

Petroleum and natural gas will go much sooner than coal. The most recent
and thorough estimate, by geologist M. King Hubbert, gives us about a century
before world petroleum reserves (including recent Alaskan discoveries) are
substantially depleted, and the outlook for natural gas is no better.[2] The
present heavy reliance on fossil fuel is shown in Table 3–2. The rise in costs
as scarcity increases will be a continuous process, possibly accelerated by
energy demands associated with limited industrial development in the UDCs.
All indications point to increasing energy costs for Americans even in the
next few years as higher extraction costs and the expense of even nominal
pollution-control efforts make themselves felt. Of course, increases in the cost

[2]"Energy Resources," M. King Hubbert, in *Resources and Man,* W. H. Freeman and
Company, San Francisco, 1969.

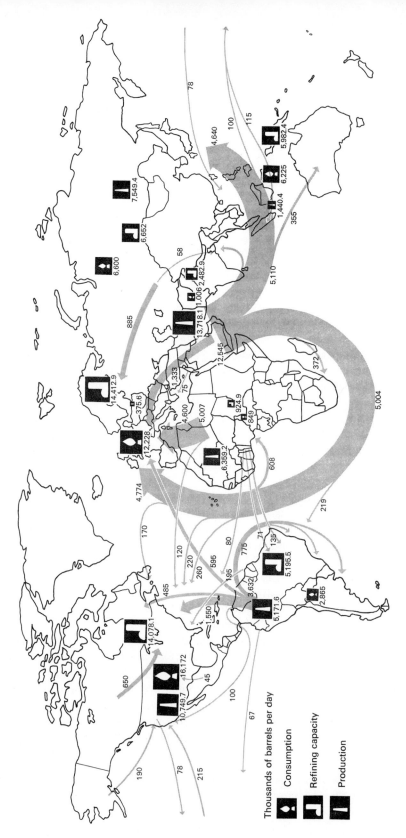

Figure 3–2 Worldwide patterns of oil production, refining, shipping, and consumption summarized from maps in the *International Petroleum Encyclopedia*. The data are for 1970. All quantities are in thousands of barrels per day. Export figures for eastern Europe, the USSR, and China refer only to exports from those areas to other parts of the world. The arrows indicate the origins and destinations of the principal international oil movements, not the specific routes. The U.S. is a heavy net importer. (From Luten, "The Economic Geography of Energy." Copyright © 1971 by Scientific American, Inc. All rights reserved.)

Thousands of barrels per day

Consumption

Refining capacity

Production

Table 3–3   Power of Inexhaustible Energy Sources

Source	Power Worldwide (Millions of Kilowatts)
Solar power incident on Earth's surface	112,000,000
Solar power (1% of land area @ 10% conversion efficiency)	32,500
Power in hydrological cycle	39,000,000
Estimated exploitable hydroelectric power	2,900
Total wind power	1,000,000
Estimated exploitable wind power	20,000
Tidal power in shallow seas	1,100
Estimated exploitable tidal power	13
1970 power consumption of civilization (for comparison)	6,000

SOURCE: *Resources and Man.*

of energy should encourage us to waste less energy in overpowered cars, in the heating and air conditioning of poorly insulated homes, and in other frivolous uses.

The threat of future shortages of liquid and gaseous fossil fuels can be relieved to some extent by converting coal to oil and gas. The liquefaction and gasification processes for coal may soon be as economical as obtaining liquid and gaseous fuels from conventional sources, and both processes seem likely to be used commercially within the 1970s. Reliance on coal for all fossil fuel needs would of course shorten the life expectancy of our coal reserves considerably. One possible alternative is the oil shales, which constitute a potential energy resource much larger even than coal.[3] However, there is vigorous disagreement about how much of the vast oil shales will ever be economically exploitable. Also, the shale must be crushed and heated to extract the oil, and the huge volume of solid residue poses an enormous disposal problem. Possibly the oil shales will serve as the eventual source of hydrocarbons for lower volume, recyclable uses, such as lubrication and the production of plastics, after the cheaper and more accessible sources of hydrocarbons have all been burned.

Water, Wind, Earth, and Sun. Hydroelectric energy and the energy of the wind and tides will always be available. The rate at which these energy sources can be exploited, however, is limited by the global flow of energy in the form of falling water, wind, and tides at any given time. It is also limited by the number of sites where these processes can be exploited economically. *Power* is the rate at which energy flows or is used. Continuous energy sources, such as the water cycle, are usually characterized in terms of power—say in kilowatts—although they could easily be characterized by the amount of energy flowing per day or per year. The power or rates of flow of the principal continuous energy sources are shown in Table 3–3.

---

[3]Hubbert estimates world oil shale resources at 2 million billion barrels, equivalent to 450 thousand billion tons of coal. He estimates world coal resources at 17 thousand billion tons. Hubbert believes only a small fraction of the oil shale will be economically recoverable, however. *(Resources and Man.)*

The world's potential production of hydroelectric power is roughly half of the amount of power now being produced by fossil fuels. There are, however, serious problems in utilizing it to the utmost. Much of the potential lies in UDCs, where the power could not be used unless those countries were industrialized; global ecological factors (to be discussed in later chapters) and the inability of the UDCs to mobilize capital and high-grade resources will impede industrialization in most of them. Furthermore, reliable hydroelectric power depends on dams, which under present conditions of technology are temporary structures. In a few hundred years — sometimes more, sometimes less, depending on the river — their reservoirs fill with silt and become useless. Thereafter, power production from the waterfall occupying the dam site hinges on the daily and seasonal variations of river flow. Finally, there is an important aesthetic question: do we really wish to impound and control all of the wild rivers of the Earth? Unfortunately, tidal power comprises only a minute fraction of all potential water power, and will presumably never be of more than local importance. Wind energy has the disadvantages of low concentration and of being unpredictable and intermittent in most locations.

There is some dispute about the exploitable power potential of the heat of the Earth's interior (geothermal energy). Some experts say that geothermal energy will never supply more than a very small fraction of civilization's energy needs. Others are much more optimistic. Geothermal energy is already important in a few countries such as Iceland, New Zealand, and Italy (Figure 3–3). A major uncertainty is the *lifetime* of the underground reservoirs of

Figure 3–3   A power plant in New Zealand that converts geothermal energy to electrical energy. The plumes are steam, not smoke. (Photo by Baum, Photofind–Rapho.)

Figure 3–4 A solar-energy-collecting device on the roof of a solar-heated house in Denver, Colorado. Use of solar energy for space heating and water heating is feasible today in most parts of the United States, *not* only in Florida and the Southwest. (Courtesy of Jerome Weingart.)

superheated water or steam that constitute the exploitable form of geothermal energy. Of course, ways to tap the heat of the Earth without relying on these reservoirs may yet be developed.

For many years men have speculated about the sun as a source of non-depletable power. Large-scale utilization of solar energy presents serious technological problems, arising mainly from intermittency (no sunshine at night, little on cloudy days, less in winter than summer) and from the low concentration of the energy. The collecting device for an electric generation plant with a capacity of 1,000 megawatts (enough power to supply electricity to a city of perhaps 750,000) would have to cover an area of about 16 square miles, assuming the solar-to-electric conversion efficiency to be 10 percent. Several recent studies have indicated that higher efficiencies and, hence, smaller collector areas are possible. Electricity generated in large solar power plants will not necessarily be prohibitively expensive, contrary to the claims of some critics. Of course, the greatest potential of solar power may be in dispersed uses—such as air conditioning and space heating—that take advantage of the fact that the sun has already distributed the power for us. Space heating, water heating, and air-conditioning for individual buildings, using simple solar collectors mounted on roofs, would probably be economically competitive with conventional electric units in many parts of the United States today (Figure 3–4). Because of its obvious environmental advantages and inexhaustible nature, the development of solar power certainly deserves more research support than it has been receiving.

Another potential source of energy, although not of the same magnitude, is the burning of garbage and agricultural wastes, including manure. If means could be devised to collect this material economically and burn it cleanly (a process that might involve converting it first to gas or fuel oil), the energy obtained could be as much as a fifth of the U.S. energy budget in 1970. Questions as to whether this is really feasible, and whether recycling garbage and returning agricultural wastes to the soil are not preferable to burning the material, remain to be answered.

Nuclear Energy.   Many people who are concerned about the rapid consumption of our fossil fuel resources, about the environmental consequences of this consumption, and about the uncertainties associated with many of the alternatives, have assumed that power from the nuclear fission (splitting) of uranium will provide the answers. Nuclear fission, it has been claimed, will be a cheap, clean, and almost inexhaustible source of power. These claims may yet prove to be true, but serious difficulties remain to be resolved. Fission power plants generate electricity, but electricity accounts for only one-quarter of the U.S. energy budget (the fraction may increase to one half by the year 2000). The fuel for fission reactors is relatively cheap, but construction costs are high compared to those for power plants operating on fossil fuel. This is perhaps not so important in the United States, where energy is already so cheap in comparison to other expenditures that we use it wastefully, but the cost factor may be very important in the poor countries. Also, fission plants are generally economically attractive only in very large sizes, and most small UDCs cannot absorb so much power in one place. Networks of transmission lines, enabling a few plants to serve large geographic areas, are expensive, and inevitable plant breakdowns are less disruptive if there are many small plants rather than a few large ones.

Another difficulty is that today's fission reactors use uranium very inefficiently, managing to extract only 1 to 2 percent of the potential energy of this fuel. The breeder reactors of the future will do much better in this respect. Contrary to a widespread impression, breeder reactors do not give us something for nothing, but they will be able to extract 40 to 70 percent of the energy in raw uranium. These reactors will probably not be ready for extensive commercial use until the late 1980s. Once they have been perfected (and this includes the assumption that their considerable environmental hazards can be held to acceptable levels), breeder reactors could provide mankind with a level of electricity consumption much larger than today's for millennia.

Another alternative that promises cheap and virtually inexhaustible fuel is controlled thermonuclear fusion. Fusion of light elements into heavy ones powers the sun and the hydrogen bomb, but we have not yet learned to harness fusion reactions for the controlled release of heat and the generation of electricity. Much progress has been made, however, and scientists working on this problem are hopeful that the scientific feasibility of this enterprise will be conclusively demonstrated within the 1970s.[4] If this occurs, actual fusion power plants might begin to come into service in the 1990s. No one knows what the construction costs of a fusion plant will be, although it seems probable that, like fission reactors, they will be most economical in large sizes. The most significant advantage of fusion over fission will be the relatively low amount of radioactivity involved and the inherent safety of the process.

Costs of Increasing Energy Production.   What are the costs of increasing energy production? Here, in fact, is the central issue in the energy field as a whole. We are limited not so much by the supply of potential fuels as by environmental costs of extracting them and converting them into the forms of energy we need. As will become apparent in later chapters, many of the most serious forms of environmental degradation stem directly from energy use. Coal mining ravages the landscape, and acid leached from the wastes is one of the most important water pollutants in the U.S. Oil spills threaten fragile coastal environments. The combustion of fossil fuels of all kinds is the dominant source of air pollution. Nuclear fission entails the possibility of accidental releases of enormous amounts of radioactivity, as well as routine emissions of much smaller quantities. The long-lived radioactive wastes from fission reactors must be safely transported and unerringly isolated from the environment for thousands of years (see Chapter 5).

The ultimate pollutant associated with energy use is heat. We refer not merely to the discharge of waste heat at electric power plants—a serious problem in its own right—but also to the eventual appearance in the environment as heat of all the energy we use. (Consider the heat from lightbulbs, from the engines and brakes of automobiles and the friction of tires against pavement, and so on.) This phenomenon is a consequence of the Second Law of Thermodynamics (Box 3–1). It cannot be evaded by technological tricks. If all the other environmental consequences of energy use could somehow be reduced to acceptable levels, the disruptive effects on climate of the resulting heat would still eventually call a halt to growth. No one can say with certainty how long the present worldwide increase in energy consumption could continue before this halt were enforced, because climate might be drastically altered by strong *local* heat sources (say in the northeastern United

---

[4]An excellent explanation of the principles of nuclear fusion and discussion of the current status of research in this field is "The Prospects of Fusion Power," by William C. Gough and Bernard J. Eastlund in *Scientific American*, February 1971, and in *Man and the Ecosphere*, P. R. Ehrlich, J. P. Holdren, and R. W. Holm, eds., W. H. Freeman and Company, San Francisco, 1971; also available as Offprint 340.

States) well before man's energy input became important on the basis of a global average.

Very optimistically, however, suppose that another 50 to 100 years of rapid growth in energy consumption is possible before heat or other environmental difficulties force a halt. (At the present rate of increase of worldwide energy consumption, 5 percent per year, 100 years of growth would produce seven doublings—a 128-fold increase over the present annual consumption.) Significantly, even the assumption that maintaining such a level of energy supply is technically and environmentally feasible does *not* permit one to conclude that a human population much larger than today's can be supported in prosperity. This is so because it is not always easy or cheap to "convert" energy into the necessities of existence—food, fiber, water, and metals. Energy is only one of the elements of production (land, labor, and machinery are some others). Moreover, the ecological side effects of the processes needed to convert energy to other consumables could overwhelm us if these processes were carried out on too large a scale. In short, energy itself may not prove to be the factor that limits growth, but it is also not a panacea for eliminating all other potential limits.

Mineral Resources Other Than Fuels

Geologist T. S. Lovering wrote in 1968: "Surprisingly enough, many men unfamiliar with the mineral industry believe that the beneficent gods of technology are about to open the cornucopia of granite and sea, flooding industry with any and all metals desired."[5] Lovering was responding to an outpouring of propaganda from technological optimists who underestimate the problems posed by civilization's enormous consumption of nonrenewable resources and by the uneven distribution of those resources. Energy resources have already been considered. What is the situation for metals and other minerals? Should we believe the technological optimists, who hold that science and technology alone can solve resource problems? Or should we heed those who argue that mineral resources, whether they be extracted from undiscovered rich deposits or from the tiny concentrations present in such common rocks as granite, are exhaustible and irreplaceable?

The answer is something like this: for the next few decades the DCs will probably not fare too badly, since they control, either directly or indirectly, most sources of (concentrated) minerals and have the capital and technology to exploit lower-grade deposits. Most UDCs will probably be unable to industrialize on any more than a modest scale. Even those UDCs which possess rich mineral or energy resources must sell most of their raw materials abroad for foreign exchange. With few exceptions, they lack the capital and technical

[5] "Non-Fuel Mineral Resources in the Next Century," T. S. Lovering, in *Global Ecology*, J. P. Holdren and P. R. Ehrlich, eds., Harcourt Brace Jovanovich, N.Y., 1971.

expertise to develop an industrial structure capable of mining and refining their own raw materials and of using them to produce manufactured goods.

After the end of this century, great difficulties in obtaining mineral resources loom for DCs and UDCs alike. Competition for the remaining rich deposits of ore will be intense. Unless population growth has drastically slowed, it will be extremely difficult to mobilize resources fast enough to provide for new arrivals, to say nothing of raising the standard of living for the population at large. As with energy resources, desperate attempts to keep up with demand for metals and other minerals will be likely to cause serious environmental mistakes.

The resources of the Earth's crust are very unevenly distributed — a result of the processes that led to their deposition and concentration. The distribution of coal, for instance, presumably represents the pattern of occurrence of certain types of plant communities that existed in swamps several hundred million years ago. Some minerals of economic value have been formed or concentrated by surface processes such as weathering and sedimentation; others have been deposited in fractures in the Earth's crust. As a result of this uneven distribution, some areas of the Earth (and thus some nations) are richly endowed with mineral wealth, while others have very little.

Despite frequently discontinuous distribution of ores as well as other factors, certain economists assume that only economic considerations determine the availability of mineral resources. They have the idea that as demand increases, mining will simply move to poorer and poorer ores, which they assume to be progressively more and more abundant. Indeed, the concentration of some minerals does vary more or less continuously from very high-grade ores to below the average abundance of the element in the crust of the Earth. Certain types of copper ores are distributed in this way, as well as ores of other important metals, such as iron and aluminum. But many metals, including ores of lead, zinc, tin, nickel, tungsten, mercury, manganese, cobalt, molybdenum, and precious metals, are not. They show sharp discontinuities in concentration. For these metals, even the availability of cheap and abundant energy (if it materializes) will not prevent extraction costs from becoming prohibitive once the rich deposits are gone.

Unfortunately, our present level of affluence cannot be sustained only by the relatively common substances with continuously varying concentrations. "Mineral vitamins" such as vanadium, tantalum, tungsten, and molybdenum — although little known to the layman — are also essential to the functioning of our industrial civilization. In some cases, common substances can be substituted for scarcer ones — aluminum for copper, for example — but in other cases no substitutes are known. For instance, we have no substitutes for mercury (with unique applications as the only metal that is liquid at room temperature). for platinum (a catalyst without equal) or for helium (indispensable in modern cryogenic technology as the substance with the boiling point closest to absolute zero).

Estimating Future Needs.   Several techniques are widely used to estimate the adequacy of mineral resources for the future. One method is to determine how long presently known reserves will last at present consumption rates. "Known reserves" refers to material whose location is known and which is thought to be extractable with present or forseeable technology. (Often reserves stand at only 20 to 50 years' supply because there is simply no incentive to spend money looking for more when this much is already at hand.) This method of estimation does not take two factors into account: (a) more material will probably be discovered in the future, and (b) the rate of consumption is now increasing and will probably continue to increase. Of course, these two factors partially offset each other.

Another method of estimation is to assume that the total exploitable resource is a multiple of presently known reserves, say, five times as much, and to ask how long this will last if the rate of consumption increases in the future as it has done in the recent past. This approach, too, is imperfect. Exponential growth in consumption rates, which is usually the historical pattern, does not really persist right up to resource exhaustion. Instead, consumption falls off gradually as scarcity and rising costs set in.

More sophisticated analyses usually result in time estimates intermediate between those given by the two approaches just described. The constant consumption and exponential growth figures for a number of important resources are given in Table 3–4.

These world figures, which are not particularly encouraging, do not reveal the most disconcerting aspects of the problem: the disproportionate share of the world's resource consumption accounted for by the United States and the proportion of the resources we consume that comes from outside our borders. The United States is highly dependent on foreign sources for many of its basic industrial raw materials, except bituminous coal (see Table 3–5). At the same

Table 3–4   World Resource Depletion

Resource	Years Supply, Static Assumption*	Years Supply, Growth Assumption†
Chromium	420	154
Coal	2300	150
Nickel	150	96
Tungsten	40	72
Petroleum	31	50
Manganese	97	94

Source: *The Limits to Growth.*
*Years to exhaust 1970 known reserves at 1970 level of consumption.
†Years to exhaust five times 1970 known reserves, assuming level of consumption increases exponentially at rate projected by U.S. Bureau of Mines.

**Table 3–5   Net U.S. Imports as a
Percentage of U.S. Consumption**

Resource	1960 Imports	1970 Imports
Chromium	94	100
Nickel	72	65
Manganese	92	94
Tin	73	69
Petroleum	16	22

SOURCE: Interim Report of the National Commission on Materials Policy, April 1972.

time, our industrial production and affluence have reached levels far beyond
those to which the UDCs can realistically aspire. Our national per capita income is some 33 times that of India, for example, and our per capita production
of energy and steel are more than 50 times those of India. In 1968 our per capita
steel *consumption* (consumption equals production plus imports minus exports) was some 342 times that of Indonesia, 86 times that of Pakistan, 68 times
that of Ceylon, 23 times that of Colombia, 9 times that of Mexico, 2 times that
of France and Switzerland, 1.4 times that of Japan, 1.5 times that of the United
Kingdom and the USSR, and marginally (10 percent) higher than that of our
nearest rival, Sweden. The United States, with less than 6 percent of the
world's people, in 1968 accounted for more than one-third of the world's
energy consumption; well over a third of its tin consumption; about a fourth
of its phosphate, potash, and nitrogenous fertilizer consumption; almost half
of its consumption of newsprint and synthetic rubber (produced from a variety
of resources); more than a fourth of its steel consumption, and about an eighth
of its cotton consumption.[6] Using the figures for energy resources, steel, tin,
and fertilizers as indicators, it seems reasonable to estimate that the United
States is currently accounting for about 30 percent of the world's consumption
of raw materials. Obviously, the United States consumes much more than its
"share" on a basis of population.

The DCs altogether account for only about 30 percent of the world's people
but consume the vast majority of the world's resources. The United States,
Canada, Europe, the U.S.S.R., Japan, and Australia in 1968 consumed about
90 percent of both the energy and the steel produced in the world.

The availability of critical resources has a considerable bearing on the
possibilities of industrialization in the UDCs. Even if world population growth
stopped in 1974, world iron production would have to be increased about sixfold, copper production almost sixfold and lead production about eightfold
to bring global per capita consumption to the present United States level.

[6]The figures in this and the following paragraph were computed from data in *The
United Nations Statistical Yearbook, 1970*, United Nations, New York, 1971.

Such considerations ignore the enormous amounts of these metals already mined, refined, and in use in the railroads, automobiles, girders, electrical wiring, and so on, in the United States. There are 10 tons of steel, 300 pounds of copper, 300 pounds of lead, 200 pounds of zinc, and 40 pounds of tin in use for every man, woman, and child in the United States.[7] If one takes into account this enormous capital stock of metals, which, far better than annual consumption alone, measures the true standard of living, the picture appears even gloomier. One then finds that to raise all of the 3.8 billion people in the world of 1972 to the American material standard of living would require the extraction of almost 30 billion tons of iron, more than 500 million tons of copper and lead, more than 300 million tons of zinc, about 50 million tons of tin, as well as enormous quantities of other minerals. These numbers represent between 75 and 250 times the present annual output of all the mines and smelters in the world.

To raise the projected world population *of the year 2000* to today's U.S. level would of course require about twice as much material as the already staggering 1972 "requirement." Whether some of the needed substances will *ever* be available in these quantities is debatable; but there is no possibility whatever of their being extracted *fast enough* to meet the rising aspirations of today's world population and the needs of tomorrow's even larger population.

Needless to say, the situation is aggravated by the high probability that most of the metals extracted in the next 30 years will be used to support wasteful practices and further industrial growth in the rich countries rather than to raise the pathetic standards of living in the poor ones. Far from concentrating on ways to help UDCs while making a maximum effort to husband limited resources, most American economists still want to *increase* the per capita rate of consumption of nonrenewable resources in the United States far above the present levels, while U.S. population growth continues. It is questionable, of course, whether even the DCs will be able to obtain the steadily increasing amounts of critical mineral resources that are projected as future "needs." In the short term, the United States may manage by increasing its imports, by developing substitutes, and, in some instances, by resorting to poor quality domestic deposits when imports become unavailable. It is already obvious that a major goal of United States foreign policy has been to assure continued access to high grade resources around the world — oil in the Middle East and Indonesia, rubber and tin in Southeast Asia, and so on. One may speculate about the consequences of continuing such policies in a world of increasing scarcity and growing military capabilities.

Setting aside the difficulties of getting through the next 30 to 50 years, many technologists seem to believe that the long-run solution to shortages

[7]"Human Materials Production as a Process in the Biosphere," Harrison Brown, in *Scientific American*, September 1970, and in *Man and the Ecosphere*, P. R. Ehrlich, J. P. Holdren and R. W. Holm, eds., W. H. Freeman and Co., 1971; also available as Offprint 1198.

of most mineral resources is to extract these materials from their very low concentrations in common rock and in sea water. This approach is beset by many difficulties, several of which we have already mentioned. Some of the materials we need are simply not found in common rock or in sea water. Even for those that are, the amounts of energy required to extract them will be enormous, probably prohibitively so both economically and environmentally; labor and machinery costs for such an enterprise would be very expensive even if energy were free; and disposing of the wastes from mining and processing will pose even more formidable environmental problems than we face today.

Bibliography

Cloud, Preston E., Jr. (ed.), 1969. *Resources and Man*. W. H. Freeman and Company, San Francisco. See especially Chapter 8 by M. King Hubbert on energy resources, Chapter 6 by T. S. Lovering on mineral resources from the land, and Chapter 7 by P. E. Cloud on mineral resources from the sea.

Holdren, J., and P. Herrera, 1971. *Energy*. Sierra Club Books, New York. Well-documented treatment of the energy situation: technology, economics, environmental impact, and a history of utility-environmentalist confrontations.

Landsberg, H. H., L. L. Fischman, and J. L. Fisher, 1963. *Resources in America's Future*. Johns Hopkins Press, Baltimore. Data pertaining to supply, demand, and technology for renewable and nonrenewable resources; also helps sort out accounting practices that sometimes render more condensed data sources unintelligible.

Meinel, A. B. and M. P. Meinel, 1971. Is it time for a new look at solar energy? *Science and Public Affairs (Bulletin of the Atomic Scientists)*, vol. 27, no. 8 (Oct.). Description of an ambitious proposal for large-scale electricity generation from solar energy.

Science and Public Affairs (Bulletin of the Atomic Scientists), 1971. The September and October issues are devoted to extensive discussion of the "energy crisis."

These huge machines are spreading fertilizer on melon fields on a farm near Mendota, California. (Ernest Lowe, Photofind, S.F.)

FOUR

Carrying Capacity: Food and Other Renewable Resources

The distinction between renewable and nonrenewable resources is not always a clear one. The Earth's supply of metals is usually considered a nonrenewable resource, not because metals are destroyed or leave the planet, but because they are lost to civilization when they are dispersed in concentrations too low for economical recovery. Water, on the other hand, is generally considered a renewable resource, although the absolute supply on the Earth is as fixed as that of metals. The difference is that water that has been made unusable by contamination or dispersal in use is restored to usable form as it passes through the various stages of the hydrologic cycle: water vapor, rain, and so on. Food, which comes from biological species that reproduce themselves, can also be considered a renewable resource. In theory there may be no limit to the amount of food that could be produced, but in fact there are very real limits to potential food production, such as the availability of suitable land, a favorable climate, and sufficient water. There are also less obvious biological constraints that manifest themselves in such phenomena as attacks by pests or outbreaks of disease. Agricultural products are special, however, in that they are dependent upon replenishment of other resources, such as soil and water.

Evidently, the appropriate question to be asked about a renewable resource is "Does the rate of production or replenishment equal the rate of consumption or loss?" (For nonrenewable resources, in contrast, the usual question is simply "How much exists?") With respect to renewable resources, then, the

Earth's carrying capacity for human beings is determined by *maximum sustainable yields* (the highest rates of harvesting that can be balanced by the processes of replenishment). If the rate of consumption of a given resource exceeds the maximum sustainable yield for long, the stocks will be exhausted, and the humans dependent on the stocks will be impoverished and may perish. In much of the world, disaster will strike if the consumption of water exceeds rainfall or the consumption of agricultural products exceeds harvests for a few months to a year. When accumulated stocks are large compared to annual consumption, as is true of forests or certain ocean fishes, consumption can sometimes exceed the sustainable yield for decades before the damage becomes obvious. In this chapter, we will consider the implications of sustainable yields, including how civilization tries to increase them and how it may exceed them in agriculture, in fisheries, in water resources, and in forestry.

A Hungry World

The most pressing factor now limiting the capacity of the Earth to support human beings is the supply of food. Perhaps as much as one-half of all the world's people are inadequately fed to some degree. Despite efforts to convince people of the need for a "balanced diet," which have continued in the United States since the 1920s and 1930s, some Americans are still convinced that the typical Asian can live happily and healthily on one bowl of rice per day. The truth is that an Asian's nutritional requirements are essentially the same as those of an American, although the total amount of some nutrients needed may be less owing to the Asian's smaller size (itself probably the result of poor nutrition during the years of growth). The traditional diets of most Asians and inhabitants of other poor areas of the world, where undernutrition and malnutrition are widespread, are indeed much less varied than the diet of the typical American, but this limited variety could still be sufficient to meet nutritional needs. The nutritional deficiencies that exist result either from insufficient supplies of some or all of the traditional foods or from poverty or ignorance.

In 1967 the President's Science Advisory Committee Panel on the World Food Supply estimated that 20 percent of the people in the underdeveloped countries (which include two-thirds of the world population) were undernourished (that is, were not receiving enough calories per day) and that 60 percent were malnourished (seriously lacking in one or more essential nutrients, most commonly protein). This means that as many as a billion and a half people are either undernourished or malnourished. This is a conservative estimate; others place the number of "hungry" people at more than 2 billion. The President's panel further estimated that perhaps a half billion people can be described as either chronically hungry or starving. These numbers do not include the hungry and malnourished millions in the lower economic strata of developed countries such as the United States, or the numbers of people who can afford to eat well but are malnourished because of their ignorance of elementary nutrition. Figure 4–1 shows the areas of the world where hunger is most widespread.

Even in the face of such staggering numbers, one might be tempted to shrug and say, "Oh well, there have always been famines and hungry people." The truth is that today's situation is totally unprecedented, in part because of the absolute numbers of people involved. Famines, which have existed throughout human history, have generally been cataclysmic, short-term events caused by weather or human intervention and have been limited to relatively small, local populations. Though such famines are undeniably tragic affairs that result in a great amount of human suffering and death, they are an entirely different phenomenon from the unceasing privation now endured by more than one billion people around the globe. Today's hunger is also unprecedented because the hungry multitudes are increasingly aware of how well the affluent few eat and have high hopes of emulating them. This situation has important political implications for the future.

This condition of widespread chronic hunger accompanied by grinding poverty has been gradually worsening for a number of years in many UDCs, as population growth has outstripped increases in food production. Before World War II, many countries in Africa, Asia, and Latin America were grain exporters. By the mid-1960s, they were importing grain in far greater quantities than they had ever exported it. Per capita food production in most of Asia, Africa, and Latin America fell and rose several times during the 1960s, as rising production, with several setbacks, barely kept pace with population growth during the decade as a whole.[1]

Although individual needs for calories vary according to age, sex, body size, and activity, the United Nations Food and Agriculture Organization (FAO) has established standard "reference" body weights and standard daily per capita calorie requirements for estimating a population's food needs in calories. Children's caloric needs, which are higher than those of adults in proportion to their body weights, are standardized according to age groups. For adults, allowances are also made for pregnancies and differences in age and sex. On the basis of these FAO standards, which were considered generous, the President's Science Advisory Committee placed 1965 world average caloric needs at 2354 calories[2] per capita per day. The FAO estimated that an average of 2420 calories per capita per day in food was available worldwide at the market level in the middle 1960s. These estimates would indicate that there was barely enough to supply each person adequately with calories.

[1] See the *FAO Food Production Yearbook* published annually by the United Nations Food and Agriculture Organization in Rome.

[2] Throughout this book, the term calorie refers to the nutritional unit, written Calorie by some authors, and equal to 1000 of the calorie units used in physical science and engineering.

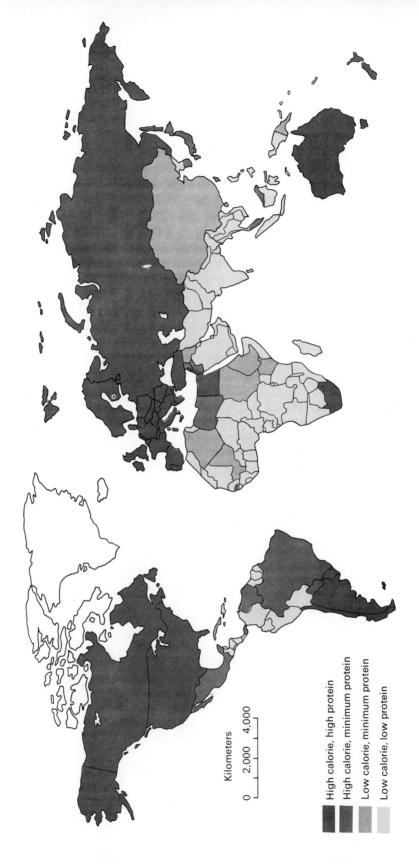

Figure 4–1 The geography of hunger. (Data derived from FAO *Production Yearbook* 1968.)

Kilometers

0   2,000   4,000

High calorie, high protein

High calorie, minimum protein

Low calorie, minimum protein

Low calorie, low protein

However, vast inequities in the distribution of food between and within countries must be taken into account. The rich get more than their share; the poor get less. If an additional loss of at least 10 percent from waste, pests, and spoilage between market and actual consumption is also taken into account, the reality of the gap between needed calories and available calories becomes clear.

Conflicting accounts of the actual food situation sometimes result from different ways of comparing figures. There is a vast difference between what is produced and what reaches the marketplace, besides the losses between the market and the family table. Estimates of losses to insect and rodent pests and to spoilage *before* food reaches the market range from 20 percent to as high as 50 percent in some areas. In addition, food-production figures are usually quoted only in calories and take no account of whether adequate protein or other nutrients are available.

Individual protein requirements also vary with body size and age, although activity makes very little difference. These needs must be calculated according to the quality of the protein sources. Where animal foods are a rare element in the diet, more protein is needed to compensate for the lower quality of the protein in vegetable sources. Maldistribution of proteins in UDCs, even within households, is an even more serious problem than maldistribution of calories (Figure 4–2). Children and pregnant or nursing women, who have greater proportionate needs for protein than men or non-reproducing women, are often left the smallest portions.

To feed the projected population of 1985 even at the inadequate 1965 level, the President's Science Advisory Committee Panel estimated that total world food production must be increased between 43 and 52 percent over 1965 production. The low estimates assume that effective population-control measures will have reduced fertility by 30 percent by 1985 and that food distribution will have been improved. The greatest increase in food needs will occur in the UDCs, which are growing most rapidly. For example, the requirements of India, Pakistan, and Brazil for calories will *more than double* unless population growth slows down. The increase in protein requirements will be even higher. In some UDCs the increased needs for protein may be as much as 150 percent.

Even if the world is successful in making these prodigious increases in available food, and if distribution is made more equitable, in 1985 there will be a population of around 5 billion, perhaps 15 percent of which will still be undernourished and 40 percent of which will be malnourished.

The present failures of food distribution are the result of a number of interacting factors, including poverty, ignorance, cultural and economic patterns, and lack of transport systems. Although the worldwide supplies of food might theoretically be adequate, the average diet within many countries in southern Asia and tropical Latin America is significantly below the minimum nutritional standards set by the FAO. Within these countries, individuals in the

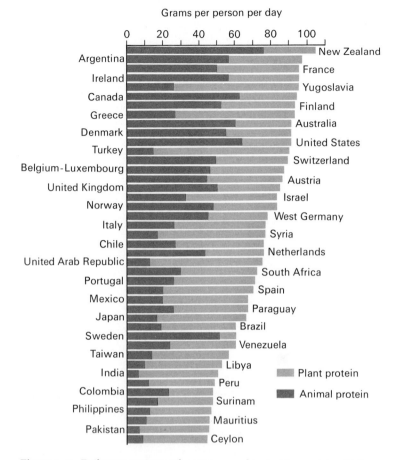

Figure 4–2 Daily per capita total protein supplies in 43 countries. (After Cole, *Introduction to Livestock Production*, 2nd ed., W. H. Freeman and Company. Copyright © 1966. All rights reserved.)

poorest quarter of the population may be receiving only three-fourths of the calories and protein of even this inadequate average diet. These shortages show up in widespread malnutrition and hunger to an obvious degree, especially among such vulnerable groups as infants, preschool children (ages 1 to 4), pregnant women, and nursing mothers. Correcting this situation alone would require a massive effort to raise total food production, since those who now consume more than their minimal share can hardly be expected to approve of a redistribution plan that would place everyone on a minimum-calorie–low-protein diet.

Deaths from starvation and malnutrition are commonplace in today's world. Of the 60 million deaths that occur each year, between 10 and 20 million are estimated by French agronomists (food specialists) Rene Dumont

Table 4–1   Child Mortality Rates 1–4 Years, 1960–1962 (Average Annual)

Continent and Country	Rate per 1,000 Children (ages 1–4) per Year	Continent and Country	Rate per 1,000 Children (ages 1–4) per Year
Africa		Philippines	8.4
Mauritius	8.7	Syria	8.3
United Arab Republic	37.9	Thailand	9.1
North and Central America		*Europe*	
Canada	1.1	Austria	1.3
Costa Rica	7.2	Bulgaria	2.4
Guatemala	32.7	Czechoslovakia	1.2
Mexico	13.8	France	1.0
Trinidad and Tobago	2.5	Germany, West	1.3
United States	1.0	Greece	1.9
South America		Italy	1.9
Argentina	4.2	Portugal	8.0
Chile	8.0	Spain	2.0
Equador	22.1	Sweden	0.8
Peru	17.4	United Kingdom—	
Venezuela	5.9	England, and Wales	0.9
Asia		Yugoslavia	5.2
Ceylon	8.8	*Oceania*	
China (Taiwan)	7.2	Australia	1.1
Japan	2.2		

SOURCE: United Nations, *Statistical Series*, K/3, 1967.

and Bernard Rosier to be the result of starvation or malnutrition.[3] The cause of death is usually officially attributed to some infectious or parasitic disease, which in most cases only dealt the final blow. Diseases that are ordinarily only minor nuisances for well-nourished individuals are devastating to the malnourished. Even if they do not kill, they tend to intensify the malnourishment by draining the individual's reserves. Extremely poor sanitary conditions further complicate the picture; intestinal diseases and infestations of various kinds of worms are commonplace. Diarrhea, dangerous even in a well-fed, well-protected baby, is disastrous to an ill-fed one. (*For our purposes, any death that would not have occurred had the individual been properly nourished is considered to be due to starvation, regardless of the ultimate "cause of death."*) Dumont's and Rosier's estimates are contested by some experts and may be too high. But even if they are five times too high, *some 2 to 4 million human beings starve to death every year*; a tragedy of vast proportions.

Malnutrition and poor sanitary conditions are a major cause of the high infant and even higher child mortality rates in the UDCs compared with those of the DCs. (See Appendix for recent infant mortality rates; Table 4–1 for

[3]In *The Hungry Future*, Praeger, New York, 1969. These authors also estimate that in 1969, 300-500 million human beings were undernourished and 1,600 million were malnourished.

examples of child mortality rates.) Infants are somewhat protected both from parasites and from severe nutritional deficiencies while they are nursing. Nevertheless, the infant mortality rate in some poor countries is two to eight times higher than that in the United States, which is by no means the world's lowest. The preschool mortality rate has been considered the best indication of the nutritional level of a population, since children of this age are usually no longer protected by nursing and are therefore the most susceptible segment of the population. In many parts of Latin America, Asia, and Africa, these rates are three to forty times higher than in the United States. Although dependable statistics are hard to obtain, India's mortality rate for children under the age of 4 (including infants) has been estimated to be as high as 250 per thousand. There is little question that at least half of these deaths are basically due to malnutrition, usually protein starvation.

The most commonly encountered deficiency diseases in UDCs are *marasmus* and *kwashiorkor*, both of which attack young children. Marasmus is probably indicative of overall undernutrition, but it is often described as a "protein-calorie deficiency." Most victims are babies less than a year old. It seems to be related to early weaning or to a failure in breast-feeding that results in the provision of inadequate substitutes for mother's milk, and it often appears following a bout of diarrhea or some other disease. Kwashiorkor is a West African word that means "the sickness the child develops when another baby is born." Kwashiorkor is the result of protein starvation and, unlike marasmus, can occur even if calories are abundantly provided. It most frequently follows weaning, when the child of one or two years is offered mainly starches or sugars for his diet. The President's Science Advisory Committee reported that the high mortality rates of children 1 to 4 years old in UDCs "suggest that moderate protein-calorie malnutrition affects at least 50 percent of these children."

Vitamin and mineral deficiencies are also widespread in UDCs, although they are found in DCs as well. The most common vitamin deficiencies are lack of vitamin A, which frequently accompanies protein deficiency and in acute cases produces blindness and damage to certain tissues, and beriberi (lack of thiamine), which is usually the result of a high carbohydrate diet based on polished rice. Iron-deficiency anemia and rickets (from lack of calcium and/or vitamin D) are also very common in UDCs. All these forms of malnutrition afflict mothers and children most frequently and most disastrously.

The serious malnutrition prevalent in our overpopulated world causes incalculable suffering, waste of human life, and loss of human productivity. Malnourishment, especially protein deficiency, inhibits the development of protective antibodies and lowers resistance to diseases. Even more alarming is the growing body of evidence that shows that protein malnutrition has permanent effects, especially on small children. It has been known for a long time that malnourishment during the years of growth and development will result in a certain amount of dwarfing and delayed physical maturity, even if the deficiency is temporary and a normal diet is later restored. What is far more ominous is the evidence that protein deficiency in infancy and early childhood may result in permanent impairment of the brain.[4]

Governments must be made aware of nutritional levels in their populations and of what these can allow them to expect and demand of people. Under-nutrition, together with parasitism and disease, typically produces apathy, listlessness, and low productivity. Well-fed Europeans and North Americans, seeing these symptoms but neither recognizing them as such nor understanding their cause, often conclude that natives of underdeveloped areas are "lazy." By contrast, the improvement of inadequate diets may lead to rebelliousness and aggressiveness — characteristic of the behavior of humans during the recovery period following starvation experiments with volunteers. The implications of the prevalence of malnutrition for the underdeveloped countries in the future, when it is more likely than not to be even more widespread and severe, are frightening to say the least. All proposals to increase food production in the UDCs are inevitably attached to elaborate plans for economic development. Can they possibly achieve either with a weakened, malnourished populace and with the prospects of physical and mental impairment in a large portion of the coming generation?

The Biology of Food Production

"All flesh is grass." This simple phrase summarizes a fundamental principle of biology that is essential to an understanding of the world food problem. The basic source of food for all animal populations is green plants. Human beings and all other animals with which we share this planet obtain the energy and nutrients for growth, development, and sustenance by eating plants or by eating other animals that have eaten plants or by eating animals that have eaten animals that have eaten plants, and so forth.

One may think of the plants and animals in a given area, together with their physical surroundings, as comprising a system (an ecosystem) through which energy passes, and within which materials move in cycles. Energy enters the system in the form of radiation from the sun. Through the process of photosynthesis, green plants are able to "capture" some of the incoming solar energy and use it to bind together small molecules into the large molecules that are characteristic of living organisms. Through digestive processes, animals that eat plants are able to break down these large organic molecules and put to their own use the energy that once bound the molecules together. Some of the energy an animal takes in is expended in its daily activities and some is used to build large molecules of animal substance (for growth or repair of tissue).

[4]*Malnutrition, Learning, and Behavior*, Nevin S. Scrimshaw and John E. Gordon, MIT Press, Cambridge, 1968.

Animals that eat other animals once again break down the large molecules and put the energy from them to their own uses. A simplified diagram of these basic energy transformations is shown in Figure 4–3. Note that photosynthesis is the basic source of energy for all plants and animals.

Thus, one may picture the flow of energy through this system as a stepwise progression along what is known as a *food chain*. A food chain starts with the green plants, which are known as the *producers*. They are the first trophic (feeding) level. Then at the second trophic level come the *herbivores* (plant-eating animals), the primary consumers. At the third trophic level are the secondary consumers, the *carnivores* (or meat-eaters), which eat herbivores. Tertiary consumers are the carnivores that eat other carnivores, and so forth. Also essential to the energetics of food chains are the *decomposers:* bacteria, fungi, small insects, and other tiny organisms that derive their energy from the wastes and dead bodies of plants, herbivores, and carnivores. This waste-disposal service is absolutely essential, since without it the cycling of elements on which all organisms, including mankind, depend would cease (see Chapter 6). Man plays many roles in food chains, but his most common one is that of a herbivore, since grains and other plant materials make up a very great proportion of the diet of most human beings. Man may also be a secondary consumer, as when he eats beefsteak (or the meat of any other herbivorous animal). When he consumes fishes, he often occupies positions even further along the food chain, because many fishes are tertiary or even quaternary consumers themselves. A food chain including man is shown in Figure 4–4.

According to the First Law of Thermodynamics (see Box 3–1), energy can be neither created nor destroyed, although it may be changed from one form to another (as in the change from light energy to the energy of chemical bonds in photosynthesis). The Second Law of Thermodynamics says, in essence, that in any transfer of energy there will be a loss of usable energy; that is, a certain amount of the energy will be degraded from an available, concentrated form (like the energy in gasoline) to an unavailable, dispersed form (like the energy

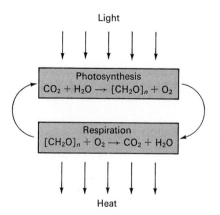

Figure 4–3 Photosynthesis and respiration, which are the basic metabolic processes of most living plants, obtain their energy from sunlight. In photosynthesis, energy from light is used to remove carbon dioxide and water from the environment; for each molecule of CO_2 and H_2O removed, part of a molecule of carbohydrate (CH_2O) is produced and one molecule of oxygen (O_2) is returned to the environment. In respiration by a plant or an animal, combustion of carbohydrates and oxygen yields energy, CO_2, and H_2O. (From Gates, "The Flow of Energy in the Biosphere." Copyright © 1971 by Scientific American, Inc. All rights reserved.)

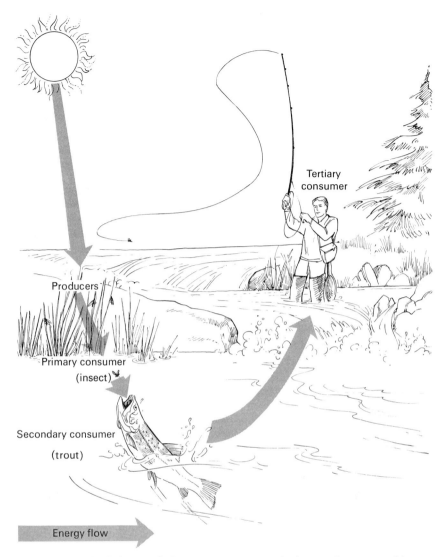

Figure 4–4 A food chain including man. A mosquito feeding on the man would be a quaternary consumer.

in exhaust fumes). The practical consequence of this law as it applies to food production is that no transfer of energy in a biological system may be 100 percent efficient; there is always some loss of usable energy at each transfer. In the photosynthetic system, usually 1 percent or less of the sunlight falling on green plants is actually converted to the kind of chemical-bond energy that is available to animals eating the plants. Roughly 10 percent of this store of energy in the plants may turn up as available energy in the chemical bonds of animals that have eaten plants. And roughly 10 percent of that energy may in turn be incorporated into the chemical bonds of other animals that eat the animals that ate the plants. Thus carnivores may incorporate about one ten-thousandth (.01 × .10 × .10) of the solar energy impinging on the green plants of an area.

It follows from this application of the Second Law of Thermodynamics that in most biological systems the *biomass* (living weight) of producers will be greater than that of primary consumers; the biomass of primary consumers in turn will be greater than that of secondary consumers; and so on. The weight of organisms possible at any trophic level is dependent upon the energy supplied by the organisms at the next lower trophic level; and some energy becomes unavailable at each transfer. For instance, as an oversimplification, it might take roughly 10,000 pounds of grain to produce 1,000 pounds of cattle, which in turn could be used to produce 100 pounds of human beings. By moving man one step down the food chain, ten times as much energy would be directly available—that is, the 10,000 pounds of grain used to produce 1,000 pounds of cattle could be used instead to produce 1,000 pounds of human beings. The energetics of both a natural ecosystem and an agricultural one are shown in Figure 4–5.

The Practice of Agriculture

Mankind has always been dependent on the process of photosynthesis for his food. Whether a primitive man ate berries, roots, fishes, reindeer, or whatever, the energy he derived from his food had the same ultimate source: the radiant energy of the sun. Not until the agricultural revolution, however, did people begin to exercise some control over plant growth and attempt to concentrate and increase the yield from desirable food plants. The earliest attempts at agriculture doubtless were based on the astute observation that certain accidental disturbances of the land by human activities increased the growth of some useful plants. Indeed, today in some tropical areas, so called "slash-and-burn" agriculture consists of little more than cutting and burning clearings in which seeds of various desirable plants are then scattered. It would have been a small step from such practices to the reduction of competition for the desired plants by the simple hoeing of weeds and the protection of the crop from animals, and to the utilization of the fertilizing effects of human and animal excreta and other organic wastes from human activities.

Modern agriculture, of course, differs completely from primitive slash-and-burn methods. (See Figure 4–6). The changes in agriculture in temperate regions over the past few hundred years could quite fairly be considered a second agricultural revolution. The science of plant breeding has produced a vast diversity of crop varieties that are adapted to various growing conditions, that are high in yield, resistant to diseases, and so forth. Mechanical cultivation and harvesting improved methods of fertilization and irrigation, the use of chemical and biological controls against plant and insect pests, weather forecasting (and, to a small degree, weather control), and many other techno-

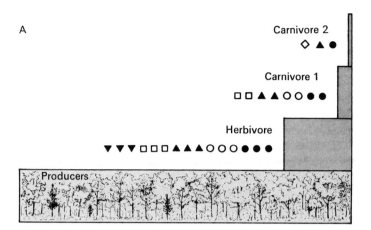

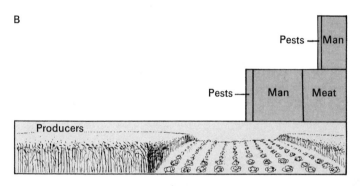

Figure 4–5 A. Intact natural ecosystem exemplified by a mature oak and hickory forest that supports several levels of consumers in the grazing food chain, with from 10 to 20 percent of the energy in each trophic level being passed along to the next level. The symbols represent different herbivore and carnivore species. Complexity of structure regulates population sizes, maintaining the same pattern of energy distribution in the system from year to year. B. Agricultural ecosystem is a special case, yielding a larger than normal harvest of net production for herbivores, including man and animals that provide meat for man. Stability is maintained through inputs of energy in cultivation, pesticides, and fertilizer. (From Woodwell, "The Energy Cycle of the Biosphere." Copyright © 1970 by Scientific American, Inc. All rights reserved.)

logical advances have greatly increased the quantity of food that can be produced on a given area of land. Technology has also increased the quality of some crops, but not of all crops. For instance, high yields of grains are sometimes gained at the expense of lowered protein content.

Figure 4–6 Above. An example of slash-and-burn agriculture. The new clearing in second-growth forest contains many stumps of trees that have been cut high for use as props for growing plants. Some, although stripped of their leaves, will survive; along with invading tree seedlings they will slowly reforest the garden site. (Photo by Ray A. Rappaport.) Below. An example of modern mechanized agriculture, which is characterized by high energy inputs to maintain stability and high yields. These machines are wheat combines. (Photo by William A. Garnett.)

Modern, high-yield agriculture can reasonably be described as a system that turns calories of fossil fuel into calories of food.[5] Fossil fuels are, of course, used extensively in both the manufacture and the operation of farm machinery. They are also used in the construction and operation of the systems that transport materials to the farm and carry farm produce to market. They are used as fuel in the mining and manufacture of fertilizers, and both as energy sources and raw materials in the production of pesticides. Recent statistics indicate, conservatively, that for each calorie of food produced in the United States, about 1.5 calories of fossil fuels are consumed by agriculture and related activities. In part, of course, this energy must be used to stabilize simple agricultural ecosystems; that is, to protect them from insect pests, plant diseases, winds, drought, or the like. This biological stability is normally provided by the complexity of natural ecosystems.

Although man is able to modify many of the conditions of plant growth, limits are imposed upon agricultural production by such factors as geographic variation in the amount of solar energy reaching the surface of the Earth, temperatures of both soil and air, and the amount of soil moisture available. And, because of the key role played by photosynthesis in agriculture, it is inevitable that farming will remain a highly dispersed human activity. Agriculture must remain spread over the face of the Earth because the energy of sunlight can only be utilized in photosynthesis at its point of arrival. Furthermore, especially when populations are large, food production cannot be considered apart from food distribution. It is not possible to concentrate agriculture in regions of need, as it is so often possible to concentrate production of other substances required by human beings.

Indeed, high concentrations of human beings tend to be inimical to agriculture. As anyone knows who has lived in the country around such cities as Philadelphia, Chicago, or Los Angeles, much farmland is taken out of production each year and "developed" into subdivisions and highways. For each additional 1,000 people in California, an average of 238 acres of arable land (that is, land suitable for farming) has been covered by buildings and pavement (Figure 4–7). By 1960 some 3 million acres of California farmland, most of which was of high quality, had been converted to nonagricultural use. A projection to the year 2020 shows that 13 million acres—half of the state's arable land—will be lost to farming by then. The figures for prime agricultural land alone are even more shocking. More than one-third of this superior land will be gone by 1980. In addition, smog kills crops. If current trends continue, California eventually will not be able to feed herself, let alone export food as she does today.

---

[5]At least 3 percent of U.S. nonfood energy consumption in 1960 took place in activities related to agriculture, according to *Resources in America's Future*, by H. L. Landsberg, L. L. Fischman and J. L. Fisher (Johns Hopkins Press, 1963, p. 218). This fraction amounted in 1960 to 5000 calories of fossil fuel energy per person per day, to produce 3200 calories of food per person per day.

Figure 4–7 An orange grove in Southern California being replaced by a subdivision. To the left are undisturbed orange groves, in the center is finished housing. To the right is housing in various stages of completion. At the lower right is a freshly cleared area with one orange tree remaining per lot. Since the photograph was taken in the 1950s, the entire area has been developed. (Photo by William A. Garnett.)

Major Food Crops.   Man has domesticated some 80 species of food plants, as opposed to only about two dozen kinds of animals. Over the centuries, most of them have been improved by selective breeding and/or hybridization. Interestingly, virtually all the original domestication of both plants and animals took place in prehistoric times. But, in spite of the diversity of available food plants, a relatively small number of crops supplies the vast majority of the world's food. If one had to pick the three most important food plants in the world, the almost inevitable choice would be three species of grasses: rice, wheat, and corn. So important are these cereal grains that slightly more than one-half of the harvested land of the world is used to grow them. Wheat and rice together supply roughly 40 percent of all human food energy (Figure 4–8).

Rice is the most important crop of all; it is the staple food for an estimated 2 billion people. Total world production in 1968 was an estimated 295 million metric tons before milling (a metric ton is 1000 kilograms or 2200 pounds). New strains of rice that produce very high yields per acre when properly cultivated have been developed at the International Rice Research Institute (IRRI) in the Philippines. The IRRI strains have been introduced to farmers in Southeast Asia, where they have had dramatic effects on rice production.

Close behind rice in importance in the diet of human beings comes wheat, with a slightly smaller total production than rice. In 1970 some 288 million metric tons were produced. Unlike rice, wheat does not grow well in the tropics, in part because one of its major diseases, wheat-rust fungus, thrives in warm, humid climates. Wheat is grown mostly in the Temperate Zones, where winters are cold and wet, and summers hot and rather dry (although in the United States wheat belt most of the precipitation is in the summer).

Corn, or maize, is the third great cereal crop, with 1970 world production being about 250 million metric tons. The long, warm, moist summers of the eastern half of the United States are ideal for corn production, and more than 40 percent of the world supply is grown there. It should be noted, though, that the bulk of U.S. corn production is fed to cattle and hogs. This process results in perhaps a sevenfold reduction in the amount of calories from corn actually consumed by human beings.

Rice, wheat, and corn together account for well over $\frac{3}{4}$ billion metric tons of grain annually. The rest of the world's crop of about 1 billion metric tons is made up by other grains: barley, oats, rye, millet, and sorghum, mainly grown in the Temperate Zones.

The protein content of modern high-yield grains tends to be about 5 to 13 percent and is not complete protein (protein with the proper balance of amino acids for human nutrition). Grains are all rich in protein, however, in com-

Figure 4–8   The sources of mankind's food energy. More than half of the calories people consume come from cereals, with wheat and rice each providing about 20 percent. (From Brown, "Human Food Production as a Process in the Biosphere." Copyright © 1970 by Scientific American, Inc. All rights reserved.)

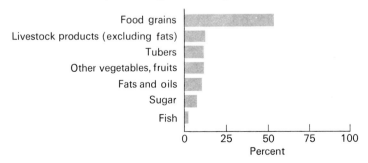

parison with the only other staple crop that approaches them in global significance: potatoes. Roughly a third of a billion metric tons of potatoes are grown annually, but the water content of the potato is so high (75 percent) and its protein content so low (1 to 4 percent wet weight) that the food value of the crop is considerably less than that of any of the "big three" grains.

Legumes (a group of plants that includes peas, beans, peanuts, and several forage crops) cannot compete in volume with grains in world food production. However, they have two to four times the protein content, and are thus critically important in human nutrition and for domestic animals as well. Bacteria associated with the roots of legumes have the ability to fix gaseous nitrogen from the atmosphere and convert it to a form that may be directly used by plants. As a result, legumes also serve mankind as fertilizer, "green manure," and thus contribute indirectly to the protein derived from other plants.

Two legumes — soybeans and peanuts — are grown primarily as oil sources. They account for about half of the world's legume production of some 80 million metric tons. Soybean oil and peanut oil are used for making margarine, salad dressings, and shortenings; they also are used in various industrial processes. The material remaining after the oils are pressed out (press cake) is valued as a feed for livestock. Little of the soybean crop is directly consumed by man, whereas a significant portion of the peanut crop is eaten in the nut form or in candy or peanut butter. Many varieties of beans and peas also provide a significant element in the human diet. Legumes are grown all over the world; soybean production is concentrated in the United States and mainland China; peanuts in India and Africa; and other beans and peas in the Far East and Latin America.

Grains and legumes are the mainstays of man's vegetable diet on a global basis, but a vast variety of other plants is cultivated and consumed. Cassava, sweet potatoes and yams (all root crops) supply starch to many people in the world, especially the poor. The roots of the sugar beet and the stem of sugar cane (a grass) supply sugar. The roots, stems, fruits, berries, and leaves of still other plants are important sources of vitamins and minerals in human diets.

Many plants are also used as forages — food for domestic animals. Although domestic animals are often just turned loose to graze and fend for themselves, many crops are grown specifically as feed for them. For instance, some 60 million acres of the world are planted in the legume alfalfa (called "lucerne" in Europe), which is the most nutritious of all forage crops and is especially rich in protein. Clovers and other legumes are also grown as forage, as are various grasses.

The primary importance of domesticated animals is as a source of high-quality protein. The selection of animals to domesticate for food has been more limited than the selection of plants. Only nine species — cattle, pigs, sheep, goats, water buffalo, chickens, ducks, geese, and turkeys — account for nearly 100 percent of the world's production of protein from domesticated animals.

Beef and pork together, in roughly equal amounts, account for some 90 percent of the nonpoultry meat production. Cows produce more than 90 percent of the milk consumed, water buffalo about 4 percent, and goats and sheep the remainder (ignoring tiny amounts from reindeer and some other domestic mammals). Although certain breeds of domestic animals are adapted to the tropics. animal husbandry is generally easier and more productive in temperate areas than in the tropics.

Recent History of Agricultural Production.   Following the Second World War, there was a steady worldwide upward trend in the amount of food produced for each person on Earth. This trend has generally continued in the DCs, with some exceptions, to the present day. In the UDCs, however, this steady increase halted between 1956 and 1960, depending on the country. Food production has fluctuated around the same per capita level ever since (Table 4–2). In 1968 the average country in Africa and Latin America grew less food per person than it had 12 years before. The average country in the Far East increased its per capita food production from 1956 to 1964, dropped back in 1965–1967, and showed a recovery in 1968. These drops in per capita production occurred in spite of substantial increases (roughly 30–35 percent) in absolute food supplies in these areas during those 12 years, because population growth offset the gains.

Figure 4–9 shows the general trends of population growth, total food production, and per capita food production in the underdeveloped areas. Much of the year-to-year irregularity in these figures is due to local weather conditions, which are crucial to food production. Overall in the UDCs, per capita food production in 1969 remained roughly what it was in the base period 1952–1956. This indicates *an enormous increase in human misery*, because something on the order of a billion people were added to those hungry populations during the 1950s and 1960s. Thus, although the average nutritional condition

Table 4–2   Index Numbers of Per Capita Food Production (1952–56 = 100)

Area	1948–52	1954	1955	1956	1957	1958	1959	1960	1961	1962	1963	1964	1965	1966	1967	1968	1969	1970
Developed Regions	92	98	101	104	102	107	108	110	109	112	113	114	114	119	121	124	121	121
Developing Regions	94	100	100	102	102	103	104	105	105	106	106	106	104	102	104	104	105	105
World*	93	99	101	103	101	105	106	106	106	108	108	108	107	109	110	112	110	109

SOURCE: Food and Agriculture Organization of the United Nations (FAO). Monthly bulletin of Agricultural Economics and Statistics, vol. 20, Jan. 1971.
NOTE: The indices are calculated as a ratio between the index numbers of food production and the corresponding index numbers of population using all data available as of November 15, 1970. For further information consult the FAO Production Yearbook.
*Excluding People's Republic of China (mainland).

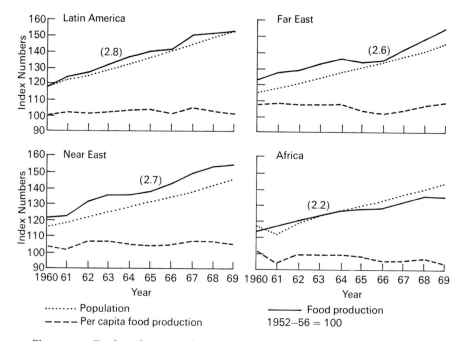

Figure 4–9 Food production and population trends in underdeveloped regions. Figures in parentheses show annual rate of growth of food production in the decade 1956–1958 to 1966–1968. Data for the Near East exclude Israel; data for the Far East exclude Japan, People's Republic of China (mainland), and other Asian communist nations; data for Africa exclude South Africa. (After FAO, *State of Food and Agriculture*, 1970.)

of the proverty-stricken of our planet may have remained about the same, both the absolute numbers of the poor and their proportion of the total world population have increased rapidly.

Of course, production figures are at best crude indicators of the food situation, since even within a single country, conditions may vary tremendously from area to area. For instance, by mid-1968 the famine conditions that had held sway in most of northern India for several years had ended. (They necessitated the shipment of vast quantities of grain to India by the United States and some other DCs.) In some areas of northern India wheat and rice were even super-abundant, and as a result prices were dropping steadily. But in spite of this surplus of food, 7 million people were in danger of starvation in one province alone, and in northern India as a whole, some 20 million people were described as being in "acute distress." These conditions were due largely to local droughts in areas adjacent to those producing surpluses. The people were so poor that they could not create effective "demand" for food, producing the spectacle of surpluses and dropping prices in close proximity to starvation.

This local situation is an example of the story of food distribution throughout the world.

To picture the UDCs simply as net food importers would be a mistake. Although the DCs annually deliver some 2.5 million tons of gross protein to the UDCs, the latter send to the DCs about 3.5 million tons of higher quality protein in fish meal, presscakes of oilseeds, and soybeans. The DCs use nearly all of it to feed poultry, livestock, and pets. More than sixty countries, including Mexico, Panama, Hong Kong, and India, supply the United States with shrimp, which could otherwise be a life saver for the protein-starved children of those countries. Peru exports to the DCs large catches of various fishes that could greatly relieve severe protein deficiencies in Latin America. Food specialist Georg Borgstrom describes the advantage held by the rich countries of the world in the present pattern of protein flow as a "treacherous exchange." That it results primarily from the present world economic system is an indictment of that system and its values.

Increasing Food Production

The food supply in the UDCs is at best marginal. *Large-scale efforts are required simply to avoid drops in per capita food production.* In order to improve the lot of the Earth's 1 to 2 billion hungry people, food production will have to increase at an unprecedented rate. What are the prospects for continuing to increase the food production of the world? Within the framework of any system of technology or any economic system, the environment imposes limits on agricultural production. As noted earlier, for the foreseeable future food production on Earth will depend on the availability of sunlight, fertile soil, water, and a growing season long enough for crops to mature. However, these conditions are unevenly distributed over the planet. For example, although many tropical forest areas have a year-round growing season and abundant rainfall, their soils are often extremely poor, making large-scale agriculture there virtually impossible at present.

Opening New Land. In 1967 the report of the President's Scientific Advisory Committee Panel on the World Food Supply estimated the amount of potentially arable land on the Earth to be 7.86 billion acres. This amounts to only 24 percent of the total ice-free land area, but is more than double the area actually planted and harvested in any given year. About 4.13 billion acres, more than half of the estimated total, lies in the tropical areas. Warm-temperate and subtropical areas account for another 1.37 billion potentially arable acres, and cool-temperate areas account for most of the rest, 2.24 billion acres. The distribution of cultivated and potentially arable land in relation to population and area of continents in 1965 is shown in Table 4–3. The majority of potentially arable land is in Africa, South America, and Asia.

But the term "potentially arable" can be misleading. Actually, almost all the land that can be cultivated under today's economic circumstances is now under cultivation. Most of the "potentially arable" land in Asia could not support one four-month growing season without irrigation; subtracting this land leaves very little additional arable land available in Asia.

Irrigation is just one factor among many that will have to be considered if the potential of this land is to be realized. Technical expertise must be available to evaluate the fertility of soils, the feasibility of irrigation, and the availability of capital and labor for both farming and support activities, such as constructing farm roads. Such surveys cost money. So do farm roads, which account for 10 to 30 percent of the cost of developing new agricultural land. Clearing land, removing stones, improving drainage, and other necessary improvements also cost money, and these costs are extremely variable from area to area. Other costs that must be considered include the expense of irrigation when irrigation is necessary, the costs of administering new developments, resettling people, supplying them with homes, schools, services, and so on. The per-acre costs of seven sample projects in UDCs ranged from $32 to $973, and the median cost was $218.

Table 4–3   Present Population and Cultivated Land on Each Continent, Compared with Potentially Arable Land

Continent	Population in 1965 (Millions of Persons) (1)	Area in Billions of Acres			Acres of Cultivated* Land per Person (5)	Ratio of Cultivated* to Potentially Arable Land (Percent) (6)
		Total (2)	Potentially Arable (3)	Cultivated* (4)		
Africa	310	7.46	1.81	0.39	1.3	22
Asia	1,855	6.76	1.55	1.28	.7	83
Australia and New Zealand	14	2.03	.38	.04	2.9	2
Europe	445	1.18	.43	.38	.9	88
North America	255	5.21	1.15	.59	2.3	51
South America	197	4.33	1.68	.19	1.0	11
U.S.S.R.	234	5.52	.88	.56	2.4	64
Total	3,310	32.49	7.88	3.43	1.0	44

SOURCE: President's Science Advisory Committee, *The World Food Problem* (1967).
*Our cultivated area is called by FAO "Arable land and land under permanent crops." It includes land under crops, temporary fallow, temporary meadows for mowing or pasture, market and kitchen gardens, fruit trees, vines, shrubs, and rubber plantations. Within this definition there are said to be wide variations among reporting countries. The land actually harvested during any particular year is about one-half to two-thirds of the total cultivated land.

How much could be accomplished in the population-food crisis by concentrating on the development of new lands? Under the optimistic assumption that one acre of land will support one person, and the even more optimistic assumption that development costs will be only $400 per acre (the cost of irrigating alone now averages almost $400 per acre), the world would have to invest *$28 billion per year* simply to open new lands to feed the people now being added to the population annually. And, since there is an inevitable "time lag" in opening up new lands, it might seem reasonable to start immediately with the financing of at least a 10-year program costing at least $280 billion. The chances are, however, that such a program would be as unsuccessful as previous attempts have been at opening "potentially arable" lands.

In 1954 large sections of the dry plains of Kazakhstan in the U.S.S.R. were put into grain production. Premier Khruschchev had great hopes for this highly promoted "virgin lands" program; but the virgin turned out to be a harlot in disguise. Rainfall in Kazakhstan is marginal, roughly 12 inches per year, and drought has afflicted the area. In the 1950s Turkey also expanded grain plantings into grassland areas that subsequently had to be allowed to revert to grass because of inadequate rainfall.

A classic example of lack of attention to the agricultural limits imposed by local conditions was the ill-fated British groundnut (peanut) project started in Tanganyika (now Tanzania) after the Second World War. Although agricultural experts predicted that weather conditions would be satisfactory in only eight years out of 19, millions of dollars were spent on the program. All the expertise of the British was to no avail; the program was a catastrophic failure.

Brazil's attempts to set up an agricultural colony in the Amazon basin have been utterly defeated by poor tropical soils. Unlike temperate soils, which are rich storehouses of nutrients for plants, tropical soils contain relatively little of the nutrients that exist in a tropical forest. Most of these are stored in the forest trees and shrubs themselves. When the forest is removed, what nutrients exist in the soil are quickly washed away by heavy rains. Small wonder forest clearing so often results in disaster! Successful agricultural development of tropical lands clearly requires a much more sophisticated approach than simply transplanting Temperate Zone agriculture.[6] New techniques will have to be developed for these areas through experimentation with various crops and methods. Quite possibly much can be learned by studying and comparing the practices of indigenous populations in similar climates. For example, the rice-growing people of Southeast Asia have learned to preserve their soil by terracing, careful fertilizing and renewing fertility with silt deposited in river valleys by floods.

Presumably progress can be made in tropical agriculture without unbearable ecological consequences, if great care is used. But the ecological risks are

---

[6]"The Unexploited Tropics," Daniel Janzen, in the *Bulletin of the Ecological Society of America*, Sept. 1970. pp. 4–7. A distinguished ecologist explains some of the problems associated with agriculture in the tropics.

great, especially of the destruction of the great reservoirs of organic diversity represented by tropical rain forests.

Perhaps the most discussed approach to bringing substantial amounts of new land under cultivation lies in the irrigation of arid (but otherwise arable) lands. This must be done with great care, as the danger of ruining the land is great. In Pakistan it has been estimated that salinization and water-logging take an acre of irrigated land out of production every 5 minutes. (See Figure 4–10 for an example of salinization.) Future attempts to bring large areas under irrigation may be limited to large-scale water projects that would include dams and canals or the removal of salt from ocean and brackish water (desalination). Supplies of usable groundwater are already badly depleted in most areas where they are accessible, and natural recharge is so low in most arid regions that such supplies do not offer a long-term solution in any case.

Large water projects are extraordinarily expensive, very time consuming to construct and bring into operation, and often seriously hampered by environmental and sociological side effects. A rough rule of thumb for large dual-purpose projects (irrigation and electricity generation) is that $1,000 goes into constructing the facility for every person who can be fed from the newly irrigated land. Construction times range from 10 to 20 years, during which period population growth may outstrip the gains in productivity. The dams may flood existing fertile land, displace substantial numbers of people,

Figure 4–10   Saline fields stand out against darker cultivated land in this aerial photograph. The related problems of waterlogging and salt accumulation in the soil have made 5 million acres of West Pakistan's irrigated farmland either impossible or unprofitable to cultivate. (Photo by Pakistan Communications Media Division.)

and diminish soil fertility downstream by interrupting the flow of nutrients in silt.

An obvious example of these shortcomings is the Aswan High Dam in Egypt. It has added only a tenth of an acre of cultivated land for each person added to Egypt's population during the construction period; Egypt had only an average of one-quarter of an acre of cultivated land per person when construction began. In addition to its probable negative effects on fertility in the Nile delta, it has apparently already damaged the sardine fishery in the eastern Mediterranean. And the associated network of irrigation canals has facilitated the spread of a serious parasitic disease, schistosomiasis, the transmission of which depends on freshwater snails.

Desalting sea water for irrigation also has serious limitations. With present technology, the cost of desalted water is five to ten times what farmers can afford to pay for use on staple crops such as wheat and rice. If the land to be irrigated is not near a coastline, the high cost of transporting water makes the enterprise unattractive even if desalting costs fall dramatically. Hopes for irrigating extensively with sea water in the future hinge on three possibilities: (1) that improvements in desalting technology will bring the cost of the water down, (2) that improvements in agricultural technology will reduce the amount of water needed to produce a pound of food, or (3) that strains of food crops that are tolerant of salty water will be developed. When and to what extent these possibilities will be realized cannot now be predicted. As with most technological rabbits-in-the-hat, elementary considerations of the time and money needed for development and deployment indicate that no major impact on the food situation can be anticipated in the next 20 years. Unfortunately, population growth will not wait. And, if and when large-scale desalting for agriculture does come about, we shall have to deal with such difficult environmental questions as how to dispose of the salt.

The Green Revolution.   A great deal of publicity has been given to the so-called Green Revolution, an agricultural transformation that some claim may enable mankind to keep agricultural production in the UDCs well ahead of population growth. There are two general components in this revolution: increased use of the new "high-yield" varieties of grain (Table 4–4), and increased use of the "inputs"—fertilizers, water (often from irrigation), and pesticides—needed to realize the potential of the miracle varieties.

The new high-yield varieties are capable of producing yields well above those of traditional strains. For instance, one miracle dwarf rice strain, IR-8, can produce two or more times the harvest of traditional rice plants from a given area, *if it is handled correctly.* Like the other new strains it is extremely responsive to fertilizers. Under some conditions it can be fertilized at three times the level of traditional varieties, and it can use that fertilizer input much more efficiently in producing grain. Given the large amounts of water that are a necessary accompaniment of heavy fertilizer inputs, and given protection from pests, the strong, short stalks of the new grains can carry a truly miraculous load of grain.

Table 4–4 Estimated Acreages Planted in New High Yielding Grain Varieties (Non-Communist Nations)

Crop Year	Wheat	Rice	Total
1965–66	23,000	18,000	41,000
1966–67	1,542,000	2,505,000	4,047,000
1967–68	10,173,000	6,487,000	16,660,000
1968–69	19,699,000	11,620,000	31,319,000
1969–70	24,664,000	19,250,000	43,914,000

NOTE: Most of wheat and all reported rice acreages were in South and East Asia; of 1969–1970 total, 59 percent was in India, 20 percent in Pakistan. Limited areas of wheat have been planted in West Asia, North Africa, and Latin America.
SOURCE: Dalrymple, 1971. *Imports and Plantings of High-Yielding Varieties of Wheat and Rice in the Less Developed Countries.* U.S. Department of Agriculture.

The new varieties mature early and are less sensitive to seasonal variations in day length (both characteristics increase the possibility of multiple cropping; that is, growing and harvesting more than one crop per year). It must be emphasized, however, that the *potential* yields of the miracle grains can only become *actual* yields if an entire complex of conditions is met, especially the proper inputs of fertilizers, water, and pesticides. Without these, yields may be well *below* those of traditional varieties.

It is clear that the Green Revolution has great potential for increasing food supplies in many UDCs; in some countries, that potential has already been realized. In 1968 the Indian wheat harvest was 35 percent above the previous record, and the Pakistani crop was 37 percent higher than any other year. There were also large gains in rice production in the Philippines and Ceylon in 1966–1968. These gains were in large part due to the new grain varieties. In Mysore State in India, farmers are growing three corn crops every 14 months. When adequate water is available, Indian, Indonesian, and Philippine farmers can now grow two and even three rice crops each year. Where there is a dry season with inadequate water available for growing rice, some farmers are growing new high-yielding grain sorghums (which require less water). In some areas of northern India and Pakistan, farmers are alternately planting rice in the summer and wheat in the winter.

Such advances do indicate that significant increases in yields are *possible* in some UDCs. There are, however, many unanswered questions about the ultimate scale and duration of the Green Revolution.[7] For instance, because the new grain varieties typically *must* have high fertilizer inputs in order to realize their potential, large amounts of chemical fertilizers are required, since sufficient natural fertilizers are not available. The production of chemical fertilizers is straightforward, and a good deal is known about their effective application. There are, however, staggering difficulties barring the implementation of fertilizer technology on the scale required. The accomplishments of Japan and the Netherlands are often cited as offering hope to the under-

[7]"How Green is the Green Revolution?" William C. Paddock, in *BioScience*, vol. 20, no. 16. pp. 892–902, Aug. 15, 1970.

developed world. Some perspective on this point is afforded by noting that, if India were to apply fertilizer as intensively as the Netherlands, Indian fertilizer needs alone would amount to nearly half the present world output. Per capita use in the Netherlands is more than 12 times that of India (but the Netherlands is nonetheless unable to feed herself).

If a UDC is to convert to fertilizer-intensive agriculture, the fertilizer must be produced within the UDC or purchased from outside, and it must then be transported to the fields. Capital is required for fertilizer plants, fertilizer purchases, and transportation facilities. Abundant water is also essential for the fertilizer-sensitive miracle grains, requiring investment in tubewells, pumps, and irrigation ditches. Similarly, pesticides and mechanized planting and harvesting are necessary to get the most out of the new varieties. These too are expensive, and capital is in chronically short supply in most UDCs.

There are many other economic problems associated with the Green Revolution. For instance, in some countries progress is hindered by a lack of farm credit. New grains are first introduced to "progressive" farmers, usually those with the largest, richest farms. They are in the best position to pay for the inputs of fertilizer, pesticides, irrigation water, and so forth. This advantage of the large landholders over small farmers is intensified when the higher yields bring in more money, which can be further invested in more land and more fertilizer. As attempts are made to spread the Green Revolution to smaller farmers, the need for credit becomes acute.

Another serious problem in spreading new agricultural technology is a critical shortage of agricultural-research workers and technicians in the UDCs. Research organizations like the International Maize and Wheat Improvement Center (CIMMYT) in Mexico and the International Rice Research Institute (IRRI) in the Philippines have already made many valuable contributions to agricultural development. Many more institutions such as these, supported by private foundations or where necessary by government funds from the DCs, should be established all over the tropical world as trained researchers become available to staff them.

In many ways the problem of revolutionizing UDC agriculture is inextricably tied up with the general problem of UDC "development." Shortages of capital, demand, resources, and trained technicians, lack of effective planning, and the absence of adequate transport and marketing systems all tend to combine with extremely high rates of population growth, malnutrition, and disease to make any kind of development extremely difficult, and thus retard agricultural development. It is a vicious cycle—one that the Green Revolution may not be able to break.

Perhaps even more important than the effects of the economic problems on agricultural development are those of potential biological problems. For instance, the new grain varieties were rushed into production in places like Pakistan, where the climate is most favorable. How they will fare in less favorable climates remains to be seen. They are also going into production without adequate field testing, which is very time consuming, so it is uncertain how resistant they will be to the attacks of insects and plant diseases. Continuous breeding efforts are, however, being carried out in order to develop varieties suitable for different conditions. In general, though, when crops are selected for high yield, something is sacrificed, such as protein content or resistance to bacteria or insects. We suspect that in the next few years escalating pest problems will cut heavily into "miracle yields."

One of the most serious side effects of the Green Revolution may be acceleration of the loss of reserves of genetic variability in crop plants, variability badly needed for continuing development of new strains.[8] This process is already well under way as old varieties, reservoirs of variability, are replaced by high yielding varieties over large areas. FAO agronomists estimate that seed stock reserves must be established for the old varieties within the next five years, or "mankind will have lost them for good and ever."

Since the new varieties may require more input of pesticides, with all of their deleterious ecological side effects, part of the price of agricultural development may be an increase in environmental pollution and a decrease in the harvest of food from the sea. And, of course, there may be serious environmental problems connected with the heavy use of fertilizers required with the new varieties. (These and similar biological problems are discussed in detail in Chapter 6.) Because biological problems usually develop over considerable periods of time, it is possible that early successes in the Green Revolution may have given the world a false impression of what rates of improvement in yield can be sustained.

The new grain varieties have been adopted primarily by the most progressive farmers in the most suitable areas; it remains to be seen whether their success will be duplicated by less progressive farmers who may not do as well with the new strains or may not even be willing or able to try them. On the other hand, it can be argued that the Green Revolution may break the crust of tradition and become self-accelerating. Only time will tell.

As promising as high-yield agriculture may be, the funds, the personnel, the ecological expertise, and the necessary time to develop its full potential are unfortunately not at our disposal. We are, among other things, faced with a *rate* problem. Revolutionizing agriculture throughout the tropics will be a time-consuming proposition, and population growth will not wait. Fulfillment of the Green Revolution's promise will come too late for many of the world's hungry, if it comes at all. Even the most enthusiastic boosters of the Green Revolution, including Norman Borlaug, who received the Nobel Prize for developing the miracle wheats, admit that it cannot possibly keep food production abreast of population growth for more than two decades or so. Since a birth-control solution to the population explosion will inevitably take much longer than that, the prospects for avoiding massive increases in the death rate from starvation are dim indeed.

[8]"Genetic Dangers in the Green Revolution," O. H. Frankel et al., in *Ceres* (FAO), vol. 2, no. 5, pp. 35–37, Sept.–Oct., 1969.

Food from the Sea

Perhaps the most pervasive myth of the population-food crisis is that mankind will be saved by harvesting the "immeasurable riches" of the sea. Unfortunately, the notion that we can extract vastly greater amounts of food from the sea in the near future is an illusion promoted by the uninformed. Biologists have carefully measured the riches of the sea, considered the means of harvesting them, and have found them wanting as a solution to the world food problem.

The basis of the food-from-the-sea myth seems to be some theoretical estimates that fisheries productivity might be increased to many times current yields. However, an analysis by J. H. Ryther of the Woods Hole Oceanographic Institution in 1969 put the maximum sustainable fish yield in the vicinity of 100 million metric tons, considerably less than twice the record 1970 harvest of perhaps 70 million metric tons.[9] (This is larger than the U.N. estimate, which does not include the harvest of the People's Republic of China, calculated to be 6–8 million metric tons.) Some marine biologists, more optimistic than Ryther, think a global fisheries yield of 150 million metric tons is attainable.

Since 1950, when the total world-fisheries production was about 21 million metric tons, production has risen each year at an average rate of about 5 to 6 percent. This rapid sustained increase was largely due both to more intensive fishing and to the increasing use of technology, and probably also in part to more accurate and complete reporting. In 1969 the rise in fisheries production came to an abrupt halt; in fact, the total catch of 63 million metric tons represented a decline of 2 percent from the previous year. There was a recovery in 1970, up to some 70 million metric tons, but preliminary 1971 reports indicated another decline. If the global fish catch should increase by the year 2000 to 100 million metric tons, Ryther's estimate of the maximum sustainable yield, there would be less fish consumed per person than in 1970 (unless the human population growth rate decreased in the meantime).

To surpass the potential annual fish production of 100–150 million metric tons would require moving down the food chain from the big fish ordinarily found in fish markets to the harvesting of plankton (tiny marine organisms). All signs at the moment indicate that this will not be feasible or profitable in the foreseeable future, if ever. More calories of fuel and human energy would be spent on harvesting the plankton than could be gained in eating it; the expenditure of money would be colossal in relation to the yield; also, the product would require considerable processing to be made palatable as human food. In addition, harvesting plankton would result in the depletion of desirable stocks of larger fish living farther up the food chain.

But two things stand between humanity and the future achievement, by

[9]"Photosynthesis and Fish Production in the Sea," John H. Ryther, in *Science*, vol. 166, pp. 72–76, 1969.

more conventional methods, of even 100 million tons of yield. The first is overexploitation, the second is oceanic pollution (which is discussed in Chapter 6). The 1969 setback may mean that these two problems have already overtaken us. The story of the whale fisheries[10] serves as a model of overexploitation. In 1933, a total of 28,907 whales was caught, producing 2,606,201 barrels of whale oil. In 1966, a third of a century later, 57,891 whales were killed, almost exactly twice as many as in 1933. But twice as many whales yielded only 1,546,904 barrels of oil, just about 60 percent of the 1933 yield. The reason can be seen in the charts of Figure 4–11. As the larger kinds of whales were driven toward extinction, the industry shifted to harvesting not only the young individuals of large species, but, with time, smaller and smaller species.

Setting aside any consideration of the aesthetics or morality of such unrestricted slaughtering of these magnificient and intelligent animals, what can be said about the whaling industry's performance? For one thing, of course, its drive toward self-destruction seems to contradict the commonly held notion that people will automatically change their behavior if they realize that it is against their own self-interest. Fully informed by biologists of the consequences of their behavior, the whaling industry has nonetheless operated against its own self-interest continually since 1963. Short-term self-interest, the lure of the "quick buck," clearly is too strong to allow the long-run best interest of everyone to prevail. Those who own the industry apparently plan to make more money in the long run by forcing both the whales and the industry to extinction and then simply investing their ill-gotten gains elsewhere after the final collapse of the whale stocks.

Space-age technology, which has been unleashed on the whales, is also being applied to other major fisheries around the world, even though many stocks are already overexploited, and others apparently soon will be. The Soviet Union and other eastern European nations have moved into big-time fishing with a vengeance. A single Rumanian factory ship equipped with modern devices caught in one day in New Zealand waters as many tons of fish as the whole New Zealand fleet of some 1,500 vessels (see Figure 4–12). *Simrad Echo*, a Norwegian periodical published by a manufacturer of sonar fishing equipment, boasted in 1966 that industrialized herring fishing had come to the Shetland Islands, where 300 sonar-equipped Norwegian and Icelandic purse-seiners had landed undreamed-of-quantities of herring. An editorial in the magazine queried, "Will the British fishing industry turn . . . to purse-seining as a means of reversing the decline in the herring catch?" Another quotation from the same magazine gives further insight: "What then are the Shetlands going to do in the immediate future? Are they going to join and gather the bonanza while the going is good—or are they going to continue

---

[10]Although whales are mammals, not fishes, the hunting of them is arbitrarily called a "fishery."

drifting and if seining is found to have an adverse effect on the herring stocks find their catches dwindling?" The answer is now clear. In January 1969, British newspapers announced that the country's east-coast herring industry had been wiped out. The purse-seiners took the immature herring that had escaped the British drifter's nets, which are of larger mesh, and the potential breeding stock was destroyed.

As biologist Garrett Hardin has pointed out, the sea is a "commons," analogous to a communal pasture open to all.[11] From the point of view of an individual herder exploiting such a pasture commons, there seems to be every reason to keep adding to his herd: although the grass is limited, he will get a larger share if he has a larger herd. If his animals do not eat the grass, someone else's will. Such reasoning is, of course, followed by each user of the commons. Individuals struggle to increase their herds until, at some point, the carrying capacity of the pasture is exceeded, and it is destroyed by overgrazing. Similarly, in the sea, each individual, company, or country exploiting a fish stock (equivalent to the grass of the pasture) strives to get a maximum share of the catch because each increment represents further immediate profit. Unless some strict agreement is reached about the degree of utilization of the fishery commons, maximum utilization seems to be the best short-range strategy from the point of view of each user. After all, reason the Japanese, if we don't get the fish, the Russians will. The Russians take a similar view, as do the Peruvians and all the others. Unhappily, the end result of all these individual optimum strategies for dealing with the commons is disaster for all.

The race to loot the sea of its protein is now in full swing. Fish catches more than doubled between 1953 and 1968. Peru, Japan, and the USSR took the lion's share in 1968, jointly landing almost 40 percent of the catch (the catch of the People's Republic of China is not included here). The United States and Norway, who came next, landed some 7 percent between them. The pressures of competition have begun to show. Soviet fishing ships make headlines by fishing close to both coasts of the United States and Canada. Between 1961 and 1971, the Peruvian government seized 30 United States tuna fishing boats, and Ecuador had taken 70 others in disputes over the limits of territorial waters. Ecuador and Peru each claim sovereignty over the ocean within 200 miles of their shores. The list of conflicts grows and will undoubtedly continue to do so unless competition is regulated.

Since only a few percent of the world's calories come from the sea, one might easily draw the conclusion that a reduction of per capita yield is not particularly important. On the contrary, it is extremely serious. Although food from the sea provides comparatively few calories, it supplies about 15 percent of the world's animal protein. For some countries, especially for those where fish provide a greater than average proportion of high quality

---

[11]"The Tragedy of the Commons," *Science*, vol. 162, pp. 1243–1248, 1968.

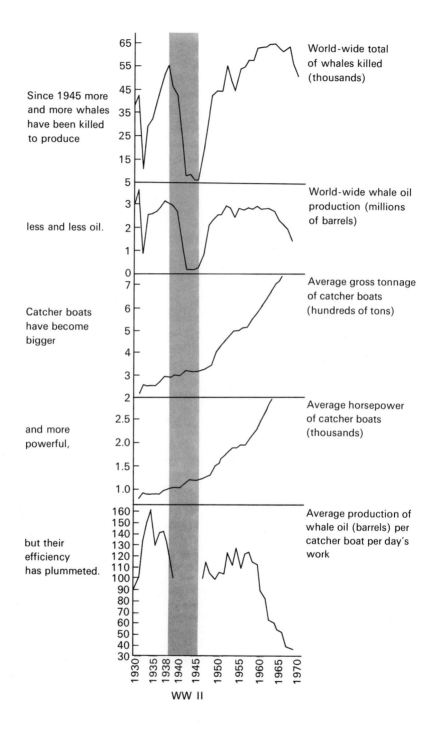

Since 1945 more and more whales have been killed to produce

World-wide total of whales killed (thousands)

less and less oil.

World-wide whale oil production (millions of barrels)

Catcher boats have become bigger

Average gross tonnage of catcher boats (hundreds of tons)

and more powerful,

Average horsepower of catcher boats (thousands)

but their efficiency has plummeted.

Average production of whale oil (barrels) per catcher boat per day's work

WW II

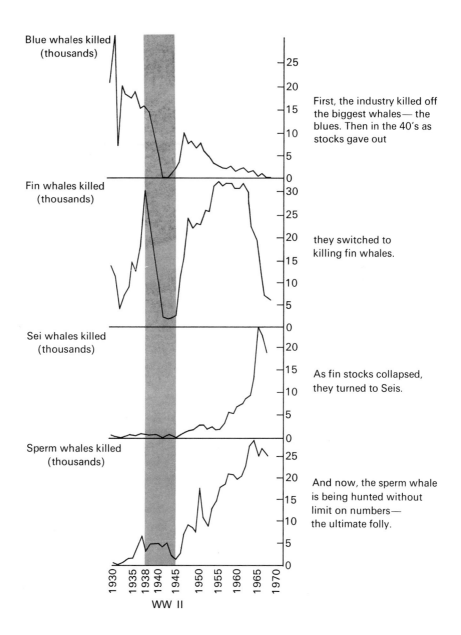

Blue whales killed (thousands)

First, the industry killed off the biggest whales— the blues. Then in the 40's as stocks gave out

Fin whales killed (thousands)

they switched to killing fin whales.

Sei whales killed (thousands)

As fin stocks collapsed, they turned to Seis.

Sperm whales killed (thousands)

And now, the sperm whale is being hunted without limit on numbers— the ultimate folly.

WW II

Figure 4–11   Overexploitation of whale fisheries. (After *N.Y. Zoological Society Newsletter*, Nov. 1968.)

Figure 4–12 Russian factory ship *Polar Star* lies hove to in the Barents Sea in June, 1968, as two vessels from its fleet of trawlers unload their catch for processing. (Photo by Sovfoto.)

protein, the loss of this protein would be catastrophic. Japan's fisheries, for instance, supply her with more than one-and-one-half times as much protein as is provided by her agriculture.

What about "farming" the sea? Unfortunately, the impression that sea farming is here today, or is just around the corner, is illusory. For the most part we still hunt the sea today, or in a relatively few cases herd its animals (for example, we herd oysters and a few kinds of fishes). Farming the sea presents an array of formidable problems, especially of fertilizing and harvesting. About the only planting and harvesting of marine plant crops done today is some seaweed culture in Japan. Perhaps if the sea is emptied of its fishes and shellfishes by mindless human exploitation and pollution, some kind of phytoplankton (tiny marine plants) farming could be attempted (if the sea is not by then too badly poisoned by pollution). The crop would be extremely costly at best, and it would not be very tasty, but in desperation mankind might give it a try. For the immediate future, however, sea-farming offers no hope at all of substantially affecting the world food problem.

Plans for increasing the yield of fishes from the sea have disregarded the effects of pollution and are based on the premise that the fish stocks will be harvested rationally. The history of fisheries so far gives little hope that rationality will prevail. (See Figure 4–13 on overfishing in the North Atlantic Ocean.) One can, for instance, expect continuation of attempts to harvest

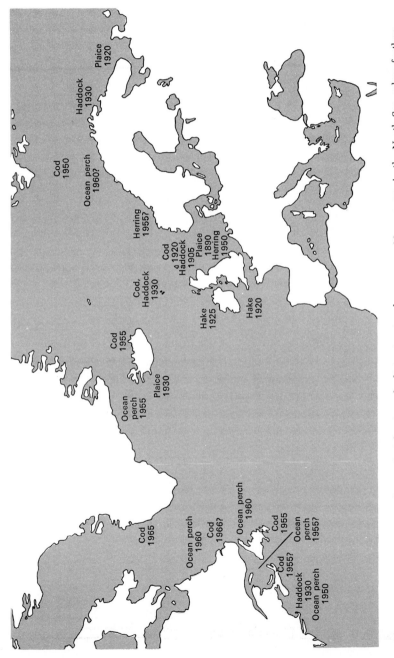

Figure 4–13 Overfishing in the North Atlantic and adjacent waters began some 80 years ago in the North Sea, when further increases in fishing the plaice stock no longer produced an increase in the catch of that fish. By 1950 the same was true of North Sea cod, haddock, and herring; of cod, haddock, and plaice off the North Cape and in the Barents Sea; of plaice, haddock, and cod south and east of Iceland; and of ocean perch and haddock in the Gulf of Maine. In the period between 1956 and 1966 the same became true of ocean perch off Newfoundland and off Labrador and of cod west of Greenland. It may also be true of North Cape ocean perch and Labrador cod. (From Holt, "The Food Resources of the Ocean." Copyright © 1969 by Scientific American, Inc. All rights reserved.)

simultaneously young and old of the same species, and both the big fishes and the little fishes that big fishes eat to live. And one can expect pollution to help reduce the size of many or all fish populations.

Thus, far from being the answer to all our food problems, the sea may not even be able to continue to support the limited yield we now extract from it. The 1969 setback may be the beginning of a long downward trend. Judging from the fishing industry's behavior toward the sea, one would suppose that if they were to go into the chicken-farming business they would plan to eat up all the feed, all the eggs, all the chicks, and all the chickens simultaneously, while burning down the henhouses to keep themselves warm.

Novel Sources of Food.   What about some of the other proposed solutions to the world food problem that are often seen in the public press? Certain food novelties do have potential for helping to alleviate the protein shortage. For instance, protein-rich material can be produced by culturing single-celled organisms on petroleum or other substrates. Theoretically, much, if not all, of the world's protein deficit in the last two decades of this century could be made up with protein from such sources. Knowledgeable people think it conceivable that single-cell protein (SCP) could be made sufficiently pure for human consumption by 1980, although whether the purification costs would make it uneconomical is another question. Factories are already producing limited amounts of SCP for use as a livestock-feed supplement. If SCP for human use were developed, the problem would become one of building plants, arranging for distribution, and solving local political and economic problems relative to the use of SCP. Perhaps most important of all, people will then have to be convinced that SCP is food. People in general tend to be extremely conservative in their food habits. The hungriest people are precisely those who recognize the fewest items as food, because they have always existed on a diet of limited variety.

Other ways of reducing the protein deficit are being actively promoted. Work is going ahead on the production of grains with higher quality proteins, those that contain a better balance of the protein building-blocks (amino acids) that are necessary for human nutrition. This is being done both by breeding new varieties and by fortifying grain grown from traditional varieties. This is critically important work, and, if successful, it could make a substantial contribution to the improvement of the human diet. The plant-breeding programs take a good deal of time, although they doubtless will be more satisfactory in the long run. Lysine-enrichment of wheat has been shown to be beneficial to rats and human babies under rigidly controlled conditions. Whether its benefits are well enough demonstrated to warrant large-scale introduction is still a matter of debate.

New protein foods have been produced by adding oilseed protein concentrates to foods made from cereals. The best known of these is Incaparina, developed by INCAP (Institute of Nutrition for Central America and Panama).

It is a mixture of corn and cottonseed meal enriched with vitamins A and B. Incaparina and similar products should be viewed more as "future hopes" than as current cures. As valuable protein and vitamin supplements, they hold considerable promise, but the economics of their production and distribution are not well worked out. More important, the question of their general acceptability remains open. Incaparina has been available in Central America for more than a decade, but its impact remains insignificant.

Other unorthodox ways of providing more food are presently being discussed or are under preliminary development. These include herding such animals as the South American capybara (a rodent) and the African eland (an antelope), converting water hyacinths and other aquatic weeds to cattle feed, making cattle feed from wood, extracting protein from leaves and little fishes, and culturing algae in the fecal slime of sewage-treatment plants. Some of these hold promise, at least to help local situations. But most are subject to serious problems, not the least of which would be to persuade people to eat sewage-cultured algae.

We must, of course, press ahead to develop novel foods and, especially, to find ways to make them acceptable to diverse peoples. But it is reasonably clear that few of them will be a major factor in the world food picture during the critical decade or two ahead. Hopefully, if mankind can survive, the most ecologically, economically, nutritionally, and aesthetically desirable of these processes will eventually be integrated into normal food supplies.

Reduction of Food Losses.   One area in which technology can greatly help to improve the food supply is in reduction of losses in the field, in transit, and in storage. For instance, the Indian Food and Agriculture Ministry estimated that in 1968 rats consumed almost 10 percent of India's grain production, and others think 12 percent is more nearly accurate. It would take a train almost 3,000 miles long to haul the grain India's rats eat in a single year. And yet in 1968 India spent $265 million on importing fertilizers, about *800 times* as much as was spent on rat control. The rats in two Philippine provinces in 1952–1954 consumed 90 percent of the rice, 20–80 percent of the maize (corn), and more than 50 percent of the sugar cane. Since 1960, birds in Africa have destroyed crops worth more than $7 million annually. Insects in UDCs may destroy as much as 50 percent of a stock of grain in a year's storage period. Spoilage from molds, mildews, and bacteria also takes a heavy toll, even in the DCs. As a guess, the development of good storage and transport facilities alone might increase UDC food supplies by as much as 10 to 20 percent.

The problems of controlling populations of insect pests in fields are discussed in Chapter 6. Reducing these losses requires great care to avoid serious ecological problems. Controlling rats, birds, rusts, and other non-insect pests in fields also presents similar problems. Protection of foods once they are harvested, however, is much more straightforward and ordinarily involves much less ecological risk. Storage facilities may be made rat-proof, be refrigerated, and be fumigated with nonpersistent pesticides that are not released into the environment until they have lost their toxicity. Transport systems may be improved so that more rapid movement, proper handling, refrigeration where necessary, and other measures greatly reduce spoilage en route. Perhaps the safest investment man could make toward improving the quantity and quality of food would be to improve methods of handling, shipping, and storing crops after the harvest.

Should We Be Pessimistic?   As must be apparent by now, we tend not to share the enthusiasm of many for various proposed "solutions" to the world food problem. The most practical solution, that of increasing yield on land already under cultivation (the Green Revolution), presents great difficulties. This and other programs are usually carried out with little consideration for their ecological consequences, and all too often they neglect the critical importance of high-quality protein in the human diet. Still, if many of these programs are simultaneously put in operation, some badly needed time may be bought to start bringing the population explosion to a halt. It is certainly evident that no conceivable increase in food supply can keep up with the current population growth rates over the long term. We emphatically agree with the report of the President's Science Advisory Committee's Panel on the World Food Supply, which in 1967 stated: "The solution to the problem that will exist after about 1985 *demands* that programs of population control be initiated now."

The basic questions for the next decade or so seem to be:

1. Will the weather be favorable?
2. Can apparent breakthroughs in UDC agriculture be sustained and converted into real revolutions in spite of the substantial problems associated with their achievement?
3. Will the ecological price paid for a Green Revolution be too high?
4. Can we rapidly develop international agreements for rational use of the sea?

Only time will bring the answers. Obviously, the most prudent course is to work for the best but prepare for the worst.

Other Renewable Resources

Besides consuming and dispersing irreplaceable mineral and fossil fuel resources, humanity is overconsuming resources that ordinarily are replenished by natural processes. Two renewable resources that are being consumed or destroyed faster than they can be restored are water and forests. The saddest

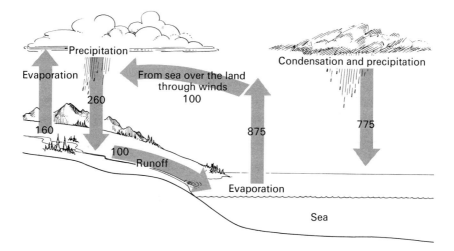

Figure 4–14 Hydrologic cycle (in cubic kilometers per day). (Data from Borgstrom, *Too Many*, Macmillan, New York, 1969.)

aspect of this is that, with careful planning and prudent use, both resources could remain available essentially in perpetuity.

Water. "Water is the best of all things," said the Greek poet Pindar. It is also, in the broad sense, a renewable resource. It circulates on the Earth in a complex series of pathways known collectively as the hydrologic cycle (Figure 4–14). But even though it circulates, the finite supply of fresh water still places limits on the numbers of people that can be supported, both in specific locations and on the Earth as a whole.

Some 97 percent of the world's water is sea water. Of the remaining 3 percent, which is fresh water, almost 77 percent is tied up in glaciers and ice caps, principally in Antarctica and Greenland. Since freeing all of this water would raise the sea level some 50 meters, flooding many of our cities and much of our crop land, it would seem best to leave most of that water tied up as it is, even if it were feasible to free it.

Water is needed in prodigious quantities just to produce food. Plants are constantly absorbing water from the soil and evaporating it from their leaves in a process known as transpiration. This is the basic reason for the great water requirements of vegetable food production and the even greater requirements of meat production. A single corn plant may take from the soil and evaporate as much as 200 quarts of water in a growing season. The water needed for the production of one pound of meat includes that necessary for growing about 10 pounds of forage plants, plus the water directly required by the animal for drinking, and further water for meat processing. To produce a pound of dry wheat requires some 60 gallons of water; a pound of rice, 200–250 gallons; a pound of meat, 2,500–6,000 gallons; and a quart of milk, about 1,000 gallons.

Industrial processes are even more water-greedy. Directly and indirectly, it takes an estimated 100,000 gallons of water to produce a single automobile. In 1900 about 525 gallons of water were used daily for each American. This increased to almost 1,500 gallons per capita in 1960, and is expected to reach almost 2,000 gallons by 1980. These figures do not include the use of rainwater by crops, but roughly 50 percent of the consumption given here is for irrigation.

These huge quantities of water are supplied almost entirely by tapping the runoff portion of the hydrologic cycle: the rivers and streams that flow over the surface, and the subsurface aquifers (water-carrying beds of rock) that are fed by percolation and underground streams. The only exception is a statistically insignificant amount of water obtained directly from the sea by desalting. Withdrawals from the runoff do not necessarily constitute consumption, because much water is simply used (for washing cooling, flushing, etc.) and returned to the river or aquifer from which it came. If suitably purified, this water can be used over and over again; in fact, the water in some river systems of developed countries is reused up to 50 times. However, almost all use involves some depletion in the form of evaporation and, in the case of irrigation, transpiration. Indeed, depletion from irrigation ranges from 60 to 90 percent of withdrawals. Water is also effectively depleted if it is discharged so polluted as to make reuse impossible, or if it is discharged into the ocean.

The second major aspect of water demand is flow requirement. This term means that after all the demands for consumption have been met, there must still be enough water flowing in the river to carry off wastes, to meet hydropower and navigational needs, and (perhaps) to maintain wildlife habitat and recreational opportunities. On the assumption that capacity to absorb wastes will be the limiting factor, and using a nominal figure for acceptable concentration of pollutants, it was estimated in a 1963 study, *Resources in America's Future*, that the U.S. flow requirements in 1980 and 2000 would be 332 and 447 billion gallons per day (bgd), respectively. Their "medium" projections for depletions in those years were 178 and 247 bgd.

At first glance, even these numbers for 2000 seem unalarming, because the U.S. runoff averaged over a year comes out 1100 bgd. In practice, however, much of the runoff occurs in a short wet season, so the *dependable* flow is much smaller than the "average." This problem can be ameliorated to some extent by building reservoirs to catch and store the high flows that would otherwise be wasted. With the storage facilities existing in the U.S. in 1954, however, the flow that was maintainable 95 percent of the time (a standard measure of "dependable flow") was only 93 bgd, or less than 10 percent of the impressive average runoff. It seems unlikely that the dependable flow can be increased fast enough to meet the projected needs for the year 2000, even setting aside the environmental costs of water projects and the reduction of older storage capacity by silting.

The situation looks even worse when one breaks it down by geographical regions. More than 75 percent of the annual runoff occurs in the eastern half of the U.S. In many parts of the western half of the country, the dependable flow is *already* inadequate. Excluding Washington and Oregon, the total runoff for the western U.S.—assuming it could *all* be exploited—will be inadequate to meet projected needs in this part of the country before the year 2000.

When needs cannot be met from dependable flow, one "solution" is to increase the concentration of wastes, with serious consequences for water quality. Another is to withdraw water from underground aquifers faster than it is replenished by runoff. Both practices are already occurring in the U.S. and other DCs. Georg Borgstrom, an authority on food production, estimates that the people of Europe extract three times what the cycle returns to accessible reserves, and that North Americans take out about twice what is returned. The groundwater supply in some areas will soon be below that necessary to meet withdrawal demands, and those branches of the water bank will fail.

Similar squeezes will occur in many other areas of the world, especially in connection with the immense water needs related to agriculture. For instance, India, in her desperate struggle to grow more food, has greatly increased her tapping of groundwater. Between July 1968 and June 1969 the government drove 2,000 new tube wells, and private enterprise drove 76,000. In addition, 246,000 new pumps were installed on old and new wells. Even in areas such as the Ganges Plain, which is underlain by a huge groundwater reservoir, the supplies are not infinite. Sustained pumping will have to be accompanied by careful planning to allow for replenishment if three-crop agriculture is to be developed over much of the plain without depleting the groundwater supply.

Forests. Intimately related to fresh water supplies is another renewable resource: forests. That deforestation results in heavy soil erosion, floods, and local changes in climate has been known for centuries—known but not always heeded. The annual floods that have plagued northern China since ancient times are due to deforestation during the early dynasties. The Chinese are now attempting to restore some of those forests. The once fertile hills of central Italy have been arid and subject to regular, occasionally devastating floods since the Middle Ages when the trees were removed. It is interesting that the results of deforestation without replanting were accurately predicted by medieval writers and by later writers as well. The ancient Greeks and Romans apparently were relatively conscientious in maintaining the forests and understood their value in protecting watersheds. But this understanding seems to have been partially lost during the Middle Ages, when the demands of a growing population for fuel, construction materials, and grazing land destroyed the forests in much of southern Europe.

Today, similar demands are encroaching on forests around the world. Many valuable tracts have disappeared entirely. Most of Europe, northern

Figure 4–15 An example of human destruction of forests. What has been replaced by the highway is permanently lost. The clear-cut area at right may eventually be reforested, but not before it and the highway construction area have lost valuable soil to erosion. This was a beautiful redwood forest south of Eureka, California. (Photo by William A. Garnett.)

Asia, the eastern one-third and vast areas of the northwestern United States were once covered with forests. Only a fraction of the forest of the eastern United States and of western Europe remains today, largely preserved through conscious conservation and reforestation policies. The Soviet Union has the greatest remaining reserves of temperate and subarctic forest, including nearly half of the world's coniferous forest. About two-thirds is virgin, largely because it is relatively inaccessible. However, the best quality trees for lumbering are in European Russia, and as a result those have been heavily exploited. Large reserves of coniferous forest also remain in North America, from Nova Scotia to Alaska. Forest management practices have been established in most

DCs, including the USSR and the United States. But reforestation takes from 50 to 100 years, depending on the tree and the climate.

What remains of temperate forests is under increasing pressure especially in the United States. Lumber interests, in an effort to meet rising demand for construction wood and paper, are increasing their harvest, often at considerable expense to the forest environment. Particularly damaging is the practice of "clear-cutting"—the wholesale removal of large tracts of mature forest. Even if this is followed by immediate replanting which it sometimes is not, a good deal of erosion and flooding can take place before the young trees are well established. Large stands of young trees are also more susceptible to disease, pests, and fire than are forests containing trees of varied age. Loggers defend the practice of clear-cutting on the grounds that certain valuable species of trees need direct sunlight and space in which to grow; that is, cleared land. Presumably some less destructive procedure can be used, such as clear-cutting of small stands, if selective cutting and replanting of individual trees are unsatisfactory.

Forests are threatened by more than a demand for lumber and fuels. Like agricultural land, much privately owned forested land disappears each year under highways, subdivisions, airports, and other development projects. Strip-mining destroys thousands of acres, in a process even more destructive of the soil than clear-cutting. Inevitable erosion and flooding follow, often accompanied by severe water pollution; reforestation is often not even attempted (although with care it can be achieved). In publicly owned tracts in National Forests, under the "multiple-use" policy, trees are cleared for access roads, powerline cuts, mining activities, sheep and cattle grazing, and recreational facilities. In the recreational areas, the trees that remain are often damaged by the crowds of visitors. And in some areas, near Los Angeles for example, trees are being killed by smog.

Vast forest reserves also still exist in the tropics, especially in the Amazon Valley, Southeast Asia, and central Africa. Inaccessibility and economic factors have until recently protected these areas from destruction, but the more accessible forests have now vanished or have been selectively depleted of the most valuable species. The rate of clearing tropical rainforests has accelerated in the past decade or so to the point that many fear that they will all but disappear by the end of the century. Brazil's forests once covered 80 percent of the country; by 1965 they had been reduced to 58 percent. Vast stretches of the Amazon forest are now being cleared for a transcontinental highway. Much of the best quality forest has been cut to clear land for agriculture and for fuel. What replanting there is has been with fast-growing, inferior trees. Tropical forests have also been exploited for lumber. The mahogany of Haiti, for example, has long since disappeared and that of Honduras is nearly gone. Replanting in tropical forests has seldom been practiced in the past, although soil damage and climate change following tropical deforestation are often even greater than in temperate areas. A few tropical countries are now becoming aware of the value of forests and are introducing forest-management practices. If tropical forests are not to vanish as did the Chinese, European and much of the U.S. forests, conservation and management policies will need to be established soon.

Many benefits are associated with forests besides the lumber and pulp that can be harvested from them. These include the maintenance of watersheds; oxygen production; their function as reservoirs for a variety of plant species, fish, and wildlife; the recreational opportunities and aesthetic pleasure they afford to people.

Careful management of forests could assure humanity of the opportunity to benefit from these values more or less in perpetuity. This management would include preservation of trees of mixed species and ages as much as possible to discourage losses from pests, disease, and fire; logging on a long-term rotation basis for the best quality of lumber; reforestation; and careful protection of the soil. Lumbering companies in the U.S. have not always strictly adhered to these principles, with the result that their abuses have been loudly protested by conservation groups. At the same time, the present and predicted housing shortage will create huge demands on American forests in the next 10 to 15 years. In 1970 President Nixon sanctioned an increase of 60 percent in National Forest logging to help meet housing needs. Conservationists find this a questionable expedient at a time when vast quantities of U.S. timber are being exported to Japan, a country that tightly restricts logging on its own soil.

At the present time, forest cutting apparently is proceeding faster than areas are being reforested. The National Forest Service estimated that demand for wood products (including paper) will have doubled between 1969 and 2000. Even if massive recycling of paper can compensate for much of this, the pressures against our forest resources are obviously growing severe. Unless a comprehensive national land-use policy, including careful management of forests, is soon established, the United States may one day find it has housed one generation rather well, but at the expense of the next.

Bibliography

Borgstrom, Georg, 1969. *Too Many*. Collier-Macmillan, Toronto. An excellent discussion of the limits of food production.

Brown, Lester R., 1970. *Seeds of Change: The Green Revolution and Development in the 1970's*. Frederick A. Praeger, New York. A current analysis of the Green Revolution and its impact on the various aspects of development strategy by an author eminently qualified to discuss the topic.

Food and Agriculture Organization of the United Nations. Source of data on world food and agriculture; several annual volumes and periodicals. See especially the annual volume, *The State of Food and Agriculture.*

Hirschleifer, J., J. C. DeHaven, and J. W. Milliman, 1969 *Water Supply Economics, Technology, and Policy.* University of Chicago Press, Chicago. Analysis of ways to meet rising demand for water.

President's Science Advisory Committee Panel on the World Food Supply, 1967. *The World Food Problem* (3 vols.). Washington, D.C. A very detailed, basic source.

Technology Review, 1970. Vol. 72, no. 4 (Feb.). Special issue on nutritional problems in UDCs and their significance in development programs. Many interesting articles.

Smog in Tokyo often reaches levels of severe eye irritation, as can be seen in this photograph taken in July, 1970. (Wide World Photos.)

FIVE

Pollution: Direct Effects on Society

The word "pollution" usually refers to harmful substances that are released into the environment as the result of human activities. (Some people would also classify the smoke from a forest fire set by lightning or the sulfur dioxide from a volcanic eruption as pollution.) A pollutant may be a single chemical element such as lead or mercury, a chemical compound such as DDT or carbon monoxide, or a more complicated combination of materials such as silt or sewage. Noise, radiation, and heat are also often regarded as pollutants.

Just as there are many kinds of pollutant, there are many different sorts of harm. It is useful to divide these into four categories:

1. Direct assaults on human health (for example, lead poisoning or aggravation of lung disease by air pollution).

2. Damage to goods and services that society provides for itself (for example, the corrosive effects of air pollution on buildings and crops).

3. Other direct effects on what people perceive as their "quality of life" (for example, congestion and litter).

4. Indirect effects on society through interference with services that are provided for society by natural ecosystems, such as ocean fish production and control of erosion by vegetation. Examples of such indirect effects are destruction of vegetation by overgrazing and logging, and poisoning of coastal waters with oil and heavy metals.

The direct effects represented by the first three categories are the most obvious consequences of pollution, and they are treated in this chapter. The less direct threats to human welfare resulting from interference with the operation of natural ecosystems may be less obvious but are perhaps even more serious. These problems are discussed in Chapter 6. They include ecological effects of some of the same pollutants that do direct damage to human beings, as well as the consequences of human activities that fall outside the narrow definition of pollution given above.

Air Pollution

The form of pollution that most Americans are aware of is air pollution. Those of us who live in or near cities can see it (Figure 5–1), and we can feel it when it burns our eyes and irritates our lungs. Pollution at times cuts down the amount of sunlight that reaches New York City by nearly 25 percent and that reaching Chicago by approximately 40 percent. But it is not strictly an American problem; virtually every major metropolis of the world has serious air-pollution problems. Moreover, it is not only the air over cities that is polluted. The *entire atmosphere* of our planet is now afflicted to some degree. Meteorologists talk about a nebulous veil of air pollution encircling the entire Earth. Smog has been observed over oceans, over the North Pole, and in other unlikely places. Mankind is taxing the capacity of the atmosphere to absorb and to transport away from areas of high population density the enormous amounts of waste exhausted into it. Air pollution is now recognized not only as an agent that rots nylon stockings and windshield wiper blades, that corrodes paint and steel, that blackens skies and the wash on the clothesline, and that damages crops; it is also recognized as a killer of people.

The major sources of air pollution in the United States are shown in Table 5–1. Emissions of carbon monoxide and hydrocarbons are the result of incomplete combustion of fuel. The dominant source of these pollutants is the internal combustion engine. Nitrogen oxides are formed any time a fuel is burned at high temperature in air. Sulfur oxides are produced in the combustion of coal and fuel oil, which contain sulfur as a contaminant. Particulate matter consists mostly of ash and includes a variety of toxic metals. Some of these, like mercury and cadmium, are natural contaminants in coal and fuel oil; others, like lead, have been added deliberately to gasoline to improve the performance of internal combustion engines. The term *photochemical smog* describes a broad variety of compounds, including ozone (O_3) and other more complex reactive chemicals, which are formed by the action of sunlight on nitrogen oxides and hydrocarbons. Ozone and other chemicals that readily give up an oxygen atom in chemical reactions are often lumped together under the term *oxidants*.

For many human beings air pollution has already proven lethal. Death rates are above normal when and where smog occurs. The death of the very old, the very young, and those with respiratory ailments is accelerated.

Table 5-1   U.S. Air Pollution Emissions in 1968 (In Millions of Tons)

Source	Carbon Monoxide	Particles	Nitrogen Oxides	Sulfur Oxides	Hydrocarbons
Fuel burned for transportation	63.8	1.2	8.1	0.8	16.6
Fuel burned in stationary sources*	1.9	8.9	10.0	24.4	0.7
Other industrial processes†	9.7	7.5	0.2	7.3	4.6
Solid waste burning	7.8	1.1	0.6	0.1	1.6
Agricultural burning, forest fires, and other	16.9	9.6	1.7	0.6	8.5
Totals	100.1	28.3	20.6	33.2	32.0

SOURCE: *Man's Impact on the Global Environment*, p. 296.
*Major components are electricity generation, industrial process heat, and space heating for homes, commerce, and industry.
†Major contributors are pulp mills, smelters, refineries, and cement plants.

Perhaps the most dramatic case thus far recorded was the London smog disaster of 1952 when some 4,000 deaths were directly attributed to the smog. But such disasters have still been of less significance to public health than have the less spectacular but ultimately more far-reaching effects that day-to-day exposure has on people living in seriously polluted localities. In 1969, sixty faculty members of the Medical School of the University of California at Los Angeles made a recommendation to the residents of southern California's smoggy areas. Their statement read, in part: "air pollution has now become a major health hazard to most of this community during much of the year." They advised "anyone who does not have compelling reasons to remain to move out of smoggy portions of Los Angeles, San Bernardino, and Riverside counties to avoid chronic respiratory diseases like bronchitis and emphysema."

What are the general effects of individual air pollutants on health?

Carbon monoxide combines with the pigment hemoglobin in our blood, displacing the oxygen that hemoglobin normally transports. When oxygen supply to the cells is reduced, the heart must work harder, as must the respiratory mechanism. These effects may produce a critical strain in people with heart and lung diseases. Spending eight hours in an atmosphere containing 80 parts per million (ppm) of carbon monoxide has the same effect as the loss of more than a pint of blood. When traffic is badly snarled, the carbon monoxide content of the air may approach 400 ppm. Symptoms of acute poisoning often experienced by people in traffic jams and on freeways include headache, loss of vision, decreased muscular coordination, nausea, and abdominal pain. In extreme cases of carbon monoxide poisoning, un-

Figure 5-1   Air pollution is a world wide problem. *Top illustration on this page:*
Smog inspectors on a rooftop in Tokyo in 1961. Despite their efforts, Tokyo's smog
is still among the worst in the world. (World Wide Photos.) *Bottom left:* Smog
covering Atlanta, Georgia in February, 1961. (Photo by William A. Garnett.) *Bottom
right:* A paper pulp mill in Port Angeles, Washington. This mill is also a source of
water pollution. (Photo by William A. Garnett.) *Opposite page, top:* An early morning
inversion blankets the Los Angeles basin in smog, while the higher Hollywood Hills
in the foreground remain clear. This picture was taken in 1949. (Photo by William A.
Garnett.) *Center:* Air pollution from a plant near Alvik, Norway, in July, 1972. (Photo
by Robert E. Van Vuren.) *Bottom:* Steel mills in an industrial area south of Sydney,
Australia, in 1962. (Photo by William A. Garnett.)

consciousness, convulsions, and death follow. An association between high concentrations of atmospheric carbon monoxide with higher mortality in Los Angeles County has been demonstrated for the years 1962–1965.[1]

Sulfur dioxide has been implicated in the increased rates of acute and chronic asthma, bronchitis, and emphysema observed in people exposed to severe air pollution. Asthma, a severe allergic disorder, and bronchitis attack many people annually. Emphysema, a progressive lung disease once thought rare, is ultimately fatal. Most sulfur compounds are harshly irritating to respiratory passages, causing coughing and choking. Their effects are thought to be a major cause of the abnormal death tolls that have occurred during smog disasters.

Nitrogen oxides have much the same effects as carbon monoxide, reducing the oxygen-carrying capacity of the blood. Studies on animals have demonstrated a variety of other toxic effects of nitrogen oxides, principally involving the lungs. A study of Chattanooga school children demonstrated an increase in respiratory infections at a concentration of nitrogen dioxide regularly exceeded in 85 percent of all U.S. cities of over 500,000 population.

The hydrocarbon pollutants are a diverse lot and, among other things, are almost certainly involved in rising cancer death rates. Similarly, some components of "particulate" pollution, such as asbestos and certain metals, are strongly suspected of contributing to the incidence of cancer in the human population. An association between particulate air pollution and mortality from cirrhosis of the liver has been shown, but it is not clear which components are the toxic agents or whether other substances present along with the particulates are also involved. Asbestos exposure is implicated in raising the incidence of lung cancer among cigarette smokers.

Unfortunately, it is difficult to make definitive statements about the precise health effects of air pollution for reasons explained in Box 5–1. In spite of these problems, the evidence pointing to the seriousness of air pollution as a definite hazard is now massive. Consider just a few sample findings. Cigarette smokers from smoggy St. Louis, Missouri, have roughly four times the incidence of emphysema as smokers from relatively smog-free Winnipeg, Canada. At certain times, air pollution increases the frequency of head colds. Ten years after a smog disaster in Donora, Pennsylvania in 1948, those residents who had reported severe effects during the smog showed the highest subsequent death rates. (This, of course, does not prove that the smog hurried them toward their graves; perhaps only previously weakened people suffered severe effects.) Pneumonia deaths are more frequent in areas of high pollution. Chronic bronchitis is more serious among British postmen who work in areas

---

[1]The original sources of most of the public-health data summarized in this and the succeeding three paragraphs are given in "Air Pollution and Human Health," L. B. Lave and E. P. Seskin (*Science*, vol. 169, p. 723, August 21, 1970). The Chattanooga study was reported by C. M. Shy et al. in *Journal of the Air Pollution Control Association* (Vol. 20, 1970, pp. 582–588). The Los Angeles carbon monoxide study was reported by A. C. Hexter and J. R. Goldsmith in *Science* (vol. 172, pp. 265–267, April 16, 1971).

of high air pollution than in those who serve in relatively smog-free areas. Emphysema death rates have skyrocketed as air pollution has increased. England has higher overall rates of air pollution than the United States, and death from lung cancer is more than twice as common among British men as it is among American men. The lung-cancer death rates in England are correlated with the density of atmospheric smoke. The lung-cancer rate for men over 45 in the smoggiest part of Staten Island, New York is 55 per 100,000. In a less smoggy area just a few miles away, the rate is 40 per 100,000.

Some of the effects just described are still the subject of controversy within the scientific community, undoubtedly owing to the sorts of difficulties described in Box 5–1. However, much of the debate resembles the cigarette-smoking-and-cancer arguments of a few years ago—the evidence is "only statistical," but to those knowledgeable in statistics, it is already persuasive and becoming overwhelming. In short, air pollution kills. Since it usually kills slowly and unobtrusively, however, the resulting deaths are not dramatically called to the attention of the public. Estimates of the annual American financial loss resulting from air pollution's effects on health run as high as

---

Box 5–1   Assaying the Hazards of Air Pollution

The effects of cigarette smoking on health might be considered a problem in personal air pollution. We now know that cigarette smoking has many harmful effects. Yet even with the great advantage of being able to measure the amount and length of exposure, and having a relatively uniform pollutant source, it took many years to do the research required to convince doctors, scientists, and eventually the general public of the extreme hazards of smoking.

In contrast, here are some of the problems of assaying the dangers of air pollution:

1. Pollutants are numerous and varied, and many of them are difficult to detect. Their concentrations vary geographically. In many areas techniques for monitoring pollutants are inadequate, and long-term records are unavailable. Long periods of study are usually needed to reveal delayed and chronic effects.

2. It is usually impossible to determine precisely the degree of exposure of a given individual to specific pollutants.

3. Degree of air pollution is correlated with other factors, such as degree of exposure to various kinds of stress, other kinds of pollution,

and food additives. Such factors must be considered in data analysis.

4. Research is complicated because pollutants that do not cause problems when tested alone may be dangerous in combination with other pollutants. For instance, many of the asbestos particles inhaled by nonsmokers are carried out of the lungs in an ever-moving sheet of mucus propelled by the beating of cilia (tiny active appendages of living cells). Smoking interferes with this natural cleansing function, and increases the chance of coming down with an asbestos-induced cancer of the lungs. Sulfur dioxide also tends to interfere with this cleaning function. It is thought that the length of exposure of lung surface to airborne carcinogenic hydrocarbons may determine whether a cancerous growth is started. When such hydrocarbons occur as pollutants in combination with sulfur dioxide, the exposure and the hazard are greatly increased. Such interactions are called *synergistic*; the danger from the two combined pollutants is greater than the sum of the individual dangers.

$14–29 billion. A 1970 study put the *lower limit* on the annual savings (in medical care and lost income) that a 50 percent reduction in air pollution in major urban areas would provide at slightly more than $2 billion.

If current trends are allowed to continue, death from air pollution *will* become obtrusive. The U.S. Public Health Service has predicted that annual sulfur dioxide emissions will increase from the 1960 level of 20 million tons to 35 million by the year 2000. Similarly, nitrogen oxides will increase from 11 to almost 30 million tons, and particulates from about 30 million to more than 45 million tons. Unless the United States alters present trends in transportation, the number of automobiles will quadruple between the years 1960 and 2000, as will the number of gallons of fuel consumed. Although population and environmental limitations make it unlikely that the trends will continue to the end of this century, these projections do give some indication of what we may have to live with as long as they do continue.

Urban Air Pollution: A Case History.   Four centuries ago, Juan Rodriquez Cabrillo recorded in his diary that smoke from Indian fires in the Los Angeles Basin went up for a hundred feet and then spread to blanket the valley with haze. Because of this phenomenon, he named what is today called San Pedro Bay "The Bay of Smokes." Cabrillo was observing the effect of a thermal inversion. Normally the temperature of the atmosphere decreases steadily with increased altitude, but during an inversion a layer of warm air overlying cooler air below severely limits vertical mixing of the atmosphere, and pollutants accumulate in the layer of air trapped near the Earth's surface (Figure 5–2). Because of the wind patterns in the eastern Pacific and the ring of mountains surrounding the Los Angeles Basin, it is an ideal place for the formation of inversions, usually at about 2000 feet above the floor of the basin. They occur there on about seven out of every 16 days.

Los Angeles has abundant sunshine, another climatic feature that contributes to its air-pollution problems. Sunlight acts on a mixture of oxygen, nitrogen oxides, and hydrocarbons to produce photochemical smog. Combustion products from well over 3 million cars are exhausted into the atmosphere of the Los Angeles Basin in addition to the wastes discharged by oil refineries and other industries. As a result, the air that residents of Los Angeles breathe contains far more than the usual mixture of nitrogen, oxygen, and carbon dioxide—it also contains carbon monoxide, ozone, aldehydes, ketones, alcohols, acids, ethers, peroxyacetyl nitrates and nitrites, alkyl nitrates and nitrites, benzpyrene, and many other dangerous chemicals.

Smog first became prominent in Los Angeles during World War II. Since then the Los Angeles County Air Pollution Control District (APCD) has pursued a vigorous policy of smog abatement. The district has imposed strict controls on industry, setting rigid emission standards for power plants, refineries, and other sources of pollution. Some 1.5 million domestic incinerators, a dozen large municipal incinerators, 57 open burning dumps, and

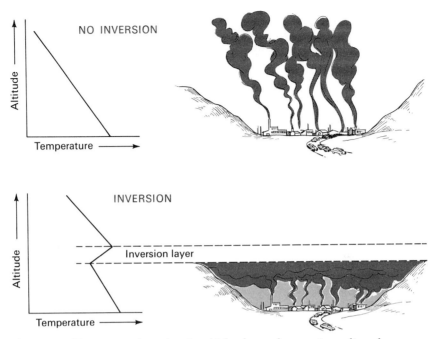

Figure 5-2   Temperature inversion, in which a layer of warm air overlies a layer of cooler air, trapping air pollution close to the ground.

most incinerators in commercial buildings have been eliminated. Coal burning has been made illegal, and so has (for most of the year) the burning of oil with a high sulfur content. Control is exercised over the escape of vapors from petroleum storage tanks and gasoline loading facilities. Commercial processes that require organic solvents are also controlled, as well as the olefin content of gasoline sold in Los Angeles County, and many other contributors to air pollution. Furthermore, all cars sold in California were required to have smog-control devices (designed to reduce crankcase emissions of hydrocarbons) before the devices were required nationwide.

The Los Angeles area has partially "controlled" its smog by generating a portion of its electricity in areas of low population in New Mexico, using low-quality coal that would not be tolerated under the air quality laws of California or Arizona. Figure 5-3 shows the volume of air pollution produced by the Four Corners Power Plant, which generates electricity in New Mexico for use in Los Angeles. This is roughly equivalent to throwing garbage in a neighbor's yard because his yard is large and he is too ignorant or weak to prevent it.

And what has all this smog control effort accomplished? At best, it has more or less permitted Los Angeles to hold the line: there has been little or no improvement in the air quality in the Los Angeles Basin since 1960. Unex-

pectedly, pollution from nitrogen oxides has soared, partly because manufacturers have increased the compression ratios of automobile engines, and
partly because of the fitting of crankcase antismog devices designed to reduce
the emission of hydrocarbons. Since 1970, nitrogen oxide emissions in new
cars have been reduced and should be further reduced by 1974. Hydrocarbon
levels remained about even during the 1960s as have those of carbon monoxide,
while levels of sulfur oxides have fluctuated. Since 1962 there has been an
increase in the number of smog alerts, in which public-health warnings are
broadcast. Furthermore, although there has been no spectacular rise in the
density of smog since 1960, the *volume* of heavily polluted air is increasing.
The concentration of ozone and other oxidants has decreased in downtown
Los Angeles since 1965, but has been constant or slowly increasing in other
parts of the basin such as Pasadena and Azusa. The smog is spreading in area
and in height as the heat generated by the city forces the base of the inversion
cap higher. According to one estimate, the Los Angeles Basin now receives

Figure 5-3   The Four Corners power plant in northwestern New Mexico produces a
stream of air pollution often visible for as far as 100 miles downwind. In the
foreground can be seen the result of strip-mining for coal to fuel the power plant.
(Photo by William A. Garnett.)

only 94 percent of its heat from the sun; fully 6 percent comes from the burning of fossil fuels. Air pollution is now reported to be causing damage to living plants growing hundreds of miles east of Los Angeles.

Why has Los Angeles experienced so much difficulty in improving its air quality in spite of the strenuous efforts of the APCD? A basic answer is population growth. Even though the per capita amount of pollution has declined, the total number of people has increased. Each new worker is faced with the virtual necessity of using an automobile to move around in an immense city that lacks an adequate public-transportation system. And, of course, more people mean more business and industry, which in turn tend to attract more people. In California the situation is especially critical, but many other urban areas of the United States face similar problems. More people and more automobiles, plus systematic resistance to smog control from industry and industry-hungry local governments have combined to work against successful abatement.

Prospects for Cleaning Up. By 1970, public concern and growing activism on the part of environmental organizations began to have a nationwide effect on government apathy and industrial resistance to pollution control. Federal and state laws against automobile and smokestack emissions were made increasingly stringent. Both federal and state governments began to prosecute companies that violated standards, imposing heavy fines or closing down offending plants. Automobile manufacturers and industrialists complained that it was impossible to keep up with constantly changing standards; what was acceptable one year was unacceptable the next. Many 1970 model automobiles failed to meet emission standards for that year. Some of the tests previously used were also found not to be sensitive enough to measure emissions accurately. To add still another complication, cars that ran "clean" enough when new were usually found to pollute too much after a few thousand miles.

In late 1970 Congress passed a new Clean Air Act, setting strict new standards for air pollution both for factories and automobiles. Most of the standards must be met by 1975. For automobiles, emissions of hydrocarbons and carbon monoxide must be reduced by 90 percent by January 1, 1975, and nitrogen oxides by 90 percent by January 1, 1976. The Environmental Protection Agency (EPA) is charged with setting national air-quality standards and enforcing the act.

One can hope that continued public awareness of the problem will lead to further change during the 1970s, that perhaps the internal combustion engine will gradually come to play a much smaller role in American life while pollution control becomes more effective. One early practical step might be to reduce the size, horsepower, and compression ratios of internal combustion engines, while making every effort to improve the control of emissions. The amount of pollution from an automobile is not necessarily related to engine size, but small engines certainly consume less fuel. The *California Tomorrow*

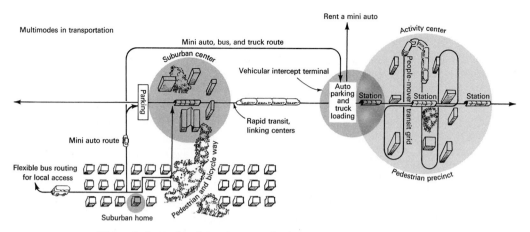

Figure 5–4 A plan for an integrated urban transportation system using mini autos, buses, and rapid transit trains. Allowance is made for pedestrians and bicyclists as well. (After Heller, *The California Tomorrow Plan.* Copyright © 1972 by William Kaufmann, Inc.)

Plan,[2] a comprehensive plan for the future of that state developed by a privately financed task force, recommended that a graduated tax be placed on automobiles exceeding 65 horsepower. If such a tax were steep enough, it would greatly encourage the use of small cars. Mandatory annual inspection of all motor vehicles to see that pollution-control devices were working properly would be another giant step toward clean air.

Eventually, the presently dominant form of the internal combustion engine may be replaced by one or perhaps a variety of less polluting alternatives: steam engines, electric motors, gas turbines, diesels, or the pistonless, rotary Wankel engines. Large-scale use of most of these potential substitutes for today's engines would create new problems, including a different spectrum of pollutants in some cases and considerable economic adjustment to new forms of fuel or power in others. Electric cars, for instance, merely shift the pollution from the air over highways and cities to the air above power plants because of the increased amount of electricity that must be generated to recharge the cars. However, it might prove easier to control the pollution in such a system. Since many of the other problems associated with automobiles — including resource depletion (both for power and materials), solid-waste disposal, and urban and highway congestion — would still remain, even the best of the alternatives can provide only a partial solution. They will ultimately have to be supplemented by efficient forms of public transportation. Perhaps the ideal situation would combine zoning regulation to curtail urban sprawl and a network of public transportation with minimum use of small private vehicles in an efficient, integrated system. (See Figure 5–4 for an example of such a plan.) Of course,

[2] *The California Tomorrow Plan,* Alfred Heller, ed., William Kaufmann, Inc., Los Altos, California, 1972.

any move to reduce substantially our dependence on large automobiles is likely to meet determined resistance not only from those who manufacture, service, and repair automobiles, but also from the American public.

Water Pollution

In many communities direct threats to human health arrive through the faucet as well as through the air. The drinking water that flows from the tap in some localities has already passed through seven or eight people. Graffiti in public washrooms in numerous towns along the upper Mississippi River read: "Flush the toilet, they need the water in St. Louis." When the water reaches St. Louis, it is chlorinated and filtered, and therefore should be safe to drink. Unfortunately, the water in many cities is often unsafe to drink. Although chlorination may help, there is growing evidence that high content of organic matter in water can somehow protect viruses from the effects of chlorine. Infectious hepatitis is spreading at an alarming rate in the United States, and a major suspect for the route of transmission is the "toilet-to-mouth pipeline" of many water systems not made safe by chlorination. Indeed, the safety of purifying water with chlorine has been questioned by geneticists because certain chlorine compounds, which are sometimes formed by the chlorination process, can cause mutations that may lead to hereditary defects. But considering the high level of dangerous germs in many of our water supplies, we probably will have to continue to accept any risks involved in chlorination.

Water pollution from sewage provides one of the classic examples of diseconomies of scale accompanying population growth. If a few people per mile live along a large river, their sewage may be dumped directly into the river and natural purification will occur. But if the population increases, the waste-degrading ability of the river becomes overstrained, and either the sewage or the intake water must be treated if the river water is to be safe for drinking. Should the population along the river increase further, more and more elaborate and expensive treatment will be required to keep the water safe for human use and to maintain desirable fishes and shellfishes in the river. In general, the more people there are living in a watershed, the higher the *per capita* costs of avoiding water pollution will be.

As the populations of many municipalities grow, their sewage-treatment facilities, though once adequate, are quickly outgrown. Funds for new sewage facilities can be obtained only at the expense of funds needed for more and better schools, police departments, water systems, roads, and other public services. Inevitably, it seems, the available funds are insufficient to meet all of these needs, which are created in part by increases in population. The sewage problem is increased by lax inspections and lax public-health standards, which permit construction of septic tanks too close together or in unsuitable soils in many of the rural and suburban areas where there are no general sewage facilities.

As the population in a DC grows, so does industry, which pours into our water supplies a vast array of contaminants: lead, detergents, sulfuric acid, hydrofluoric acid, phenols, ethers, benzenes, ammonia, and so on. As the population grows, so does the need for increased agricultural production, which results in a heavier water-borne load of insecticides, herbicides, and nitrates (from fertilizers). A result is the spread of pollution not just in streams, rivers, lakes, and along seashores, but also (and most seriously) in groundwater, where purification is almost impossible. With the spread of pollution goes the threat of epidemics of hepatitis and dysentery, and of poisoning by exotic chemicals.

A particular hazard is the problem of nitrate pollution. The heavy use of inorganic fertilizers results in the flow of a heavy load of nitrates into our water supply; nitrates also accumulate in high concentrations in our crops. Nitrates themselves are not especially dangerous, but when certain bacteria are present in the digestive tract, they convert the nitrates into highly toxic nitrites. Farm animals and human infants are particularly likely to have in their digestive tracts these types of bacteria and the appropriate conditions for the conversion of nitrate to nitrite. In addition, conversion of nitrates to nitrites can occur in any opened container of food, even if it is subsequently refrigerated. Nitrate water pollution in lakes, streams, and wells probably is more dangerous in the Central Valley of California, where it is a severe public-health hazard and where doctors often recommend that infants be given only pure bottled water. It is also serious, however, in some other states, such as Illinois, Wisconsin, and Missouri.

The direct relation between energy consumption and air pollution is widely appreciated, but it is not as well known that some of our most serious water-pollution problems are also directly caused or aggravated by our mobilization and use of energy resources. Both strip mining and underground mining of coal create large volumes of wastes that are exposed to the weather. Rain leaches sulfur from these wastes, yielding acidic runoff that renders streams and rivers uninhabitable by fish and unusable by man. Piles of ash from the combustion of coal in electric-power plants are also a source of acidic runoff. Wastes from uranium mining and processing have led to pollution of waterways with radioactive materials. Refining wastes from the petroleum industry are a major source of water pollution. Oil spills in transportation by pipeline and tanker will be discussed in the next chapter. Thermal pollution, also discussed in Chapter 6, aggravates other water-pollution problems in two ways: (1) it increases the rate of oxygen consumption of aquatic organisms while lowering the actual dissolved oxygen content of the water, thus reducing the amount of waste that biological systems in the waterway can degrade, and (2) it increases the rate of evaporation, which raises the concentration of pollutants that are left behind (Figure 5–5).

The history of water pollution abatement in the U.S. has largely paralleled that of air pollution: generally too little effort applied too late. By the later

Figure 5-5   The nuclear power plant at Haddam on the Connecticut River empties up to 370,000 gallons of coolant water a minute through a discharge canal (bottom) into the river. Temperature is represented by shades of gray. The hot effluent (white) is at about 93 degrees F.; ambient river temperature (dark gray) is 77 degrees. The line across the picture is a time marker for a series of absolute measurements. (Aerial thermogram by HRB Singer, Inc., for the U.S. Geological Survey's Water Resources Division.)

1960s, despite a growth of federal involvement in setting standards and providing financial assistance, the situation was getting out of control. Since 1969, the emphasis has been on pouring money into municipal waste-treatment plants. These are certainly needed, but inadequate to solve all our water pollution problems.

The Environment Protection Agency and the Army Corps of Engineers have been given the joint task of regulating industrial water pollution under the 1899 Refuse Act, a strict law that was rarely enforced until recently.

The Public Health Service, which monitors municipal water supplies for drinking safety, is empowered only to set standards to prevent the introduction or spread of disease organisms. As of 1970, it had no power against any of the myriad of known dangerous or possibly dangerous chemicals that have been appearing in increasing amounts in U.S. waters, including various kinds of pesticides. The PHS is presumably revising its standards to include such chemicals in its monitoring, and hopefully steps will be taken to remove them as much as possible from our drinking water.

National standards for water quality and federal regulation and enforcement of them have long been needed to replace a hodgepodge of state, local, and federal standards. A Water Pollution Control Act was passed in late 1972 with the goal of ending water pollution by 1985. The act allows for the development of strict, progressively tightening national guidelines for the control of effluents from municipal and industrial sources.

Solid Wastes

A serious problem facing the United States and other affluent countries is the accumulation of solid wastes in open dumps or inadequate fills. These dumps are not just eyesores (Figure 5–6). If the wastes are burned they contribute to air pollution; water filtering through them may pollute groundwater supplies; they serve as breeding grounds for such annoying and disease-bearing organisms as rats, cockroaches, and flies. Each year in the United States we must dispose of some 55 billion cans, 26 billion bottles and jars, 65 billion metal and plastic bottle caps, and more than half a billion dollars

Figure 5–6   Solid wastes are a problem even in such remote areas as the Sahara Desert. (Photo by George Gerster, Photofind–Rapho.)

worth of other packaging materials. Seven million automobiles are junked each year, and the amount of urban solid wastes (trash and garbage) collected annually is approximately 200 million tons. Every man, woman and child in the United States is, on the average, producing nearly a ton of refuse annually. In addition to junked cars, some 10 million tons of iron and steel are scrapped each year, more than 3 billion tons of waste rock and mill tailings are dumped near mine sites, and huge amounts of slag, ash, and other wastes are produced by smelters, power plants, other industries, and agriculture.

It is becoming universally recognized that current methods of dealing with the solid-waste problem are utterly inadequate.[3] Many cities are facing disposal crises as population growth simultaneously produces more waste and reduces the available land for dumping. Waste disposal is another classic case where per capita costs tend to go up as population grows. San Francisco considered having its refuse hauled to distant dumping sites by train, and cities on the eastern seaboard considered hauling their wastes to the coalfields of Pennsylvania for disposal in abandoned mines. But people living near the selected sites opposed the idea, and costs would have been very high. Sanitary landfill, where space is available, is a more satisfactory (and expensive) solution than dumping, but it also generates many problems. Water pollution continues, dust pollution is created, and nonbiodegradable materials (those not quickly broken down by microorganisms), which do not compact easily, lessen the utility of the fill. Incineration of wastes is another answer, which in France and other European countries has been combined with power production in trash-fired power plants. Unless great care is taken, of course, this answer may merely substitute air pollution for land pollution.

Besides the obvious necessity of limiting the size of the human population, a number of other measures would help solve the solid-waste problem. Laws might be passed that would place heavy taxes upon any product or wrapping that is designed to be discarded rather than returned or recycled, and the manufacture of nonbiodegradable products could be prohibited. Heavy deposits, perhaps 5 or 10 cents per beer can or "pop" bottle, could be required to encourage the return of such containers and to give a boost to those recycling programs already under way. Even those containers that might be discarded would no doubt be collected from roadsides and beaches by ambitious children. Many of our products, as well as our refuse-collection system, could be so designed that the materials that might be used as soil conditioners could be separated from those to be recycled in other ways. New apartment buildings could be equipped with separate disposal chutes for different kinds of wastes. Automobiles could be designed not only to minimize air pollution but also for ease of disassembly into recyclable components. Indeed, in view of the obvious need to minimize the wasteful scattering of nonrenewable resources, the

[3]*Cleaning Our Environment: The Chemical Basis for Action*, American Chemical Society, Washington D.C., 1969, p. 165.

design of all of man's manufactured devices, from home appliances to computers, should take into account the possibility of recycling their components.

Pesticides and Related Compounds

Some substances—such as chlorinated hydrocarbons (DDT and similar organic chemical compounds), lead, mercury, and fluorides—reach us in so many ways that they must be considered as general pollutants. Chlorinated hydrocarbons are among the most ubiquitous manufactured chemicals in the environment. Of these, DDT has been employed the longest, having been put into mass use late in World War II. It is the most commonly used and most thoroughly studied of all synthetic insecticides. It often occurs in concentrations of more than 12 parts per million (ppm) in human fat, and as high as 5 ppm in human milk (though the usual range is some 0.05 to 0.26 ppm). Most mother's milk in the United States contains so much DDT that it would be declared illegal in interstate commerce; the permissible level in cow's milk is set by the FDA at 0.05 ppm. Other chlorinated hydrocarbon insecticides, including aldrin, dieldrin, and benzene hexachloride, have also been found in human milk.

Recently, another class of chlorinated hydrocarbon compounds, polychlorinated biphenyls (PCBs), has also been found to be a serious pollutant. These compounds are used in a variety of industrial processes and are released into our environment in a variety of ways. They vaporize from storage containers, are emitted from factory smokestacks, are dumped into rivers and lakes with industrial wastes, and, along with a number of other hydrocarbons, are added to the load of particulate atmospheric pollutants as automobile tires are worn down. Like the pesticides, they show up in the milk of nursing mothers. Zoologist Robert W. Risebrough has stated that PCBs "are highly toxic to man when inhaled as vapors, and the more heavily chlorinated components have greater toxicity. No tolerance limits have been set for human food supplies, and their cancer-causing properties remain to be determined."

Chlorinated hydrocarbons are present in very low concentrations in our drinking water, in our fruits and vegetables, and in the air we breathe. Greater amounts are present in meat, fish, and eggs. At times the dosage is direct and high. Farmers sometimes far exceed legal residue levels of insecticides on their crops and get away with it because inspection is inadequate. Some ill-informed grocers spray their produce to kill fruit flies. In view of the possibilities for leakage or other accidents, the sale of all pesticides should be prohibited in food stores.

A colleague of ours has observed massive anti-roach spraying—presumably of chlordane—in a restaurant kitchen, where the spray drifted over exposed food. Some restaurants formerly used lindane vaporizers; these have now been banned. Regardless of whether such practices and the resultant heavy doses are common or not, continuous "light" exposure is virtually unavoidable.

For example, at least a dozen states have reported that residual pesticide levels in fishes may be well above the FDA recommended limits, and in some individual fishes DDT concentrations are 10 times higher.

Can this "light" exposure be dangerous? Doesn't the government specify how much exposure to these chemicals is safe on the basis of long-term experiments? Haven't the medical and biological sciences protected us? Isn't it true that DDT has been proven to have no adverse effects on humans unless taken in massive doses? Unfortunately, the answer to the last three questions is a resounding "No!". But there is no reason why the average citizen should know that, even though the dangers of pesticide poisoning have been given increasing and much-needed attention in the news media during the past decade. Because of problems similar to those enumerated in the discussion of air pollution, it has been very difficult to evaluate the long-term and chronic effects of pesticides. Biologists have long been warning that DDT and related compounds might have such effects, even though the damage is not immediately obvious. But, as often happens, the possibility of subtle chronic effects has been discounted by industry, ignored by the government, and forgotten by the public. That DDT has very low immediate toxicity to mammals, including humans, has been known since it was first put in use, and this has never been questioned. Promoters of pesticides have even resorted to the dangerous extreme of eating spoonfuls of pure DDT in an effort to prove how harmless it is, but such actions in no way demonstrate that DDT is safe for human consumption *over the long run.*

People can see and understand acute poisoning, but they cannot see the subtle physiological changes of slow poisoning, and they thus find it difficult to grasp. Why should it matter if high concentrations of chlorinated hydrocarbons are being stored in our bodies? Haven't scientists carried out experiments in which convicts ate DDT without apparent harm? Hasn't one study of workers in a DDT plant and another done with convicts shown that no ill effects resulted from heavy exposure? The answer is that these two studies attesting to the "safety" of DDT were poorly designed and utterly inadequate to assure us of its long-term safety. Both were done with people whose first exposure occurred as *adults,* and the convict study followed individuals over *less than two years.* The study of exposed workers did not investigate what had happened to workers who were no longer employed. The effects on the delicate developmental systems of fetuses and infants were not investigated, nor were there any women or children in the study. No attempt has ever been made to investigate the possible effects of DDT exposure on large populations over several decades, and the causes of death in large numbers of people with high and low exposures have not been statistically compared.

Biologists have just started to get an inkling of what our "harmless" chlorinated hydrocarbon load may be doing to us over the long run. Animal studies give us some clues. In high doses, DDT has recently been shown to increase the incidence of cancers, especially liver cancers, in mice. This indicates that

DDT might also be carcinogenic (cancer-inducing) in human beings. At concentrations of roughly 10 ppm, DDT in rats has been shown to induce abnormally high levels of certain liver enzymes that break down many prescribed drugs and render them ineffective. It also increases the weight of the uterus and the deposition of dextrose in the uterus. We know that DDT affects the sex hormones of rats and birds and may produce sterility in rats. We also know that rat reproductive physiology shows many similarities to human reproductive physiology. DDT induces the same liver enzymes in humans, but we do not know whether hormonal changes occur or what their effects are if they do.

Findings of other recent studies are even more ominous. One study, the data for which were obtained in autopsies, showed a correlation between DDT levels in fat tissue and cause of death.[4] Concentrations of DDT and its breakdown products, DDE and DDD, as well as dieldrin (another chlorinated hydrocarbon pesticide), were significantly higher in the fat of patients who died of softening of the brain, cerebral hemorrhage, hypertension, portal cirrhosis of the liver, and various cancers than in groups of patients who died of infectious diseases. The histories of the patients in the study showed that concentrations of DDT and its breakdown products in their fat were strongly correlated with home use of pesticides, heavy users having much higher concentrations than light or moderate users.

More conclusive investigations of these effects are urgently needed. But in the light of what is known about the deleterious effects of chlorinated hydrocarbons on laboratory animals, the results of this study alone leave little room for complacency. Neurophysiologist Alan Steinbach claims that DDT differs from many other nerve poisons in that its effects tend more often to be irreversible. There is also evidence that chlorinated hydrocarbon exposure can cause abnormal changes in brain-wave patterns. These observations are not surprising, since experiments with other animals indicate that exposure to chlorinated hydrocarbons causes changes in the central nervous system. For example, in experiments conducted by biologists J. M. Anderson and M. R. Peterson, trout exposed to 20 parts per *billion* DDT showed a complete inability to learn to avoid an electric shock, whereas *all* unexposed fishes learned to do so quite easily. Furthermore, previously trained fish lost their ability to avoid electric shock after exposure to DDT.

There is evidence that the amount of DDT stored in human tissue has not increased over the past decade or so in the United States, but has probably reached a mean concentration of some 7–12 ppm. At a given exposure level it apparently takes about one year for a balance to be established between intake and loss through excretion and breakdown, after which continued exposure produces no increase in DDT storage. The mean concentration of DDT in human populations varies widely from one geographic location to

---

[4]"Pesticide Concentrations in the Liver, Brain and Adipose Tissue of Terminal Patients," J. L. Radomski, W. B. Deichmann, E. E. Clizer, and A. Rey, *Food and Cosmetic Toxicology*, vol. 6, pp. 209–220, 1968.

another, both within and among countries. It also varies with diet, race, age, and undetermined individual differences. There is evidence that other pollutants may interfere with the excretion of DDT. In one experiment, dogs exposed to DDT and aldrin at the same time stored twice as much DDT as dogs exposed to DDT alone.

It is difficult at this juncture to evaluate the magnitude of the direct threat to human health represented by the present level of chlorinated hydrocarbon contamination. Most analyses have dealt with DDT, although human beings are also being exposed to a wide range of related compounds, some of which have considerably higher immediate toxicity. There are indications that dieldrin, perhaps four times as toxic as DDT, may also be involved in portal cirrhosis of the liver, and that benzene hexachloride may contribute to liver cancer. The critical question is not immediate toxicity, but *long-term effects*. The oldest people who have been exposed to high concentrations of DDT since conception are now in their twenties. It is possible that their life expectancies may already have been greatly reduced; it is also possible that there will be no significant reduction of life expectancies. No one will know until more time has passed.

It will also take some time to discover what the overall effects of the chlorinated hydrocarbon load will be. We may be in for an unpleasant surprise, since the slow rate of natural breakdown of these compounds guarantees decades of further exposure even after their use has been discontinued. The continued release of chlorinated hydrocarbons into our environment amounts to a reckless global experiment and we humans, as well as all other animals that live on this globe, are playing the role of guinea pigs.

Pollution by Heavy Metals

Lead. Although biologists are just beginning to understand the effects of chlorinated hydrocarbons on people and are beginning to realize that they previously underestimated the danger, there is no lack of understanding with regard to acute lead poisoning. We *know* what lead can do, although we do not know what the results of chronic exposure to low levels of lead are, especially the atmospheric lead that comes from automobile exhausts. Lead-poisoning symptoms include loss of appetite, weakness, awkwardness, apathy, and miscarriage; it causes lesions of the neuromuscular system, circulatory system, brain, and gastrointestinal tract. It is a sobering thought that overexposure to lead may have been a factor in the decline of both the Greek and Roman civilizations. The Romans lined their bronze cooking, eating, and wine-storage vessels with lead. They thus avoided the characteristic unpleasant taste of copper and the obvious symptoms of copper poisoning trading them for the pleasant flavor of lead and the more subtle symptoms of lead poisoning.

Our civilization too is constantly exposed to lead in our environment, in the form of air contamination from lead smelting and the combustion of gasoline containing tetraethyl lead. We are exposed to lead in various other ways as well—via pesticides, paints, solder used to seal food cans, lead pipes, abraded particles of lead-containing ceramics and glassware, and so forth. Clair C. Patterson, a geochemist, stated in 1965,[5] "There are definite indications that residents of the United States today are undergoing severe chronic lead insult. The average American ingests some 400 millionths of a gram of lead per day in food, air, and water, a process which has been viewed with complacency for decades."

The pattern of increase in the lead contamination of the atmosphere has been revealed by studies of the lead content of the Greenland ice cap. The ice cap "lead load" increased about fivefold between 1750 and 1940, and twentyfold between 1750 and 1967. By comparison, studies show that the content of sea salts in the Greenland ice cap have not changed since 1750, indicating that changes in the overall pattern of deposition of materials in the ice is not the cause of the lead increase. That similar patterns of lead contamination are not found in the Antarctic ice cap lends strong support to the thesis that atmospheric lead pollution originated first with lead smelting and then more recently with the combustion of gasoline, two sources of contamination that are concentrated in the Northern Hemisphere. The spread of pollution to the Southern Hemisphere is largely blocked by atmospheric circulation patterns.

It is now suspected that airborne lead is becoming a major source of exposure, at least for people in urban areas, although the overall exposure from food and beverages is still higher. But in Los Angeles and a few other cities, it is possible that more lead is now being absorbed through the lungs than through the digestive tract. The average concentration of lead in the blood of Americans in 1968 was about 0.25 ppm, which is a little less than half the level at which removal from exposure is recommended for people who work with lead in industry. Garage mechanics and parking lot attendants tend to have about 0.34–0.38 ppm in their blood.

Lead is a cumulative cellular poison. It seems hardly prudent to wait until much of the population begins to show chronic or acute symptoms before we attempt to lower its level in the environment. Chronic lead poisoning is unusually difficult to diagnose, and low-level effects could be quite common already. Moreover, there is always the possibility of synergistic interactions with the other poisons to which we are exposed.

Low-lead and lead-free gasolines were offered for sale in the U.S. by most major oil companies during 1970. By mid-1971, they still accounted for only about 5 percent of sales. Possibly the public was still largely unaware of lead's role in air pollution. But the major reasons for the low sales doubtless were

[5]"Contaminated and Natural Lead Environments of Man," Clair C. Patterson, *Archives of Environmental Health*, vol. 11, pp. 344–360, September 1965.

the price difference — from 2 to 6 cents per gallon more than leaded gasoline — and the fact that many cars, especially older ones and high-powered models, could not operate well without lead. Cars produced since 1970 are more tolerant of unleaded gas. Engines designed to meet the 1975 pollution requirements will be unable to use leaded gasolines, so a conversion to nonleaded gas will certainly take place during the next few years. Presumably the cost differential can be eliminated as the new gasolines come into wider use. Even at a penny or two more per gallon, unleaded gasoline is quite a bargain, provided that substitute additives do not cause other problems.

Mercury.   Mercury is added to the environment in many ways. It leaks from industrial processes, especially those that produce chlorine (which, in turn, is used in large quantities in the manufacture of plastics) and caustic soda (which has many industrial uses). It is also emitted by the pulp and paper industry. It is a prime ingredient of agricultural fungicides, which have been used extensively for treating seeds. Small amounts of mercury are found in fossil fuels and are released when the fuels are burned. Despite the low concentration, the enormous volume of fossil fuels consumed each year may make this the dominant manmade source of mercury in the environment. Medicines flushed down drains and even broken medical thermometers may also make significant contributions to the environmental mercury load.

The natural "background" level of mercury in waters is a matter of some dispute. The mercury content of seawater varies with such things as salinity and depth and seems to average close to 1 ppb (part per billion). Calculations indicate that man's activities have not added significantly to the mercury already present in the open ocean from natural sources, and mercury levels in oceanic fishes caught almost a century ago seem to be comparable to those caught today. Of course, just because mercury may come from natural sources does not mean that it is harmless. Indeed, modern fishing techniques may be increasing human intake of mercury simply because they permit the wider marketing of large oceanic fishes. Human contributions are probably an important factor in raising oceanic mercury levels only in estuarine and coastal waters.

The picture in fresh water is quite different: mercury concentrations in fresh water are correlated with sources of mercury pollution. The Saskatchewan River in Canada was found to have .05 ppb above the city of Edmonton and .12 ppb below. Sediment below a plant using mercury to produce chlorine and caustic soda had 1800 ppm (parts per million). Measurements taken in many North American streams show a similar picture. Mankind has made substantial contributions to the mercury load in lakes, rivers, and streams.

Metallic (elemental) mercury is relatively nontoxic to humans. Certain microorganisms, however, are able to convert metallic mercury to more toxic organic forms such as methylmercury. This process goes on continuously, so that the metallic mercury deposited in freshwaters serves as a reservoir from which the more poisonous form may continually be added to ecosystems for decades or even centuries *after release of mercury is halted.*

Methylmercury is concentrated by organisms and amplified by food chains. Fishes, for instance, seem to absorb it both from their food and through their gills, and may show concentrations in their bodies thousands of times higher than that of the water in which they live. Methylmercury is far more easily absorbed than inorganic mercury and excreted far more slowly. Buildup in the food chains also occurs, as indicated by high levels of mercury in tuna, swordfish, and in other animals that live near the tops of marine food chains. Concentrations in tuna are often in the 0.13–0.25 ppm range, and concentrations in swordfish average even higher. The FDA in 1971 found that most of its tested samples of swordfish exceeded the maximum allowable concentration, and 8 percent of the samples had three times more than the maximum allowable concentration.

The symptoms of methylmercury poisoning are varied. Blindness, deafness, loss of coordination, madness, or death may be the fate of those exposed to high concentrations. Individuals vary both in their sensitivity to methylmercury and in their exposure. Populations that eat large amounts of fish are, for instance, likely to have a much higher exposure than those that do not.

There have been local disasters connected with high levels of mercury pollution. For instance, in 1953 a chemical plant in Minamata City, Japan, greatly increased its production and its release of mercury. The result was the appearance of "Minimata disease" in the population eating seafood from Minamata Bay. More than 100 people died or suffered serious damage to their nervous systems.

In spite of this and similar cases it seems unlikely that we are on the verge of an epidemic of mercury poisoning. But in the light of our lack of knowledge of many aspects of the problem (including the long-term effects of exposure to subclinical mercury loads and possible interactions of methylmercury with other chemicals now assaulting our cells), extreme caution is clearly required. The fact that some of our mercury exposure is due to the natural "background" is no reason to ignore the problem. Small man-induced increases over the background level may be extremely serious. Some steps are being taken to limit release of mercury into the environment, and a few foods (such as swordfish) may disappear from the market. We hope mankind has recognized the mercury menace in time to avoid disaster.

Cadmium, Arsenic, and Other Heavy Metals.   Lead and mercury are the best studied of the heavy-metal pollutants, but some others also pose environmental threats. Cadmium is now being detected in suspicious concentrations in oysters and elsewhere, but we are ignorant both of the significance of these levels and of the pathways cadmium follows in the environment. Cadmium poisoning causes a serious disease called *itai-itai* (ouch-ouch) in Japan because it is so painful. Fatal cases have been reported in Japan, where cadmium pollution of food supplies is now a recognized problem. The U.S. Geological Survey found concentrations of cadmium above U.S. Public Health Service standards in the raw water supplies (before treatment) of 20 cities. The amounts ranged from 10 to 130 ppb. Unacceptably high levels of both cadmium and chromium have been found in groundwaters in one part of Long Island. The contamination originated with wastes deposited during World War II, and the polluted zone is slowly expanding. Contamination should not reach the nearest well being used for a public water supply until around 2000 A.D., but the situation plainly calls for careful monitoring. This is an excellent example of the degree to which groundwater supplies are vulnerable to long-term contamination.

Arsenic is another pollutant found both in food and in water supplies in trace amounts. The main sources of this pollutant are arsenical pesticides and detergents, which contain a possibly less toxic form, arsenate. But there is a real possibility that under conditions of heavy water pollution the arsenate may be broken down to the more toxic arsenite. Moreover, arsenic is concentrated in the tissues of many plants and animals, including some used for human food.

The metals characterized by the M.I.T. Study of Critical Environmental Problems as being "the most toxic, persistent, and abundant in the environment" are lead, mercury, cadmium, chromium, arsenic, and nickel. We are seriously in need of more information on environmental effects and short- and long-term human toxicity of all of these. Until such information is available, the intelligent course is to limit as stringently as possible their release into the environment.

Radiation

Radioactive substances are those whose atoms undergo spontaneous nuclear disintegration, emitting both high-speed particles and penetrating electromagnetic rays (virtually identical to X-rays) in the process. For reasons that need not concern us here, both the particles and the rays are usually termed *ionizing radiation*. We live all our lives in what has been called a "sea" of such radiation. Known as the natural background, this radiation comes from cosmic rays, from radioactive substances in the Earth's crust, and from other such substances (such as potassium-40) that circulate through the living world. It amounts to an average of from 0.08 to 0.15 rad per person per year. (The "rad" is the customary measure for doses of ionizing radiation.) That man has evolved in the presence of this inescapable background does not mean that it should be regarded as "safe," however, nor does it mean that we should take lightly any manmade additions to the background that happen to be smaller than or comparable to it.

Actually, there is no reason to doubt that a burden of genetic defects, cancers, and stillbirths has always been and will continue to be associated with the natural background, and that any additional radiation exposure that mankind brings upon itself will increase this burden. We know, for example, that ionizing radiation causes *mutations*. Mutations are random changes in the structure of DNA, the long molecule that contains the coded genetic information necessary for the development and functioning of all organisms, including humans. The vast majority of mutations are harmful, just as a random change in any complex apparatus, such as a TV set, is much more likely to do harm than good. When a mutation occurs in reproductive cells, which produce sperm or eggs, the mutation may be passed on to future generations.

Unlike mutations, the adverse effects of which are felt only in later generations, other consequences of radiation exposure are suffered by the individuals who are exposed. Such consequences include cancer and shortening of lifespan irrespective of cause of death. The mechanisms by which radiation induces these forms of damage are not well understood. It is clear that the incidence of such effects increases with the dose, although disagreement exists over whether this is in direct proportion to exposure or whether there is some more complicated relationship at the lower doses.

Naturally, all these costs of increased radiation exposure must be balanced against whatever social benefits are derived from the activities generating the exposure. We will nevertheless dwell here on the costs, secure in the knowledge that the promoters of the activities in question will focus ample attention on the benefits.

At the moment, by far the bulk of manmade radiation exposure (over 90 percent) is attributable to the medical and dental uses of X-rays for diagnosis and therapy. Health physicist Karl Z. Morgan has argued that superfluous medical radiation exposures today may be causing between 3,000 and 30,000 unnecessary deaths annually in the U.S. alone.[6]

Another source of radiation exposure is fallout from nuclear weapons. This source has equalled (for Americans) only 1 or 2 percent of the natural background. However, the rate of increase when the test-ban treaty was signed in 1963 (stopping above-ground testing by the U.S., U.K., and USSR) was such that we should be grateful to have stopped the testing when we did. Unfortunately, both the French and the Chinese have continued surface testing. We cannot assume that there have been *no* adverse consequences of fallout, particularly since the doses in some cases have been unevenly distributed. (Averaging radiation doses over the entire population is often deceptive—it is a bit reminiscent of the old story of the statistician who drowned in a lake averaging only 2 feet deep.)

A potentially important source of radiation exposure is the use of nuclear

[6]Testimony of Dr. Karl Z. Morgan, Director of Health Physics, Oak Ridge National Laboratory, in *Environmental Effects of Producing Electric Power*, part 2, vol. I, U.S. Government Printing Office, Washington, D.C., 1970, p. 1257.

reactors to provide electric power (Chapter 3). While nuclear reactors accounted for less than 1 percent of all the energy consumed in the United States in 1970, the amount seems to be doubling roughly every 2 years. Such a rate, if it persists, means a tenfold increase every 6.5 years, which very quickly becomes a great deal of nuclear power. Figure 5–7 shows the locality of a proposed but now abandoned reactor site near San Francisco, California.

Nuclear power can result in the release of radioactivity to the environment in a number of ways: from mining and processing the fuel, from the operation of the power plant itself, from the transportation and reprocessing of spent fuel elements, and from storage of the long-lived radioactive wastes. In addition to these "routine" processes, there is the possibility that an accident at a nuclear plant will release much larger quantities of radioactivity – potentially as much as the fallout from hundreds of Hiroshima-sized fission bombs.

Obviously, no one would like to see such an accident occur, and the Atomic Energy Commission (AEC) and reactor builders assure us that the probability is near zero. But because the consequences would be so great – ranging from thousands to perhaps millions of casualties, depending on the location of the reactor, and billions of dollars in property damage – assurances that a

Figure 5–7   Bodega Head in California, the proposed site for a nuclear reactor to have been built for Pacific Gas and Electric Company. The San Andreas Fault runs through the bay in the background, and the site is within 50 miles of San Francisco. Note the scars from excavations begun before environmental groups forced a halt to the project. (Photo by Aero Photographers.)

major accident is almost impossible are not very satisfying. After all, "impossible" things have happened before, including the sinking of "unsinkable" ships and the cascading failure of "fail-safe" power grids. An AEC document on reactor safety published in 1964 records 11 "criticality accidents" in *experimental* reactors, which resulted in unusual radiation exposure to personnel, damage to the reactor, or both. An accident at the Fermi fast-breeder reactor near Detroit in 1966 was worse than the "maximum credible accident" specified in the official Hazards Summary for that installation. Partly by good luck, no injuries resulted. This "near miss" for the people of Detroit casts suspicion on the system of checks and balances in the AEC regulatory bureaucracy, which permitted this highly experimental and potentially very dangerous device to be built near a population center in the first place.

The complexities of reactor safety make this a difficult area for judgments by nonscientists or even by scientists trained in other fields. It is instructive, though, that the Western Hemisphere's largest insurance companies (which presumably can afford competent advice) have refused, even as a coalition, to underwrite more than about 1 percent of the potential liability for a major nuclear power plant accident. This has led to the curious situation in which, by act of Congress (the Price-Anderson Act), the bulk of the liability is absorbed by the American public, who would pay up to some $478 million from the U.S. Treasury in the event of an accident, and by the victims, who would be uncompensated for any damages beyond that.

The issues are hardly simpler when it comes to the routine storage of radioactive wastes produced by nuclear fission. Highly radioactive liquid wastes are presently stored in steel tanks at several locations around the country. This is acknowledged to be a temporary measure, since these wastes must be isolated from the biosphere for centuries. Some two hundred thousand gallons (out of about 80 million gallons stored) are known to have leaked already from the "tank farm" at Hanford, Washington. The AEC's plan to reduce the high-level wastes to solid form and store them in salt beds deep underground has been blocked, perhaps permanently, by unresolved technical questions and a growing public climate of skepticism.

In dealing with less radioactive but still very dangerous "low-level" wastes, it would appear that the desire to save money has dominated prudence. The Committee on Resources and Man of the National Academy of Sciences/ National Research Council summarized the situation concerning these low-level wastes as follows: "In fact, for primarily economic reasons, practices are still prevalent at most Atomic Energy Commission installations with respect to these latter categories of waste that on the present scale of operations are barely tolerable, but which would become intolerable with much increase in the use of nuclear power."

Another avenue by which radioactivity from nuclear fission reaches the public is the release of small quantities of radioactive substances during routine operation of the powerplants and reprocessing facilities. (Spent reactor fuel is reprocessed to extract the valuable plutonium and uranium it contains for later use.) Following a vigorous controversy among scientists working in the field of radiation protection, the AEC in 1971 changed the guidelines for emissions of radioactivity from certain kinds of nuclear reactors during routine operation, reducing the level of permissible emissions by 100-fold. If enforced, these new guidelines would effectively solve the routine emissions problem for the plants affected. However, the AEC chose to exclude from the new guidelines all new types of reactors now under development, and reprocessing plants.

The controversies surrounding nuclear energy have raised a number of more fundamental issues that are relevant to all of the matters discussed in this section and to which the AEC has offered no satisfactory answer. Why should both the promotion and the regulation of a technology be entrusted to the same agency? If it is not the AEC's intention to expose the public to a hazard permitted by present regulations, why doesn't the AEC tighten the regulations to be sure the public is not so exposed? Where the data admit the *possibility* of serious harm to public health, does the public have the right to halt a commercial project before harm is proven conclusively? On the other hand, does the promoter have the right to proceed with a project before he can prove its safety?

In the matter of atomic-power generation and in all matters relative to the protection of the environment, we are faced with problems so new that we are forced to examine our basic rules for individual and collective protection. Traditionally, our legal system has assumed that a person or group has the right to proceed so long as their activities are not harmful to others. When a person claimed that he was in danger of being harmed, the burden of proof lay upon him to demonstrate the nature of the harm. Today, our society has a technology that bombards the air we breathe, the water we drink, and the natural processes upon which we depend with a volume and variety of substances the exact consequences of which are unknown. It is clear that when we are dealing with forces of unknown but certainly profound and longlasting effect on all human beings, including the unborn, the burden of proof must in some part be shared by those who are releasing the forces. Not knowing the consequences of one's actions must be a reason for restraint in this vital area.

Chemical Mutagens

Recently, biologists have become seriously concerned about sources of mutations other than radiation, namely chemical *mutagens* (substances known to cause mutations). Increased interest in the causes of birth defects, combined with the progress being made toward an understanding of the chemical basis of heredity and development, have led to an awareness that mankind is being exposed to many thousands of synthetic chemicals whose mutagenic potential is unknown. Such chemicals as caffeine and LSD have been alleged to be dangerously mutagenic in man, but the results of tests on experimental animals have been variable and therefore inconclusive. Caffeine has been shown to be mutagenic in fruit flies, but not in mice. Among the many other chemicals that have been shown to be capable of causing mutations are nitrogen mustards (from which organophosphate insecticides are derived), hydrogen peroxide, formaldehyde, cyclohexylamine (a breakdown product of the artificial sweetener, cyclamate), and nitrous acid (this is what the food additive sodium nitrite becomes in the stomach). In 1971, DDT was shown to be mutagenic in mice.

In order to keep civilization intact during the next few decades, we will have to focus our attention primarily on the *quantity* of *Homo sapiens*. But it would be foolish for us to neglect, even in the face of crisis, the question of the future *quality* of the human population. Every reasonable effort should be made to determine the extent of mutational hazards and to reduce them.

Noise Pollution

People everywhere have become aware of a new kind of pollution — noise pollution. The problem has been brought into sharp focus by the discovery that many teenagers have suffered permanent hearing loss following long exposures to amplified rock music, and by public concern about the effects of sonic booms that would be caused by supersonic transports (SST) if they were put into commercial service.

Noise is usually measured in decibels. A tenfold increase in the strength of a sound adds 10 units on the decibel scale, a 100-fold increase adds 20. The human threshold of hearing is represented by zero decibels. (Table 5–2 gives the decibel values of some representative sounds.)

Even a brief exposure to intense noise can cause temporary loss of hearing acuity. Permanent loss of hearing follows chronic exposure to high noise levels. Noise levels as low as 50–55 decibels may delay or interfere with sleep and result in a feeling of fatigue on awakening. Recently there has been growing evidence that noise in the 90-decibel range may cause irreversible changes in the nervous system. These forms of damage, including permanent hearing loss

Table 5–2   Noise Levels

Noise Level	Decibels
Threshold of hearing	0
Normal breathing	10
Whispering	30
Homes	45
Conversation	60
Food blender	80
Heavy automobile traffic	100
Jet aircraft taking off	120

Figure 5-8 Street scene in a New York City slum. (Photo by Emilio Labrador, Photofind, S.F.)

such as that suffered by fans of rock music, can occur at noise levels well below those that are painful. Noise may be a factor in many stress-related diseases, such as peptic ulcer and hypertension, although present evidence is only circumstantial. In any case, noise pollution is clearly a growing threat to our health and happiness. Even if we are not subjected to the booms of the SST, the problem of noise abatement will continue to be a serious one for our society. Unless action is taken against the proliferation of motorcycles, "tote-goats," snowmobiles, power lawnmowers, motor boats, noisy appliances, and the like, they will make aural tranquility, even in the wilderness, a thing of the past. Fortunately, however, this problem is more readily soluble with technology, imagination, and determination than most pollution problems.

The Urban Environment

The deterioration of the environment, both physically and aesthetically, is most apparent in our cities. The dehumanizing effects of life in the slums and ghettoes particularly, where there is little hope for improving conditions (Figure 5-8), have often been cited as causes contributing to urban rioting and disturbances. Crime rates usually reach their zenith in these neighborhoods. Such symptoms of general psychological maladjustment suggest that modern cities provide a less than ideal environment for human beings.

There seems to be abundant evidence that traditional cultural patterns break down in cities, and also that the high numbers of contacts with individuals not part of one's circle of regular social acquaintances may lead to mental disturbance (defined here merely as behavior generally considered "disturbed" by the majority of the society). It is important to note that antisocial behavior and mental illness are found in all cultures, and that indeed the same disorders recognized by psychiatrists in the West are found even in primitive peoples. Therefore, we can be reasonably certain that lack of a "natural" environment (where "natural" refers to the sort of environment in which *Homo sapiens* evolved) is not the sole cause of such behavior. Nevertheless, that lack may well serve to aggravate the problems of people living in our most crowded, smoggy, and impersonal metropolises.

Crime rates are some five times as high in urban as in rural areas. Though some of this difference may be due to disparities in reporting. not all of it can be explained on this basis. Such factors as unemployment, poverty, and a poor social environment undoubtedly contribute as well. Rates for violent crimes have been shown to be positively correlated with actual population densities in American cities.[7] This general correlation held for statistics taken in three different years, 1940, 1950, and 1960, in the same cities. Interestingly, crime rates in the suburbs have also been rising in the past few years, especially among teenagers from relatively affluent areas, although their crimes are more often acts against property than crimes of violence.

However, none of these data show that crowding alone causes crime. Recent studies suggest that crime is more closely associated with high rates of migration into cities than with population density itself. On the other hand, work by psychologist Jonathan Freedman and his colleagues indicates that increased mental illness does tend to be associated with increased population density.

The environmental deterioration of American cities is most obvious to the poor who live in them. For them, "environmental deterioration" has nothing to do with the disappearance of fish and wildlife in national forests or litter in campgrounds. Their concern is "ghetto ecology," including the wildlife in their homes—rats, mice, and cockroaches. Air pollution reaches its highest levels in city centers; here also are there most likely to be inadequate sewage and solid-waste disposal systems. Heat in winter is often insufficient, space is at a premium, crime rates and vandalism are high, food is often inadequate, medical care is poor at best, opportunities for recreation are virtually nil, schools are at their worst, and public transportation is expensive and inconvenient. In short, all the problems and disadvantages of cities are

[7]"Crime Rate vs. Population Density in United States Cities: A Model," R. L. Kyllonen, *Yearbook of the Society for General Systems Research*, vol. 12, pp. 137–145, 1967.

greatly intensified for the poor. This environmental syndrome is reflected by higher death rates among the poor (especially infant and child mortalities) than for the general population.

Of course, many, if not most, of the present hazards and discomforts of city life could be eliminated or mitigated by more creative design of houses and neighborhoods (Figure 5–9), by the development of alternative, less-polluting means of transportation, by finding solutions to the problems of racial minorities and the poor in general, and by more efficient and equitable forms of administration. If urban areas were planned and developed so that people could live near their places of employment, many problems related to transportation would be alleviated, including congestion and pollution from automobiles. Making the vicinities of factories pleasantly habitable would present some problems but would result in considerable pollution abatement. Similarly, the social problems created by the separate existence both of suburban bedroom communities and city-center ghettoes might also be relieved (Figure 5–10). Of course, all of this requires vast infusions of time,

Figure 5–9   Attempts at urban renewal to provide housing for the poor are not always successful. This huge project in St. Louis was so badly designed that some buildings have been abandoned and are scheduled for demolition only 15 years after they were built. (Photo by William A. Garnett.)

imagination, and money. But no amounts of these, however vast, can bring lasting success as long as our urban centers continue to grow as rapidly as they have in the last twenty years.

Figure 5-10   Many urban problems are largely the result of unplanned, haphazard development. Planning could avoid the serious problems of congestion, transportation, and destruction of valuable land that accompany urban sprawl as exemplified here. Mass production techniques are used to cover huge areas in the Los Angeles basin with houses in a few months. Upper left: land cleared for building. Upper right: foundations poured and lumber stacked neatly for each unit. Lower left: siding and roofs in place. Lower right: the result. (Photos by William A. Garnett.)

Bibliography

Council on Environmental Quality. Annual reports, 1971 and 1972. *Environmental Quality*. U.S. Government Printing Office, Washington, D.C.

Environmental Quality Laboratory, California Institute of Technology, 1972. *Smog: A Report to the People of the South Coast Air Basin*. Ward Ritchie Press, Los Angeles.

Esposito, John C., 1970. *Vanishing Air*. Grossman Publishers, New York. Ralph Nader's Study Group's report on air pollution.

Gofman, J. W., and A. R. Tamplin, 1971. *Poisoned Power*. Rodale Press, Emmaus, Pa. Livermore scientists present their case on radiation and the hazards of nuclear power.

Holdren, John and Phil Herrera, 1971. *Energy*. Sierra Club Books, New York.

Murdoch, William W., ed., 1971. *Environment: Resources, Pollution, and Society*. Sinauer Associates, Inc., Stamford, Conn. A topnotch collection.

Study of Critical Environmental Problems (SCEP), 1970. *Man's Impact on the Global Environment*. MIT Press, Cambridge. An excellent assessment of some of the most important environmental problems.

Whyte, William H., 1968. *The Last Landscape*. Doubleday, Garden City, New York. An important book on refurbishing our urban disaster areas.

A view of San Francisco Bay Area on a clear day, looking south to San Jose. This sprawling urban area has seriously altered the original ecosystem in a great many ways, some obvious, others not so apparent. Much of it, of course, has been completely replaced by buildings and roads. The flora and fauna of the land and of the bay are very different from that of only twenty years ago; even the climate in many places has changed. Most of the development along the shore has taken place on dirt fills, destroying valuable marshes in the process. (Photo by William A. Garnett.)

SIX

Disruption of Ecological Systems

The direct effects of pollution on property, on human health, and on the quality of life are varied and important, but they may ultimately prove to be less critical for society as a whole than the less obvious effects of pollution and other human activities on the ecological systems that sustain human life. (See Box 1–1 for a review of ecological terminology.)

Green plants are the basic energy source for all other forms of life on Earth, and green plants are provided with the material ingredients of growth by the nutrient cycles of the biosphere. These cycles do routinely what human society as yet cannot do—convert wastes completely into resources, using energy from the sun. The crops of civilization are watered, nourished, and protected from potential pests with considerable help from natural processes, including the formation and preservation of soil itself. The agents and carriers of human disease, like crop pests, are controlled more often by natural enemies or by environmental conditions than by human action. Climate and the composition of the atmosphere itself are regulated by geophysical and biological processes that may be susceptible to human interference.

These and other "public services" of the global ecosystem cannot be replaced by technology now or in the foreseeable future. This is so in many cases because the process is not understood scientifically. And, even where scientific knowledge might be adequate, the sheer size of the tasks performed by natural ecosystems dwarfs civilization's capacity to finance, produce, and deploy the necessary new technology. If, as we say, the support provided for human life by ecosystems is indispensable and irreplaceable, it is essential that the mechanisms behind these vital functions—and the potential for disrupting them through pollution and other human activities—be carefully examined. This chapter is an introduction to these critical issues.

Biochemical Cycles

Energy from the sun is constantly entering and passing through the Earth's ecosystems. But our ecosystems have no similar extraterrestrial source of the carbon, nitrogen, phosphorus, potassium, and sulfur, and many other substances that are required for life. These substances must be continually recycled through the ecosystem if the ecosystem is to persist. The carbon, nitrogen, and phosphorus cycles will be described in detail.

The Carbon Cycle.   Carbon is the basic constituent of all the large molecules characteristic of living beings. In a real sense life on Earth is based on carbon;

Figure 6–1   Carbon cycle. Solid arrows represent flow of CO_2.

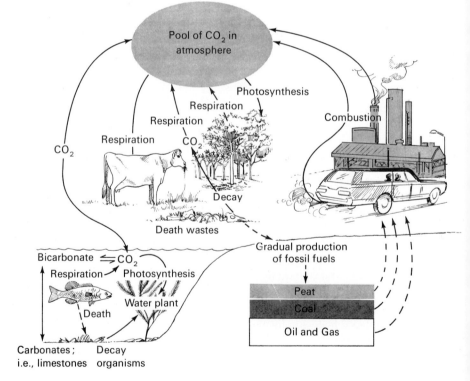

life is possible only because of the properties of this element. The major reservoir of carbon is carbon dioxide gas (CO_2), which occurs in the atmosphere of our planet and in solution in its waters. As shown in Figure 6–1, the process of photosynthesis is the primary pathway by which carbon (as CO_2) is withdrawn from the carbon dioxide "pool" and is used by plants to build carbohydrates and other organic (carbon-containing) compounds. In photosynthesis, energy from the sun is used to form the bonds of chemical energy that hold organic molecules together, and oxygen is released into the atmosphere as a byproduct. The carbon contained in the compounds produced by photosynthesis then moves up the food chain from plants to herbivores to carnivores. Both plants and animals extract energy from these organic compounds by means of the complex biochemical process called *cellular respiration*. In this process, the organic molecules are broken down by oxidation (a slow combustion), and the energy of their chemical bonds is extracted. The end products of respiration, water and carbon dioxide, are the raw materials of photosynthesis.

Thus an essential part of the carbon cycle is the movement of carbon containing molecules from the pool of CO_2 in air and water to plants and to animals farther up the food chain. From plants and animals at various positions along the chain, respiration returns CO_2 to this pool. Carbon is also returned to the pool through the agency of the bacteria and fungi that cause decay. These microorganisms serve as the ultimate link in food chains, reducing the complex carbon-containing molecules of dead plant and animal matter, and animal wastes, to their simple components.

The amount of carbon bound up into compounds by photosynthesis each year is called the *gross primary production* of an ecosystem (usually measured in grams of carbon per square meter of the Earth's surface per year). The gross primary production, less the carbon reoxidized to carbon dioxide by respiration in the primary producers (photosynthetic plants), is called the *net primary production*. This figure is easily converted to a measure of the energy available to the food chains; about 600 million billion calories per year for the entire biosphere, roughly 5 percent of which flows through agricultural ecosystems.[1]

The amount of carbon extracted from the CO_2 pool by photosynthesis is balanced, on the average, to within one part in 10,000 by the amount added to the pool through respiration and decay. Part of the small imbalance leaves the carbon cycle for millions of years and enters the crust of the Earth. This happens when incompletely decomposed organic matter accumulates and is transformed by geologic processes into fossil fuels — coal, oil, and natural gas. Carbon also is temporarily withdrawn from the cycle by the formation of limestone, often through the life processes of organisms (as in the formation of

[1]"The Energy Cycle of the Biosphere," George M. Woodwell, *Scientific American*, September 1970.

coral reefs). Such carbon is returned to the CO_2 pool by the burning of fossil fuels and by the weathering of limestone rocks.

The Nitrogen Cycle. Air is almost 80 percent nitrogen, another element required by all living systems (it is an essential ingredient of proteins). Nitrogen moves within ecosystems through a series of complex pathways, some of which are shown in Figure 6–2. Unlike the oxygen and carbon dioxide of the atmosphere, gaseous nitrogen cannot be used directly by most organisms. But some microorganisms, such as certain bacteria and blue-green algae, can convert gaseous nitrogen into more complex compounds that can be utilized by plants and animals. The best known of these nitrogen-fixing organisms are the bacteria associated with the special nodules on roots of legumes such as clover and alfalfa. These and other nitrogen-fixing bacteria that live free in the soil use the atmospheric nitrogen directly in making their own proteins. Nitrogen-containing compounds become available to plants and eventually to animals that eat the plants when these bacteria die.

Figure 6–2   Nitrogen cycle.

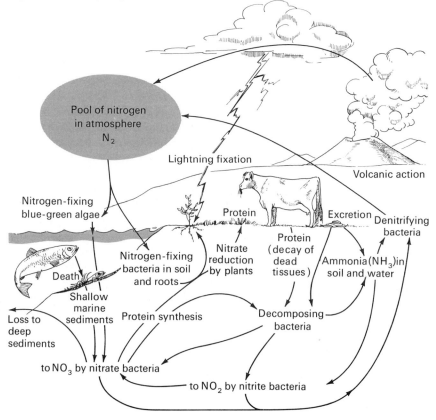

Decay of dead plants and animals (by bacteria and fungi) leads to the production of ammonia, as does animal excretion. A special group of bacteria, nitrite bacteria, utilizes the energy in the chemical bonds of the ammonia, degrading it to nitrites (compounds containing nitrogen atoms each combined with two oxygen atoms — in the shorthand of the chemist, NO_2). Then another group of bacteria, nitrate bacteria, changes the nitrites to nitrates (compounds with combinations of single nitrogen atoms with three oxygen atoms, NO_3). The nitrate bacteria remove more energy in degrading NO_2 compounds to NO_3. Nitrates are the commonest form in which plants obtain nitrogen from the soil; thus a loop of the nitrogen cycle may be completed without the formation of gaseous nitrogen.

Nitrogen, then, enters the living part of the cycle in two ways: directly from the atmosphere via nitrogen-fixing bacteria, and as nitrates taken up from the soil by plants:

$$NO_3 \rightarrow protein \rightarrow ammonia \rightarrow NO_2 \rightarrow NO_3.$$

Another kind of bacteria, denitrifying bacteria, returns nitrogen to the atmosphere. These bacteria break down nitrates, nitrites, and ammonia, and liberate gaseous nitrogen.

Some nitrogen is lost to the system. Nitrates, which are highly soluble, are washed from the soil and eventually become deposited as deep-sea sediments.

The Phosphorus Cycle.   Phosphorus is also required for life. It is an essential element in the DNA and RNA molecules involved in the transmission of genetic information (heredity) of all organisms, and phosphorus compounds are the prime energy-manipulating devices of living cells. Phosphorus does not cycle in ecosystems as readily as nitrogen does. The principal phosphorus reservoirs are phosphate rocks, deposits of guano (sea-bird excrement), and deposits of fossilized animals (Figure 6–3). Phosphorus is released from these reservoirs through natural erosion and leaching, and through mining and subsequent use as fertilizer by man. Some of this released phosphorus becomes available to plants in the form of phosphates in the soil, and thus enters the living part of the ecosystem. It may pass through several animals and microorganisms before returning to the soil through decay. Much of the phosphate washed or dug from rock deposits eventually finds its way to the sea, and human mining and distributing activities accelerate this process. There it may be utilized by marine ecosystems or deposited in shallow or deep marine sediments. Although some of this may be returned by upwelling currents, much of it is lost to the ocean depths. It can be returned by geological processes leading to the uplifting of sediments, but it seems unlikely that these will be sufficient to balance the loss in the near future. Obviously, mankind should make an effort to recycle phosphates and to extend the life of the reserves rather than permitting phosphates to become pollutants as now commonly occurs.

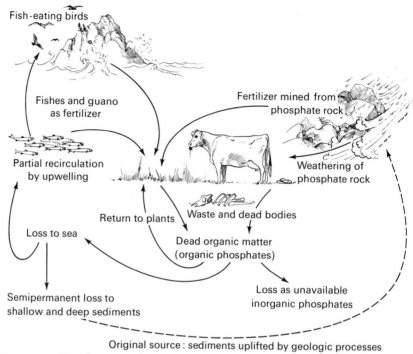

Fish-eating birds

Fishes and guano as fertilizer

Fertilizer mined from phosphate rock

Partial recirculation by upwelling

Weathering of phosphate rock

Return to plants

Waste and dead bodies

Loss to sea

Dead organic matter (organic phosphates)

Semipermanent loss to shallow and deep sediments

Loss as unavailable inorganic phosphates

Original source : sediments uplifted by geologic processes

Figure 6–3 Phosphorous cycle.

Food Webs: Ecological Complexity and Stability

The concept of the food web was introduced in Box 1–1. Food webs of various kinds obviously play a central role in the operation of the nutrient cycles just described. The food web of a Long Island estuary has been thoroughly investigated by biologists George M. Woodwell, Charles F. Wurster, and Peter A. Isaacson.[2] The relationships they discovered are illustrated in Figure 6–4; their study illustrates several important characteristics of most food webs. One is complexity. Although only some of the kinds of plants and animals in this ecosystem are shown in this figure, it is evident that most of the consumers feed on several different organisms, and that most prey organisms are attacked by more than one predator. To put it another way, the food chains are inter-linked. This intricate interlacing of most biological food chains provides a form of insurance against disruptions. If one species of plant in a complex community is eradicated by disease or drought, the herbivores in the community can survive on other kinds of plants that may be less susceptible. If a

[2]"Toxic Substances and Ecological Cycles," George M. Woodwell, *Scientific American*, March 1967. Reprinted in *Man and the Ecosphere*, edited by Paul R. Ehrlich, John P. Holdren, and Richard W. Holm, W. H. Freeman, San Francisco, 1971.

population of predators dwindles for one reason or another, an outbreak of the prey species is unlikely if there are other kinds of predators to fill the gap.

For example, suppose that the marsh-plant–cricket–redwing-blackbird section of Figure 6–4 represented an entire isolated ecosystem. If that were the case, removing the blackbirds–say, by shooting them–would lead to a cricket plague. This in turn might lead to the defoliation of the plants, and then to the starvation of the crickets. In short, a change in one link of such a simple chain would have disastrous consequences for the entire ecosystem.

Figure 6–4 Portion of a food web in a Long Island estuary. Arrows indicate flow of energy. Numbers are the parts per million of DDT found in each kind of organism. (After Woodwell, "Toxic Substances and Ecological Cycles." Copyright © 1967 by Scientific American, Inc. All rights reserved.)

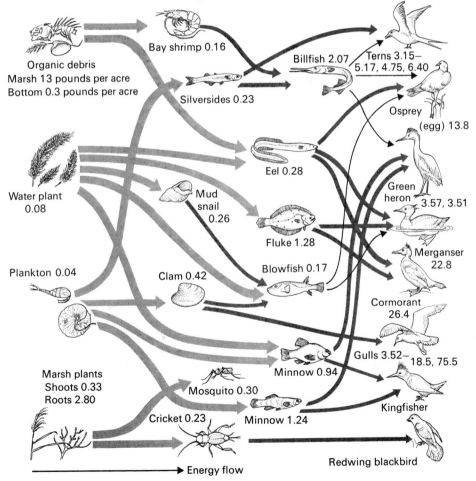

Organic debris
Marsh 13 pounds per acre
Bottom 0.3 pounds per acre

Bay shrimp 0.16

Billfish 2.07

Terns 3.15–5.17, 4.75, 6.40

Silversides 0.23

Osprey (egg) 13.8

Eel 0.28

Water plant 0.08

Mud snail 0.26

Green heron 3.57, 3.51

Fluke 1.28

Plankton 0.04

Clam 0.42

Blowfish 0.17

Merganser 22.8

Cormorant 26.4

Gulls 3.52–18.5, 75.5

Marsh plants
Shoots 0.33
Roots 2.80

Minnow 0.94

Mosquito 0.30

Kingfisher

Cricket 0.23

Minnow 1.24

Redwing blackbird

Energy flow

Suppose, however, that the cormorants were removed from the larger system. Populations of flukes and eels would probably increase, which in turn might reduce the population of green algae (*Cladophora*). But there would be more food for mergansers and ospreys, and their populations would probably enlarge, leading to a reduction of eels and flukes. In turn, the algae would recover. Of course, things do not normally happen this simply and neatly in nature, but the basic stabilizing role of cross-connecting links in food chains is apparent. As was mentioned in Box 1–1, ecological stability may be defined as the ability of an ecosystem that has suffered a disturbance to return to the conditions that preceded the disturbance; or, alternatively, as resistance to large rapid changes in the sizes of the populations in the ecosystem.

There are many kinds of biological complexity and many mechanisms by which complexity may impart stability. Species diversity presumably imparts stability by providing alternative pathways for the flow of nutrients and energy through the ecosystem. Another possible advantage of there being a large number of species in a community is that there will then be few empty "niches." (A *niche*—to a biologist—is a biological role, and an *empty niche* is an opportunity for invasion by a new species from outside the community, with possible disruptive effect.)

Sheer number of species is not the only factor that determines stability, however; a degree of balance in population sizes among the species is also required if the capacity of the alternative pathways is to be adequate and if the niches are to be solidly occupied. To take an oversimplified example, consider two communities, each containing 1,000,000 organisms divided among 1,000 species. A situation with 1,000 populations of 1,000 individuals each should be more stable than a situation where one population contains 900,100 individuals and the other 999 populations contain 100 individuals each.

Measures of complexity exist at the population level as well as that of the community. One measure of complexity in a population is genetic variability, which provides the potential for evolving resistance against new threats. A highly variable population is most likely to contain individuals with heritable characteristics that may protect them from, for instance, a new type of predator or parasite, scarcity of food, or a sudden change in climate. Another form of complexity in populations is physiological variability in the form of a mixed age distribution. Here the advantage of complexity works against threats that are specific to a particular stage in the organism's life cycle; say, a disease that strikes only juveniles. There are other forms of complexity as well, including physical variation in habitat and differences in the geographic distribution of a given species.

The causal links between complexity and stability in ecological systems are by no means firmly established or well understood, and exceptions do exist. The evidence of a general correlation between these properties is growing. however, and consists of (*a*) theoretical considerations of the sort summarized above, (*b*) general observations of actual ecosystems of widely varying complexity (the relatively simple ecosystem of the boreal coniferous forest — the "north woods" — is observed to be less stable than the complex tropical rain forest), and (c) a limited number of controlled laboratory and field experiments.

Modifying Ecosystems

Like any other creature, human beings have always had some effect on the ecological systems of which they were a part, but the history of deliberate and significant modification of ecosystems doubtless began with the development of agriculture. Since then, human influence has reached to the remotest areas of the planet and has been intensified by increased numbers of people and the development of modern technology.

What are some of the ways in which mankind modifies ecological systems? Obviously, some ecosystems are destroyed outright by such diverse activities as planting crops, logging forests, starting fires, building dams, applying defoliants to jungles, constructing buildings, and laying pavement. (See Figure 6–5 for an example of how activities on land can damage an ecosystem in an adjacent bay.) The ecological results of human activities are as varied as the activities themselves. When prairie is converted to cornfield, an unstable, simple ecosystem replaces a stable, complex one. Attempts to stabilize such systems artificially can lead to further destabilization and bring about changes elsewhere as well.

Abuses of Soil. Wholesale logging of forests creates extreme changes that effectively destroy the forest ecosystem. Numerous animals that depend on the trees for food and shelter disappear. Many of the smaller forest plants depend on the trees for shade; they and the animals they support also disappear. With the removal of trees and plants, the soil is directly exposed to the elements, and it tends to erode faster. Loss of topsoil reduces the water-retaining capacity of an area, diminishes the supply of fresh water, causes silting of dams, and has other serious consequences for man. The flooding along many of the world's rivers, from the Yang-tse in China to the Eel River in California, is greatly aggravated by heavy deforestation in their watersheds. Deforestation also reduces the amount of water transferred from ground to air by the trees in the process known as transpiration. This modifies the weather downwind of the area, usually making it more arid and subject to greater extremes of temperature. Finally, if reforestation is not carried out, the deforested area is invaded by "pioneer" weedy plants that often have much less desirable characteristics for human use than did the forest that was removed.

Human activities have already produced a great increase in the amount of desert and wasteland. The vast Sahara Desert itself is in part manmade, the result of overgrazing, faulty irrigation, and deforestation, combined with

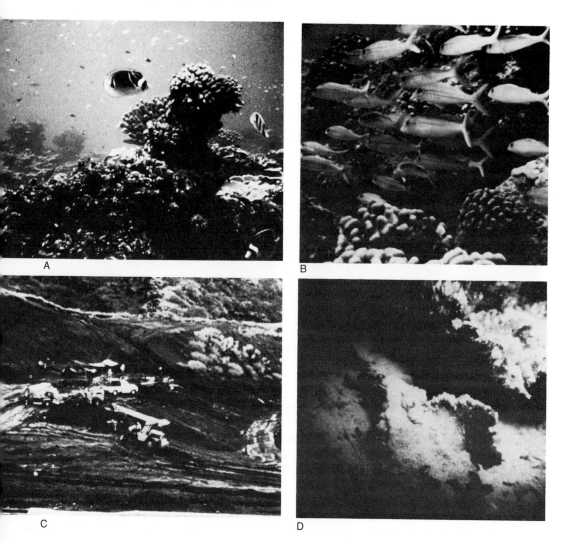

A   B

C   D

natural climatic changes over centuries. Today the Sahara is advancing south-ward on a broad front at a rate of several miles per year. The great Thar Desert of western India is also partly the result of man's influence. Some 2,000 years ago, what is now the center of this desert was a jungle. The spread of this desert has been aggravated by poor cultivation practices, lumbering, and overgrazing.[3] Similar activities can lead to repetition of the Sahara and Thar stories in many parts of the globe.

[3]The Sahara and Thar desert situations are described in "Desertification versus Poten-tial for Recovery in Circum-Saharan Territories," M. Kassas, in *Arid Lands in Transi-tion.* American Association for the Advancement of Science, Washington, D.C., 1970; and "Problems of Environment in India," B. R. Seshachar, in *Proceedings of Joint Colloquium on International Environmental Science*, Report 63–562. U.S. Govt. Printing Office, Washington, D.C., 1971.

E

Figure 6–5   Destruction of coral reefs at Kaneohe Bay, Oahu, Hawaii, as a result of
the building of subdivisions. A and B, "before." A. Complex reef community before
intrusion of silt and sewage; prominant are butterfly fishes (*Chaetodon lunula*), which
are characteristic of coral communities, feeding on the reef fauna of invertebrates.
B. A school of goatfishes (*Mulloidichthys samoensis*), which are prized as food. They
feed on small animals in sandy bottoms among the coral growths. C. Construction of
subdivisions on slopes above the bay with inadequate erosion control. Heavy
downpours wash large amounts of silt into Kaneohe Bay. D and E, "after." D. Silt
settling on and killing coral growths by overloading the self-cleaning abilities of the
tiny animals that secrete the hard coral skeletons. E. "Graveyard" of coral killed by
silt and sewage from subdivisions. Note the greatly reduced diversity of life and the
presence of sea cucumbers, which are regarded by some marine biologists as
indicators of heavy pollution. The complex, stable reef system, which once provided
edible fishes and aesthetic values for people, has been replaced by a destabilized
simple system featuring the population explosion of a "garbage" organism. (From the
film "Cloud Over the Coral Reef" by Dr. Lee Tepley and Dr. R. E. Johannes.)

Erosion, another problem that probably has plagued humanity since the
agricultural revolution, is becoming increasingly serious. It is estimated that
today one-half of the farmland in India is not adequately protected from erosion, and, on fully one-third of the farmland, erosion threatens to remove the
topsoil completely. As Georg Borgstrom has observed, soil conservation procedures are especially difficult to institute in areas where the population is
poorly fed. He cites a study that recommended a one-fifth *reduction* in the
amount of cultivated land and a one-third *reduction* in the size of livestock
herds in Turkey.[4] It was hoped that these reductions would help to diminish
the danger of catastrophic erosion caused by overgrazing. Unfortunately, the

[4]*Too Many*, Georg Borgstrom, Collier-Macmillan, New York, 1969.

program was not initiated, presumably because the local people were dependent upon the land and the herds for food and other necessities. As so often
happens, a short-run need took precedence over long-run wisdom.

In most tropical areas the soils are extremely poor. They cannot maintain
large reserves of minerals needed for plant growth, such as phosphorus, potassium, and calcium, primarily because heavy rainfall and the resultant
leaching cause a high rate of water flow through the ground to the water table.
Also as a result of heavy leaching, these soils have very high contents of iron
and aluminum oxides in their upper levels. Most of the nutrients in a tropical
jungle are concentrated not in the soil, but in the vegetation. Nutrients that
are released to the soil through the decay of dead plant parts are quickly returned to the living vegetation. The extensive shallow root systems of the
forest trees absorb the nutrients as soon as they are released. Since most jungle
trees are evergreen, the process is continuous. There is no chance for nutrients
to build up in the soil as they do in temperate deciduous forests, which are
dormant each year following a general leaf fall.

When a tropical forest is defoliated or cleared for agriculture, this continual recycling of nutrients is interrupted. Heavy rains wash away the thin
supply of soil nutrients, and the last substances to leach out are iron and
aluminum oxides. The soil is exposed to sun and oxygen, and a series of
complex chemical changes takes place, often resulting in the formation of a
rocklike substance called *laterite*. Such laterization has occurred over wide
areas of the tropics, starting long ago and continuing in recent years. Those
who have been fortunate enough to visit Angkor Wat in Cambodia (Figure 6–6)
have seen magnificient cities and temples built by the Khmers some 800 to
1,000 years ago. But visitors seldom realize that the construction materials
were sandstone and laterite, and that laterization may have been a principal
reason for the disappearance of the Khmer civilization.

Farming small clearings for a year or two and then letting the jungle reclaim
them is the ancient method of agriculture in many areas where soils are subject
to laterization. Tropical forests are usually able to reinvade small areas before
laterization is complete. Whether large areas that have been kept cleared for
substantial periods of time can be reforested is an open question. Reforestation has been successful in some areas where the soil crust has been carefully
broken up, fertilizers applied, and the whole system carefully cultivated.
But natural reforestation seems unlikely, and even most of the attempts supported by man have failed. Laterization is continuing throughout the tropics
and will doubtless proceed more rapidly as mankind grows increasingly desperate for food. According to geologist Mary McNeil, "The ambitious plans
to increase food production in the tropics to meet the pressure of the rapid
rise of population have given too little consideration to the laterization problem and the measures that will have to be undertaken to overcome it."[5] Along

---

[5]"Lateritic Soils," Mary McNeil, *Scientific American*, November 1964. Reprinted in
Man and the Ecosphere (see footnote 2).

with other data supporting her contention, she provides a description of the fiasco at Iata in the Amazon Basin, where the government of Brazil attempted to found a farming community. Laterization destroyed the project when, "in less than five years the cleared fields became virtually pavements of rock."

Agriculture and Instabilities.   The practice of agriculture, even where quality of soils, erosion or salt accumulation do not pose problems, may cause ecological difficulties. The most basic one is that agriculture is a simplifier of eco-systems, replacing relatively complex natural biological communities with relatively simple manmade ones based on a few strains of crops. Being less

Figure 6-6   Laterite construction in the temple of Angkor Wat near Ankor Thom, a major city of the ancient Khmer civilization in what is now Cambodia. Laterite on exposure to air turns into a bricklike form of rock still widely used for construction. (Photo by United Nations.)

complex, agricultural communities tend to be less stable than their natural counterparts: they are vulnerable to invasions by weeds, insect pests, and plant diseases, and they are particularly sensitive to extremes of weather and variations in climate. Historically, mankind has attempted to defend agricultural communities against the instabilities to which they are susceptible by means of vigilance and the application of "energy subsidies" (for example, by hoeing weeds and more recently by applying pesticides and fungicides). The effort has not always been successful. The Irish potato famine of the last century is perhaps the best-known example of the collapse of a simple agricultural ecosystem. The heavy dependence of the Irish population on a single, highly productive crop led to the deaths of one-and-a-half million people (in a population of 8 million) when the potato monoculture fell victim to a fungus in the 1840s.

Advances in agricultural technology in the last hundred years have not resolved the ecological dilemma of agriculture; they have aggravated it. The dilemma can be summarized in this way: agriculture tries to manage ecosystems in such a way as to maximize productivity, nature "manages" ecosystems in such a way as to maximize stability, and the two goals are incompatible. In short, productivity is achieved at the expense of stability.

Of course, mankind must practice agriculture to support even a fraction of the existing human population. A degree of instability in agricultural ecosystems must therefore be accepted and, where possible, compensated for by technology. However, the trends in modern agriculture, associated in part with the urgent need to cope with unprecedented population growth and in part with the desire to maximize yields (amount of harvest per acre) for strictly economic reasons, are especially worrisome ecologically. The three major liabilities are:

1. As larger and larger land areas are given over to farming, the unexploited tracts available to serve as reservoirs of species diversity and to carry out the "public service" functions of natural ecosystems become smaller and fewer.

2. Even in parts of the world where land area under agriculture is constant or (for economic reasons) dwindling, attempts to maximize yields have led to dramatic increases in the use of pesticides and inorganic fertilizers — increases that have far-reaching ecological consequences themselves.

3. The quest for high yields has led also to the replacement of a wide variety of traditional crop varieties all over the world with a few, specially bred, high-yielding strains. Areas of unprecedented size are now planted to a single variety of wheat or rice. Because of this enormous expansion of monoculture, the chances are much greater for an epidemic crop failure from insects or disease — one that might occur over an area far greater than any crop failure in the past.

Types of Pollutants

The expansion and intensification of agriculture has been accompanied by a continuing industrial revolution that has multiplied many times over both the magnitude and variety of the substances introduced into the biological environment by mankind. It is useful to classify these substances as *qualitative pollutants* (synthetic substances produced and released only by man) and *quantitative pollutants* (substances naturally present in the environment but released in significant additional amounts by man).

Well-known qualitative pollutants include the chlorinated hydrocarbon pesticides, such as DDT, the related class of industrial chemicals called PCBs, and some herbicides. These substances are biologically active in the sense that they stimulate physiological changes. But, since organisms have had no experience with them over evolutionary time, the substances are usually not biodegradable. Thus, they may persist in the environment for years and even decades after being introduced and be transported around the globe by wind and water. Their long-term effects will be discovered only by experience.

Within the category of quantitative pollutants, there are three criteria by which a contribution made by mankind may be judged significant:

1. Man can perturb a natural cycle with a large amount of a substance ordinarily considered innocuous, either (a) by overloading part of the cycle (as we do to the denitrifying part of the nitrogen cycle when we overfertilize, leading to the accumulation of nitrates and nitrites in ground water); (b) by destabilizing a finely tuned balance (as we may do to the global atmospheric heat engine that governs global climate, by adding CO_2 to the atmosphere via combustion of fossil fuels); or (c) by swamping a natural cycle completely (as could happen to the climatic balance in the very long term from human input of waste heat).

2. An amount of material negligible compared to natural global flows of the same substance can cause great damage if released in a sensitive spot, over a small area, or suddenly (for example, the destruction of coral reefs in Hawaii by silt washed from construction sites).

3. Any addition of a substance that can be harmful even at its naturally occurring concentrations must be considered significant. Radioactive substances fall into this category, as does mercury.

Concentration of Toxic Substances in Ecosystems. Nowhere is human ecological naiveté more evident than in popular assumptions about the capacity of the atmosphere, soils, rivers, and oceans to absorb pollution. These assumptions all too often take the following form: if one gallon of poison is added to one billion gallons of water, then the highest concentration of poison to which anything will be exposed is about one part per billion. This might be approximately true if complete mixing by diffusion took place rapidly, which it often does not, and *if only physical systems were involved*. But because *biological systems* are involved, the situation is radically different.

For example, filter-feeding animals may concentrate poisons to levels far higher than those found in the surrounding medium. Oysters capture food by constantly filtering the water they inhabit, and they live in shallow water near the shore, where pollution is heaviest. Consequently, their bodies often contain much higher concentrations of radioactive substances or lethal chemicals than the water in which they live. For instance, they have been found to accumulate up to 70,000 times the concentration of chlorinated hydrocarbon insecticides found in their environment.[6] Food chains may lead to the concentration of toxic substances; they act as a kind of "biological amplifier." The diagram of the Long Island estuary food web (Figure 6–1) shows how the concentrations of DDT and its derivatives tend to increase in food chains from one trophic level to another. This tendency is especially marked for the chlorinated hydrocarbons because of their high solubility in fatty substances and their low water solubility. Although the clam and the mud snail are at the same trophic level, the filter-feeding clam accumulates more than half again as much DDT as the mud snail because of the difference in their food-capturing habits.

The mechanism of concentration in food chains is simple. As one would expect from the Second Law of Thermodynamics, the mass of herbivores normally cannot be as great as the mass of plants they feed on. With each step upward in a food chain the *biomass* is reduced. Energy present in the chemical bonds of organisms at one level does not all end up as bond energy at the next level, because much of the energy is degraded to heat at each step. In contrast, losses of DDT and related compounds along a food chain are small compared to the amount that is transferred upward through the chain. As a result, the concentration of DDT increases at each level. Concentrations in the birds at the end of the food chain are from tens to many hundreds of times as high as they are in the animals farther down in the chain. In predatory birds, the concentration of DDT may be a *million* times as high as that in estuarine waters.

Insecticides and Ecosystems

Besides being direct threats to human health, synthetic insecticides (Box 6–1) are among man's most potent tools for simplifying and thus destabilizing ecosystems. The increase in the concentration of the most persistent of these compounds with each upward step in a food chain exposes the populations *least* able to survive poisoning to the highest concentrations.

There are several reasons why the organisms that occupy positions near

---

[6]"The Significance of DDT Residues in Estuarine Fauna," Robert van den Bosch, in *Chemical Fallout: Current Research on Persistent Pesticides*, edited by M. W. Miller and G. G. Berg, Charles C. Thomas, Springfield, Illinois, 1969.

the upper end of food chains are less able to cope with the poisons than are, for example, herbivores. The first reason traces back again to the Second Law of Thermodynamics. Because of the loss of energy at each transfer, the higher the position that a given population occupies in a food chain, the smaller that population will be. This means that if a poison were applied that would kill most of the predators and herbivores in an area, it would be more likely to exterminate the population of predators than the population of herbivores, simply because there are fewer predators. Purely by chance, members of the larger population would be more likely to survive. It would not be necessary to kill all individuals of any one species of predator to force it to extinction. If survivors were too scattered for the sexes to find one another and produce offspring, extinction would surely follow. Or, if survivors were few, various genetic problems might result from inbreeding and cause the population to dwindle to zero.

Another reason that small populations of animals occupying high positions in food chains are more vulnerable is that smaller populations tend to have less *genetic variability*. The individuals of a population are not all genetically alike; there is a great deal of variation in the inherited characteristics among them. Suppose for instance, that one individual per hundred thousand in each of two species of insects by chance carries a mutant gene that makes it naturally resistant to a certain pesticide. Assume that one species is a herbivore—a pest for our purposes—and its population in a field consists of one million individuals, while the second species is a predator of the first, with a population of one hundred thousand individuals. If the field is thoroughly treated with the pesticide, ten individuals of the pest species will survive, but only one of the predator species will survive; each of these survivors being naturally resistant mutants. In this oversimplified example, the consequences are obvious. The small group of resistant pest insects can quickly reproduce a large population, free from attack by its predator. But because most individuals of the new pest population will be resistant, the next treatment with insecticide will have little effect. If dosage of the insecticide is increased, the pest species will respond by becoming more and more resistant with each new generation. Not only herbivorous pests but other large populations can easily develop such resistance; for example, resistance to DDT has developed in many mosquito populations and has hampered malaria control programs.

There is an additional reason why our artificial poisons are so much more effective against predators and parasites than they are against herbivores. For many millions of years plants have been evolving defenses against the assaults of herbivores. Many of these defenses are familiar to everyone. They include the spines of the cactus, the thorn of the rose bush, and a wide variety of chemical compounds ranging from the irritants in poison ivy and poison oak to such useful substances as quinine and pepper. These plant substances are natural pesticides; in fact, mankind has utilized some of them, such as nicotine (extracted from tobacco) and pyrethrins (extracted from a small marigoldlike flower), for their original purposes—as insect poisons. Although the use of nicotine as an insecticide has fallen off since the introduction of synthetic pesticides, pyrethrins are still the active ingredient in many insect sprays intended for home use.

Insects, of course, have in turn evolved mechanisms for evading the plants' chemical defenses. Long before man appeared, this "coevolutionary war" was being waged between the plants and insects; the plants continually building better defenses, the insects countering with better attacks. Small wonder that herbivorous insects have had little trouble in dealing evolutionarily with man's recent attempts to poison them. Indeed, pesticides may often lead to *higher* concentrations of pests rather than lower, either because they directly

---

Box 6-1   Synthetic Insecticides

Two groups of compounds contain the majority of synthetic insecticides: chlorinated hydrocarbons and organophosphates.

Chlorinated Hydrocarbons

This group includes DDT, benzene hexachloride (BHC), dieldrin, endrin, aldrin, chlordane, lindane, isodrin, toxophene, and similar compounds designed to kill insects. DDT is the most thoroughly studied of the chlorinated hydrocarbons, and much of the following discussion is based on it. In its behavior it is more or less typical of the group, although other chlorinated hydrocarbons may be more soluble in water, more toxic, less persistent, etc. In insects and other animals these compounds act primarily on the central nervous system in ways that are not well understood, but the effects range from hyperexcitability to death following convulsions and paralysis. Chronic effects on vertebrates include fatty infiltration of the heart, and fatty degeneration of the liver which is often fatal. Fishes and other aquatic animals seem to be especially sensitive to chlorinated hydrocarbons. Oxygen uptake is somehow blocked at the gills, causing death from suffocation. That chlorinated hydrocarbons apparently can influence the production of enzymes may account for their wide range of effects.

Chlorinated hydrocarbons tend to be selectively soluble in fats and fatty tissues. In animals this means that they may be stored in tissues far removed from the sensitive nervous system and thus rendered relatively harmless. Chlorinated hydrocarbons vary a great deal in their toxicity to plants. They are known to slow the rate of photosynthesis, but the exact cause of this effect is unknown. The greater toxicity of chlorinated hydrocarbons in insects as compared to mammals is primarily a function of the greater ease with which these compounds are absorbed through insect cuticle compared with mammalian skin. Four properties make chlorinated hydrocarbons a particular threat to ecosystems:

1. Chlorinated hydrocarbons have a wide range of biological activity; they are broad-spectrum poisons, affecting many different organisms in many different ways. They are toxic to essentially all animals including many vertebrates.

2. They have great stability. It is not clear, for instance, how long DDT persists in ecosystems. Fifty percent of the DDT sprayed in a single treatment may still be found in a field 10 years later. This does not mean, however, that the other 50 percent has been degraded to biologically inactive molecules; it may only have gone somewhere else. Probably DDT (including its biologically active breakdown product DDE) has an average half-life (time

poison the natural enemies of the pest, or because they indirectly decrease the efficiency of those enemies as controlling agents.

There are many actual cases in which differential kill of predators has released some of their prey species from their natural restraints. It is fair to say, for instance, that mites, as pests, are a *creation* of the pesticide industry. Careless overuse of DDT and other pesticides has promoted many of these little insect-like relatives of spiders to pest status by killing the insects that previously preyed on the mites and kept them under control. The emergence of the European red mite as a major pest in apple orchards followed the use of DDT to control the codling moth. This is only one of many examples in

required before 50 percent has been degraded) of much more than a decade. Indeed, DDE may be virtually indestructable.

3. Chlorinated hydrocarbons are very mobile. For example, the chemical properties of DDT cause it to adhere to dust particles and thus get blown around the world: four different chlorinated hydrocarbons have been detected in dust filtered from the air over Barbados; frog populations in unsprayed areas high in the Sierra Nevada of California are polluted with DDT. Furthermore, DDT co-distills with water; when water evaporates and enters the atmosphere, DDT goes with it. Chlorinated hydrocarbons thus travel in the air and surface waters.

4. Finally, chlorinated hydrocarbons become concentrated in the fats of organisms. If the world is considered as being partitioned into nonliving and living parts, then these pesticides may be thought of as moving continually from the physical environment into living systems. To attempt to monitor DDT levels merely by testing water (as has frequently been done) is ridiculous. Water is saturated with DDT — that is, can dissolve no more — when it has dissolved 1.2 parts per billion. Besides, the chemical does not remain for long in water; it is quickly removed by any organisms that live in the water.

It is these four properties — extreme range of biological activity, stability, mobility, and affinity for living systems — that cause biologists' fears that DDT and its relatives are degrading the life-support systems of our planet. If any *one* of these properties were lacking the situation would be much less serious, but in combination they pose a deadly threat.

Organophosphates

This group includes parathion, malathion, Azodrin, diazinon, TEPP, phosdrin, and several others. These poisons are descendants of the nerve gas Tabun (diisopropylfluorophosphate), developed in Nazi Germany during World War II. All of them are cholinesterase inhibitors; they inactivate the enzyme responsible for breaking down a nerve "transmitter substance," acetylcholine. The result is, in acute cases of poisoning, a hyperactivity of the nervous system; the animal dies twitching and out of control. Unlike chlorinated hydrocarbons, organophosphates are unstable and non-persistent; thus, they tend not to produce chronic effects in ecosystems or to accumulate in food chains.

Organophosphates inhibit other enzymes in addition to cholinesterase. Indeed, some of those that show relatively high insect toxicity and low mammalian toxicity do so because they poison an enzyme that is more critical to the functioning of insect than of mammalian nervous systems.

which pesticides intended for one pest have led to the flourishing of others. The usual response of the pesticide industry to such situations is to use more of the original pesticide, or to develop more potent poisons which then create another array of pollution problems; for instance, some miticides seem to be powerful carcinogens.

In such cases one or more pests were being held in check by natural biological controls, which were upset by the introduction of the chemical. That so many organisms can be "promoted" to pest status by the killing of predators and parasites with pesticides is itself a powerful testimonial for biological controls. These controls are constantly at work suppressing potential pests at no economic cost. The destabilizing effect of pesticides on ecosystems is so common that it is often cited in the scientific literature as evidence that ecosystem simplification leads to instability. Unfortunately, the farmer's frequent response to an instability in the form of a pest outbreak is to apply higher doses of pesticides, thus aggravating the situation still further.

Of all the synthetic organic pesticides, probably more is known about DDT than any other. It is the oldest and most widely used chlorinated hydrocarbon insecticide. It is found everywhere—not only where it has been applied, but all over the Earth. Virtually every kind of animal on Earth has been exposed to it, and so have people. Concentrations in the fat deposits of Americans average about 12 ppm (parts per million), and the people of India and Israel have much higher concentrations. More startling and significant in some ways has been the discovery of DDT residues in the fat deposits of Eskimos, and in Antarctic penguins and seals. Seals from the east coast of Scotland have been found to have concentrations of DDT as high as 23 ppm in their blubber. Pesticide pollution is truly a worldwide problem.

Because DDT breaks down so slowly, it lasts for decades in soils. For instance, in the Long Island estuary studied by Woodwell and his colleagues, the marsh had been sprayed for 20 years for mosquito control. Up to 32 pounds per acre of DDT were found in the upper layer of mud there. Such concentrations in U.S. soils are not unusual. As a result of the concentration of DDT as it moves up food chains, the danger to the life and reproductive capacity of fish-eating birds is extreme. Nesting failures among bald eagles attributable to DDT have now reached proportions that bring the survival of the species into severe jeopardy. In addition, reproductive difficulties in populations of such diverse birds as the peregrine falcon, the brown pelican, and the Bermuda petrel have been traced to residues of DDT and other chlorinated hydrocarbon insecticides. These chemicals interfere with the birds' ability to metabolize calcium, which results in the laying of eggs whose shells are so thin that they are crushed by the weight of the incubating parents. Figure 6–7 shows thinning of eggshells in brown pelicans. Similar effects have been suggested for the polychlorinated biphenyls (PCBs—chlorinated hydrocarbons used extensively in industry), which are closely related to the insecticides. They may share with the insecticides the blame for high rates of nesting failure in predatory

Figure 6–7 Crushed egg in the nest of a brown pelican off the California coast. This egg had such a thin shell that the weight of the nesting parent's body destroyed it. The concentration of DDE in the eggs of this 300-pair colony reached 2,500 parts per million; no eggs hatched. (Photo by Joseph R. Jehl, Jr.)

birds, and they may be five times more potent as killers than DDT.

The evidence against DDT in the case of birds' eggs is now overwhelming. Studies have been done of the thickness of predatory bird eggshells in museum collections. Among those species investigated that feed high on food chains, there is virtually always a sharp drop in eggshell thickness for the period 1945–1947, when DDT was generally introduced (Figure 6–8). In Britain a strong correlation has also been shown between the level of chlorinated hydrocarbon contamination in various geographical regions and eggshell thickness in peregrine falcons, sparrowhawks, and golden eagles nesting in those regions.

The exceptions make the case even more convincing. The shells of one Florida population of bald eagles first thinned in 1943, not in 1945–1947. Investigations disclosed that this population lived in a county where large-scale DDT testing took place in 1943. One pair of peregrine falcons on the coast of California was an exception to the general rule of nesting failure. Examination of their nest revealed that they were feeding inland on mourning doves. Mourning doves are herbivores; thus the peregrines were feeding much lower

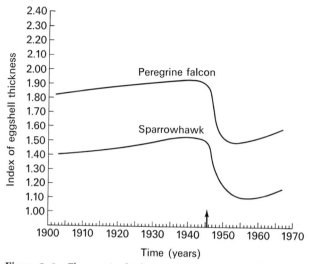

Figure 6–8   Changes in thickness of eggshells of peregrine falcon and sparrowhawk in Britain. Arrows indicate first widespread use of DDT. (After Ratcliffe, *J. Appl. Ecol. 7,* 67–115, 1970.)

in the food chain than if they had been feeding on fish-eating sea birds. They picked up less DDT, and were therefore able to reproduce successfully.

Pest Control: Success or Failure?   World agriculture today is an ecological disaster area. We carefully breed out of plants their natural chemical defenses. The poisons usually taste unpleasant to us, although some of our spices, which we use in small quantities, are produced by plants to serve as insecticides. We plant our crops in tight, simple monocultures, inviting pest outbreaks, to which we then respond with synthetic pesticides, often killing a higher proportion of some nontarget populations than of the target population of pests. Because synthetic pesticides, whether intended for insects or pest plants, have toxic effects on so many nontarget organisms, they are more accurately called "biocides." There are a few hopeful signs that ecologically sound agricultural practices may eventually be adopted, but so far the general trend has been in the opposite direction.

The percentage of crop losses to insects in the U.S. seems to have remained about the same for more than 20 years, despite enormously increased use of pesticides. In 1948, ecologist William Vogt noted in his book, *Road to Survival,*[7] that "one-tenth of all crop plants are destroyed by insects in the U.S. every year." Vogt based his comment on statistics published by the USDA. In 1969, Georg Borgstrom, also using USDA figures, observed that crop losses

[7]Sloane Publishers, New York.

due to insects amount to the yield from about a fifth of our total acreage, or about a sixth of the cash value of our total crop production.[8] When the storage-loss component is subtracted, the field losses amount to slightly more than a tenth of total production, about the same as in 1948. The President's Science Advisory Committee Panel on the World Food Problem estimated insect losses in the field during the 1950s as between 4 percent and 14 percent, depending on the crop. In 1948, according to zoologist Robert L. Rudd, DDT, benzene hexachloride, and lead arsenate were the only insecticides of any significance used.[9] By the 1960s, chlorinated hydrocarbons had largely replaced the latter two, and insecticides were being used at a rapidly escalating rate. Overall, pesticide usage in the United States more than doubled between 1960 and 1970, with about one billion pounds being used in 1970. Of course, it is difficult to get accurate estimates of pest losses, and standards of pest damage have changed through time. Nevertheless, the consistency of insect loss estimates over time is rather striking. Despite huge inputs of insecticides, insects still claim a substantial share of the American farmers' greatly increased agricultural production.

What proportion of this increased production is due to the use of synthetic pesticides? Certainly not as much as the pesticide industry would like us to believe, but synthetic pesticides may play a more significant role than is indicated in the relatively constant percentage-loss figures. High-yield strains of crops, heavily fertilized, probably require more protection per acre than lower yield strains. Therefore, one might expect a higher percentage loss in fields today if we were still using the control techniques of 1940.

Could similar or greater yields have been achieved since the Second World War with control methods that are more ecologically sophisticated than current pesticide practices? It is the opinion of systems ecologist K. E. F. Watt that, when measured against successful biological and integrated control programs, "most pesticide projects have been failures." We believe that the procedures in use in the 1950s and 1960s will eventually be seen as one of mankind's most tragic blunders, and that when the total accounting is done, it will be found that other methods of control would have provided higher yields at less direct cost and with fewer deleterious consequences for mankind.

Some Pest-Control Programs. The history of attempts to control cotton pests in the coastal Cañete Valley of Peru has been reported by entomologist Ray F. Smith. Against the advice of ecologically sophisticated entomologists, who recommended the use of cultural control methods and inorganic and botanical insecticides, synthetic organic pesticides were widely introduced in the valley in 1949. At first the use of these pesticides, principally the chlorinated hydrocarbons, DDT, BHC, and toxaphene, was very successful. Cotton

[8]See footnote 4.

[9]*Pesticides and the Living Landscape*, Robert L. Rudd, University of Wisconsin Press, Madison, 1964.

yields increased from 494 kilograms per hectare (440 lbs/acre) in 1950 to 728 kilograms per hectare (648 lbs/acre) in 1954. The cotton farmers concluded that if more pesticide were applied, more cotton would grow. Insecticides "were applied like a blanket over the entire valley. Trees were cut down to make it easier for the airplanes to treat the fields. The birds that nested in these trees disappeared. Other beneficial animal forms, such as insect parasites and predators, disappeared. As the years went by, the number of treatments was increased; also, each year the treatments were started earlier because of the earlier attacks of the pests."

Trouble started in 1952 when BHC proved no longer to be effective against aphids. In 1954 toxaphene failed against the tobacco leafworm. Boll weevil infestation reached extremely high levels in 1955–1956, and at least *six new pests had appeared*, pests that were not found in similar nearby valleys that had not been sprayed with organic pesticides. In addition, the numbers of an old pest, larvae of the moth *Heliothis virescens*, exploded to new heights, and showed a high level of DDT resistance. Synthetic organophosphates were substituted for the chlorinated hydrocarbons, and the interval between treatments was shortened from one or two weeks down to three days. In 1955–1956, cotton yields dropped to 332 kilograms per hectare, in spite of the tremendous amounts of insecticide applied. Economic disaster overtook the valley. In 1957 an ecologically rational "integrated control" program was initiated in which biological, cultural, and chemical controls were combined. Conditions improved immensely, and yields rose to new highs.

This example should not be taken to mean that ecologically unsound pesticide programs have been instituted only in other places and in former times. Many examples can be cited of mistakes made here in the United States. For example, in both California and Arizona, profit margins have been dropping for cotton farmers because of insect attacks and the rising costs of chemical pesticide applications. In an attempt to evaluate the control measures used by agriculturalists, biologists uncovered some astounding facts. One study reported that "controlled experiments on small plots suggest that cotton growers in California may have spent thousands of dollars to fight an insect, the lygus bug, that has no appreciable effect on the final production per acre." Reduction of the number of lygus bugs per acre *did not lead to increased yields*, apparently because the bugs fed on "surplus" bolls of cotton, which would not ripen in any case. Spraying for lygus bugs early in the season with some pesticides not only did not help yields, but lowered them by killing insect predators of the bollworm, which caused outbreaks of bollworms. What is still more intriguing is that recent research has begun to indicate that the bollworm itself may not be a threat to yields even at population levels considerably higher than what had previously been considered a dangerous infestation.

Most disturbing of all is the Azodrin story. Azodrin is a broad-spectrum organophosphate insecticide manufactured by the Shell Chemical Company (a subsidiary of the Shell Oil Company). Azodrin kills most of the insect popu-

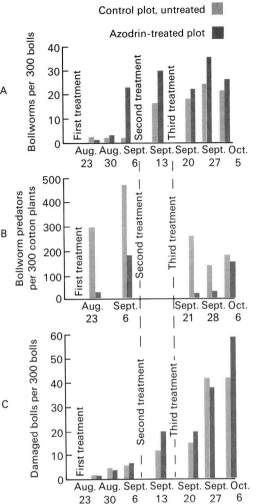

Figure 6–9 Results of experiment using Azodrin to "control" bollworms. A. Number of bollworms in untreated control plot compared with number found in plot treated with Azodrin. B. Number of bollworm predators in control plot and plot treated with Azodrin. C. Number of damaged cotton bolls in control plot and plot treated with Azodrin. These results indicate that Azodrin is more effective against bollworm predators than against bollworms, so that the pesticide treatment *increases* the damage to the crop. (After Shea, "Cotton and Chemicals," *Scientist and Citizen*, 1968, based on data from van den Bosch et al., *Pest and Disease Control Program for Cotton*, Univ. Calif. Agricultural Experiment Station, 1968.)

lations in a field, but like other organophosphates (and unlike the chlorinated hydrocarbons) it is not persistent. Its effects are devastating to populations of predatory insects. Therefore, when the field is reinvaded by pests, or when pest survivors make a comeback, their natural enemies are often absent, and overwhelming population booms of the pest may occur. Experiments by University of California entomologists clearly indicated that, rather than controlling bollworms, Azodrin applications, through their effect on the bollworms' natural enemies, actually *increased* bollworm populations in treated fields.[10] Figure 6–9 summarizes the experimental results.

Other Azodrin experiments, and the similar results obtained with the use of other broad-spectrum pesticides, make it clear that the control procedure,

[10]"Cotton and Chemicals," Kevin Shea, *Scientist and Citizen*, November 1968.

rather than helping the farmer, often has precisely the opposite effect. One might reasonably expect the pesticide manufacturer to withdraw his product, or at least warn customers and advise them how to avoid these disastrous effects. However, this was not the case. Although aware of the University's findings, Shell proceeded to mount a massive advertising campaign to promote Azodrin for use against cotton pests in California.

Shell further has been promoting the use of Azodrin on a fixed schedule, whether pests are present or not. But fixed-schedule spraying unnecessarily damages non-target organisms, destabilizes the agricultural ecosystem, and creates pest problems that otherwise would not arise. Aside from enhancing these effects, such programs of course promote the development of resistant strains of pests and the destruction of natural enemies. This guarantees the "need" for heavier and heavier doses of Azodrin. As one Azodrin advertisement put it, "even if an overpowering migration [sic] develops, the flexibility of Azodrin lets you regain control fast. Just increase the dosage according to label recommendations." The pesticide manufacturer is clearly the only beneficiary of such practices.

Insect ecologist Robert van den Bosch has written that in California a conservative estimate would be that twice as much insecticide is used as is actually needed. Since the insecticide market in California probably amounts to some $70–80 million a year, one can understand the reluctance of the petrochemical industry to see a sensible use-pattern emerge that would reduce this market by at least 50 percent.

But it would be unfair to blame the petrochemical industry alone for the misuse of pecticides. The United States Department of Agriculture has also contributed heavily to environmental deterioration by promoting pesticides, often displaying a high degree of ecological incompetence in the process. An outstanding example can be found in the history of the fire-ant program, in which the USDA, against the advice of most biologists, attempted to "exterminate" this insect over a large portion of the United States during the 1950s by spraying a huge area with chlorinated hydrocarbons. The program caused a great deal of environmental damage, but failed utterly to exterminate the fire ant. In the 1960s, following the first failure, a second fire-ant program was undertaken. Fortunately, there was even greater resistance to the new program, not only from biologists, but from other government agencies and from citizens of the affected areas. As a result, the program was not completely halted, but it was considerably reduced.

Not all pest-control programs initiated by the USDA are ecologically incompetent. Perhaps the Department's most brilliant program was that against the screwworm, a fly whose larvae (maggots) can be an extremely serious pest on cattle. Annual losses in livestock have been estimated to be as high as $40 million a year. Under the leadership of entomologist E. F. Knipling, the USDA embarked on a massive program of sterilizing male screwworm flies by irradiation and releasing them in infested areas. The female screwworm only mates once. By flooding the infested areas with sterile males, the screwworm was essentially eradicated from the southeastern United States. The effectiveness of this biological control program makes an interesting contrast with the futile and destructive fire-ant fiascos.

Alternatives to Present Patterns of Insect Control.   It is commonly claimed that only current patterns of chemical control stand between us and starvation or death from insect-borne disease. Nothing could be further from the truth. First of all, there is a wide variety of highly effective insecticides that are not persistent and that are thus much less dangerous ecologically (although some may cause considerable environmental disruption and may have much higher immediate toxicity for human beings who are using them). These nonpersistent insecticides include the organophosphates, carbamates, and botanical compounds, such as pyrethrum and rotenone. Some of these compounds may be more expensive now than the chlorinated hydrocarbons, but, if the chlorinated hydrocarbons are banned, it seems likely that the petrochemical industry will find ways to reduce the costs of producing the other compounds.

Another method of pest control, widely used long before the development of synthetic pesticides, is biological control. This method primarily involves the active encouragement or introduction of a pest's natural enemies, usually either predators or parasites. Such techniques today are favored by "organic" gardeners and farmers, but have been neglected by most farmers in industrialized countries since the introduction of DDT.

One of the most successful biological controls ever used was the introduction of vedalia beetles to attack the cottony cushion scale—a pest that threatened the existence of California's infant citrus industry in the 1880s. Complete control was achieved by the beetles in the 1890s, and no further problems arose until DDT was used on or around citrus in the 1940s. The DDT killed the vedalia beetles, and the scale insects became pests again. When DDT use was stopped and the beetles reintroduced, control of the pest was regained.

Biological controls have been tried against 223 out of about 1,000 recognized important insect pests, with some success against 55 percent of them. Clearly, much more attention should be given to promoting these ecologically more sensible techniques for keeping pest populations at a reasonable level.

The most desirable alternative of all is to shift as completely as possible to ecological pest management—to what is often called "integrated control." Integrated control has as its goal the maintenance of potential pest populations below the level at which they cause serious health hazards or economic damage. It does not attempt to exterminate pests—a goal that, incidentally, has never been accomplished by chemical control programs. Integrated control involves using one or more techniques appropriate to the particular pest situation. Mosquitos may be controlled by draining swamps in which some of the larvae live, stocking lakes with mosquito-eating fishes, applying a coat of oil, or perhaps applying small amounts of nonpersistent insecticides to any standing water that will not support fishes and cannot be drained.

Similarly, a crop could be protected by practices such as planting it in mixed cultures with other crops, destroying pest reservoirs adjacent to fields, introducing and encouraging appropriate predators and parasites, breeding more resistant crop strains, luring pests from fields with baits, and using nonpersistent insecticides. Insect development may be disrupted by the use of hormonal insecticides. These and other practices may be combined to achieve both a high level of desirable control and a minimum of damage to the ecosystems of the world. Sometimes, as in the successful screwworm program, no chemical control will be necessary; at other times chemical methods may play a major role.

Integrated control programs have been enormously successful in cases where they have been tried. Outstanding examples are the programs in alfalfa and cotton in California, which are discussed in detail in a book edited by Carl Huffaker, *Biological Control*.[11] Robert van den Bosch and his co-authors write (Chapter 17, p. 393) of the control of pests on cotton in California's Central Valley: "Existing pest-control practices are both inefficient and expensive, and because of this they are directly contributing to the economic crisis [among cotton growers]. Accumulating evidence indicates that integrated control is much more efficient and less expensive, and the hard-pressed growers are beginning to realize this."

The transition away from the relatively simple chemical techniques will require planning and training, and will perhaps produce some temporary economic stress. Since we must not delay banning the chlorinated hydrocarbons, more expensive methods may have to be used temporarily. But there is no reason that the transition should lead to serious consequences for human health or nutrition. The step would be necessary even if such consequences *were* foreseen as serious, since continued use of persistent insecticides will result sooner or later in an unprecedented catastrophe for the entire planet. In fact, in many areas positive benefits would be immediate, particularly where the development of DDT-resistant mosquitoes is reducing the effectiveness of mosquito-control programs.

Above all, the consequences of any control programs, integrated or not, require intelligent surveillance and periodic re-evaluation. *Any* tinkering with ecosystems may result in unforeseen and unpleasant consequences.

Pollutants in the Soil

The effects of pollutants on soils are difficult to evaluate. Soils are not just collections of crushed rock; they are extraordinarily complex ecosystems in

[11] Plenum Publishers, New York, 1971.

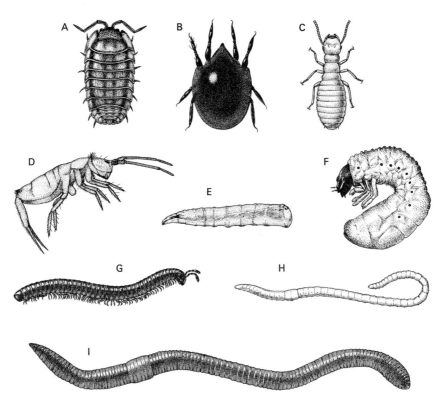

Figure 6–10 Nine soil-dwelling animals that are the chief consumers of plant debris and that are primarily responsible for the fertility of the soil. Seven of them belong to the phylum Arthropoda; they are (A) the wood louse, a crustacean; (B) the oribatid mite, an arachnid; (C) a termite, (D) a springtail, (E) a fly larva, and (F) a beetle larva, all insects; and (G) a millipede, a myriapod. The other two are worms of the phylum Annelida, (H) an enchytraeid worm; and (I) the common earthworm, the largest animal in the community. (From Edwards, "Soil Pollutants and Soil Animals." Copyright © 1969 by Scientific American, Inc. All rights reserved.)

their own right. The animals of the soil are extremely numerous and varied (Figure 6–10). In forest communities of North Carolina, an estimated 125 million small invertebrates live in each acre of soil, more than 30,000 per square meter. Some 70 percent of these are mites, a group of creatures related to insects that may eventually prove to be as diverse. In a study of pasture soils in Denmark, up to 45,000 small oligochaete worms, 10 million nematodes (roundworms), and 48,000 small insects and mites were found in each square meter. Even more abundant are the microscopic plants of the soil. More than a million bacteria of one type may be found in a gram (0.035 ounce) of forest soil, as well as almost 100,000 yeast cells, and about 50,000 bits of fungus. A gram of fertile agricultural soil has yielded over 2.5 billion bacteria, 400,000 fungi, 50,000 algae, and 30,000 protozoa.

**Table 6–1   Persistence of
Insecticides in Soils**

Insecticide	Years Since Treatment	Percent Remaining
Aldrin	14	40
Chlordane	14	40
Endrin	14	41
Heptachlor	14	16
Dilan	14	23
Isodrin	14	15
Benzene hexachloride	14	10
Toxaphene	14	45
Dieldrin	15	31
DDT	17	39

SOURCE: Nash and Woolson, *Science*, vol. 157, pp. 924–927 (1967).

In most natural situations, the plants, animals, and microorganisms of the soil are absolutely essential for its fertility. The roles that some of these organisms play in the ecology of the soil were indicated in the discussion of the nitrogen cycle. Everyone is familiar with the beneficial effects of earthworms, but most people are completely unaware of the myriad other complex (and in many cases still poorly understood) ecological relationships within the soil that make it a suitable substance for the growth of oak trees, chaparral, corn, or any other plants. The soil contains microorganisms that are responsible for the conversion of nitrogen, phosphorus, and sulfur to forms available to the plants. Many trees have been found to depend on an association with fungi. The fungi get carbohydrates and other essential substances from the roots, and the root-fungus complex is able to extract from the soil minerals that could not be extracted by the root alone. Such associations are just beginning to be understood, but it is clear that in many areas the "visible" plant community would be drastically altered if the fungi were absent from the soil.

Recognizing as they do that most of the complex physical and chemical processes responsible for soil fertility are dependent upon soil organisms, environmental biologists are appalled by continuing treatment of soils with heavy dosages of deadly and persistent poisons. Consider, for instance, a recent study of persistence of chlorinated hydrocarbons in a sandy loam soil at an experimental station.[12] Table 6–1 summarizes the results, which, because of the conditions of the study, may be close to the upper limits for persistence. Of half of these insecticides, more than one-third of the amounts applied remained in the soil 14 or more years after treatment. Under normal agricultural

[12]"Persistence of Chlorinated Hydrocarbon Pesticides in Soils," R. G. Nash and E. H. Woolson, *Science*, vol. 157, pp. 924–927, 1967.

conditions, chlorinated hydrocarbons seem to persist for 3 to 5 years, whereas organophosphates and carbamates are gone in 1 to 3 months or less.

Considerable evidence already exists that the use of insecticides may reduce soil fertility, especially in woodland soils that are subject to spraying but not to cultivation. Populations of earthworms, soil mites, and insects are dramatically changed, and these in turn affect the soil fungi, which are their principal food. Even if bacteria were not affected directly, there is no question that the general effects on the soil ecosystem would carry over to these and other microorganisms. But it would be unwarranted to assume that the bacteria are not directly affected. It is known that some microorganisms can degrade DDT to DDD under the proper conditions; a few can degrade dieldrin to aldrin and several other breakdown products of unknown toxicity. Our ignorance of the interactions of insecticides, herbicides, and other environmental poisons with soil microorganisms is immense. Our general lack of attention to the possible long-range effects of these and similar subtle problems in our environment could ultimately prove to be fatal to mankind.

Herbicides and Ecosystems

In recent years there has been an enormous upsurge in the use of herbicides as a substitute for farm machinery and labor in cultivating crops, for keeping roadsides, railroad rights of way, and powerline cuts free of shrubs. They have also been used by the military as defoliants in Vietnam. The rate of increase in herbicide use has far outstripped that of synthetic insecticides. Two kinds of herbicides are in wide use. Members of one group (2,4-D; 2,4,5-T; picloram, etc.) are similar to plant hormones and cause metabolic changes in the plant that lead to death or leaf drop (*defoliation*). The other group (simazin, monuron, and so forth) interferes with a critical process in photosynthesis, causing the plant to die from lack of energy. Although their direct toxicity to animals is low, herbicides have great impact on animal populations through their modification and eradication of plant populations, since all animals depend, at least indirectly, on plants for food. Furthermore, as a result of the coevolutionary interactions discussed earlier, many herbivorous animals are specialized to feed on one kind or just a few kinds of plants.

In the light of these considerations, it is possible to evaluate the statements that American government officials have made concerning the lack of danger to animals or the uncertainty of effects on animals of our defoliation activities in Vietnam. The reasons for concern on the part of biologists become very plain. Defoliation of tropical jungles inevitably leads to the local extinction of many populations of insects, birds, arboreal reptiles, and arboreal mammals. But, of course, "animals" in official statements can all too often be translated "elephants, tigers, and other large mammals." Figure 6–11 shows damage to Vietnamese forest from herbicide attacks, which were finally ended in 1971.

In temperate forests there is generally a less distinct canopy fauna than in tropical ones, but changes in animal populations in response to large-scale defoliation would certainly be tremendous.

Recent evidence suggests that herbicides may produce birth defects in mammals (including humans), and it has been shown that 2,4-D can kill bird embryos or induce defective or sterile young. It has been suggested that widespread use of 2,4-D may be responsible for a decline in populations of European gamebirds.

We know very little about direct effects of herbicides on soil microorganisms. Recent research in Sweden indicates that herbicides destroy bacteria that are symbiotic with legumes, although the bacteria apparently are capable of developing some resistance. Some herbicides, such as 2,4-D, are quickly degraded by bacteria and persist for only a few weeks or months; others (2,4,5-T and presumably picloram) are more persistent. Soil microorganisms (primarily bacteria and fungi) do not photosynthesize; they are consumers, not producers. Therefore, they probably are not affected by herbicides that block photosynthetic processes, although there could, of course, be other metabolic effects. Herbicides that function as simulated plant hormones are unlikely to disturb the growth processes of the soil flora, since there is no evidence that the plant hormone simulated by these substances functions in bacteria or fungi. These herbicides may of course have other physiological effects, since some are metabolized by soil bacteria.

Herbicides have also been adopted by organisms other than man. A flightless grasshopper has been discovered to secrete 2,5-dichlorophenol, apparently derived from 2,4-D, along with other naturally occurring disagreeable substances derived from plants, in its defensive fluid. This unusual ingredient appears to be very successful in discouraging predatory ants; thus, man attacking weeds inadvertently encourages a herbivore. The subtlety of the side effects of biocides is difficult to overestimate.

We know too little also about the effects of herbicides on aquatic life, but the evidence is mounting that they are substantial. Members of the group including 2,4-D particularly are toxic to fish, although less so than most insecticides, and they have also been found toxic to freshwater crustacea.

Figure 6–11 These aerial photos show the extent of damage to South Vietnamese mangrove forests from U.S. military herbicide spraying. Top photo is of an unsprayed mangrove forest about 60 miles from Saigon. Middle photo, taken in 1970, shows a once-similar forest five years after spraying. Dark spots are surviving trees. Bottom photo shows an herbicide-damaged rubber plantation about 40 miles north of Saigon. The dead trees in the foreground have been cut down. In the background, among other dead rubber trees is a plantation workers' resettlement. (Wide World Photos.)

The runoff of herbicides, especially those that interfere with photosynthesis, into inland and coastal waters could be more serious than the effects of herbicides on soil fertility. The photosynthetic processes of phytoplankton, as well as the growth of other plants, could be disturbed. Again, it is important to remember that changes in basic producer populations will inevitably affect populations higher up in the food chains.

Even with the small amount of information that exists, it is hard to be complacent about widespread indiscriminate use of herbicides under any circumstances. The spraying of potent biocides over large areas because it is easier and quicker than cultivating or weeding is a practice that ecologists can only deplore. The herbicide story may turn out to be a repetition of the insecticide story, but the case for dependence on chemicals is even weaker for weed killers. Like insecticides, they should be used with discretion and only when necessary. More attention should be paid to developing integrated control methods for weeds, and in recalcitrant cases where these methods or mechanical weeding proves infeasible, a return to weeding by human labor should be considered. Adjustment of our economic system so that more labor can be profitably employed in agriculture might help solve social and economic problems ranging from unemployment to overurbanization.

Nitrogen and Phosphates

Much of the nitrogen in natural soils is contained in humus, the organic matter of the soil. Humus is a poorly understood complex of compounds of high molecular weight. Inorganic nitrogen in such soils normally accounts for less than 2 percent of the nitrogen present; often the majority is tied up in the large organic molecules of humus, which are derived from such varied sources as the fibrous remains of woody plant tissues, insect skeletons, and animal manure. These substances, in addition to their chemical value, increase the capacity of the soil to retain water. The presence of humus makes the soil a favorable medium for the complicated chemical reactions and mineral transport needed for the growth of higher plants. Bacteria in the soil decompose humus to form nitrates and other nutrient substances required by plant roots.

Roots require oxygen in order to do the work necessary for the uptake of nitrates and other nutrients, but oxygen is not available if the soil is tightly compacted. Thus another important benefit of humus is to maintain soil porosity and so permit oxygen to penetrate to the roots of plants.

In natural soil systems the nitrogen cycle is "tight." Not much nitrogen is removed from the soil by leaching or surface runoff. It has been shown experimentally that by maintaining the supply of humus the fertility of the soil can be perpetuated. This is not possible when fertilizers containing inorganic nitrogen are employed, unless organic carbon (in such forms as sawdust or straw) is supplied to the soil microorganisms. The undesirable decline of humus which often occurs under inorganic fertilization is due to the failure of the farmer to return crop residues (and thus carbon) to his fields. The decline is not caused by any deficiency in the fertilizers themselves. Indeed, if carbon is supplied in the proper proportion with inorganic nitrogen, the supply of humus can be increased and the quality of the soil improved.

If attempts are made to maintain soil fertility by continued applications of inorganic nitrogen fertilizers alone, the capacity of the soil to retain nitrogen is reduced as its humus content drops. In humus, nitrogen is combined into nonsoluble forms that are not leached from the soil by rainwater. Depletion of humus "loosens" the soil cycles and permits large amounts of nitrate to be flushed into rivers and lakes. The use of inorganic fertilizers in the United States has been multiplied some twelvefold in the past 25 years. One result of this dramatic increase has been a concomitant rise in the content of nitrate in surface water, atmosphere, and rain. Another has been a 50 percent reduction of the original organic nitrogen content of Midwestern soils.

The results of the added nitrogen content of our waters are exemplified in part by the now well-documented fate of Lake Erie. The waters of Lake Erie are so polluted that the U.S. Public Health Service has urged ships on the lake not to use lake water taken within 5 miles of the United States shore. The water is so badly contaminated that neither boiling nor chlorination will purify it; although the organisms in it would be killed, the dangerous chemicals it contains would not be removed or broken down.

The sources of Lake Erie's pollution are many. A report to the Federal Water Pollution Control Agency in the late 1960s cited as the main source of pollution the raw sewage dumped into the lake by lakeside municipalities, especially Cleveland, Toledo, and Euclid, Ohio; and Wayne County (Detroit), Michigan. The report cited industry as another major source of pollution, and named the Ford Motor Company, Republic Steel, and Bethlehem Steel as significant polluters. Finally, the basin of Lake Erie contains an estimated 30,000 square miles of farmland, and another important source of pollution is runoff from these farmlands.

Let us examine the last source first. The waters draining the farmlands of the Middle West are rich in nitrogen as a result of the heavy use of inorganic nitrogen fertilizers. Indeed, they have an estimated nitrogen content equivalent to the sewage of some 20,000,000 people—*about twice the total human population of the Lake Erie basin.* Thus, besides fertilizing their farms with nitrogen, the farmers are also fertilizing Lake Erie; their nitrogen contribution is of the same order of magnitude as that of the municipalities and the industrial pollutors. The nitrogen balance of the lake has been seriously disturbed, and the abundance of inorganic nitrates encourages the growth of certain algae. In recent years these algae have produced monstrous blooms—big masses of algae that grow extremely quickly, cover huge areas, foul beaches, and then die.

The bacterial decay of these masses of algae consumes oxygen, reducing the amount of oxygen available for fishes and other animals. Such blooms and oxygen depletions are characteristic of lakes undergoing *eutrophication*, which may be loosely translated as "overfertilization." Phosphates, as well as nitrates, are implicated in this problem. Phosphate levels in U.S. surface waters have increased 27-fold in recent years. Sources include fertilizer run-off and industrial waste, but 60 percent of the phosphate entering U.S. waters comes from municipal sewage. The primary source of phosphates in sewage is household detergents.

The basic sequence of eutrophication is simple in outline. Inorganic nitrates and phosphates are washed into the lake and converted into organic forms as huge blooms of algae develop. The subsequent decomposition of the algae depletes water of oxygen and kills off animals that have high oxygen requirements. Much of the nitrate and phosphate remains in the lake, settling to the bottom with the decaying mass of algae. The bottom of Lake Erie now has a layer of muck that varies from 20 to 125 feet in thickness; this layer is immensely rich in phosphorous and nitrogen compounds. These compounds are bound by a "skin" of insoluble iron compounds that covers the mud. Unfortunately, the iron compounds change to a more soluble form in the absence of oxygen. Thus the oxygen depletion itself may cause the release into the lake of more of the nutrients responsible for the lake's troubles, and eutrophication may take place even more rapidly. If this breaking down of the mud skin should continue and result in the release of large amounts of nitrogen and phosphorus, the lake may face a disaster that would dwarf its present troubles.

Lake Erie is just one outstanding example of a general problem that is well known to most Americans — the gross pollution of our lakes, rivers, and streams. All manner of organic and inorganic wastes end up in our inland waters: raw sewage, manure, paunch manure (the stomach contents of slaughtered animals), detergents, acids, pesticides, garbage; the list goes on and on. All of these substances affect the life in the water, all too often exterminating much of it, and at the very least modifying the ecosystems in profound ways. This pollution problem is worldwide; many of the rivers of the Earth are quickly approaching the "too thin to plow and too thick to drink" stage.

In the United States and some other areas, serious attempts have been made to clean up fresh-water systems. These have met with mixed success. It is impossible to know whether we are gaining, holding our own, or losing at the moment, but the situation is bad, and the outlook for the future in the United States is not encouraging.

The eutrophication problems in the United States have now even spread to estuarine and inshore waters where sewage is dumped. Many oyster and clam beds have been damaged or destroyed, and some fisheries have all but disappeared. Oxygen depletion and accompanying changes in water quality have been shown to induce marked destabilizing changes in local marine ecosystems.

Similar problems exist in many other parts of the world. Lake Baikal in the Soviet Union seems slowly to be headed for a fate similar to Lake Erie's, despite the protests of Russian conservationists. Many lakes and rivers in Europe and Asia are beginning to show signs of eutrophication, often within 10 to 20 years after the start of human pollution. Parts of the Rhine River may be too polluted to support life by 1973. Strenuous efforts to curb pollution in the Rhine and its tributaries have been outstripped by the growth in the volume of pollutants. The rivers in Italy are so badly polluted that Italian scientists fear that marine life in the Mediterranean is endangered.

In most UDCs, rivers are simply open sewers. Eutrophication is not usually a problem there except in a few areas where some industrial development has taken place. However, the Green Revolution, with its required high levels of fertilization, may change the situation.

Inorganic nitrate and phosphate fertilizers must be considered a technological success because they do succeed in raising the amounts of free nutrients in the soil, but it is precisely this success that has led to eutrophication as those nutrients are leached out of the soil by groundwater. It has been predicted that in 25 to 50 years the ultimate crisis in agriculture will occur in the United States. Either the fertility of the soil will drop precipitously, because inorganic fertilizers will be withheld, throwing the nation into a food crisis, or the amounts of inorganic nitrates and phosphates applied to the land will be so great as to cause an intractable water-pollution problem. One would hope that before this comes to pass the rate of fertilizer use will be moderated and laws will require return to the soil of plant residues or other means of supplying the organic carbon necessary to build humus. Even these steps might not avert a water crisis produced by two other technological successes: high-compression automobile engines, which produce an inorganic nitrogen fall-out, and modern sewage-treatment plants, which produce an effluent rich in inorganic nitrates and phosphates. The significance of these inorganic nutrients has only recently been widely recognized.

In the light of these and many other assaults on the environment, it would behoove us to begin immediately to head off future threats. As is becoming apparent, use of the internal combustion engine will have to be greatly reduced. It is imperative that either our present sewage treatment plants be completely redesigned to eliminate nutrients from the effluent, or that a way be found to reclaim the nutrients for fertilizer. Also needed are new sewage plants for the many communities that still pour raw sewage into our waters. Such a program requires money and effort, some of which might be provided immediately by employing the Army Corps of Engineers and the Bureau of Reclamation for such projects.

The problem of controlling the runoff of nutrients from farms is more difficult, but it is known that nitrates leach from soil because they are anions (negatively charged groups of atoms), and the capacity of the soil to retain anions is low. Mixing a resin with high binding affinity for anions into the soil would increase its capacity to hold nitrates. Certainly, experimental work in this area should be initiated immediately, but "solutions" of this sort must be monitored very carefully. Often they have a tendency to create problems more serious than those they solve.

A more immediately available approach to controlling agricultural runoff might be to halt by law the practice of handling manure from farm animals as a waste product. Roughly 80 percent of American cattle are produced on feedlots, (Figure 6–12), and most of their manure is treated as sewage, which more than doubles the sewage volume of the nation. Even if costs prove to be higher, manure should be returned to the land to help build humus.

Sterile, concentrated sewage (sludge) can also be used to improve soil. Sludge from Chicago is now being employed to restore strip-mined land in southern Illinois. Crops are being grown very successfully on the reclaimed

Figure 6–12   A large cattle feedlot in California. The wastes from such congregations of animals result in serious sewage problems in many agricultural areas. (Photo by William A. Garnett.)

land. Recycled sewage has long been used as fertilizer in England, Australia, and other countries with excellent results. The prejudices of American farmers seem to be the major obstacle to the development of similar practices in the United States on a wide scale.

Pollutants and Oceanic Ecosystems

The effects of insecticides and other poisonous substances in water are not confined to aquatic animals. Perhaps the most frightening ecological news of 1968 was contained in a short paper entitled "DDT Reduces Photosynthesis by Marine Phytoplankton," which was published in the journal *Science*.[13] The author, environmental scientist Charles F. Wurster, reported that DDT reduced photosynthesis in both experimental cultures and natural communities of marine phytoplankton (algae, diatoms, and so forth), the tiny green plants that float free in the waters of the oceans. Effects were noted at DDT concentrations of only a few parts per billion (ppb), quantities that are commonly found in waters near land sites treated with DDT. Water at a distance from treatment sites ordinarily has DDT concentrations averaging less than 1 ppb, but biological systems clearly can and do amplify these amounts.

The effects of DDT on phytoplankton in nature are difficult to evaluate. Phytoplankton are the primary producers responsible for most of the food mankind takes from the sea. If photosynthesis were significantly reduced in marine phytoplankton, the amount of life in the sea would be reduced; if marine photosynthesis ceased, all sea life would die. But significant qualitative changes in the phytoplankton community seem a more probable effect of DDT than large quantitative changes. Phytoplankton populations are differentially susceptible to DDT; even extremely low DDT concentrations might result in shifts of dominance, leading to huge blooms of one or a few species. These shifts would in turn, produce serious consequences throughout oceanic food webs. One possibility is that phytoplankton less acceptable to large herbivores would dominate, so that larger animals would be affected. This shortening of food chains might leave man only microscopic plants and animals as a source of food from the sea. Another possibility is that phytoplankton communities near the shore could become dominated by smaller species, lengthening food chains and dramatically reducing the size of populations of fishes at the upper trophic levels.

Similarly, the problems besetting our inland waters (discussed above) may be aggravated by the effects of DDT on freshwater phytoplankton. As Wurster wrote, "Such effects are insidious and their cause may be obscure, yet they may be ecologically more important than the obvious, direct mortality of larger organisms that is so often reported."

[13]Vol. 158, pp. 1474–1475.

Another pollutant was found in 1970 to reduce photosynthesis in phytoplankton, both marine and freshwater. This was mercury, which in organic forms such as methylmercury proved to be extremely toxic to these tiny plants. Photosynthesis was significantly inhibited at concentrations in water of 0.1 ppb, one-fiftieth the amount now tolerated by U.S. Public Health standards (5 ppb). When concentrations reached 50 ppb, growth essentially stopped completely. Mercury's effects on phytoplankton resemble those of DDT; like the chorinated hydrocarbons, it also tends to be concentrated in food chains. Thus, its potential impact on oceanic food webs may be serious and of a similar nature to that of DDT. Enough inorganic mercury has already accumulated on lake and stream beds in North America to provide a serious mercury threat (if converted to the soluble organic form) to freshwater and estuarine life for decades to come, unless a way is found to remove it. San Francisco Bay alone was estimated by the U.S. Geological Survey in 1971 to have some 58 tons of mercury on its bottom, with concentrations ranging from 0.25 to 6.4 parts per *million* parts of bottom sediment.

The long-term ecological effects in the seas of other heavy metals, such as lead, cadmium, and chromium, are not known. But since they are known to be toxic to many forms of life, it would be unreasonable to assume their effects to be negligible.

One ocean pollutant that has received a great deal of publicity, mainly because much of it is the result of spectacular accidents, is oil. In 1970, when Thor Heyerdahl sailed a papyrus raft across the Atlantic Ocean, he reported that, "Clots of oil are polluting the mid-stream current of the Atlantic Ocean from horizon to horizon." The oil has reached the sea in a variety of ways. Among them are the massive accidental spills from tankers that have received so much publicity, as well as many smaller spills. These probably account for less than 0.1 percent of the total oil transported at sea. But that total volume is so huge, about 360 billion gallons per year (60 percent of all sea-transported goods), that the spills amount to a considerable quantity. Still more is spilled as fuel oil from ships not involved in transporting oil, especially in connection with refueling operations, and is discharged from the pumping of bilges. In addition to shipping spills, there are accidents in extraction from sea-floor drilling, of which the Santa Barbara leak is the best known example. Finally, some oil reaches the sea in sewage wastes. Natural oil pollution of the oceans occurs from undersea faults and joints. But this is greatly outweighed by the quantities now injected, accidentally or otherwise, by mankind.[14]

The potential effects of oil pollution on oceanic ecosystems, beyond the immediate and obvious decimation of populations of fish, shellfish, and sea birds at the site (Figure 6–13), are now being discovered, thanks to a relatively small spill that occurred in 1969 near the Wood's Hole Oceanographic Institute in Massachusetts. Effects vary with the type of oil, the distance from shore where it is spilled, how long it can "weather" (be degraded by micro-

---

[14]See "Oil Pollution" by Gene Coan in *Sierra Club Bulletin*, March 1971, pp. 13–16. Coan describes Blumer's findings as well as other aspects of pollution from oil spills.

Figure 6–13 An aerial photograph of the 1971 oil spill from a tanker collision in San Francisco Bay. Some of the oil has already washed out the Golden Gate to the left. One tanker is in the center of the picture, Sausalito to the upper left, Angel Island and the Richmond–San Rafael Bridge to the upper right, and Alcatraz Island to the lower right. Lower photographs show volunteers cleaning a beach fouled by the spilled oil and some of the birds that were killed. (Top, courtesy of Western Aerial Photos, Inc.; lower left, photo by Klink, Photofind, S.F.; lower right, photo by Robert Schen, Photofind, S.F.)

organisms, dissolve, and evaporate) before reaching shore, and what organisms live there. Some components of oil are toxic, others are known carcinogens; weathering can reduce their toxicity, but the carcinogenic components are long-lasting. Oil washed to shore lingers on rocks and sand for months or years, but the marine life may need a decade or more to recover, even after the oil is no longer obvious.

Entire populations of some sea birds, especially the diving birds, which are most susceptible, have been drastically reduced in recent years, probably largely due to oil contamination. Besides killing thousands of them directly, oil toxins may also reduce egg viability and affect reproduction in these birds.

Detergents used to clean up oil spills have been found to make the situation worse in many cases. Not only are the detergents themselves toxic to many forms of life, they disperse the oil and spread it into new areas. They may also, by breaking up the oil into droplets, render it more easily absorbable by small marine organisms.

Immediately after the Massachusetts spill, there was a 95 percent mortality of fish, shellfish, worms, and other sea animals. Nine months later, repopulation had still not taken place. Surviving mussels failed to reproduce. Some constituents of the oil were still present and killing bottom-dwelling organisms 8 months later. Surviving shellfish and oysters took in enough oil to be inedible and retained it even months after distant transplanting. According to marine biologist Max Blumer, there is a possibility that the carcinogenic constituents of oil, absorbed unchanged by phytoplankton and other small organisms, may in time be incorporated into and contaminate entire food chains.[15] Thus there is a chance that at levels too low to alter the flavor and aroma of seafoods, some of these oil components could invade a substantial part of the human diet.

Some effort is being made to develop bacterial strains that can quickly degrade spilled oil; more efficient technical means of collecting it before it reaches shore are also being studied. In view of the amount of oil already polluting the oceans and the increasing potential for further spills represented by the rising volume of oil transportation by sea and the increasing size of tankers, efforts to deal with such accidents should be vigorously pursued. At the same time much can be done in the area of prevention without further research. Oil can and should be removed from sewage; safety regulations both for drilling platforms and tankers can be tightened and enforced; the flushing of tankers can be prohibited, and other ships can be forbidden to waste or discard oil products of any kind.

No one knows how long we can continue to pollute the seas with chlorinated hydrocarbon insecticides, polychlorinated biphenyls, oil, mercury, cadmium, and thousands of other pollutants, without bringing on a collapse of ocean productivity. Subtle changes may already have started a chain reaction in that direction, as shown by declines in many fisheries, especially those

---

[15]*Ibid.*

in areas of heavy pollution caused by dumping of wastes. There is now an international movement toward regulation of ocean dumping.

Pollutants and the Atmosphere

Because the atmosphere is maintained in its present state to a large degree by biological systems, it is an indicator of the health of all ecosystems — in fact, of the entire ecosphere. The climate in a given area is partly a function of the organisms in that area, primarily the plants. The pattern of airflow near the ground is affected by the presence or absence of forests. The amount of water vapor in the air, the rates at which the ground heats up during the day, and thus the occurrence of updrafts, vary according to the vegetation that is present.

Many air pollutants, including hydrofluoric acid, sulfur dioxide, ozone, and ethylene, injure or kill plants, and these changes in plant life lead to drastic changes in the animal populations dependent upon the plants. Other dangerous air pollutants that can also upset ecological systems are the nitrogen oxides. It is thought that the eutrophication of Lake Mendota in Wisconsin is largely attributable to phosphates, but part of the problem can be traced to the automobiles of nearby Madison; rains deposit heavy amounts of nitrogen from auto exhausts, and the nitrogen ends up in the lake. In New Jersey the rains annually bring to earth an estimated 25 pounds of nitrogen per acre from industrial and automobile sources. Where this lands on soil it amounts to very modest fertilization and is a benefit to the vegetation — a rare example of a positive effect from pollution.

Ecologists are very concerned about changes in the atmosphere that may occur, or may be occurring, as a result of human interference with the Earth's complex biogeochemical cycles. The possible effects of general atmospheric pollution on the climate will be discussed below. But human influence on biogeochemical cycles could pose other lethal threats. Picture, for instance, what would happen if one of the biocides that we are adding to our environment should show a special lethality for microorganisms that live by degrading ammonia to nitrites in the soil. The death of these microorganisms could be followed not only by a serious decline in soil fertility but by a buildup of poisonous ammonia in the atmosphere.

On the average, the amount of oxygen produced by photosynthesis is balanced to within one part in 10,000 by the amount consumed when the plant matter is later metabolized in the food chain or by decomposers. The accumulation of oxygen in the atmosphere took place over hundreds of millions of years, and resulted from the relatively exceptional circumstances in which carbon fixed in photosynthesis was preserved in sediments without being oxidized. This is the origin of graphite in older geological deposits and fossil fuels in younger ones. Because the production and consumption of oxygen in photosynthesis and decay is so nearly in balance on a year-to-year basis, and because of the vast reservoir of atmospheric oxygen that has been built up over geological time, there is no danger that man's destruction of forests and other plant communities will cause an oxygen shortage. In the short term, plants are most needed as the basis of everything we eat, rather than as sources of oxygen.

The most substantial drain on atmospheric oxygen comes from the combustion of the fossil fuels. However, given the present estimates of how much of the fossil fuels will actually prove to be exploitable, even this effect is negligible. The 1970 M.I.T. Study of Critical Environmental Problems concluded that the combustion of all known exploitable reserves of fossil fuels would reduce the atmospheric concentration of oxygen by only fifteen-hundredths of 1 percent.[16] Clearly, the central issue in the quality of the atmosphere is not changes in the concentrations of the two main constituents, nitrogen and oxygen. Rather, the dangers lie in the addition of poisonous or otherwise significant trace contaminants. The carbon dioxide produced by combustion of all the fossil fuels, for example, could have a measurable effect on world climate.

Thermal Pollution and Local Climates. Thermal pollution, as the term is most often applied today, refers to waste heat from the generation of electrical power. The adverse consequences of discharging such heat to rivers, lakes, and estuaries is indeed a matter for serious concern, but it is only one aspect of a more fundamental problem. Specifically, *all* human activities—from metabolism to driving (and stopping) an automobile—result in the dissipation of energy as heat. In the case of a power plant, the heat delivered to the environment ultimately includes not only the waste heat at the site, but all the useful output as well: the electricity itself is transformed to heat in wires, filaments, the bearings in electric motors, and so forth. That all the energy we use—electrical and otherwise—is eventually degraded to heat is a consequence of the Second Law of Thermodynamics (see Box 3–1); no technological gimmickry or scientific breakthrough can be expected to relieve this constraint. Thus the thermal load imposed upon the surroundings where energy is consumed can be moderated only by manipulating the number of consumers or the per capita consumption. Of course, the thermal load at the place where power is generated can be reduced somewhat by devising more efficient power plants.

The consequences of man's introduction of heat into his environment can usefully be classified as local, regional, and global. Local effects (cities, the vicinities of power plants) are already prevalent, although not always well understood. Regional effects (river basins, coastlines) could become important before the turn of the century; their exact form is speculative. Global thermal effects could become significant within 70–100 years if current rates of increase persist. They will be considered in the next section, together with the climatic consequences of man's input into the atmosphere of CO_2, particulate matter, and aircraft contrails.

[16]*Man's Impact on the Global Environment*, Report of the Study of Critical Environmental Problems, M.I.T. Press, 1970.

The climate of cities differs appreciably from that of the surrounding countryside in several respects, due in part to the dissipation of heat from the human activities concentrated there. The annual mean temperature in cities in the U.S. is .9 to 1.4° F higher than that in rural surroundings, cloudiness and precipitation are 5 to 10 percent greater, and fog is 30 to 100 percent more prevalent. In the Los Angeles Basin, the rate of energy dissipation by man is equal to 5.5 percent of the solar energy absorbed over the same area.[17] However, it is difficult to separate the climatic consequences of the dissipation of heat from other man-induced effects that accompany it (for example, the haze of gaseous and particulate pollutants for which Los Angeles is noted).

Better understood and more clearly dangerous thermal effects are those at the installations where electrical power is generated. All such plants in commercial operation today, whether powered by fossil fuels or nuclear fission, employ a steam cycle that, at the condenser stage, transfers heat to water. The water is warmed by from 12° to 25° F. The 2000 cubic feet per second of water needed for one of today's larger plants amounts to the entire flow of a moderate sized stream.

There are several effects of an increase in water temperature on aquatic life. The dissolved oxygen content of the water is reduced while the metabolic rate of its animal inhabitants increases. Thus, when the animals need more oxygen, they have less available. Some die forthwith, others become more susceptible to chemical toxins or disease. Bacterial decomposition is accelerated, further diminishing the dissolved oxygen content. The ultimate consequences of artificial warming are a reduction in species diversity (with the large species of greatest benefit to man usually being the first to go) and a reduction in the ability of the water to absorb organic waste.

Nuclear-fission power plants present these problems to a greater degree than do their fossil-fueled counterparts, because, at the present stage of technology, the former are thermally less efficient; that is, they produce more heat per unit of electricity. Modern coal-fired plants operate near 40 percent efficiency, fission plants at about 32 percent. This 8 percent difference in overall efficiency means that a nuclear plant discharges about 40 percent more waste heat at the site than does a fossil-fueled plant. Moreover, about 25 percent of the fossil-fueled plant's discharged heat goes up the stack, further reducing the burden on aquatic systems.

It is possible to transfer *all* of the waste heat to the atmosphere at either type of plant, but power companies claim that this is expensive. Cooling ponds require 2 acres of land per megawatt of installed capacity, the cost varying with location. Evaporative cooling towers increase construction costs by some 4 percent and operating costs by 10 percent. Closed-cycle cooling towers increase construction costs by perhaps 12 percent and operating costs by an amount not

---

[17]The figures on heat and those on temperature, cloudiness, precipitation and fog are from *Inadvertent Climate Modification*, Report of the Study of Man's Impact on Climate, M.I.T. Press, Cambridge, Mass., 1971. This is the best source on most aspects of man's influence on climate.

yet established. In no case, however, should such measures increase the actual price of electricity to consumers by more than about 5 percent. This is so partly because generation costs are only half the cost of delivered electricity, the rest being accounted for by transmission and distribution.

In considering regional effects, the distinction between discharging waste heat to bodies of water or into the atmosphere with cooling towers or ponds becomes less important. The principal concern here is that man's energy input will become a significant climatic perturbation over large areas, and this can occur whether the heat goes into water (and, inevitably, into the atmosphere eventually) or directly into the atmosphere.

It should also be emphasized that such measures as heating homes and apartments with the warm effluent of power plants or using it for irrigation in cold climates do not completely solve even local thermal pollution problems. No matter how it is used, the heat ultimately reaches the atmosphere, where it contributes to the regional heat balance. Also, if it is used to heat buildings, it will contribute to the urban thermal effects mentioned above. However, using waste heat this way does help with the larger problem to the extent that it substitutes for other heating, reducing overall fuel consumption and hence the environmental heat load. For these reasons, using waste heat from power plants for residential heating or irrigation is worth doing where it is feasible. Finally, as already suggested, all of man's *useful* energy consumption must be added to the waste heat from power plants in the reckoning of regional climatic effects.

In posing the thermal pollution question for systems larger than a single stretch of river or coastline, some observers have reassured themselves by comparing mankind's contribution with the input of energy from the sun. Such analyses overlook the fact that climate is the result of numerous powerful forces operating in a rather finely tuned balance. Put another way, the climate we perceive often results from small differences in large forces. Thus, the important determinants of regional climate include: (a) the variation of solar heating with latitude, (b) the winds and ocean currents driven by this variation in solar heating, (c) the variation in the heat balance between land and adjacent bodies of water, (d) the role of river systems, lakes, bays, and oceans as thermal buffers, and (e) updrafts over mountain ranges. While many of the complexities of the meteorological system are still not understood, a few observations indicate that man's energy input will soon be a force to be reckoned with on these sorts of scales.

For example, if the trends of the past 20 years persist for another 10 to 15 years, one-fourth of the annual freshwater runoff of the United States could be employed in the cooling of electric-power stations (the problem will not be quite this bad, since some plants will be located on the seacoast). But, since much of the runoff occurs in short flood seasons, the relevant number for 1980 is actually one-half of the *normal* flow. Projecting the same trends for 30 years, to about the year 2000, shows that the equivalent cooling demand will correspond to raising the *entire* annual runoff of the United States by 20° F. (Consumption of electric power in the United States is doubling roughly every 10 years). In view of the role of river systems in determining regional climates and the economic and aesthetic importance of their aquatic life, these numbers are not comforting.

Finally, heavily populated regions such as the Boston-to-Washington megalopolis seem likely to be in climatic difficulty by the turn of the century, even according to the conservative criterion that compares man's energy input to the sun's. In a review of manmade climatic changes, meterologist Helmut E. Landsberg cites projections that, by the year 2000, "Boswash" (the Boston-Washington complex) will contain 56 million people on 30,000 square kilometers, dissipating heat at a rate equal to 50 percent of the solar power received at the surface in winter, and 15 percent in summer.[18]

Global Climate and Human Influences.   Global climate cannot be thoroughly understood without a study of atmospheric physics and circulation patterns far too complicated to be presented here. Nevertheless, some of the most important phenomena and their vulnerability to interference by mankind can be illustrated in terms of a simplified energy balance for the Earth-atmosphere system. Most of the sun's energy reaches the top of the Earth's atmosphere in the form of radiation of relatively short wavelengths—namely, visible and near-ultraviolet light. About 35 percent of this incident radiation is returned directly to space, either by reflection from clouds, dust particles in the atmosphere, and the surface of the Earth, or by scattering from the air itself. The total reflectivity of the planet due to all these contributors is called the *albedo*. Clouds reflect an average of 50 to 60 percent of the light that actually strikes them, and the surface of the Earth reflects 5 to 10 percent. The local surface value depends strongly on the angle of the sun and on the terrain: deserts reflect more than farmland and forests, and ice and snow may reflect as much as 90 percent.

Of the incoming solar energy not directly reflected, about 30 percent is absorbed by the atmosphere and warms it; 35 percent evaporates water at the surface and is released to the atmosphere when the water vapor later condenses to become rain; and 35 percent is absorbed by and warms the ground or surface of the sea. On an annual average over the whole Earth, of course, as much energy must leave as enters. If this were not true, the planet would be steadily warming up. The energy leaves as long-wavelength infrared radiation emanating from the surface and from the atmosphere. The atmosphere's role here is very important. Water vapor, water droplets, and carbon dioxide in the atmosphere absorb infrared radiation outbound from the Earth's surface and re-radiate about half of it back downward. If this "trapping" of heat did not occur, the surface of the Earth would have an average temperature around $-10°$ F instead of about $+60°$ F.

[18]"Man-made Climatic Changes," Helmut E. Landsberg, *Science*, vol. 170, pp. 1265–1274, 1970.

This phenomenon of heating, which is due to the differential transparency of the atmosphere to long and short wavelengths, is called the *greenhouse effect*. Glass in a greenhouse lets light in, but absorbs the infrared radiated by the warmed plants and soil of the greenhouse. The glass reradiates some of the infrared back into the greenhouse, which is one reason that greenhouses normally have higher daytime temperatures than their surroundings (that the glass shelters the interior from the wind is also a factor). Similarly, cloudy nights tend to be warmer than cloudless nights, other things being equal. At night the Earth's surface radiates heat accumulated during the day, and clouds absorb part of the heat and reradiate it toward the surface, adding to the greenhouse effect. Clouds thus play an important dual role in the heat balance, contributing to the albedo during the day and to the greenhouse effect night and day.

That is a simplified outline of the major factors affecting the average temperature of the Earth's surface. Energy from the sun is partly reflected and partly absorbed by the surface. In the process of absorption the surface is warmed and radiates infrared radiation, part of which is trapped by the greenhouse effect. Calculations based on this simplified picture show that, if present rates of increase in human energy use persist for about a century, the mean global surface temperature would increase by more than a degree Fahrenheit.

As has already been observed, of course, the average temperature is not the whole story of climate. Many other factors determine how the energy received from the sun actually drives the global weather system. These are not entirely understood, but it is known that differential heating is very important, especially the degree of contrast between the equator and the poles. This means that the probable continued input of most of man's energy dissipation in the temperate latitudes could have effects much greater than if the dissipation were evenly distributed. It also means that raising the overall temperature of the planet a degree or two would not necessarily mean a warmer climate for all the world's population. The main effect might be to speed up circulation patterns and to bring arctic cold farther south and antarctic cold farther north.

Man has the potential of altering global climate significantly even before his thermal impact becomes important, however. For instance, when fossil fuels are burned, carbon dioxide (CO_2) is added to the atmosphere, and CO_2 contributes to the greenhouse effect described above. Since 1880 the CO_2 content of the atmosphere has increased about 12 percent, and until the 1940s there was a concomitant rise in temperature. All of this increase in CO_2 may not be accounted for by burning of fossil fuels, since some increase in the amount of radioactive carbon (carbon-14) in the atmosphere has been reported. Much more carbon-14 is present in living and recently dead plant materials than in fossil fuels. Therefore the release of CO_2 by burning of fossil fuels would not significantly increase the atmospheric load of carbon-14. Part of the increase in CO_2 undoubtedly has come from agricultural burning, and part from the slow oxidation of peat bogs which occurred as the climate warmed.

The whole CO_2 picture is made immensely complex by interactions between the atmospheric pool of CO_2 and plant life (which uses CO_2 in photosynthesis) and the oceans (which absorb CO_2 at different rates in different areas). Unquestionably, man is influencing the climate when his activities add CO_2 to the atmosphere, but the degree and significance of that influence are uncertain.

Since the 1940s there appears to have been a slight decline in the average temperature of the Earth, in spite of a continued increase in the CO_2 content of the atmosphere. This could have been a result of increases in the albedo caused by volcanic ash, dust, other particulate pollution, and also increased cloud cover produced by the contrails of high-flying jet aircraft. This increase in reflectivity may have more than counterbalanced the increased greenhouse effect from the CO_2. These effects are at present difficult to pin down unequivocally. The "average temperature of the Earth" is itself an elusive quantity, because of the limited number and distribution of measurement stations, and because large year-to-year fluctuations that vary from one region to another tend to mask trends. One should scarcely take comfort from our ignorance in these matters, although some people do—apparently on the grounds that what we don't know won't hurt us.

One major source of atmospheric dust is agriculture; thus food-growing activities could, in principle, change the weather. Automobiles, aircraft, power plants, trash burning, deforestation (leading to wind-erosion of soil) and many other devices and activities of mankind add to the turbidity of the atmosphere.

Many experts believe that at this time the influence of volcanic activity on climate is still greater than the effect of man's contribution of particulate matter. A look into history can give us some idea of what might be in store if particulate pollution continues to increase or if there should be an upsurge in volcanic activity. In 1815, the eruption of Mount Tambora on the island of Sumbawa in Indonesia put an estimated 150 cubic kilometers of ash into the atmosphere. The climatic effects were staggering. In 1816 there was "no summer" in the northern United States, and the English summer was one of record cold. The mean July temperature in England was 13.4° C (56° F), in contrast with a 250-year average of 15.7° C (61° F). In fact, the three coldest decades in England's summary weather statistics were 1781–1790, 1811–1820, and 1881–1890, the decades of the eruptions of Mount Asama in Japan and Mount Skaptar in Iceland (both 1783), Mount Tambora (1815), and Krakatoa (1883). It is sobering to consider what a Tambora-scale eruption today would do the world food supply.

Increases in the planetary albedo resulting from man's activities are not limited to those caused by particulate pollution. Contrails, the long thin clouds produced by the passage of high flying aircraft, also add to the albedo. Contrails often dissipate rather rapidly, but sometimes they apparently trigger the formation of high cirrus clouds.

Unfortunately, it is impossible to predict exactly what will happen to the overall temperature of the Earth over the next few decades, or what the local effects of changes will be. We are especially ignorant of trigger or threshold effects in climatic systems. An increase in a mean summer temperature from 16° C to 18° C might produce little effect, but a further .5° C rise to 18.5° C might bring on a catastrophe. Moreover, it is not even known whether the amount of radiation produced by the sun is a constant — and that is essential information if changes in the heat budget of the planet are ever to be predicted. As a result, although we can be certain that man is affecting the climate (and probably accelerating change), we cannot yet isolate man's contribution to changes we observe.

Climate, of course, is an ever-changing thing. The past million and a half years have shown a pattern of glacial advances and retreats, changes in sea level, changes in rainfall pattern, and so forth — all having tremendous impact on the men alive at the time. Many areas of our planet show the traces of mankind flooded out, frozen out, or forced to migrate because of drought. The man-induced climatic changes that now seem possible might be viewed merely as a continuation of age-old processes of change and therefore held to involve risks that have always been present in one form or another. But, unhappily, there is a difference. At just the time that man has populated the planet to the point of stretching his food resources to the maximum, he is almost certainly accelerating climatic changes. When climate changes, so must agriculture, and man is conservative in his agricultural behavior. Consequently, any *rapid* change of climate in whatever direction is certain to decrease food supply. Should rapidly accelerating air pollution, a new volcanic incident, or civilization's heat production perturb climate enough to damage the Northern Hemisphere's granaries, enormous famines would be inevitable.

Ecological Accounting

Many existing and potential forms of ecological disruption have been described in this chapter, sometimes in rather technical detail. It may be helpful to review at this point the relevance of these considerations to human welfare. In other words, just what could an ecological catastrophe mean for human beings?

The various ways the biosphere supports human life were outlined at the beginning of the chapter. The loss of one or more of these vital services would kill or seriously impair the health of a significant fraction of the human population. Such a loss could be the result of any large-scale ecological breakdown. As we have seen, there is a great variety of possible causes for such a breakdown, but there are relatively few forms that its human consequences can take. Probably the most likely of these would be a widespread shortage of food. This could result from the disruption of oceanic food webs, from progressive loss of soil fertility or of soil itself, from outbreaks of crop pests brought about by misuse of pesticides, from crop failures initiated by changed climate conditions or plant diseases attacking vast monocultures, or from a combination of such factors.

Perhaps the second most likely event would be a deterioration of public health resulting from an accumulation of toxic or disease-harboring substances at overloaded links in nutrient cycles (for instance, surface waters overloaded with organic matter or the accumulation of nitrites in ground water and soil), and including the possibility of epidemic disease.

A third might be a dramatic rise in the incidence of birth defects and cancers, brought about by the individual or combined effects of the array of persistent mutagens and carcinogens that society continues to disperse in the biosphere.

The role of population size and distribution in generating ecological problems has been touched upon here already and is treated more systematically in Chapter 7. A point that should be obvious but is often overlooked is that population factors can also govern the seriousness of a disruption once one is underway. For example, it is largely because the growing population has stretched food production to its limits that there is little reserve against temporary crop failures caused by pests, plant disease, or weather variations. The sheer size and density of the human population in many parts of the world makes external aid almost impossible in time of local famine or other disaster. Epidemic diseases can spread more readily through dense populations, especially, of course, when malnourishment has made resistance low.

Moreover, as the population grows, a larger proportion of people tend to live in hazardous locations. For instance, since the famous 1906 earthquake, a growing proportion of the population of the San Francisco Bay area has been housed on landfill, on seacliffs and even along the fault itself (Figure 6–14). The homes on landfill have not been built to withstand the extraordinary shaking to which structures on fill are subjected in an earthquake. When the next big earthquake occurs in this overpopulated area, a great many people are likely to die simply because they are living in geologically marginal locations.

On the Ganges Delta of East Pakistan (now Bangladesh), a large, mostly destitute population lives exposed on flat lowland, in spite of the ever present danger of climatic disaster for which the region is famous. They live on the delta because there is no room for them elsewhere in grossly overpopulated Bangladesh. In November 1970, 300,000 people perished when a huge tidal wave driven by a cyclone swept over the delta. Most of the victims would not have died if their nation had not been overpopulated. Because of the poverty and overcrowding of their nation, evacuation following the flood was impossible. And, since the region was already nutritionally marginal, people began to starve to death immediately after the disaster. This cataclysm has been described as the greatest documented national disaster in history.

Governmental and other decision makers, whose job it is to weigh the costs and benefits of alternative courses of action, have rarely given much weight to the considerations discussed in this chapter. In the past, the environmental consequences of human activities have usually not been linked in the minds

Figure 6-14 Development near the San Andreas Fault on the San Francisco Peninsula. The dashed white line shows the approximate location of the fault. A manifestation of excessive population density (and the irresponsibility of developers) is the location of homes and schools virtually astride major earthquake faults and on coastal bluffs subject to periodic slides (left foreground). (Photo by William A. Garnett.)

of policy makers to the specific kinds of actions (or lack of them) that caused the problems. As environmentalists now strive to bring such costs into society's balance sheets, they find themselves bearing a heavy burden of proof. After all, say the defenders of the status quo, environmentalists cannot show exactly when or how an ecological disaster will take place, or how many human lives will be lost. Without solid evidence, how is one to act? This point of view is leading society to treat a grave risk that is poorly understood as if it were no risk at all. In any balance sheet of costs and benefits, this is faulty accounting. One does not need to know the date of a future flood to avoid development on flood plains, nor the exact magnitude of a possible earthquake to keep nuclear reactors away from major faults. If a risk entails the potential for major impact on human welfare, and if actions that increase the risk are identifiable, then it is only prudent to avoid or restrain such actions as far as possible, even when knowledge concerning the risk is incomplete. Ecological disruption clearly entails such risks, and it is time to shift the burden of proof. Where, for example, are the *benefits* of population growth that justify the ecological risks accompanying it?

Bibliography

Kennedy, Donald and John Hessel, 1969. The biology of pesticides. *Cry California*, vol. 4 no. 3, pp. 2–10 (Summer). Reprinted in Holdren, J. P. and P. R. Ehrlich, eds., 1971. *Global Ecology.* Harcourt Brace Jovanovich, N.Y.

Murdoch, W. W., 1971. Ecological systems, in Murdoch, W. W., ed., *Environment: Resources, Pollution, and Society.* Sinauer, Stamford, Connecticut.

Odum, Eugene P., 1972. *Fundamentals of Ecology*, 3rd ed. Saunders, Philadelphia.

Sears, Paul, 1971. An empire of dust, in Harte, J. and R. H. Socolow, *Patient Earth.* Holt, Rinehart and Winston, N.Y.

Woodwell, George M., 1970. Effects of pollution on the structure and physiology of ecosystems. *Science*, vol. 168, pp 429–433 (24 April). Reprinted in Holdren, J. P. and P. R. Ehrlich, 1971, *Global Ecology.* Harcourt Brace Jovanovich, N.Y.

This auto junkyard symbolizes many of the interacting elements of the environmental crisis in the United States: resource depletion, growth of population and affluence, and faulty technology. (Photo by Walt Mancini.)

SEVEN

Understanding the Web of Blame: The First Step to Solutions

Pressures related to the size of the human population are already large and are growing rapidly. There is pressure on our physical resources—food, water, forests, metals. There is pressure on the biological environment, whose ability to remove and recycle human wastes and to provide other vital services from pest control to fish production is being sorely taxed. There is pressure on society's ability to dispense services—education, medical care, the administration of justice. Indeed, there is even pressure on such important values as privacy, freedom from restrictive regulations, and the opportunity to choose from a variety of life styles.

Population size is not the only cause of these pressures. The consumption of materials and energy per person are also important factors. So is the type of technology that people employ to make the consumption possible. So are the economic, political, and social forces that influence personal and institutional decision making. Can these factors be disentangled? Can one or another be identified as the dominant culprit in creating the present human predicament? It would be convenient if the answer were yes, for this would imply that a simple-minded, single-faceted solution exists.

Unfortunately, the answer is no. All the factors are important, and often they are inextricably linked by an array of cause-and-effect connections. Mankind's predicament has deepened so rapidly because a number of the contributing factors—population, consumption per person, the careless use of technology—have been growing simultaneously, and the ability of individuals and governments to adapt their behavior to ever more rapidly changing conditions and problems has not kept pace. Obviously, in considering the causes of mankind's plight, we are confronted not by a single culprit but by a complex and tightly woven web of blame. If we are to find adequate and rational *solutions*, it is essential that we investigate more carefully the factors that interact to cause our problems.

Multiplicative Factors

Some aspects of the human predicament, such as pressure on values, are difficult to discuss in very informative or specific terms because so little is known about the subjects. The problems of resources and the environment, although very difficult, are often easier to describe quantitatively. We shall therefore use these latter problems to illustrate in more detail what we mean by a "web of blame."

The most fundamental point is that the factors that contribute to growing resource consumption and environmental degradation are multiplicative rather than additive. This idea is expressed by a simple equation,

$$\text{resource consumption} = \text{population} \times \text{consumption per person,}$$

$$\text{(Equation 1)}$$

and by the slightly more complicated one,

$$\text{environmental impact} = \text{population}$$
$$\times \text{consumption of goods per person}$$
$$\times \text{environmental impact per}$$
$$\text{quantity of goods consumed.}$$

$$\text{(Equation 2)}$$

Since consumption of goods per person is a measure of affluence, and since environmental impact per unit of goods consumed depends on the technologies of production, Equation 2 has sometimes been abbreviated as "impact equals population times affluence times technology." Note also that there is a distinction between consumption of resources and consumption of goods. Producing a good such as food may require large or small amounts of a resource such as phosphate fertilizer, depending on the form of agricultural technology being employed.

For problems described by multiplicative relations like Equations 1 and 2, no factor can be considered unimportant. The consequences of the growth of each factor are amplified in proportion to the size and the rate of growth of each of the others. Rising consumption per person has greater impact in a large population than in a small one—and greater impact in a growing population than in a stationary one. A given environmentally disruptive technology, such as the gasoline-powered automobile, is more damaging in a large, rich population (many people own cars and drive them often) than in a small, poor one (few people own cars, and those who do drive them less). A given level of total consumption (population times consumption per person) is more damaging if it is provided by means of a disruptive technology, such as persistent pesticides, than if provided by means of a relatively nondisruptive one, such as integrated pest control.

Quantitatively, the important point about Equations 1 and 2 is that slowly growing factors, when they multiply each other, lead to rapidly growing totals. Consider the following example for the resource equation. Suppose we wish to know whether population growth or rising consumption per capita played a greater role in the growth of total energy consumption in the United States between 1880 and 1966. In this period, total energy consumption increased about twelvefold, and the population increased fourfold.[1] It may therefore appear that consumption per capita was a more important factor than population growth. It was not. Consumption per capita increased threefold, versus fourfold for population. The twelvefold increase in the total consumption of energy arose as the *product*, not the sum, of the fourfold increase in population and the threefold increase in consumption per capita.

The results may be even more deceptive when there are three contributing factors, as there are in the environment equation. In a hypothetical case where population, per capita consumption of some commodity, and the impact of technology per unit of consumption all increase threefold, the total impact increases *27-fold*. The contributing factors here are equally important, but each seems quite small compared to the total.

Needless to say, the numerical quantities in the resource and environment equations will vary greatly depending on the problem under scrutiny. For example, there are many different kinds of environmental impact, and different forms of consumption and technology are relevant to each. The population factor itself may refer to the population of a city, a region, a country, or the world, depending on the problem being considered. Our formulas, then, represent not just two calculations but many. We shall give a number of examples below—but first a few comments about the individual factors are in order.

Population.   The U.S. and world population situations have already been discussed in detail in Chapter 2. For the purposes of elucidating the role of population growth and the other factors in the web of blame, we shall focus on the United States over various time periods in the span from 1900 to 1970. The total population and urban population of the United States for several years in this period are given in Table 7–1. The table shows that the U.S.

[1]These and most other statistics in Chapter 7 are from *Historical Statistics of the United States, Colonial Times to 1957*, U.S. Dept. of Commerce, U.S. Govt. Printing Office, 1957, and *Statistical Abstract of the United States, 1971*, U.S. Dept. of Commerce, U.S. Govt. Printing Office, 1971.

**Table 7–1   United States Total and
Urban Population in Selected Years**

Year	Total Population	Urban Population
1900	76,094,000	30,160,000
1910	92,407,000	41,999,000
1940	132,122,000	74,424,000
1946	141,389,000	——
1968	201,177,000	——
1970	205,200,000	149,279,000

SOURCE: *Statistical Abstract of the United States,
1972.*

population in 1970 was 2.70 times as large as in 1900 and 1.55 times as large
as in 1940. The urban population has increased even faster: in 1970 it was
4.95 times as large as in 1900 and 2.00 times as large as in 1940.

Affluence and Consumption.   How does one measure affluence? This is
certainly a more difficult task than counting people. A conventional but
much criticized measure of affluence is Gross National Product per capita.
Gross National Product (GNP) consists of expenditures by consumers and
government for goods and services, plus investment. So that figures for different years can be meaningfully compared in spite of inflation, they are
usually converted to their equivalent in the dollars of some reference year.
GNP per capita in the United States, measured in 1958 dollars, is given for
selected years between 1900 and 1970 in Table 7–2. Evidently, GNP per person,
corrected for inflation, was 3.75 times as large in 1970 as in 1900 and 2.02
times as large as in 1940.

**Table 7–2   United States
GNP Per Person in
1958 Dollars**

Year	GNP Per Person
1900	$ 940
1910	$1150
1940	$1740
1946	$2240
1968	$3515
1970	$3525

SOURCE: *Statistical Abstract
of the United States, 1972,
and Historical Statistics of
the United States: Colonial
Times to 1956.*

It is easy to find fault with GNP as a meaningful index of affluence. In one sense it includes too much. Dollars spent on catching and prosecuting a growing number of violators of a growing number of laws contribute to GNP, as do the costs of wars and attempts to clean up pollution. Since these expenditures reflect or are necessitated by a declining rather than an improving quality of life, they should hardly be regarded as an indication of affluence. In another sense, GNP takes too little into account. Perhaps the "cost" of decaying cities, now being paid not in dollars but in the misery of those who must live and work there, should somehow be *subtracted* from GNP.

Despite the shortcomings of GNP as a measure of affluence, no alternative measures have yet gained wide acceptance. One possible approach is to use production or consumption of certain basic materials as an indicator of affluence. Typically, steel and energy are chosen as representative commodities, simply because large quantities of both are essential to running an industrial civilization. Another critical material in this connection is water. Figures for steel, energy, and water are given in Table 7-3. Note that the per capita use or production of these commodities in the United States has increased between twofold and fourfold since 1900. The figures are not entirely unrelated, of course. It takes water and energy to produce steel; steel and water to make energy available; steel and energy to make water available.

Using flows of materials as an index of affluence has the drawback that it is often not *flow* that measures well-being but rather the stock of goods maintained by the flow. Owning a refrigerator is an indication of affluence; having to replace it frequently is not. Thus the amount of steel or the number of refrigerators and automobiles in existence in a society is a better measure of affluence than the annual consumption or sales of these things. The quantity of goods, machinery, and materials owned or in existence is often referred to as *capital stock*; the annual consumption, or *throughput* as it is sometimes

**Table 7-3   Flows of Basic Resources
in the United States**

Year	Annual Steel Production (Lbs/Person)	Annual Energy Consumption (Million BTU/Person)	Daily Water Use (Gal/Person)
1900	300	96	—
1910	635	154	875
1940	1020	181	1030
1946	941	205	1170
1970	1285	336	1600

SOURCE: *Statistical Abstract of the United States, 1972*, and *Historical Statistics of the United States: Colonial Times to 1956*.

**Table 7–4   Stock of Consumer Durables
in the United States**

Item	1940s	1960s
Automobiles in use per capita	.208 in 1940	.416 in 1968
Refrigerators in use per capita	.145 in 1946	.277 in 1960
Clothes dryers in use per capita	.001 in 1949	.053 in 1960
Percentage of households with air conditioners	0.2% in 1948	13 6% in 1960

SOURCE: *Resources in America's Future.*

called, measures additions to the stock itself and replacement of losses (for example, junked automobiles that are not reclaimed). To the extent that a part of GNP is just flows of goods and materials measured in dollars, GNP shares the defect of focusing on throughput rather than on capital stock.

Changes over the last few decades in the capital stock of a number of goods known as *consumer durables* are shown in Table 7–4. Such figures are rather good indicators of rising affluence.

In some instances, of course, a flow rather than a stock is the appropriate measure of affluence. This seems to be the case for the necessities of existence — food, clothing, and shelter. In the case of food, calories and grams of protein per day measure adequacy, and, beyond that, annual dollar expenditures on food measure variety and quality. To some extent, rising expenditures on food may also reflect increasing costs of production (to be discussed below). On the average, diets have been adequate in terms of quantity in the United States throughout this century. But increasing affluence, as reflected in expendi-

**Table 7–5   Annual Per Capita
Expenditures on Necessities in
the United States in 1958 Dollars**

Year	Food	Housing (Rent or Equivalent)	Clothing
1910	$175	$131	$ 87
1940	$231	$104	$ 87
1946	$346	$ 95	$133
1970	$440	$328	$214

SOURCE: *Statistical Abstract of the United States, 1972,* and *Historical Statistics of the United States: Colonial Times to 1956.*

tures on food, is very apparent in Table 7–5. Since clothing wears out rather rapidly, annual expenditure (a flow) is a reasonable measure of the quality of the stock. In the case of shelter, annual per capita expenditure in the form of rent or mortgage payments is probably a reasonable index of quality, after correction has been made for inflation. Statistics like "housing units" per capita do not help much; they measure the size of living groups, but they do not distinguish between one-room apartments and palatial mansions. Clothing and housing expenditures are shown along with those for food in Table 7–5.

Obviously, there are many ways to define and measure affluence, none of them completely satisfactory. Nevertheless, the picture that emerges from all the admittedly imperfect measures is a consistent one: affluence, by *any* reasonable definition, has increased dramatically in the United States in this century and especially in the last 30 years.

Technology.   As noted above, society's emphasis on throughput in economic accounting sometimes leads to oversimplifying the connection between consumption and affluence. The factor most responsible for the real complexity of this connection is the character of the technology used to transform flows into benefits.

The relations among consumption, affluence, and technology are well illustrated by the example of energy. Some of our energy consumption provides direct benefits in the form of heat for cooking, water heating, and space heating (the heating of homes, offices, etc.) Even in space heating, however, the real benefit is the "stock" of heat maintained inside, and the flow of energy is needed only to replace losses through walls, windows, and so on. The amount of energy flow needed to maintain a given temperature depends on technology, particularly the efficiency with which fuel is converted to heat and the quality of the insulation in the building being heated.

Another substantial part of society's energy consumption is needed simply to make possible the large throughput of other materials in our economy — steel, water, glass, plastics, and paper, to name some important ones. For given rates of consumption of these materials, the amount of energy required again depends on the technology used: the details of mechanical and chemical processing; whether or not recycling is employed; whether the process uses electricity or direct combustion of fuel; and so on. Transportation is yet another component of affluence in which energy consumption depends strongly on the sort of technology employed — small cars or large ones, trains or planes, gasoline engines or electric motors, and so on.

Technology is constantly changing. Such changes are stimulated largely by economic factors, such as the desirability of cheaper methods of production of existing kinds of goods; the profitability of inventing and marketing new kinds of goods; and the need to find substitutes for materials made scarce by heavy demands. Partly because ecological values have not been properly accounted for in our economic system, the changes in technology stimulated by that system have sometimes been profoundly disruptive of the environment.

The rapidly rising reliance on plastics in American manufacturing is a technological change that can be attributed partly to the quest for cheapness, partly to the desire for durability (which is admirable as long as the plastic is not being used in throwaway goods), and perhaps partly to scarcity of alternate materials such as certain kinds of wood. Of course, if the economic system is functioning "properly," scarcity leads to rising prices, so the cheapness of plastic and scarcity of the alternative reinforce each other.

Increasingly heavy use of fertilizers and synthetic organic pesticides in agriculture is another technological change stimulated partly by increased total demand for food and partly by economic forces that dictate *how* a greater demand will be met. In this case, alternatives would have been to bring more land into production, to promote labor-intensive rather than technology-intensive high-yield agriculture or to use more expensive integrated pest control.

Environmental Impact.   Only in a relatively few cases is it easy to assign an exact numerical value to the third factor in Equation 2—the environmental impact associated with a particular amount of consumption. It is possible to record the emissions of lead and oxides of nitrogen per vehicle mile, the pounds of sulfur dioxide released per kilowatt-hour of electricity generated, and other similar data. Even when such numbers are available, however, really good analysis is made difficult by several factors:

1. Most forms of consumption give rise to many different forms of environmental impact. For example, electricity production from coal causes air pollution, water pollution, solid waste, defacement of the landscape, and disruption of local ecosystems. Changes in technology may reduce some aspects of impact while increasing others.

2. The different kinds of impact associated with alternative technologies to meet the same need are hard to compare. For example, how does one compare the environmental impact of oil spills with that of coal mining?

3. Most of our knowledge concerns what man puts into the environment, but not how the environment responds. This accounts for much of the difficulty associated with the previous two points. It is not enough to know how much lead is emitted by man; we must know how to put numerical values on the human health effects in the short and long term, on any impairment in the functioning of individual species of plants and animals, and on the general ecological effects resulting from the simultaneous action of lead on many organisms at once. It is not enough to know how much nitrogen man applies to his fields; we must also know in detail what the health effects and ecological effects are when it gets there. In short, it is *response*, not *input*, that really defines environmental impact. In almost every case, our knowledge is far from adequate to assess this response quantitatively.

All this is not to say that we are too ignorant to take corrective action. The evidence of damage is overwhelming, and many of the basic causes are clear. But one must be cautious about using selected numbers to draw sweeping conclusions about the numerical increase in environmental damage over a given time span, and about the assignment of blame among the many factors that play a role.

The United States since World War II

The pitfalls of underestimating the complexity of the web of blame are well illustrated by the statement frequently heard that "faulty technology" developed since World War II has been the principal culprit generating the environmental crisis in the United States.[2] Examination of this hypothesis is a useful way to look more deeply and specifically into some of the points raised above.

The main evidence offered to show that technology has been the dominant environmental villain is the observation that some indices of pollution in the United States have increased by 200 percent or more since World War II, while the population and affluence were growing much more slowly. Among the usual examples of dramatically increasing sources of pollution in the postwar period are emissions of lead and nitrogen oxides in auto exhausts, the use of synthetic pesticides and nitrogen fertilizer in agriculture, and the use of phosphates in detergents. But these examples would prove the hypothesis only if *all* of the following conditions were met:

1. The calculations for these examples showed that population growth and rising affluence have been minor contributors to the total increase, arithmetically speaking.

2. The changes in technology that led to rapid growth in these indices of pollution were not sometimes *caused* by increases in total demand (population times consumption per capita) that could not be met by earlier technology.

3. The examples represented a valid sampling of all important kinds of environmental impact.

In actuality, *none* of these conditions is met by examples that have been said to demonstrate a dominant role for faulty technology.

Arithmetic of Growth. Because the contributing factors — population growth, per capita consumption, and technology — are multiplicative, each factor is important no matter how fast the other factors have grown. According to Table

---

[2]The most vigorous exponent of the "faulty technology" hypothesis has been biologist Barry Commoner, whose book *The Closing Circle* (Knopf, New York, 1971) contains a number of the specific fallacies we describe in this chapter.

7–1, the U.S. population grew 45 percent between 1946 and 1970. In purely arithmetic terms (ignoring all possible cause-and-effect connections between population growth and the other factors), this says that our impact would only have been about two-thirds as large in 1970 as it actually was if the population had not grown in this interval. (The ratio of the 1946 population to that in 1970 is 1/1.45 = .69, or slightly over two-thirds). Of the large total increase in impact, the one-third that is "explained" by population growth is an important contribution.

Table 7–2 shows that by one measure, GNP per person corrected for inflation, affluence grew 57 percent between 1946 and 1970. If GNP per capita were in fact a valid measure of the contribution of affluence to environmental impact, these figures would indicate that the 1970 impact would have been only 64 percent as large as it actually was if affluence had not grown in the 1946–

Box 7–1   Automotive Lead: A Case Study

The emissions of lead from automobile exhausts increased 415 percent in the period between 1946 and 1968. Does this mean that the 42 percent increase in the population was responsible for only one-tenth of the increase in emissions? Not at all, because the contributing factors are multiplicative, not additive. Let us rewrite the equation given in the text symbolically (using · as a multiplication sign):

$$I = P \cdot C \cdot T,$$

where I denotes environmental impact, P is population, C is consumption per person, and T is the technological impact per unit of consumption. If, in a given time period, the increases in the various quantities are denoted ΔI, ΔP, ΔC, and ΔT, then the equation for the later time is

$$I + \Delta I = (P + \Delta P) \cdot (C + \Delta C) \cdot (T + \Delta T).$$

Percentages emerge when the equation is rewritten in the form

$$1 + \frac{\Delta I}{I} = \left(1 + \frac{\Delta P}{P}\right) \cdot \left(1 + \frac{\Delta C}{C}\right) \cdot \left(1 + \frac{\Delta T}{T}\right),$$

where $\Delta I/I$ times 100 is the percentage increase in environmental impact, $\Delta P/P$ times 100 is the percentage increase in population, and so on. (Note that an increase of 100 percent means

a doubling of the initial quantity, an increase of 200 percent a tripling, and so on.)

The 42 percent increase in population between 1946 and 1968 means that $\Delta P/P$ for this period is .42 and the population factor, $1 + \Delta P/P$, is 1.42. In considering automotive emissions, the quantity "consumed" is vehicle miles per capita, which doubled in the period in question. Thus $\Delta C/C = 1.00$, $1 + \Delta C/C = 2.00$. The complete impact equation for lead emissions from automobiles therefore is

$$1 + \frac{\Delta I}{I} = 1 + 4.15 = 5.15$$

$$= \left(1 + \frac{\Delta P}{P}\right) \cdot \left(1 + \frac{\Delta C}{C}\right) \cdot \left(1 + \frac{\Delta T}{T}\right)$$

$$= 1.42 \cdot 2.00 \cdot 1.81.$$

In this example, the technology factor, emissions of lead per vehicle mile, is intermediate in importance between the population factor and the consumption factor. Population is not unimportant (without population growth, the total increase would have been 252 percent rather than 415 percent); technology is not dominant. This is so even though the emission of lead by automobiles is one of the *best* available examples of faulty technology in the postwar period.

1970 interval, again ignoring cause-and-effect connections among the factors. (The ratio of the 1946 per capita GNP to that in 1970 is $1/1.57 = .64$.) If neither population nor affluence had grown since the Second World War, the total environmental impact in 1970 would have been only 44 percent of that actually experienced (within the limitations of GNP per person as a measure of the contribution of affluence to environmental impact, and ignoring cause-and-effect connections among the factors).

The point here is not that the relative impact of technology has not grown substantially since World War II; in some cases, it has. But *especially* in such cases the total impact has been made that much greater because population and affluence were growing too. Some arithmetic calculations pertaining to growing environmental impact are shown in full detail in Box 7–1, using the actual example of automotive lead emissions since World War II.

Cause-and-Effect Relations

Increases in total consumption, brought about by population growth and rising affluence, can cause changes in the technology factor in several ways. Consider the use of manmade fibers such as nylon in clothing. The rapidly growing synthetic fiber industry is often cited as an example of an ecologically faulty technology, since these materials require large quantities of energy in their production and degrade only slowly in the biosphere. However, providing today's total U.S. demand for fiber *without* the synthetics would have required nearly a doubling in production of cotton and wool by 1972 over the 1945 levels (which were higher than more recent ones). Whether this would have been practical at all is questionable. And, if it had been done, what would have been the ecological costs in terms of pounds of fertilizer and pesticides applied to cotton fields, the side effects of irrigation projects, and the erosion of farmland resulting from overgrazing? Clearly, technology changes with demand, and it is meaningless to consider the environmental impact of one kind of technology without also considering the impact of alternative technologies that would permit the same material consumption.

Aluminum is another material whose consumption is increasing rapidly and which requires a great deal of energy to obtain from ore. Its use in cans is certainly a faulty technology unrelated to population growth or real affluence, but containers comprise only 10 percent of U.S. aluminum use. Thirteen percent is used in the electrical industry, where aluminum has been substituted for copper, which has been made scarce by heavy demands. Twenty-three percent is used in building and construction, partly to replace wood in siding, window frames, awnings, and so on.[3] Meeting the demands of a growing popu-

---

[3]Figures on aluminum use are from *The Minerals Yearbook, 1968*, U.S. Department of the Interior, U.S. Govt. Printing Office.

lation for better housing with wood alone would put additional pressure on forests already being too intensely exploited. Substitutions of one material for another—nylon for cotton, aluminum for copper, aluminum and plastics for wood—are inevitable as a growing, increasingly affluent population presses on a finite resource base. Obviously, any additional environmental impact that results from such substitutions cannot justifiably be blamed on "faulty technology" alone.

Another way in which population growth and rising per capita consumption cause increases in technological impact is through the *law of diminishing returns*. This refers to a situation in which, in the jargon of the economist, the additional output resulting from each additional unit of input becomes less and less. Here "output" refers to a desired good (such as a food or metal), and "input" refers to what must be supplied (say, fertilizer, or energy, or raw ore) to obtain the output. Suppose that consumption of goods per person is to be held constant while the population increases. If the law of diminishing returns prevails, the per capita consumption of inputs needed to provide the fixed per capita level of goods will increase. Since environmental impact is generated by the inputs (such as energy) as well as by the use and disposal of the goods themselves, the per capita impact will also increase.

To see how the law of diminishing returns operates in a specific example, consider the problem of providing nonrenewable resources such as minerals and fossil fuels to a growing population, even at unchanging levels of per capita consumption. More people means more demand, and thus more rapid depletion of resources. As the richest supplies of these resources and those nearest to centers of use are consumed, it becomes necessary to use lower-grade ores, to drill deeper, and to extend supply networks. All these activities increase the *per capita* use of energy and hence the *per capita* impact on the environment. In the case of partly renewable resources such as water (which is effectively nonrenewable when groundwater supplies are mined at rates far exceeding natural replenishment), per capita costs and environmental impact escalate enormously when the human population demands more than is locally available. Here the loss of free-flowing rivers and other economic, aesthetic, and ecological costs of massive water-movement projects represent increased per capita penalties directly connected to population growth. These effects would, of course, also eventually overtake a stationary population that demands more than the environment can supply on a perpetual basis; growth simply speeds up the process and allows less time to deal with the problems created.

The law of diminishing returns is also at work when society tries to increase food production to meet the needs of growing populations. Typically, attempts are made both to overproduce on land already farmed and to extend agriculture to marginal land. Overproduction requires increased energy use out of proportion to the gain in yield, through the processes of obtaining and distributing water, fertilizer, and pesticides. Farming marginal land also increases per capita energy use, since the amount of energy invested per unit of yield increases as less desirable land is cultivated. Both activities often "consume" the fertility built into the natural soil structure. Similarly, as the richest fisheries stocks are depleted, the yield per unit of effort drops, and more and more energy per capita is required to maintain the supply. Once a stock is depleted it may not recover—it may be nonrenewable.

Substitutions and diminishing returns are examples of the way in which population growth and rising consumption generate disproportionate increases in the *input* side of environmental impact—in what man *does to* the environment. Mankind's environmental predicament is also greatly aggravated by situations where relatively small changes in inputs may cause dramatic changes in the environment's *response*.

Threshold effects are one such type of situation. For example, below a certain level of pollution, trees will survive in smog. But when a small increment in the local human population produces a small increment in smog, living trees become dead trees. Perhaps 500 people can live around a certain lake and dump their raw sewage into it, and its natural systems will be able to break down the sewage and keep the lake from undergoing rapid ecological change. But 505 people may overload the system and result in a polluted or eutrophic lake.

Such thresholds characterize the responses of many organisms or groups of organisms to many different kinds of environmental changes: fish die when water temperature exceeds a certain threshold or when dissolved oxygen content falls below a certain threshold; different crops have different thresholds for tolerance of dissolved salts in irrigation water; carbon monoxide is fatal to humans at high concentrations, but, as far as we know, causes only reversible effects at low concentrations. Scientists describe such situations as displaying a *nonlinear dose-response relation.* Nonlinear in this context means that a graph plotting response (say, percentage of deaths in a population of fish) versus dose (say, temperature in the habitat) will not be a straight line. The difference between linear and nonlinear dose-response relations is shown schematically in Figure 7–1.

Another form of nonlinear behavior in dose-response relationships is *synergism.* Here one is concerned with the simultaneous interacting effects of two or more kinds of input, where each kind of input acts to intensify the effects of others. For example, sulfur dioxide and various cancer-causing kinds of particulate matter are found at the same time in city air and for hundreds of miles downwind. One of the effects of sulfur dioxide is to impair the cleaning mechanisms of the lungs, thus increasing the time that the carcinogenic particles spend in the lungs before being discharged. Thus the joint effect is *synergistic*: it exceeds the sum of the individual effects expected if sulfur dioxide and cancer-causing particles had been present separately.

Synergisms also occur in environmental systems that influence human health less directly than the incidence of disease. A particularly disturbing

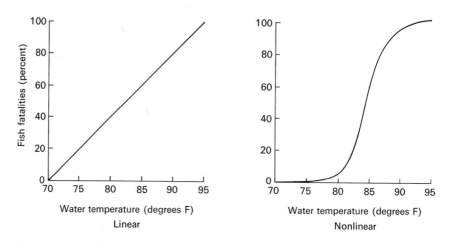

Figure 7-1 Idealized linear and nonlinear dose-response relations. In the real world, graphs like that on the right usually apply.

example is the combined effect of DDT and oil spills in coastal waters. DDT is not very soluble in sea water, so the concentrations to which marine organisms are ordinarily exposed are small. However, DDT is very soluble in oil. Oil spills therefore have the effect of concentrating DDT in the surface layer of the ocean, where much of the oil remains, and where many marine organisms spend part of their time. These organisms are thus exposed to far higher concentrations of DDT than would otherwise be possible. As a result, the combined effects of oil and DDT probably far exceed the individual effects. Many other synergisms in environmental systems are possible. Investigation of such effects is one of the most difficult (and neglected) areas of environmental analysis.

Other Forms of Impact. It is possible to get the impression from some of today's discussions of environmental problems that our troubles began with the advent of the internal combustion engine, DDT, and nuclear fission. Although these are significant problems, we have shown in previous chapters that they are far from the whole story. Loss of good land to erosion, to faulty irrigation practices, and to overgrazing dates back thousands of years and is still serious today. Overexploitation of commercially valuable species of plants and animals has driven some to extinction and threatens many others — whales, a dozen species of fishes, several kinds of wild cats, birds, butterflies, redwoods, and so on. Ocean fisheries are threatened by destruction of breeding grounds through dredging and filling operations in estuaries and marshes, as well as by overfishing and pollution. The extension of monocultures of a few, selected high-yield varieties of grain over large areas is increasing the vulnerability of world agriculture to disruption. In the United States, some of the best agricultural land is continually disappearing under suburbs, airports and highways. In short, there is a great deal more to environmental deterioration than pollution.

There is no single index that measures these numerous forms of environmental impact, nor even for many of them, any statistics at all from which to derive some allocation of "blame" among population growth and the other contributing factors. Many observers agree, however, that consumption of energy is the best single measure available of human impact on natural surroundings. The use of energy is central to most of the activities in question, and it is a direct contributor to many of the most obvious environmental problems. Moreover, as noted above, energy consumption per capita combines within a single statistic a measure both of affluence and of the impact of the technology that provides the affluence. It may not be possible to unravel the numerous connections *between* population size and per capita energy consumption. Nevertheless, it is useful to weigh the purely arithmetic contributions of these two factors to the recent growth of *total* energy consumption.

In an earlier example we showed that population growth was a greater contributor than rising consumption of energy per capita to the increase in total U.S. energy consumption over the past 90 years. During a more recent period, 1940 to 1969, the population increased by 53 percent while energy consumption per capita increased by 80 percent Worldwide, energy consumption has recently been increasing at about 5 percent per year—about 2 percent per year due to population growth and 3 percent per year due to rising consumption per capita. Obviously, if energy consumption is a good measure of environmental impact, population growth has continued to be an important contributor to that impact both in the U.S. and in the world as a whole.

Perfect Technologies and Shifting Impact

It is sometimes claimed that dramatic improvements in technology will compensate for continued growth in population and consumption per person. That is, if the per capita impact on the environment due to technology can be sufficiently reduced, growth in population and consumption per capita need not lead to increased environmental degradation. This is certainly true for some kinds of activities and for a limited time. Some kinds of air pollution in the Los Angeles Basin, such as hydrocarbons and carbon monoxide, are currently decreasing, even though both the population and the consumption of fuels are increasing. Installation of sewage treatment facilities has improved water quality in Seattle's Lake Washington and Wisconsin's Lake Mendota despite growing populations in these areas.

Such technological improvements should certainly be sought and applied, but they are not complete cures. One reason is that many technological "fixes" for environmental problems simply shift the impact to somewhere else, rather than removing it. Incinerating garbage pollutes the air, and available techniques for removing oxides of sulfur from power-plant exhaust gases generate either solid wastes or water pollution. Switching from internal combustion engines to electric automobiles simply shifts part of transportation's pollution burden from the air over highways to the air over power plants. Removing the lead from gasoline has apparently increased particulate emissions and may have increased the proportion of emitted hydrocarbons that are carcinogenic as well.

Even the approaches that successfully relieve one problem without creating another one are nevertheless imperfect. There is no such thing as "zero emissions." As we strive to reduce the percentage of contaminants per unit volume of effluent (say, treated water or stack gases from power plants) to very small levels, the costs of the control measures in dollars and energy become very large. In fact, reducing contaminant concentrations to zero would require an infinite amount of energy. Long before we got there, of course, the environmental impact associated with supplying the energy for pollution control would exceed the impact of the pollution we were trying to clean up. This is the law of diminishing returns at its worst.

A good example is the economics of sewage treatment. The cost of removing 80 to 90 percent of the biochemical and chemical oxygen demand (standard indices of pollutants in water), 90 percent of the suspended solids, and 60 percent of the resistant organic material by means of secondary treatment is about 8 cents per thousand gallons in a large plant. But if there is so much sewage that its nutrient content creates a serious eutrophication problem (as is the case in much of the United States today), or if water is in such short supply that sewage water must be reused for industry, agriculture, or groundwater recharge, advanced treatment is necessary. The cost ranges from 2 to 4 times as much as for secondary treatment (17 cents per 1000 gallons for irrigation of food crops, 34 cents per 1000 gallons to yield a drinkable supply).[4] This story could be repeated for many other forms of environmental impact.

There is good reason to believe, therefore, that a rapidly rising fraction of national income will have to be spent during the next few decades to hold pollution to tolerable levels. Even then, some important aspects of the problem may go unnoticed until irreversible damage has been done, and other aspects may worsen for the lack of available technology to deal with them at any price. At the moment, for instance, no technology has been developed to control emissions of nitrogen oxides from electric power plants, and it is not practical to control emissions of carbon dioxide from all combustion of fossil fuels because the volume of the effluent is so great. Tilling the soil and mining operations may accelerate the rate at which mercury is given off from the Earth's crust.[5] More mercury may be released to the environment this way than by industrial processes, and no remedy is known.

As already noted, the ultimate pollutant is heat. All other forms of pollution control and all recycling require energy, and all the energy we use ulti-

---

[4]Figures on cost of sewage treatment are from *Cleaning Our Environment: The Chemical Basis for Action* (American Chemical Society, Washington, D.C., 1969).

[5]See "Fossil Fuel Combustion and the Major Sedimentary Cycle," by K. K. Bertine and Edward D. Goldberg (*Science* vol. 173, p. 233, July 16, 1971).

mately turns up in the environment as waste heat. Efficient generation and utilization of energy can relieve this problem somewhat, but they cannot eliminate it. If miraculously, all other environmental defects of our technology could be remedied, this one would remain.

One may conclude from all of this that improving technology to reduce its contribution to total environmental impact is worthwhile but is not the entire answer. Under any set of technological conditions, there will be some impact associated with each unit of consumption, and therefore some level of population size and consumption per person at which the total impact becomes unsustainable.

The Prospects

The tightly interlocked and simultaneously growing factors that comprise what we have called the web of blame must *all* be attacked if we are to weather the environmental crisis. The misappropriation of the world's resources by the rich countries, which accompanies and contributes to our environmental plight, must also be directly confronted, as must the more general problems of poverty and the maldistribution of wealth. A strategy that treats only some of the factors is bound to fail.

The most dramatic improvements in technology will ultimately be cancelled out by rising population and consumption levels. At the same time, control of population will be of no avail if technology and consumption are not controlled as well. It has been claimed that we should attack the technology factor *first* because it is the easiest to deal with. As should be clear from the preceding analysis, this is a completely misleading idea.

The momentum inherent in population growth commits us to years of further increase even under the most optimistic assumptions. The momentum of economic growth makes it equally unlikely that this trend will be quickly halted — particularly as long as economic growth is incorrectly perceived as a substitute for eliminating gross inequities in the distribution of wealth. If humanity ignores population growth, overconsumption, and maldistribution of wealth now because these problems are tough ones, choosing instead to deal with the relatively easy technological questions, the prospects twenty or thirty years hence will be gloomy indeed. The momentum of population and consumption trends will still be committing us to even more growth, but most of the easy technological tricks to soften the environmental impact of growth will have already been exploited. The prospects for eventual prosperity in the UDCs, already slim, will be hopeless after a few more decades of the present pattern of the rich countries looting the world's high-grade resources for their own extravagant consumption.

Obviously, the time is long past for quibbling about which factor in the human predicament is "most important." They are all important. Failure to come to grips with all the factors — *simultaneously, now* — will surely sabotage the future.

Bibliography

Ehrlich, P. R., and J. P. Holdren, 1971. Impact of population growth, *Science*, vol. 171, pp. 1212–1217, 26 March.

Ehrlich, P. R., and J. P. Holdren, 1972. One-dimensional ecology, *Science and Public Affairs: The Bulletin of the Atomic Scientists*. vol. 28, no. 5, pp. 16–27 (May).

Meadows, Donella H., D. L. Meadows, J. Randers, and W. W. Behrens III, 1972. *The Limits to Growth*, Universe Books, Washington, D.C.

U.S. Commission on Population Growth and the American Future, 1972. *Population and the American Future*. Report of the National Commission. Signet Books, New York.

Part Two
SOLUTIONS

This machine makes oral contraceptive pills at the rate of 10,000 tablets per minute. The operator wears a protective mask to avoid inhaling steroids which could cause hormonal changes. (Courtesy of Syntex Laboratories, Inc.)

EIGHT

Population
Limitation

Any set of programs that is to be successful in alleviating the set of problems described in the foregoing chapters must include measures to control the growth of the human population. The potential goals of such measures, in order of possible achievement are:

1. Reduce the *rate* of growth of the population, although not necessarily to zero.

2. Stabilize the *size* of the population; that is, achieve a zero rate of growth.

3. Achieve a negative rate of growth in order to reduce the size of the population.

Presumably, most people would agree that the only humane means of achieving any of these goals on a global basis is by reducing the birth rate. The alternative is to permit the death rate to increase, which, of course, will eventually occur by agonizing "natural" processes already described if mankind does not rationally limit its birth rate in time.

Even given a consensus that limiting births is the preferred means to limit population, however, there is much less agreement as to how far and how fast limitation should proceed. Acceptance of the first goal listed above requires only that one recognize the obvious adverse consequences of rapid population growth—for example, dilution of economic progress in the UDCs, and aggravation of environmental and social problems in the DCs faster than solutions can be brought to bear. Economists and demographers, many of whom will not accept the third goal at all and ascribe no urgency to the second, generally do espouse the first one (at least for the UDCs).

Accepting the second goal simply means recognizing that the Earth's capacity to support human beings is limited and that, even short of the limits, many problems are related to population size itself rather than only to the rate of growth. Accepting the urgency of stabilizing the size of the population requires recognizing that the limits are already being approached and that, although technological and cultural change may push the limits back eventually, the prudent course is to halt population growth until existing problems are solved. Virtually all physical and natural scientists accept the eventual inevitability of halting population growth, and most accept the urgency of this goal. Much of the first part of this book has been an exposition of why the "inevitable-and-urgent" position is reasonable.

The most controversial goal is the third one listed above—reducing the size of the human population. Accepting this goal implies a belief that there is an optimum population size and that this optimum has already been exceeded (or will have been exceeded by the time population growth can be stopped). Of course, the mere use of the words "overpopulation" or "underpopulation," whether with reference to a city, a country, a region or the world, also implies the existence of optimal population sizes that have been either exceeded or not reached. The question of how optimum population size is to be determined is a complicated one, and deserves some discussion before we move on to specific methods for limiting births.

The Optimum Population

The maximum size the human population can attain is determined by the physical capacity of the Earth to support people. This capacity, as discussed in earlier chapters, is determined by such diverse factors as land area, availability of mineral resources and water, potential for food production, and ability of biological systems to absorb civilization's wastes without breakdowns that deprive mankind of essential services. No one knows exactly what the maximum carrying capacity is, and it will certainly vary with time in any case. The capacity may be maintainable at a very high value for a short period by means of rapid consumption of nonrenewable resources. In the longer term, a smaller capacity will be determined according to the rate of replenishment of renewable resources and the accomplishments of technology in employing very common materials. Whatever the maximum sustainable population may be, however, few thoughtful people will argue that the maximum and the optimum are the same. The maximum implies a bare level of subsistence for all. Unless sheer quantity of human beings is seen as the ultimate good, this situation cannot be considered optimal.

The minimum size of the human population, on the other hand, is that of the smallest group that can reproduce itself. Like the maximum, the minimum size is also certainly not the optimum. It would be too small to permit the many benefits of specialization and division of labor, of economies of scale in the use of technology, of cultural diversity, and so on. The optimum population size, then, lies somewhere between the minimum and maximum possible sizes. Since decisions concerning the population size are made, consciously or unconsciously, by the people alive at a given time, it seems reasonable to define the optimum size in terms of their interests. Accordingly, one might define the optimum as the population size below which welfare per person is increased by further growth and above which welfare per person is decreased by further growth.

Like most definitions of elusive concepts, this one raises more questions than it answers. How is welfare to be measured? How does one deal with the uneven *distribution* of welfare and, particularly, with the fact that population growth may increase the welfare of some people while decreasing that of others? What if a region is overpopulated with respect to one aspect of welfare but underpopulated with respect to another aspect? What about the welfare of future generations? Can one define an optimum population for any part of the world without reference to the situation in all other parts of the world?

No complete answers are possible, but it is time that such questions be seriously addressed. The following observations are intended to stimulate further discussion.

Priorities.   The physical necessities — food, water, clothing, shelter, a healthful environment — are the most indispensable ingredients of welfare. A population too large to be supplied adequately with these has exceeded the optimum, regardless of what other aspects of welfare might in theory be enhanced by further growth. Similarly, a population so large that it can only be supplied with physical necessities by rapid consumption of nonrenewable resources or by activities that irreversibly degrade the environment has also exceeded the optimum, for it is reducing the Earth's carrying capacity for future generations. With respect to the distribution of welfare, if an increase in population decreases the welfare of a substantial number of people in terms of necessities while increasing the welfare of others in terms of luxuries, the population has exceeded the optimum. The same is true when population increase leads to a larger absolute number of people denied the necessities — even if the fraction of the population so denied remains constant (or even shrinks).

Density.   Population density in itself is not a good measure of overpopulation or underpopulation. Shortages of many resources other than physical space — such as water, fertile soils, suitable climate or mineral resources — may make it difficult to supply even a sparse population in a given area with the necessities of existence. Large parts of Africa, North and South America, and Australia are or could quickly become overpopulated in this respect despite low densities measured in people per square mile. Some people have claimed that prosperous, densely populated countries such as the Netherlands, which has almost 1000 people per square mile, show that the world as a whole (averaging 55 people per square mile of land area) is underpopulated. This "Netherlands Fallacy" is an example of what is known in philosophy as the "fallacy of composition"—the fallacy that what is true of a part must be true of the whole. The Netherlands can support 1000 people per square mile only because the rest of the world does not; the Dutch rank second in the world (behind similarly densely populated Denmark) in imports of protein per person, and they import most of their fiber, almost all of their industrial metals, and 45 percent of their energy.[1]

Human Values.   The concept of an optimum population size must account for human values that go beyond physical necessities and economic purchasing power. Such values include an environment that is psychologically as well as physiologically agreeable, a satisfying degree of contact with other people, a variety of educational opportunities, freedom from excessive external interference in personal behavior and from crime, and access to means of resolving conflicts and distributing justice. Many questions can be raised concerning these aspects of the human environment. What degree of contact is satisfying and what amount of interference excessive? How important is solitude for psychological well-being? What are the effects of population density, levels of noise, or colors in the environment on human behavior? There is little experimental evidence on most of these questions (although it is known, for example, that the color green has a soothing effect), and there is little consensus between cultures or even within a given culture on what constitutes an agreeable environment.

These uncertainties and lack of consensus suggest that a population size can be considered optimum only if it is far enough from physical limits to permit a good deal of environmental, social, and cultural diversity. Near the limits, diversity must be sacrificed in order to maximize production of physical necessities. Recall from Chapter 6 that productivity and diversity also conflict in agricultural and other biological systems. More generally, as soon as population growth begins to close more options than it opens, one can say that the population size has exceeded the optimum. In the United States, there is reason to believe that people's lives have already been made more regimented, regulated, and restricted, owing in part to increases in the size of the population.

Certain values conflict directly with numbers, although numbers may also be considered a value by some people, such as businessmen (who see bigger markets), politicians (who see more political power), and parents of large families. Those who promote numbers of people as a value in itself, however, may be overlooking the cheapness such abundance often brings. One form of con-

[1]Figures from the United Nations *Statistical Yearbook* for 1970.

flict between values and numbers arises in the choice between having many deprived children or having fewer who can be raised with the best care, education, and opportunity for successful adulthood. This dilemma is equally acute whether it is posed to a family or to a society. It is surely no accident that so many of the most successful individuals are first or only children; nor that children of large families (particularly with more than four children), whatever their economic status, on the average perform less well in school and show lower I.Q. scores than their peers from small families.[2]

Although human beings are capable of adapting themselves to a wide variety of environments, it is plain that people do much better in some sets of circumstances than others. A vitally important point is how we measure success — whether by the number of individuals who can barely survive in a given area, or by the number that can live healthy, productive, reasonably happy, and comfortable lives.

The Time Factor.   The optimum population size is a dynamic quantity, not a static one, and the concepts of overpopulation and underpopulation, therefore, are also dynamic. "Optimum" means "optimum under existing social and technological conditions." To argue that a region is not overpopulated by pointing out that certain hypothetical social and technological changes could relieve the stresses on resources, environment, and society is to misunderstand the biological meaning of overpopulation, which has always been defined in terms of creatures *as they are*. In this context, the conclusion is inescapable that, in terms of present patterns of human behavior and level of technology, *the planet Earth as a whole is overpopulated.*

With the passage of time, both technological change and cultural evolution will inevitably change the population sizes regarded as optimum. In the face of such changing conditions, governments should be ready to encourage appropriate population trends, just as they now attempt to produce desired economic trends. In other words, the size of the human population must be brought under rational control, but not with the idea of establishing some sort of permanently frozen optimum. Actually arriving at population sizes regarded as optimum at any given time will involve extraordinary changes in human attitudes — attitudes that have been produced by eons of biological and cultural evolution. These changes will inevitably trouble men's minds; limiting deaths goes with the grain of tradition, but limiting births goes against it. Changing people's views of birth control and desired family size to coincide with the goal of a better future for all mankind is one of the greatest challenges humanity has ever faced.

[2]See *Rapid Population Growth; Consequences and Policy Implications*, Roger Revelle et al. (Johns Hopkins Press, 1971). Report of a National Academy of Sciences Study Panel. It includes several articles on the advantages to children of being first-born or in small families.

Birth Control

An essential feature of any humane program to regulate the size of the human population, and to achieve the goal of a world optimum, is the control of births. Many birth-control practices are at least as old as recorded history. The Old Testament contains obvious references to the practice of withdrawal (removal of the penis from the woman's vagina before ejaculation). The ancient Egyptians used crude barriers to the womb made from leaves or cloth, and even blocked the entrance to the womb with cotton fibers. The ancient Greeks practiced population control through their social system as well as through contraception; they discouraged marriage and encouraged homosexual relationships, especially for men. The idea may be distasteful to most of us, but it undoubtedly worked. The condom, or penis sheath, dates back at least to the Middle Ages. Douching, the practice of flushing out the vagina with water or a solution immediately after intercourse, has had a similarly long history. The simplest, the most effective, and perhaps the oldest method of birth control is abstention; but this method seems to have been favored mainly by older men, particularly unmarried members of the clergy.

Attempts to limit family size by one means or another appear to be a universal phenomenon. Abortion has a very long history and is believed to be the single most common form of birth control in the world today, despite its illegal status in most countries. Infanticide, which is viewed with horror by prosperous people in industrialized societies, has been a rather common practice in a great many societies.

The modern family-planning movement began around the turn of the century in the United States and England as an outgrowth of the women's rights campaign. In the beginning it was intended primarily to relieve women of the burdens of too many children, which not uncommonly included a threat to the mothers' very lives. In the early years of this endeavor, men (including members of the medical profession), generally opposed the idea or were indifferent to it. Later, when the economic advantages and the benefits to conjugal and family life became evident, more men began to support family planning, and the medical profession developed more modern and effective methods of birth control. Nevertheless, more often than not, the wife still holds the primary responsibility for birth control in the family. This is reflected by the fact that the majority of modern birth-control methods, particularly those used by most married couples, are designed to be employed by the woman.

Methods of Birth Control.   Among the so-called conventional methods and devices for birth control are the condom, the diaphragm, and the cervical cap; various creams, jellies, and foams; the douche; and the rhythm system. All of these operate to prevent the meeting of sperm and ovum.

Rhythm.   Also referred to as "periodic abstention," the rhythm method is the only method of birth control now sanctioned by the Roman Catholic

Church. The basic idea is to abstain from sexual relations during the several days each month when a woman might be capable of conceiving. One difficulty is that this period is often hard to determine, particularly in women with irregular menstrual cycles. The rhythm method therefore is one of the least effective of birth-control methods. Approximately one woman in six has a cycle so irregular that the system will not work at all for her.

The Pill. The modern steroid oral contraceptive, generally known as "the pill," is the most effective means of birth control generally available today, other than sterilization and abortion. When taken without fail according to instructions, it is virtually 100 percent effective. It is believed to act by suppressing ovulation.

The advantages of an oral contraceptive are obvious, even apart from its effectiveness. Its use is far removed in time from the act of intercourse, and there are no mechanical devices or chemicals except the pill to deal with. On the other hand, the woman must remember to take it each day, which requires a fairly high degree of motivation. The chances of pregnancy increase with each forgotten pill.

As is inevitable with any drug, particularly a hormonal drug, there may be undesirable side effects. Most of these, however, wear off within a few months or can be dealt with by adjusting the dosage or changing brands.

A serious possible hazard associated with the use of the pill is the risk of thromboembolism. Research published in England in 1968 revealed that women who were using the pill had a significantly higher chance (about 8 times higher) of dying of thrombophlebitis (inflammation of veins together with blood clots) or pulmonary embolism (blood clots in the blood vessels of the lungs) than women of the same age who were not using the pill. However, the risk of death from thromboembolic disease while using the pill is still considerably less than that of death resulting from pregnancy. Newer versions of the pill appear to reduce the incidence of thrombosis by a quarter and deaths by half.

Much more time will have to pass and much more data will have to be gathered before definite statements can be made about the long-term risks involved in the use of oral contraceptives. We are in somewhat the same position as we were when DDT first came into use. The risks must be weighed against the benefits, and the long-term risks are still unknown. From what we know now, it appears that for most women the benefits outweigh the risks; the latter can be minimized through close supervision by an alert physician. Obviously, continued monitoring of the long-term effects of the pill (or any future hormonal contraceptives) is essential.

The IUD. The intrauterine device, or "IUD" as it is generally known, is a plastic or metal object that is placed inside the uterus (womb) and left there for as long as contraception is desired. The advantages of an IUD over other contraceptives for the user are several; the primary ones are that once in place it can be forgotten, and it is very inexpensive. These are great advantages for a woman whose lack of motivation, educational background, or financial resources would make other forms of birth control unreliable or beyond her means. However, it must be inserted by and subsequently checked by a physician or a paramedical person.

About 10 percent of women spontaneously expel the device, sometimes without knowing that they have. This tendency varies greatly with age and with the number of children previously borne. Many women have to remove the IUD because of such side effects as bleeding and pain. Less frequently, the IUDs may be associated with pelvic inflammation, though there is some question whether the device is primarily responsible or only aggravates a pre-existing condition. There is no evidence that IUDs lead to the development of cancer. In very rare cases perforation of the uterus occurs. Nevertheless, for the women who can successfully retain the IUD, it is a highly effective contraceptive. In its present stage of development it is probably most suitable for women over 30 who have completed their families; they are least likely to have a birth-control failure, to have problems with side effects, or to expel the device.

Various methods of birth control are compared in Table 8–1. The effectiveness of techniques is calculated on the basis of 100 woman-years — that is, the

Table 8–1   Failure Rates of Contraceptive Methods

Method	Pregnancy Rates for 100 Woman-Years of Use	
	High	Low
No contraceptive	80	80
Aerosol foam	—	29
Foam tablets	43	12
Suppositories	42	4
Jelly or cream	38	4
Douche	41	21
Diaphragm and jelly	35	4
Sponge and foam powder	35	28
Condom	28	7
Withdrawal	38	10
Rhythm	38	0
Lactation	26	24
Steroid contraception (the "pill")	2.7	0
Abortion	0	0
Intrauterine contraception (averages)		
Lippes loop (large)		
0–12 months	2.4	
12–24 months	1.4	

SOURCE: After Berelson et al., *Family Planning and Population Programs*, University of Chicago Press, 1966.

number of women per 100 who will become pregnant in a one-year period while using a given method. Among 100 women using no contraception, 80 can expect to be pregnant by the end of one year. The failure rates are based on actual results, no distinction being made whether the method failed or the individuals were careless in using it. The lower rates are generally achieved by highly motivated individuals under close medical supervision.

Sterilization.   For couples whose families are complete and who wish to rid themselves of concern about contraceptives, sterilization is often the best solution. This procedure can be performed on either partner, but it is much simpler for the male. A vasectomy takes only fifteen or twenty minutes in a doctor's office or a clinic. The procedure consists of cutting and tying off the vas deferens (sperm ducts), thus making it impossible for sperm to be included in the ejaculate (although the absence of the sperm may only be detected by microscopic examination). The female's operation, called a salpingectomy or tubal ligation, is somewhat more complicated, involving internal surgery. In this operation a section of each fallopian tube is cut and removed so that the ova (eggs) cannot pass through. Both the sperm and the eggs are resorbed by the body.

Contrary to the beliefs of many people, sterilization does not in any sense end one's sex life. Vasectomy is *not* castration. The hormonal system is left intact, and sperm are still manufactured by the body; they are simply prevented from leaving it. Sexual performance, including orgasm and ejaculation, is normally unchanged. In the few cases in which psychological problems develop, they usually are found to have grown out of previously existing disturbances. In many cases, psychological improvement is reported as worry over unwanted children ends.

The same is true for the sterilized female; her hormones still circulate, ova are still brought to maturity and released, the menstrual cycle goes on. All that is changed is that the ova and sperm can never meet. Adverse psychological reactions to this operation are extremely rare.

Many individuals hesitate to take so final a step as sterilization. Although in actual practice only a very small percentage of sterilized people ever ask to have the operation reversed, many want some assurance beforehand that it can be done. Successful reversal of the operation can now be achieved in 50 to 80 percent of cases. For men who still have lingering doubts about taking the final step of sterilization, it is now possible to preserve a sample of sperm in a frozen-sperm bank for up to 10 years, perhaps even longer. Thus, if a second wife years later wishes children, they can be provided by artificial insemination. Another possibility is that live sperm can be removed from the father's testes and used for insemination.

Sterilization is perfectly legal in the United States, although it is restricted in Utah to cases of "medical necessity." Nevertheless, in some places it is still difficult for an individual to find a doctor who is willing to perform these operations. Apparently many physicians have been relectant to perform sterilizations because of a fear of lawsuits, although no lawsuit over sterilization has ever been won in a case where a release was previously signed by the patient.

Since 1969, as a result of several court decisions, hospital restrictions against sterilizations have been loosened to a considerable degree in many states, and many more doctors now accept sterilization requests. National publicity about vasectomies has resulted in a spectacular increase in the number of men obtaining them. A medical survey revealed that 750,000 men in the United States received vasectomies in 1970, approximately a sevenfold increase in only a few years. The rate for female sterilization is about one-third as high.

Abortion.   Abortion is the arrest of a pregnancy. When performed under appropriate medical circumstances by a qualified physician, abortion is much safer than a full-term pregnancy. But if it is delayed beyond the twelfth week, the risks of complication or death rise considerably. The dangers are also very great when the abortion is illegal, as it is in much of the world. In the United States, as in many parts of the world, bungled illegal abortions have been the greatest single cause of maternal deaths.

Abortion is practiced in some form in all societies today, and there are records of it throughout history. It was made illegal in the nineteenth century on the grounds that it was dangerous to the mother. In those days before sterile medical techniques were developed, it was. In China, India, Japan, England, the USSR, Sweden, several countries in eastern Europe, and a few states in the United States, abortion today is available either on request or under fairly liberal circumstances.

But most of the United States, virtually all of Latin America, many Asian countries, and southern and western Europe still have very restrictive abortion laws. It is allowed, if at all, only when the mother's life is threatened. However, this situation may change rapidly in the next few years, as more countries reform their abortion laws either to ease their population pressures or to put an end to the tragic deaths from botched illegal abortions.

Illegal abortions can probably be obtained in every country in the world and are most prevalent where contraceptive and abortion laws are most restrictive. The poor and ignorant, who make up the bulk of the population in most UDCs, are generally unaware of the existence of birth control other than by ancient folk methods, and could not afford modern methods even if they knew of them. There are some exceptions where governments and volunteer organizations have established free birth-control clinics. But, although these help, they as yet reach only a small fraction of the population. In areas where hunger and malnutrition are widespread, a failure of primitive birth-control methods leaves women with no alternative but to practice equally crude forms of abortion.

In the United States, 17 states had moderated their abortion laws by the end of 1970. Most of these new laws permit abortion in cases where bearing the child presents a grave risk to the mental or physical health of the mother, where the pregnancy is a result of incest or rape, and where (except in California) there is a substantial likelihood that the child will be physically or mentally defective. Four states, Hawaii, Alaska, Washington, and New York, now essentially have abortion on request, although Hawaii and Alaska have residency requirements. Several states with partially reformed laws have begun to interpret their laws much more liberally, and the legal abortion rate has risen.

The rich have always been able to obtain safe abortions. Under the new liberalized laws, safe abortions have now become available to the poor (who have also to a large degree been denied access to contraceptives).

In the first year after passage of the new abortion law in 1970 there were 200,000 legal abortions in New York. It is clear that the number of illegal abortions was comparatively very low. New York maternal death rates, which include those from abortion, dropped by nearly one-half. The infant mortality rate also declined, as did the number of illegitimate births and the birth rate overall for the state. There were only 15 deaths, several of which were from illegal abortions, and all of which occurred in the first eight months after the law was passed. The death rate has remained very low.

The controversy about abortion was certainly not ended by passage of the law. Anti-abortion groups have actively lobbied to have the laws tightened up. The greatest opposition to freely available, medically safe abortion comes from the Roman Catholic Church and other religious groups that consider abortion immoral. The crux of the Catholic argument is that the unborn child is, from the moment of conception, a complete person with a soul. In the Catholic view, induced abortion is a form of murder.

By contrast many Protestant theologians hold that the time when a child acquires a soul is unknown and perhaps unimportant. They see no difficulty in establishing it at the time of "quickening." when movements of the fetus (unborn child) first become discernible to the mother; or at the time, around 28 weeks, when the infant, if prematurely born, could survive outside its mother's body. To them, the evil in abortion is far outweighed by the evil of bringing into the world an unwanted child under less than ideal circumstances.

To a biologist the question of when life begins for a human child is almost meaningless, since life is continuous and has been since it first began on Earth several billion years ago. The precursors of the egg and sperm cells that create the next generation have been present in the parents from the time they were embryos themselves. To most biologists, an embryo (unborn child during the first two or three months of development) or a fetus is no more a complete human being than a blueprint is a building. The fetus, given the opportunity to develop properly before birth, and given the essential early socializing experiences and sufficient nourishing food during the crucial early years after birth, will ultimately develop into a human being. Where any of these essential elements is lacking, the resultant individual will be deficient in some respect.

From this point of view, a fetus is only a *potential* human being.[3] Historically, the law has dated most rights and privileges from the moment of birth, and legal scholars generally agree that a fetus is not a "person" within the meaning of the United States Constitution until it is born and living independent of its mother's body.

From the standpoint of a terminated fetus, it makes no difference whether the mother had an induced or a spontaneous abortion. On the other hand, it subsequently makes a great deal of difference to the child if an abortion is is denied, and the mother, contrary to her wishes, is forced to devote her body and life to the production and care of the child. In Sweden, studies were made to determine what eventually happened to children born to mothers whose requests for abortions had been turned down. When compared to a matched group of children from similar backgrounds who had been wanted, more than twice as many of these unwanted youngsters grew up in undesirable circumstances (illegitimate, in broken homes, or in institutions), more than twice as many had records of delinquency, or were deemed unfit for military service, almost twice as many had needed psychiatric care, and nearly five times as many had been on public assistance during their teens.

There seems little doubt that the forced bearing of unwanted children has undesirable consequences not only for the children themselves and their families but for society as well, apart from the problems of overpopulation. The latter factor, however, adds further urgency to the need for preventing unwanted births. An abortion is clearly preferable to adding a child to an overburdened family or an overburdened society, where the chances that it will realize its full potentialities are slight.

Those who oppose abortion often raise the argument that a decision is being made for an unborn person who "has no say." But unthinking actions of the very same people help to commit future unheard generations to misery and early death on an overcrowded planet.

One can also challenge the notion that anyone—a medical doctor, a legislator, or a celibate clergyman—has the right to make decisions whose consequences are borne largely by young women and their families.

There are those who claim that free access to abortion will lead to genocide. It is hard to see how this could happen if the decision is left to the mother. A mother who takes the moral view that abortion is equivalent to murder is free to bear her child. If she cannot care for it, placement for adoption is still possible.

Few people would claim that abortion is preferable to contraception, not only because of moral questions, but also because the risk of death or injury to the mother is usually greater. But until more effective forms of contracep-

---

[3]See "Abortion—Compulsory Pregnancy?" by Garrett Hardin in the *Journal of Marriage and Family*, vol. 30, no. 2, 1968, for a full discussion of abortion from a biologist's point of view.

tion are developed and made fully available, abortion will remain a common method of birth control when contraceptives fail.

Attitudes on abortion have changed before, and they can reasonably be expected to change again in the future. Only a few years ago public disapproval of abortion for virtually all possible reasons, except to save the life of the mother, was very strong. Over the past decade, there has been a progressive reversal in attitudes. In 1972, for the first time, a majority of Catholics agreed that "the decision to have an abortion should be made solely by a woman and her physician." In the general population, 57 percent agreed.

In March 1972, the U.S. Commission on Population Growth and the American Future issued its final report. On the subject of abortion, the majority of the Commission recommended:

> . . . that present state laws restricting abortion be liberalized along the lines of the New York State statute, such abortions to be performed on request by duly licensed physicians under conditions of medical safety.

In a democratic country like the United States, there is good reason to question the legality of denying women the right of access to abortion. The female half of the world's population has already cast its silent vote. Every year perhaps one million women in the United States and an estimated 30 to 40 million more elsewhere make their desires abundantly clear by seeking and obtaining abortions, more often than not in the face of their societies' disapproval and of very real dangers and difficulties.

Birth Control in the Future.   Many possible ways of interfering with the reproductive process have yet to be explored; some of the most promising of these are under investigation in laboratories or are being tested clinically in humans. Within the next decade or two a variety of new methods of birth control may become available for general use. Some of the methods currently being developed show considerable promise as practical approaches for population control in underdeveloped countries, where only the simplest and cheapest methods are likely to result in a substantial lowering of birth rates.

Among the developments most likely to prove useful soon are various forms of low, continuous dosages of progestin (a synthetic hormone, also used in the pill). These appear to be potentially as effective a contraceptive as the pill, and without some of its hazards. They may also prove to be less expensive. Research has now been carried out with several forms of low-dose progestins: a "mini-pill," taken daily with no "time off" to keep track of; intramuscular injections at three-month or six-month intervals; and an implanted "time capsule," which is implanted under the skin by a hypodermic needle. The implant releases the steroid at a constant rate over a long period of time, potentially as long as 25 or 30 years.

"Morning-after" birth control consists of taking a substantial oral dose of estrogens within a few days after coitus. Pregnancy is prevented, but the woman usually feels quite sick for a day or two. It is therefore not suitable for regular use, at least in this form. This method is still being clinically tested, but is available in some medical centers in the United States.

One of the newest and most fascinating developments in drug research has been the discovery of prostaglandins, a group of hormone-like substances related to fatty acids and normally found in many mammalian tissues. They appear to have beneficial applications in many areas of medicine, one of which is in birth control. Intravenous injections of prostaglandins induce menstruation or labor, depending on the stage of pregnancy. Their action is therefore actually abortifacient (abortion-inducing). Experimental work with women on this new method is being carried on in several countries with intravenous, oral, and vaginal applications. If either of the latter methods proves successful, prostaglandins may become a safe, self-administered form of birth control, whose use would probably not be required more than a few times a year. Some temporary side effects have been reported with prostaglandins, but further development may reduce or eliminate their incidence. Of course, it is far too early to know what, if any, long-term effects will attend the use of prostaglandins, and many years of research lie ahead before they will be generally available.

Besides experiments with a variety of chemicals, some other new ideas being tested in laboratories are more sophisticated versions of contraceptives already in use. Attempts to find new forms of contraceptives for men have so far been remarkably unsuccessful. Among the most promising are removable mechanical devices, now only in the experimental stage, which may provide reversible sterilization. If successful, these devices would satisfy the objections to sterilization from those who fear taking an irreversible step.

Research and Development. In the light of the current world-population situation, it is clear that research on means of birth control has been neglected for too long. Although some potentially valuable possibilities for birth control have come out of recent research, obviously we are still many years away from having an ideal contraceptive—one that is cheap, easy to use, effective, and free from unpleasant or dangerous side effects. In the United States, a *minimum* of 8 to 10 years of testing is required before a new contraceptive agent can be released to the general public.[4] Since contraceptive chemicals, unlike most other drugs, are intended for continuous or regular use over long periods of time, perhaps decades, by large numbers of people, the need for exhaustive testing is genuine. But there is no question that it requires a great deal of

[4]See "Birth Control After 1984," by Carl Djerassi in *Science*, vol. 169, pp. 941–951, Sept. 4, 1970, for a detailed discussion of the problems of contraceptive research and development.

time and increasing quantities of money. Unless some incentives, including governmental support, are soon established to encourage research and development in the birth-control field, new contraceptive agents may be delayed in their appearance on the market even beyond the middle 1980s. In view of the world's great need for cheap, simple, and effective means of birth control, the United States and other DCs have an obligation to make positive efforts to encourage their development.

Family Planning

What is being done in the world today to limit human population size? How can today's efforts be converted to genuine population control? Family-planning programs are the only programs now in existence that claim to have as a goal the regulation of human numbers. However, family planning is traditionally oriented to the needs of individuals and families, not of societies. *Family planning and population control are therefore not synonymous.*

Family Planning in the DCs.   Birth rates in the United States and Europe had already begun to decline as a result of the demographic transition long before the establishment of the first birth-control clinics before World War I. But the early Planned Parenthood movement, especially in the United States, played a significant role in popularizing the idea of birth control and making information and contraceptive materials available to the public. This was accomplished not so much through their clinics, which never reached more than a small fraction of the population, as through the removal of restrictive laws against birth control, the development of medical and religious support for family planning, and the creation of a social climate in which birth-control information could circulate freely.

By 1965, survey results showed that some 85 percent of married women in America had used some method of birth control, most of them favoring the more effective methods such as the pill. This represents virtual saturation, since most of the remainder were subfertile, pregnant, or planning to use contraceptives only when their families were complete. Catholic women in the sample showed a level of use of "artificial" contraceptives nearly as high as that of non-Catholic women.

In Europe, withdrawal seems still to be the most widely known and practiced method, followed by rhythm and the condom. However, use of the pill is increasing in most countries. Only in England and Scandinavia do modern contraceptive devices approach being as well known and readily available as they are in the United States. In France, Belgium, and the Netherlands, laws restrict the dissemination of contraceptive information and materials. Birth control is still entirely illegal in Spain, Portugal, and Ireland, although a movement for change has begun. Italy has legalized the pill for "medical

Table 8-2 Family Planning in UDCs

Size of Population (in millions)	Have an Official Family Planning Policy and Program	Have Limited Governmental Involvement or Support of Family Planning	Are Doing Nothing Official in Family Planning
400+	People's Republic of China (1962) India (1952, reorganized 1965)	——	——
100–400	Indonesia (1968)	——	——
50–100	Bengladesh (1971) Pakistan (1960, reorganized 1965)	Nigeria (1970)	Mexico Brazil
25–50	Turkey (1965) Egypt (1965) Iran (1967) Philippines (1970) Thailand (1970) South Korea (1961)	——	Burma Ethiopia
15–25	Morocco (1965) Colombia (1970)	North Vietnam (1962) South Vietnam (1968) Afghanistan (1971) South Africa (1966) Sudan (1970)	Zaire
10-15	Taiwan (1964) Nepal (1966) Ceylon (1965) Kenya (1966) Malaysia (1966)	Venezuela (1965) Chile (1965) Tanzania (1970) Uganda (1972)	Algeria North Korea Peru Iraq
Less than 10	Tunisia (1964) Barbados (1967) Dominican Republic (1968) Singapore (1965) Jamaica (1966) Trinidad and Tobago (1967) Ghana (1969) Mauritius (1965) Puerto Rico (1970) Fiji (1971)	Cuba (early 1960s) Nicaragua (1963) Costa Rica (1968) Hong Kong (1965) Panama (1969) Honduras (1956) Dahomey (1969) Gambia (1969) Rhodesia (1968) Bolivia (1968) Ecuador (1968) El Salvador (1967) Botswana (1971) Guatemala (1969) Haiti (1971) Western Samoa (1971)	Algeria Madagascar Khmer Republic (formerly Cambodia) Jordan Laos Lebanon Saudi Arabia Syria Yemen Upper Volta Mali Senegal

SOURCE: Berelson, *Studies in Family Planning* no. 39, (supp.) 1969, and Nortman, *Reports on Population/Family Planning*, no. 2, 1972, The Population Council.

purposes" (presumably to combat the high illegal abortion rate), condoms are available "for disease prevention," and birth-control information is now legally available. The Soviet Union and eastern European countries distribute contraceptives through government maternal health clinics, but people there are still heavily dependent on abortion for birth control.

Throughout its history, the emphasis and primary concern of the family-planning movement has been the welfare of the family; it has stressed the economic, educational, and health advantages of well-spaced, limited numbers of children. Its policy has been to provide information and materials for birth control in volunteer-staffed clinics for the poor, serving any interested client. Once the movement was established in the United States, little effort was made to recruit clients beyond the routine promotion that accompanied the opening of a new clinic.

Family Planning in the UDCs. In response to rising alarm during the 1950s over the population explosion in underdeveloped countries, both private and governmental organizations in the United States and other nations began to be involved in population research and overseas family-planning programs. The 1960s brought a great proliferation of family-planning programs in UDCs (Table 8–2), assisted or administered by one or another of these organizations. So far these are the only programs that have been brought into action against the population problem in UDCs, except in the People's Republic of China and a few other countries where other policies supplement family planning.[5]

Studies conducted in UDCs typically reveal that knowledge of birth control is very limited in these populations, especially outside the cities and the educated classes, and the practice of birth control is even more limited. A major difficulty is that people in UDCs generally want more children for various reasons than do people in DCs. Table 8–3 gives figures on average desired family sizes in both UDCs and DCs.

Family-planning programs in UDCs are usually carried out through independent clinics or in cooperation with maternal and child-health agencies. In some countries, mobile units are used to carry workers and equipment to remote villages. Unlike the traditional planned-parenthood organizations in DCs, these programs actively recruit clients, employing specially trained field workers for this purpose and utilizing whatever forms of mass communication and promotion seem effective. The primary emphasis of the propaganda is on preventing "unwanted births." Family-planning programs generally offer a variety of birth-control methods including sterilization, although the latter has only been used or promoted on a large scale in India and Pakistan. In addition, they provide counseling services for marriage, parenthood and child-spacing, and assistance for subfertile and sterile couples.

[5]See "Report from China—III: Population Care and Control," by Edgar Snow in *The New Republic*, vol. 164, no. 18, pp. 20–23, May 1, 1971.

Table 8-3   Desired Family Size Compared to Birth Rate

Area	Date	Average Number of Children Desired	Percentage Desiring:		1972 Birth Rate
			4 or More	5 or More	
Austria	1960	2.0	4		15.2
Czechoslovakia	1959	2.3			15.8
Great Britain	1960	2.8	23		16.2
France	1960	2.8	17		16.7
Japan	1961	2.8	22	8	19.0
Italy	1960	3.1	18		16.8
Norway	1960	3.1	25		16.6
U.S.A.	1960	3.3	40	15	17.3
Colombia	1963	3.5			44.0
Turkey	1963	3.5	42	25	40.0
Taiwan	1962–1963	3.9	62	22	28.0
Thailand	1964	3.8	54	26	43.0
Pakistan	1960	3.9	65	26	51.0
Chile	1959	4.1	58	26	28.0
Canada	1960	4.2	70		17.5
India	1952–1960	3.7–4.7	57–63	25–34	42.0
S. Korea	1962	4.4	77	44	31.0
Ghana	1963	5.3	88	56	47.0

SOURCE: Data from *Studies in Family Planning No. 7*, Population Council, 1965. Birth rates from 1972 *World Population Data Sheet*, Population Reference Bureau.

With the single exception of India, no UDC had an official family-planning program prior to 1960. Since 1965 the program in India has accelerated, and it is now using considerably stronger measures than are employed in most such programs. These include the establishment of clinics (associated with maternal-health facilities where possible), temporary camps, and mobile units (Figure 8-1), all accompanied by a very active education campaign to promote small families. Vasectomy and the IUD are the most used methods, although female sterilization and traditional contraceptives are also available. Men who accept vasectomies, and any person who persuades a man to have one, are paid small fees.

But India has run into some problems with her policies, particularly in rural areas. Aside from the monumental logistic difficulty of taking family planning to every village, a good deal of resistance has been met in some places, which has even led occasionally to riots and the destruction of camps and mobile units. This resistance results in part from the existence of three active medical traditions in India—ayurvedic, unani, and homeopathic—besides Western medicine. So far the family-planning program has been implemented only through Western medicine, a circumstance that naturally results in resentment and opposition from the others. Resistance also comes from religious and ethnic minority groups, who may perceive family planning as discrimination. This opposition has begun to show itself in a drop in the vasectomy and contraceptive acceptance rates because of lack of candidates.

By 1972, some 28 UDCs had established official antinatalist policies and were supporting family-planning programs. Another 26 countries were supporting family planning at least to a limited extent. The earlier and more vigorous programs have made considerable progress in terms of reaching a large proportion of the reproductive population. Yet, as reflected by current birth and growth rates, most show remarkably little progress toward fulfilling their own short-term goals of birth rate and growth rate reduction (Table 8–4).

Taiwan and South Korea have shown a considerable drop in birth rates since their programs were initiated, but birth rates in both countries had begun to decline before then. How much of the recent decline is due to the family-planning program is extremely hard to determine, as the administrators of the programs themselves admit. Neither country has made much effort to promote small families until recently. Taiwan may achieve its 1973 birth rate goal, although the growth rate goal seems farther away. South Korea failed to meet its growth rate goal for 1971. These two nations have given us some

Figure 8–1   A mobile vasectomy clinic in Bombay, India. This bus brings birth control information and materials to men in cities and remote villages. (Courtesy of Carl Purcell, Agency for International Development.)

Table 8-4 Family Planning Effects Measured Against Goals

Country	Program Begun	Birth Rate per 1,000		Growth Rate in Percent		Population of Married Couples	
		Goal[a]	1972[b]	Goal[a]	1972[b]	Target[c] (Millions)	Protected by 1970 (Percent)
India	1965	40 to 25 (in 10 years)	42	—	2.5	96	12
Pakistan	1965	50 to 40 (by 1970)	51	—	3.3	20	> 11
S. Korea	1961	——	31	2.9 to 2.0 (1962–71)	2.0	4.5	32
Taiwan	1964	36 to 24 (by 1973)	28	3.02 to 1.86 (1965–73)	2.3	1.8	36
Ceylon	1965	33 to 25 (in 8–10 years)	31	1.6 (by 1976)	2.2	1.7	> 8.2
Turkey	1965	——	40	3.0 to 2.0 (by 1972)	2.5	5.6	3
Singapore	1965	30 to under 20 (in 5 years)	23	—	2.2	0.3	45
Malaysia	1966	——	37	3.0 to 2.2 (by 1987)	2.8	1.6	7
Dominican Republic	1968	48 to 40 (by 1972) to 28 (by 1978)	49	3.4 to 2.7 (by 1972)	3.4	—	—
Morocco	1965	50 to 45 (by 1973)	50	—	3.4	2.6	1
Trinidad and Tobago	1967	38 to 19 (by 1978)	23	—	1.1	—	—

[a]Data on birth and growth rate goals, which have been set by the national family planning programs, are from Berelson, Studies in Family Planning, no. 39 (supp.), 1969.
[b]Data for 1972 birth and growth rates are from the Population Reference Bureau.
[c]The "target population" is the number of married couples in the reproductive ages (15–44). The "protected population" refers to the percentage of the target population which is sterilized or using some form of contraception, whether provided by a government program or through private services. Data from Studies in Family Planning, 1965–1970.

measure of the potential effectiveness of family planning alone for reducing population growth in UDCs, although both started with some advantages over most other UDCs. Taiwan, and to a lesser degree Korea, were fairly highly urbanized (for Asia), relatively literate, beginning to industrialize, and had governments favorable to the idea of family-planning programs.

Hong Kong and Singapore are also considered to have "successful" family-planning programs, although neither has come close to controlling its population growth. Both are islands, are overwhelmingly urban, and have fairly high literacy rates and well-organized medical services. Apparently the need to limit population when it is confined to small islands is as obvious to citizens as to the government, and progress in lowering birth rates may be more easily achieved under these special conditions.

Attitudes and Birth Rates

Unquestionably the single most important factor in a country's reproductive rate is the motivation of the people toward the regulation of family size. The strength of the desire for a small family is critical. If a couple is determined not to have more than two children, they usually will not, regardless of whether there is a birth-control clinic down the street. Conversely, if motivation is weak, the practice of birth control is likely to be a sometime thing, although the motivation often grows with the number of children in the family.

The overriding importance of motivation is made clear by the example of Europe, particularly in predominantly Catholic countries. The continent as a whole has the lowest birth rates of any comparable area in the world, and most European countries have had low birth rates for at least two generations. The population of Europe is growing at considerably less than 1 percent per year (0.8 percent); only Albania, Rumania, and Iceland have growth rates of 1.2 percent or more. Moreover, birth rates are just as low in countries where contraceptives and birth-control information are banned or restricted as they are in neighboring countries where information and devices are generally available and in moderately wide use.

Studies in various countries with different levels of development and different population densities indicate that people tend to have the number of children they say they want. Therefore, even if there were no unwanted babies at all, each country's growth rate would probably be little reduced. Surveys show (Table 8–3) that the average number of children wanted per family varies from 2.0 to 3.3 in most European countries. In the United States it was about 3.3 during the 1960s, but dropped to 2.3 by 1971. By contrast, the average ideal family size in most UDCs ranges between 3.5 and 5.5 children. In the United States, a significant decline in the birth rate accompanied the drop in desired family size.

Given the death rates characteristic of DCs, it would require an average of only 2.2 children per married couple over the long run to result in a steady population size. Obviously, population growth, especially in UDCs, cannot be stopped merely by preventing unwanted births, although that is certainly a desirable first step.

A great many socioeconomic factors affect the reproductive goals of individuals and of a society. Among these are the general educational level, the degree of urbanization, the social status of women, the opportunities open to women for employment outside the home, and the costs of raising and educating each child. The higher or greater each of these factors is, the lower fertility generally will be. Other factors, such as the average age at marriage (especially of women), the degree of social tolerance for illegitimate births, or the usual length of time of breast-feeding, also can directly affect the fertility rates. Later marriage, lower tolerance for illegitimacy, and extended breast-feeding all operate to reduce fertility.

Family-planning programs in general have made little effort to influence these factors. Most of them try only to influence people by emphasizing the economic and health advantages of small families to themselves and their children. Government officials, economic advisors, and many demographers tend to believe that the process of economic development will automatically bring about the conditions that lead to the desire for fewer children and in turn cause a demographic transition in UDCs. Family planning has therefore been introduced in many countries where extremely high population growth rates were impeding the rate of economic development. This is a move in the right direction, but unfortunately this great faith in the possibilities of industrial development, the demographic transition, and the prevention of unwanted children too often encourages governments in these countries to relax under the illusion that their population problems are being solved. (Conversely, many officials are lulled into the equally illusionary belief that family planning alone will automatically bring about a solution to their social and economic problems.)

A demographic transition would at best merely reduce growth rates in UDCs to the level of those of the DCs. Thus it cannot be expected to *solve* any country's population problem. In most UDCs, moreover, lack of resources and overpopulation may combine to prevent sufficient development for a demographic transition to occur. At worst, then, the demographic transition is no solution at all to UDC population problems, and at best it is an insufficient one.

If vigorous family-planning programs had been initiated just after World War II, when death control and the ideas of economic development were introduced in UDCs, the population situation might be of much more manageable dimensions today. But it plainly would still be with us. Even if the strongest feasible population-control measures were everywhere in force today, our runaway population growth could not be appreciably slowed, let alone arrested, for a discouragingly long time.

Population Growth and Policies in the United States

Some people seem to believe that in order to stop population growth there should be no reproduction at all. Actually, to reduce the 1971 United States birth rate of 17.3 per 1,000 population to where it would ultimately balance the death rate would require only a reduction to about 13 per 1,000. This is so, even though the current death rate is 9.3 per 1,000, because such low birth rates would with a few decades change the age composition of the population. The average age of the population would rise from the present 28 to about 37, and with a greater proportion in the older age classes, the death rate would rise significantly.

Looking at it another way, if the average desired size of the American family were shifted downward to 2.2, and if there were no net immigration, the growth rate of the United States population would be reduced to zero after about 70 years. If American families were to produce less than an average of 2.2 children each, the growth rate would decline more rapidly and would reach zero sooner.

Economist Stephen Enke has calculated a hypothetical model for the distribution of family sizes that would achieve the desired replacement rate. In this model, 50 percent of married women could have two children, which might be considered the norm or the ideal. Some 10 percent would have only one child, and 5 percent remain childless. Above the norm, 30 percent might have three children, and another 5 percent more than three, with an average of five. Obviously, this distribution still allows for a few large families, but the vast majority of families would have one, two, or three children. Another hypothetical distribution that would have the same demographic result would have greater proportions of both childless couples and families with more than three children.

How much of today's U.S. population growth is due to unwanted births is a matter for debate among demographers. The evidence is that the proportion has declined considerably since the early 1960s, especially among the poor, who have only recently been given access to contraceptives and, in some states, to safe abortion (see Box 8–1).[6] There is, however, no question that providing better contraceptives, legalizing abortion in the remaining states, and ensuring that both are easily available to all members of the population could further reduce the incidence of unwanted pregnancy—a desirable end in itself. But the complete elimination of unwanted pregnancies is probably not possible, and a significant additional lowering of U.S. birth rates without a reduction in family-size goals seems improbable.

Surveys taken between 1965 and 1971 revealed a growing awareness on the part of the American public of the population problem. In 1971, as polls showed an abrupt drop in the desire for large families among Americans, the fertility rate also dropped precipitously. The time span for this decline is too short to allow interpretation. Whether this is only a brief dip in fertility or the beginning of an important trend, and exactly what factors are producing it, only time will reveal. If postponement of marriage and family for economic or war-related reasons proves to be the major cause, the reduction of fertility will be only temporary. If, on the other hand, this decline in fertility heralds a genuine, lasting change in family-size goals, population growth will as a result be slowed. But, because of the age composition of the U.S. population, unless the average family size drops to less than two children, it will still require a minimum of 70 years to bring growth to an end.

Reflecting this rising public consciousness of population growth and the lowered fertility rates of the 1960s, the Census Bureau in 1971 issued two new projections of U.S. population growth based on the attainment of replacement rates of completed fertility in the 1970s. One projection, Series E, assumes that

---

[6]See "The Modernization of U.S. Contraceptive Practice," by Charles F. Westoff in *Family Planning Perspectives*, vol. 4, no. 3, July, 1972.

Box 8–1   Poverty, Race, and Birth Control

The entrance of the United States government into the field of birth control through the extension of family-planning services to the poor has aroused a controversy quite out of proportion to its potential effect on the national birth rate, particularly in the black community, some members of which perceive it as a policy of "genocide" against racial minorities.

In the United States, birth rates are higher among the poor and among nonwhites (Negroes, Orientals, and American Indians) than they are among the nonpoor and among whites, but in recent years the birth rates of the poor and nonwhites have been declining even more rapidly than those of the population as a whole. High birth rates are strongly associated with low economic and educational levels in the United States, and the poorest and least educated have somewhat higher birth rates than the rest of the population. At the same time, the poor and nonwhites also have consistently higher death rates, especially among infants and children. Above the poverty level, the birth-rate difference between races diminishes, and college-educated nonwhites have *fewer* children than their white peers.

Although there is conflicting evidence regarding desired family sizes among the poor, several surveys conducted in the 1960s indicate that they wish to have only slightly more children than do middle-class couples, and nonwhite couples in most socioeconomic classes want fewer children than comparable whites do. This is especially true among the younger couples in their prime childbearing years.

At the same time, the incidence of unwanted children among the poor and near-poor in the early 1960s was estimated to be as high as 40 percent. For nonpoor couples the incidence was about 14 percent. The reasons for this disparity between desires and actual reproductive performance appear to lie less in the lack of knowledge of contraceptives than in the unavailability of effective ones. The poor who used birth control tended to use less reliable methods than did members of the middle class.

Because poor people cannot usually afford contraceptives, and because no family-planning information or services were provided through welfare health services until the late 1960s, most poor people were until then deprived of effective methods of birth control.

Between 1965 and 1970, fertility among the poor and near-poor declined by 21 percent, doubtless due in part to the new services which were by then reaching an estimated 1.5 million women. The greatest fertility decline occurred among nonwhite women below the poverty level.

Despite the tendency of black militants to regard the provision of birth-control information and services to the poor as a policy of "genocide" against Negroes, it should be emphasized that the government's present program is basically intended to benefit the poor, and poor children in particular. In this connection it is unfortunate that the government chose to label its policy as a "population control" measure, which it is not; rather, it is a logical and long overdue extension both of the family-planning movement and of the welfare program.

Fears of discrimination have been aroused in areas where middle-class social workers or people operating birth-control clinics in poor neighborhoods have put pressure on women to accept birth-control services. The best way to avoid either the appearance or the actuality of such discrimination is to have these services administered by residents of the same neighborhoods they serve.

Although many middle-class Americans favor population control for others, especially the poor, they must realize that it is really their own excessive reproduction that accounts for most of the U.S. population growth rate. Furthermore, the middle class and the wealthy are responsible for the high rate of consumption and pollution, which are the most obvious symptoms of overpopulation in the United States.

net immigration will continue at the present rate (400,000 per year); the other, Series X, assumes no net immigration. In Series X, the U.S. population would be only about 250 million in 2000 and would stabilize in 2037 at about 276 million. Series E would put the U.S. population at 266 million in 2000 and at 300 million and still growing shortly after 2020. Earlier projections for the year 2000, Series B, C, and D, assumed higher fertility rates and ranged between 280 million and 420 million for that year. See Figure 8–2 for a comparison of the impact of different rates of fertility on the future size of the United States within 50 years.

The growth of the women's liberation movement in the United States since 1965 may well have become an important influence on birth rates. Young women are expressing more interest in careers and equal opportunities and pay with men in business and the professions and less interest in "home-making" than they did in earlier years. The movement has been an important force behind the liberalization of abortion laws and campaigns for the estab-lishment of low-cost day-care centers for children and tax deductions for the costs of child care and household work. Many young women are refreshingly honest about their personal lack of interest in having children, an attitude that would have been virtually unthinkable 15 years ago in the United States. Should these attitudes become widespread in the female population, and

Figure 8–2 Population growth in the United States, past and projected. (From the U.S. Bureau of Census, "Projections of the Population of the United States, by Age and Sex: 1970 to 2020," *Current Population Reports*, Series P-25, no. 470, 1971.)

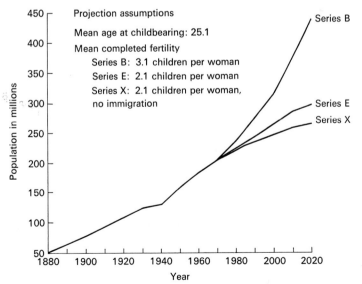

should the political goals of women's liberation be achieved, the result might well be significantly lower fertility rates.

In late 1968 Zero Population Growth was founded; the purpose of this organization is to promote an end to U.S. population growth through lowered birth rates as soon as possible and, secondarily, to do the same for world population. The organization hopes to achieve this (1) by educating the public to the dangers of uncontrolled population growth and its relation to resource depletion, environmental deterioration, and various social problems, and (2) by lobbying and taking other political action to encourage the development of antinatalist policies in the government.

Distribution and Zoning Policies.   Obscuring the population controversy in the United States has been the recent tendency of some demographers and government officials to blame our population-related problems on "maldistribution." The claim is that pollution and urban problems such as crime and unrest are the result of uneven distribution, that troubled cities may be over-populated while other areas of the country are losing population. The cure most often suggested to resolve this situation is the creation of "new cities" to absorb the 80 million or so people that are expected to be added to the U.S. population by 2000.

It is of course true that there is a distribution problem in the United States. However, population maldistribution is a different, although related, problem from that of absolute growth, and it demands a different set of solutions. Nevertheless, if growth is not curtailed, the distribution situation will certainly be aggravated.

Unfortunately, the proposal to create new cities—which would need to be built at the improbable rate of one the size of Spokane (Figure 8–3), Washington, *per month* until the end of the century if *all* expected population growth were to be absorbed—suffers from a number of serious drawbacks. In order to provide space alone, the United States would probably have to sacrifice substantial amounts of land now in agricultural production. Wasteland or grazing land could be used instead, but most people would find such areas less desirable places to live, and shortage of water might be a limiting factor. New cities would not necessarily reduce pollution; rather, they would provide additional foci of environmental deterioration. Thus the net effect on *total* environmental impact, aside from redistributing it, would be beneficial only if careful planning were used to minimize commuting and other destructive activities in the new communities. Moreover, the costs of the undertaking would be enormous. And it is doubtful that such a solution would ameliorate the social problems associated with such a mobile population; rather, they seem likely to intensify many of them. These potential disadvantages of new population centers must be weighed against the difficulties of revitalizing existing cities. The best strategy may prove to be a mixture of the two approaches.

A few states and local governments have become aware of the possibilities of limiting local population growth due to immigration by restricting or discouraging industrial and other development. The state of Delaware has banned

Figure 8–3 An aerial view of Spokane, Washington. If the population of the U.S. continued to grow at its present rate, a city of this size would have to be built each month from now until the end of the century to accommodate the additions to the population. (Courtesy of the Spokane Chamber of Commerce.)

the further establishment of heavy industries along its shoreline, and other industries must be approved before they can be established. One of the reasons cited for the ban, apart from the severe pollution such industries would bring, was the influx of population they would attract. The Colorado Environmental Commission has proposed that a population size limit be established for the Denver metropolitan area. The city of Los Angeles, which is presently zoned for a completed population size of 9.9 million, is considering a massive zoning rollback to achieve a completed city size of 4.1 million. (The 1970 population was about 2.8 million.) Oregon and Florida have stopped their former policies of encouraging immigration and are restricting industrial development.

Many other areas are changing or reconsidering their zoning regulations as a means of limiting growth. Since zoning merely restricts the use of land, it does not constitute a taking of property by the public for public use, and therefore the landowner is not entitled to compensation. Thus, socially undesirable development may be stopped, without cost to taxpayers, by means of restrictive zoning. The trend toward restrictive development policies can be expected to accelerate as more local governments become aware of the consequences of excessive growth.

U.S. Population Policies. Until 1970 the only population policies that the United States had were pronatalist policies implicit in tax and other laws, and the regulation of immigration. In 1970 Congress passed the Family Planning Services and Population Research Act, established the Commission on Population Growth and the American Future, and passed the Housing and Urban Development Act, which authorized urban redevelopment and the building of new towns. In 1972, an amendment to the Constitution affirming equal rights for women passed Congress.

A resolution was introduced in Congress in 1970 that called for a national goal of zero population growth:

> That it is the policy of the United States to develop, encourage, and implement, at the earliest possible time, the necessary policies, attitudes, social standards and actions which will, by voluntary means consistent with human rights and individual conscience, stabilize the population of the United States and thereby promote the future well-being of the citizens of this Nation and the entire world.

This resolution died in committee but has been reintroduced. Bills have also been introduced in Congress to limit tax exemptions for children to two per family, and to legalize abortion nationwide, but neither piece of legislation has gone very far. Other proposed legislation which, if enacted, might directly or indirectly affect American reproduction, includes bills to equalize tax rates between single and married people, to grant tax deductions for adoption fees, and to grant tax deductions for and to provide for child care.

The 1970 Family Planning Act provided for family planning information and services for all women in the U.S. who cannot afford them, provides grants for training and research, and established a national Center for Population and Family Planning in the Department of Health, Education and Welfare.

President Nixon has so far shown less leadership in dealing with population growth than many members of Congress, despite verbal expressions of concern. Budget requests for the Family Planning Act have been far below what was authorized. In early 1971, the President reversed an earlier Armed Services policy of providing abortion in military hospitals regardless of local laws, thus imposing his personal moral views on the women members and female dependents of the armed forces.

In early 1972, the Commission on Population Growth and the American Future released its final report. After two years of study, the Commission concluded that there were "no substantial benefits" to be gained from continued population growth, and indeed they found many serious disadvantages. Besides recommending the liberalization of abortion laws and numerous other population-related policies, the report strongly recommended that contraceptives should be made available to all who need them, including minors, that hospital restrictions on voluntary sterilization should be relaxed, that sex education should be universally available, and that health services related to fertility should be covered by health insurance. It also recommended policies to deal with immigration, population distribution and land use. Perhaps most important, the Commission stated:

> *Recognizing that our population cannot grow indefinitely, and appreciating the advantages of moving now toward the stabilization of population, the Commission recommends that the nation welcome and plan for a stabilized population.*

President Nixon rejected the Commission's recommendations that abortion laws be liberalized and that contraceptives be provided to sexually active minors without parental consent. He made no comment on any of the other recommendations or on any of the findings of the two-year study. We hope that all Americans will nonetheless give this report the serious attention it deserves, and that its recommendations will be adopted.

Population Control

Population control is the planned regulation of population size by society. No nation has yet adopted as a goal the reduction of its population growth rate to zero, let alone a reduction in absolute population size. In fact, governments in some UDCs—especially in Africa, where the death rate is still well above the average DC level—are hotly pursuing a high birth rate in the belief that their countries need more people in order to develop! These countries, needless to say, generally do not have official family-planning programs.

Before any really effective population control can be established, the political leaders, economists, national planners, and others who determine such policies must be convinced of its necessity. Most of the measures beyond traditional family planning that might be effective have never been tried because they are considered too strong and too restrictive, and because they run counter to traditional attitudes. In many countries these measures may never be considered until massive famines, political unrest, or ecological disasters make their initiation imperative. In such emergencies, whatever measures are economically and technologically expedient will be the likeliest to be imposed, regardless of their political or social acceptability.

We should long ago have begun exploring, developing, and discussing all possible means of population control. But we did not, and time has nearly run out. Measures that may seem totally unacceptable today to the majority of people at large or to their national leaders may be seen as very much the lesser of evils only a few years from now. It must be remembered that even family planning, easily justified on humanitarian grounds alone and economically feasible for even the poorest of countries, was widely considered totally unacceptable as a government policy only 15 years ago.[7]

Most of the objections to population control can be overcome or are likely to disappear with time and changing conditions. Promising methods of birth control that are not now technologically possible should be developed, so that they would be available if and when the need for them arose. Generous assistance from developed countries could remove many economic and lack-of-personnel barriers to population-control programs in UDCs. Effectiveness can really only be evaluated after a method has been tried. Moral acceptability is very likely to change as social and economic conditions change in most societies. The struggle for economic development in the UDCs is producing considerable social upheaval, which will particularly affect such basic elements of society as family structure. Radical changes in family structure and relationships are inevitable, whether population control is instituted or not. Inaction, attended by a deterioration in living conditions, will bring changes everywhere that no one could consider beneficial. Thus, it is beside the point to object to population-control measures simply on the grounds that they might change the social structure or family relationships.

[7]See "Beyond Family Planning," by Bernard Berelson (in *Science*, vol. 163, pp. 533–543, 1969), for a conservative view of possible measures for population control.

Measures for Population Control. Among proposed general approaches to population control are family planning, the use of socioeconomic pressures, and compulsory fertility control. Maximum freedom of choice is provided by traditional family planning, which allows each couple to plan the number and spacing of their children. But family planning alone should not be regarded as "population control," because it includes no consideration of optimum population size for the society, nor does it influence parental goals. Although population growth may be substantially slowed by family planning where personal motivation favors low birth rates and family planning is for relatively few children, family planning in other areas is likely to result in average family sizes too large to produce the desired level of population growth, stability, or decline.

The use of abortion and voluntary sterilization to supplement other forms of birth control can quite properly be included, wherever acceptable, as part of family planning, and made available at costs everyone can afford. Such an extension of family planning might be a first step toward population control. Although many DCs may have very nearly achieved saturation with the completely voluntary approach, there is still a good deal of room for expansion in the UDCs. Family-planning programs provide the means of contraception and, through their activities and educational campaigns, can spread awareness of the idea of birth control among the people. These programs should be expanded and supported throughout the world as rapidly and as fully as possible, but *other programs should be instituted immediately as well.* Given the family size aspirations of people everywhere, additional measures beyond family planning will unquestionably be required in order to halt the population explosion.

Socioeconomic Measures. Population control through the use of socioeconomic pressures to encourage or discourage reproduction is the approach advocated by, among others, demographer Kingsley Davis, who originated many of the following suggestions.[8] The objective of this approach would be to influence the attitudes and motivations of individual couples. An important aspect would be a large-scale educational program through schools and other communications media to persuade people of the advantages of small families to themselves and to society. Information on birth control, of course, must accompany such educational efforts. This is one of the first measures that could be adopted in all countries, UDC or DC.

As United States taxpayers know, the government uses economic pressure in its present income-tax laws to encourage marriage and child-bearing, a pronatalist bias that is no longer appropriate. In countries that are affluent enough that the majority of citizens pay taxes, tax laws could be adjusted to favor (instead of penalize) single people, working wives, and small families. Other tax measures might also include high marriage fees, taxes on luxury baby goods and toys, and removal of family allowances, where they exist.

Other possibilities include the limitation of maternal or educational benefits

[8]See "Population Policy: Will Current Programs Succeed?" by Kingsley Davis in *Science*, vol. 158, pp. 730–739, 1967, for a detailed discussion.

to two children per family. These proposals, however, have the potential disadvantage of heavily penalizing children (and in the long run society as well). The same criticism may be made of some other tax plans, unless they can be carefully adjusted to avoid denying at least minimum care for poor families, regardless of the number of children they may have.

A somewhat different approach might be to provide incentives for late marriage and childlessness, such as paying bonuses to first-time brides who are over 25, to couples after five childless years, or to men who accept vasectomies after their wives have had a given number of children. Lotteries open only to childless adults have also been proposed. The savings in environmental deterioration, education, and other costs would probably justify the expenditure. All of these measures, of course, suffer the drawback of influencing the poor to a greater degree than the rich. That would be unfortunate, since the addition of a child to an affluent family (which has a disproportionate impact on resources and environment) is in many ways more harmful to society than the addition of a child to a poor family.

Adoption to supplement small families for couples who especially enjoy children can be encouraged through subsidies and simplified procedures. It can also be a way to satisfy couples who have a definite desire for a son or daughter, and further research on sex determination should be pursued for the same reason. A special kind of social-security pension or bond could be provided for aging adults who have few or no children to support them in their old age.

There are many possibilities in the sphere of family structure, sexual mores, and the status of women that can be explored. Anything that would diminish the emphasis upon the traditional feminine roles of wife and mother and would provide women with equal opportunities in education, employment, and other areas is likely to reduce the birth rate. Any measures that postpone marriage and then delay the first child's birth would also encourage a reduction in birth rates. Provision of child care for working mothers seems more likely to encourage employment outside the home and discourage childbearing than to encourage it.

Social pressures on both men and women to marry and have children must be removed. If society were convinced of the need for low birth rates, no doubt the stigma that has customarily been assigned to bachelors, spinsters, and childless couples would soon disappear. But alternative life-styles should be open to single people and childless couples.

Somewhat more repressive measures have also been proposed, such as assigning public housing without regard for family size and removing dependency allowances from student grants or military pay. The idea behind these proposals is the observation that people in the past have voluntarily controlled their reproduction most stringently during periods of great social and economic stress and insecurity, such as the Depression of the 1930s. Studies by demographer Judith Blake and by economist Alan Sweezy, however, have cast serious doubt on the belief that economic considerations are of the greatest importance in determining fertility trends. If this view is correct, then severely repressive economic measures might prove to be both ineffective and unnecessary as a vehicle for population control, as well as socially undesirable. Clearly, much more needs to be learned about the determinants of fertility trends.

Involuntary Fertility Control.   The third approach to population control is that of involuntary fertility control. Several coercive proposals deserve discussion, mainly because societies may ultimately have to resort to them unless current trends in birth rates are rapidly reversed by other means. Some involuntary measures may prove to be less repressive or discriminatory, in fact, than some socioeconomic measures that have been proposed.

One idea that has been seriously proposed in India is to vasectomize all fathers of three or more children. This was defeated not only on moral grounds but on practical ones as well: there simply were not enough medical personnel available even to start on the eligible candidates, let alone deal with the new recruits added each day! But India's government may well have to resort to some coercive method sooner or later, unless famine, war, or disease takes the problem out of its hands. There is little time left for educational programs and social change, and the Indian population is probably too poor for economic measures (especially penalties) to be effective.

Other proposals include compulsory sterilization of mothers after two or three children, or compulsory implantations of steroid capsules at puberty with removal for childbearing by official permission only, perhaps combined with baby licenses. These are technically feasible, but suffer from a number of drawbacks. Technically impossible today, although theoretically feasible, are suggestions that sterilants or fertility-reducing agents be added to staple food or drinking water. These possibilities are generally the least acceptable to most people, although they might have advantages over the others in being far easier and more economical to administer and much less likely to be discriminatory in their consequences.

Compulsory control of family size is an unpalatable idea, but the alternatives may be much more horrifying. As those alternatives become clearer to an increasing number of people in the 1970s, we may well find them *demanding* such control. A far better choice, in our view, is to begin *now* with milder methods of influencing family size preferences, while ensuring that the means of birth control, including abortion and sterilization, are accessible to every human being on Earth within the shortest possible time. If effective action is taken promptly, perhaps the need for involuntary or repressive measures can be averted.

Population Control: The Outlook.   No form of population control, even the most coercive or repressive, will succeed for long unless individuals understand the need for it and accept the idea that humanity must limit its numbers. Therefore, the ultimate key to population control lies in changing human attitudes concerning reproductive behavior and goals in all societies. Achieving this throughout the world would be a gigantic task even if it became the world's first-priority goal, as many believe it should be.

But human survival seems certain to require population-control programs, at least in some places, even before the necessary changes in attitudes can be brought about in the population. In fact, the establishment of such programs might in itself help to convince people of the seriousness of the population problem.

Most of the population-control measures discussed here have never been tried; we know only that their *potential* effectiveness may be great. The socio-economic proposals are based on knowledge of the sort of social conditions that have been associated in the past with low birth rates. We need to know how reproductive attitudes are affected by various living conditions, including some that seem virtually intolerable to us. Even more, we need to know what influences and conditions will lead to changes in these attitudes in favor of smaller families. How can we convince a poor Pakistani villager or a middle-class American that the number of children his wife bears is of crucial importance, not just to himself and his family, but also to his society? How can we make everyone care?

Bibliography

Behrman, S. J., L. Corsa, Jr., and R. Freedman, eds., 1969. *Fertility and Family Planning; a World View.* Univ. of Michigan Press, Ann Arbor. A basic source on family planning.

Blake, Judith, 1971. Reproductive motivation and population policy. *BioScience*, vol. 21, no. 5, pp. 215–220 (1 March). An analysis of what sorts of policies might lower U.S. birth rate.

Ehrlich, P. R., and J. Freedman, 1971. Population, crowding, and human behavior. *New Scientist*, 1 April, pp. 10–14. On crowding studies.

Hardin, Garrett, 1970. *Birth Control.* Pegasus, New York. Excellent up-to-date discussion.

Johnson, Stanley, 1970. *Life Without Birth.* Little, Brown & Co., Boston. A personal and vivid exploration of the population explosion and family-planning programs around the world, particularly UDCs.

Population Council, New York. *Studies in Family Planning.* A monthly series. An excellent account of family planning programs around the world.

Tietze, Christopher, and Sarah Lewit, 1969. Abortion. *Scientific American*, vol. 220, no.1 (Jan.). Available as Offprint 1129 from W. H. Freeman and Company. Good general discussion, including some public-opinion survey results.

United States Commission on Population Growth and the American Future, 1972. *Population and the American Future.* U. S. Govt. Printing Office. Also available in paperback, Signet, New York. The Commission's final report after a two year study.

Westoff, L. A., and C. F. Westoff, 1971. *From Now to Zero: Fertility, Contraception and Abortion in America.* Little, Brown & Co., Boston. Excellent, comprehensive account of demographic structure and population policies in the United States, although estimates of incidence of unwanted births are out of date. Includes an interesting discussion of fertility in the black population and the impact of population policies on it.

Willing, Martha Kent, 1971. *Beyond Conception: Our Children's Children.* Gambit, Inc., Boston. A woman biologist's view of the population explosion and the future.

An outdoor classroom in Los Tropicos, Colombia. Such simple arrangements and use of traveling teachers may go a long way to reduce the high rates of illiteracy in UDCs. (Nicholas Sapieha, Photofind, Rapho.)

NINE

Changing Human Behavior: Toward the Environment and Toward Our Fellow Man

The last chapter discussed population control, one necessary element in the solution of mankind's problems. Although population control is necessary in this regard, it is far from sufficient. If the population were stabilized immediately around the world, mankind would still be faced by a vast array of problems, many of them potentially lethal. War, racism, maldistribution of income and resources, resource depletion, and environmental deterioration will not be solved by population limitation alone. For example, even 208 million Americans by themselves, continuing along their present course, could in the space of several more decades consume the richest and most accessible of the world's supplies of nonrenewable resources and in the process irreparably damage its life-support systems. Evidently, achieving a prosperous, humane, and environmentally sustainable civilization will require not only population limitation, but also fundamental changes in the social and political institutions that influence other aspects of human behavior.

Economics, Resources, and the Environment

Economist Kenneth Boulding has described the present economic system of the United States as a "cowboy economy."[1] The cowboy metaphor refers to a reckless, exploitive philosophy based on two premises: more resources are waiting just over the horizon, and nature has a boundless capacity to absorb garbage. For practical purposes, these premises were valid in the days of the American frontier. In that world it made some sense to seek rapid improvements in human welfare strictly through economic growth, with little regard for what *kind* of growth or for the sorts of waste that accompanied it. But today the old premises are wrong. It is now clear that physical resources are limited, and that mankind is straining the capacity of the biological environment to absorb abuse on a global scale. The blind growth of a cowboy economy is no longer a viable proposition—although an astonishing number of economists (and others) still cling to the belief that it is.

The accepted measure of success in a cowboy economy is a large "throughput." Throughput refers to the rate at which dollars flow through the economy and, insofar as dollar flow depends on the sale of physical goods rather than services, to the speed with which natural resources are converted into artifacts and rubbish. A conventional indicator of throughput is the gross national product (GNP)—the sum of personal and government expenditures on goods and services, plus expenditure on investment. Although GNP can be a very useful economic indicator, it is important to understand what GNP is *not*. It is not a measure of the degree of freedom or health of a nation's people, nor of the equity of its distribution of goods and resources. It is not a measure of the state of depletion of natural resources nor of the stability of the environmental systems upon which life depends. It is not a measure of security from the threat of war. It is not, in sum, a comprehensive measure of the *quality* of life, although it is often misused as such a measure.

Boulding has described a rational alternative to the GNP-oriented cowboy economy, calling this alternative the "spaceman economy" in harmony with the emerging concept of "Spaceship Earth." Consistent with the finiteness of this planet's supply of resources and the fragility of the biological processes that support human life, such an economy would be nongrowing in terms of the size of the human population, the quantity of physical resources in use, and mankind's impact on the biological environment. The spaceman economy need not be stagnant, however; human ingenuity would be continually at work increasing the amount of actual prosperity and well-being derivable from the fixed amount of resources in use.

Quite the opposite of the cowboy economy, which thrives on throughput, the spaceman economy would seek to minimize the throughput needed to

[1] "The Economics of the Coming Spaceship Earth," Kenneth Boulding, in *Environmental Quality in a Growing Economy*, Henry Jarrett, ed., Johns Hopkins Press, Baltimore, 1966.

maintain its stable stock of goods. Note that this is an obvious goal for any economy as regards population. A given population size can be maintained by a high birth rate balanced by a high death rate (high throughput) or by a low birth rate balanced by a low death rate (low throughput); almost everyone would agree that the low throughput situation is preferable. When one speaks of material goods, the "birth rate" is the production rate and the "death rate" is the rate at which the goods wear out or become obsolete. A given level of affluence, measured in terms of the stock of goods per person, can be maintained by very different levels of resource flow. Thus a society with one refrigerator for every three people can maintain this level of affluence with refrigerators that need replacement every 10 years (high throughput) or every 40 years (low throughput).

Could people's desires for material comforts and a high "quality of life" be met in a spaceman economy? There are good reasons to believe the answer is yes. With an unchanging number of people, society's efforts can be devoted entirely to improving conditions for the population that exists, rather than to struggling to provide the necessities of existence for new additions. Moreover, focusing attention on the *quality* of a fixed stock of goods in a spaceman economy is in many respects a more direct route to prosperity than emphasizing throughput in a cowboy economy. This is so because, as Boulding has argued, *quality* of stock is often a better measure of well-being than throughput. Most people would rather own one Rolls Royce than a succession of Fords.

Furthermore, once a good diet and a certain basic level of well-made material goods has been provided, quality of life becomes largely a matter of the availability of services and personal options. Services include education, medical care, entertainment and recreation, fire and police protection, and the administration of justice. Such services do involve the use of material resources and do affect the environment. For example, commercial office space, much of it associated with the provision of services, is a major consumer of electricity for lighting, heating and air conditioning. Nevertheless, there is great potential for improving and extending services while reducing the associated material and environmental demands. Consider the possibilities offered by communication, whereby many services that now require heavy energy use in transporting people about can be performed better, faster, and using much less energy by moving information rather than people (e.g., business meetings via videophone).

"Personal options" consist of access to a variety of landscapes, living accommodations, career possibilities, cultural environments, recreational opportunities, interpersonal relationships, degrees of privacy, and so forth. Personal options are an important part of the quality of an individual's life even when they are not exercised — it pleases us to know we *could* live in the country, even though we may choose to live in cities. Options also have value beyond the preferences of the majority of people in any given society. That the majority of citizens may prefer an urban environment is not sufficient reason to transform all living areas of the planet into urban environments — this is tyranny of the majority. Even those who enjoy neither canoeing nor golf should concede that a society with room for golf courses and free-flowing rivers is preferable to a society without those options. It is even reasonable to suppose that in human society, as in ecosystems, diversity on a small scale (individual choice) promotes stability on a large scale (society as a whole).

Insofar as personal options are part of quality of life, the spaceman economy is a clear choice over the cowboy economy. Population growth and the transformation of an ever larger fraction of the biosphere to maintain the growth of throughput are destroying options in the United States now and for the future. By stabilizing the population and reducing the level of environmentally disruptive activities associated with throughput of resources, the spaceman economy would preserve remaining options; by focusing on services, it would create new ones.

The Economy in Transition.   How can human society make the transition from a cowboy economy to a spaceman economy? How do we get from here to there? One problem that must be faced squarely is the redistribution of wealth within and between nations. Otherwise, fixing the quantity of physical goods in use would "freeze" the majority of human beings in a state of poverty. In rich countries such as the United States, a moderate degree of redistribution would alleviate this problem. It would then be justifiable to implement a transition to a spaceman economy as quickly as possible. In the poor countries, a degree of careful expansion of productive activities, as well as massive transfers of goods and technical assistance from the rich countries (see below), will be necessary before the notion of a spaceman economy can be seriously entertained. In the remainder of this section, we will confine ourselves to some aspects of an economic transition in the United States.

The Automobile: A Candidate for Change.   In the transition from a cowboy to a spaceman economy, manufacturing industries will have to undergo vast changes. The largest manufacturing industry in the United States is the automobile industry, and its product is a dominant factor in the depletion of resources and the destruction of the environment. The industry therefore makes a particularly suitable case study for economic change.

The introduction of annual automobile model changes by General Motors in 1923 quickly pushed most competitors out of business, reducing the number of American automobile manufacturers from 88 in 1921 to 10 in 1935. Only four of any economic significance remain today. A few companies therefore have been able to manipulate both demand and quality in a way that has resulted in a continual high output of overpowered, overstyled, underengineered, quickly obsolescent, and relatively fragile automobiles. These characteristics of the automobile, together with the domination of this form of personal mobility over many more sensible alternatives, are responsible for a remarkable array of resource demands and environmental problems. For example, immediate relief from a major portion of our air-pollution problems and substantial reduction in demand for steel, lead, glass, rubber, and other materials would result from the replacement of our present automobiles with small, low-horsepower, long-lasting cars designed for recycling. To this end, the U.S. government might start by removing tariffs and import restrictions on automobiles that meet strict exhaust-emission standards, so that small foreign cars would become even more attractive to American buyers. Exhaust emissions and the components of air pollution produced by the wear of tires on asphalt and from the asbestos of brake linings would be reduced by the use of smaller, lighter cars. Recycling old automobiles and building longer-lasting ones would reduce both the consumption and the environmental impact of obtaining resources, as well as reducing the pollution directly associated with automobile production. The rewards of such a program would not be limited to pollution abatement and the saving of petroleum and other resources. Because small cars need less room on the highway and in parking lots, transportation would through that change alone become pleasanter, safer, and more efficient.

Of course, there would be several adverse consequences of a general program of "automobile control." Between 10 and 20 percent of the American population derives its living, directly or indirectly, from the automobile: its construction, fueling, servicing, selling, and the provision of roads and other facilities for it. Not all of these jobs would be affected by conversion to smaller, more durable automobiles and to other forms of transportation, but many would be. Unless there were careful planning to ameliorate the consequences, such a conversion could have extremely disruptive effects on the national economy. The economy, however, is demonstrably capable of accommodating itself to very far-reaching changes. Even without extensive planning the United States economy during the period from 1946 to 1948 converted almost 50 percent of its productive capacity from war-related products to peacetime products. The flexibility of our economic institutions is often grossly underestimated.

We believe a Federal task force should be established immediately to do the planning and to lay the groundwork for dealing with the automobile problem without great disruption of the national economy. Such a task force might be part of a larger institution with the responsibility to devise policies for making the transition to a stable, ecologically sound economy. The task is enormous, but it is both possible and necessary. In the short term, alternative activities must be found for various industries, including those related to the automobile. Some of the productive capacity of the automobile manufacturers, for example, might be diverted to meeting other pressing national and international needs. Many Americans need new housing, and many localities need mass-transit systems; many UDCs need modern systems of food storage and transport. Detroit is surely capable of making important contributions in these areas.

Reducing Throughput.   The strategy of converting productive capacity from frivolous and wasteful enterprises to legitimate social needs should be accompanied, even in the short term, by efforts to minimize the throughput of resources associated with production. Economist Herman Daly, a persuasive advocate of moving from a cowboy to a spaceman economy, has suggested a specific mechanism for accomplishing such a reduction.[2] To be specific, Daly has proposed putting strict *depletion quotas* on the natural resources of the United States. That is, upper limits would be placed on the total amount of each resource that could be extracted or imported by the United States each year. This would not only directly reduce the pressure Americans place on the resources of the planet, but would also automatically generate a trend towards recycling and pollution abatement. With resources scarce (and thus expensive), a premium would be placed on the durability of goods, recycling, and the restriction of effluents (which often contain "resources" not now economically recoverable). Environmental deterioration from the processes of resource extraction and transport would be reduced, as would that resulting from manufacturing resources into finished goods. Less energy is usually required to recycle materials than to start anew from basic resources. And depletion quotas on fossil fuels and fissionable materials would encourage the frugal use of energy.

Limiting the amount of energy available would, of course, also tend to limit the size and number of automobiles, encourage the use of mass transit, and promote the substitution of efficient high-speed trains for energetically wasteful short and medium-haul jet airplanes. As Daly notes, a basic system of depletion quotas would have to be supplemented to some degree with such devices as taxes on effluents, but we agree with him that operating at the resource rather than the rubbish end of the system is fundamentally the best approach. It requires controls at many fewer points and thus would be simpler to institute, and it has the basic appeal of tackling the system where the materials are still concentrated rather than dispersed.

One of the most difficult problems in implementing the Daly system will be dealing with imports. Obviously quotas will have to be established on imported raw materials, or the primary result of the system would be simply to shift pressure from U.S. resources to the resources of the rest of the world. If American manufacturers alone were strictly rationed, there would surely be an upsurge in manufactured imports. Restrictions would therefore have to be placed on the import of manufactured goods, perhaps based on their "resource content." Those restrictions might best be put only on imports from other developed countries, to encourage them to establish depletion quotas also. Restrictions could be omitted for certain manufactured goods from underdeveloped countries, wherever it seemed that access to American markets would be a genuine economic help to the exporter.

[2]"The Stationary State Economy," Herman Daly, Distinguished Lectures, No. 2, University of Alabama, 1971.

Much additional effort by economists and others will be required to work out details of the changes required in order to minimize throughput in our economic system. One further step, however, is already clear. Both before and after depletion quotas are established, ways must be found to control advertising. Advertising now functions in large part to keep the economy growing by creating demand for a wide variety of often useless, dangerous, or environmentally destructive products. Its most dangerous abuses might be halted immediately by legislative action. For instance, it could be made illegal for any utility to advertise in such a way as to promote greater demand for power. Also, references to size, power or sexual potency (direct or implied) could be banned from automobile advertising. Certainly, every effort should be made to expunge from advertising the idea that the quality of life is closely related to the rate at which new products are purchased or energy is consumed. On the other hand, advertising could be encouraged to put effort into promoting socially desirable trends. Even indirectly, it could present small families in a favorable light, put less emphasis on overconsumption than at present, and foster a sense of responsiblity toward the environment.

The Employment Problem.   Redirecting production into more useful channels and reducing the throughput associated with production will entail considerable retraining and temporary unemployment in the work force. These problems will be all the more difficult because of the employment problem that already exists in the United States. The 4 to 6 percent unemployment figures commonly quoted do not indicate the true seriousness of the problem. First of all, this overt unemployment is very unevenly distributed in the population. Racial minorities, young workers, and, above all, young minority workers suffer disproportionately. The pressure of unemployment at the younger end of the labor pool is probably a major reason that American society has been so rigid about retirement around the age of 65. Many talented people are removed from the labor force even though they may still be capable of 10 years or more of productive work and do not wish to be "put out to pasture." The enforced separation of older people from their economic life is also clearly a factor that contributes to their problems.

Added to these components of the employment problem is disguised unemployment: people doing jobs that are either unnecessary or detrimental to society or both. Anyone familiar with government, big business, universities, the military, or any large bureaucracy, knows how many people are essentially "feather-bedding" or just "pushing paper." When those people are combined with the workers who are engaged in such fundamentally counterproductive activities as building freeways, producing oversized cars and unneeded appliances, devising deceptive advertising, manufacturing napalm and jet fighters, or being slum landlords, the number of people who are unemployed, underemployed or misemployed is a substantial portion of the work force.

Of course, the whole employment problem would be badly aggravated if society attempted to discontinue too abruptly those jobs that are unnecessary or socially and environmentally destructive. Maintaining some of these activities is probably necessary in the short run while changes in employment patterns are worked out. But now is the time to start planning and maneuvering to phase out both disguised unemployment and destructive products without damaging society and without creating enormous levels of overt unemployment.

The transition should be greatly assisted by the obvious potential for expanded employment in services such as health care and education (including adult education); in the development of energetically efficient transportation systems for people and freight; in recycling and pollution-control industries; in environmental improvement activities such as reclamation of strip-mined land, reforestation, and the construction of urban parks; in the devising and implementing of cleaner energy technologies; and in the development, production, and distribution of better contraceptives. The transition should also be eased somewhat because the numbers of new young job seekers will be somewhat smaller in the late 1970s than previously, owing to the decreasing numbers of births in the United States in the 1960s relative to the 1950s.

In the longer term, it may be that the solution to the employment problem will require a reduction in the amount of work done by each worker in order to create more jobs. Gradually shortening the work week (ultimately to 20 hours or less) or decreasing the number of work weeks per year (companies could have different spring-summer and fall-winter shifts) would accomplish this. The result would be more leisure, which might be better enjoyed by a more educated population. It would also provide the time for people both to obtain that education and to put it to good use participating in the running of society. There should be few but positive consequences from such a reduction in working time. Pay would perhaps be reduced, but so would many expenses if material goods were built to endure and there was no longer social pressure to consume for the sake of consuming. If people can be diverted from the speedy, mechanized forms of leisure activity now promoted by advertising, the pace of life would undoubtedly slow down, with attendant psychological and physical benefits. If a stable economic system could be achieved, life would indeed be different from and conceivably much improved over what it is today.

The Social System

Numerous fundamental changes will be necessary in our values and institutions if a stable population and a steady-state economy are to be made acceptable goals to a majority of Americans, not to mention citizens of other nations. Among those institutions likely to be most profoundly involved are religious organizations and the educational system.

The Religious Element.   Many of a society's attitudes toward humanity and the environment tend to be embodied in its religions. Throughout the industrial revolution, the West was in the grip of an orthodoxy that put work, material gain, and exploitation of the environment among its highest goals. The world was thought to exist for mankind's benefit alone, to be populated and exploited by the cleverest and hardest-working individuals. Inequity was justified by envisioning a lovely Heaven where the poor and meek could look forward to their reward.

Today, some progressive changes can already be detected in some of our religious institutions with respect to population, and among younger clergy there seems to be a healthy trend towards human rather than material values. Many other young people are also turning away from the old materialistic orthodoxy and espousing love of their fellow men and a simpler life in harmony with nature rather than in domination over it. Of course, a change in religious attitudes will hardly suffice to bring about the required changes in American society. The hard realities of overpopulation and fragile environmental systems must be communicated, comprehended, and translated into commitment to constructive action. The change in cultural philosophy that religion can help provide must be accompanied by a revolution in education.

Toward a Realistic Educational System.   In order to avoid a massive rise in the death rate, a highly technological society will have to be perpetuated indefinitely, but it will have to be run very differently from the society of today. Our system of education needs to be redesigned, updated, and firmly connected with the mass media. This combined educational apparatus can be used to inform people of the realities of life on this finite and fragile planet, and to prepare them for more informed and extensive participation in charting the course of their society.

While the potential for expanded employment in education could be realized very rapidly, other results would be much slower in being felt. Even with a crash program of rehabilitation for education in the United States, there will inevitably be a lag of decades before a general overhaul can be completed. In a few subject areas such as sex education, only the existence of restrictive laws prevents the widespread application of the considerable expertise and curriculum planning that already exist. In other areas, only a lack of financial support stands in the way. For example, in spite of a serious imbalance over the past two decades in the training of biologists, which has resulted in a shortage of ecologists and population biologists, sufficient personnel do exist to train large numbers of people to teach the relevant aspects of biology at all levels, if funds and programs were available.

In the social sciences, however, the picture is different. There is, for instance, only a small group of reality-oriented economists; the discipline itself is still largely in the grip of those committed to the perpetuation of growth in economic throughput. Yet few things will be more important to citizens of the future than knowledge of the workings of the economic system, as well as of the physical and biological constraints within which it operates. Moreover, where can we find teachers who will educate their students about the real workings of our political system and those of other nations? Too many political scientists seem to have been unwilling to dirty their hands on the practical problems of increasing the responsiveness and accountability of government, and of communicating its present shortcomings and the possible solutions to the public.

So, while we know how to make the population aware of contraception, the laws of thermodynamics, the functioning of ecosystems, and the relationship between birth and death rates, the problem of educating our citizens to the economic and political functioning of society is much more severe. Where are they to learn that Congress has in many ways nearly ceased to function, paralyzed by the power of obstructionist committee chairmen and increasingly overshadowed by the executive and judicial branches of government? Who will show them in detail that the U. S. income tax is a regressive tax, part of a system which Ferdinand Lundberg described as "the great tax swindle"?[3] How will they find out who really runs the United States? How, indeed? For a move to revitalize the educational system would seem to require the cooperation of precisely those elements in the society that such revitalization would hurt — from the small group of ultra-rich who control much of the power in the United States to the entrenched university professors whose doctrinaire defense of rigid boundaries between their separate disciplines is a major obstacle to solving the world's problems.

For the education system to be dramatically changed and the mass media to reach those not touched by the system in other ways will require a major societal decision. Can such a decision be made without massive reeducation? This society seems to be caught in a vicious circle, and the answer, if there is one, would seem to lie in the realm of politics.

The Political System

When major decisions by society are discussed, the topic is politics. And when solutions to the problems of human ecology are considered, all roads seem to lead to the political arena. Society as a whole will have to decide to institute resource-depletion quotas. Society as a whole will have to reject the present system of advertising. Society as a whole will have to decide it wants first-rate education. Society as a whole will have to decide to end racism and poverty. Society as a whole will have to determine how many people should live in the United States. Although individual efforts in these and other areas can be helpful, the problems will only be ultimately solved when the entire nation turns on a new course.

If you alone decide to do your part by driving a small car, you would take a tiny step towards saving the environment. But your chances of suffering seri-

[3]*The Rich and the Super-rich*, Ferdinand Lundberg, Bantam Books, New York, 1968.

ous injury or death in an accident would be higher than average until such time as *most* people chose to drive small cars. If you further decided to buy a small car that would last 30 years, be easily repairable and recyclable, and have a low-compression engine, you would find it impossible to do. A manufacturer who *wanted* to produce such a car today probably could not; no one would put up the huge amount of capital required for fear that the "Eco-special" would not sell. Only when society makes other kinds of cars illegal (or too expensive) will the money become available for such ventures.

Correspondingly, although you can accomplish something by talking against American military involvement in UDCs or by dealing with people without regard for the color of their skin, imagine how helpful it would be if the government was firmly on your side. Think how unlikely future Vietnams would be if the military-industrial complex were diverted to useful purposes. Imagine how quickly race relations would improve if politicians openly espousing unequal treatment for different races were removed from office.

Changing the System. It is often claimed that political action against entrenched special interests has been tried and has failed. When Eugene McCarthy was beaten by Hubert Humphrey at the establishment-controlled Democratic Convention in 1968, many of McCarthy's embittered supporters felt that efforts to change national policy were hopeless. Similarly, Paul McCloskey's failure against Richard Nixon in the New Hampshire primary in 1972 left many anti-war Republicans without hope. When an advertising agency, heavily funded by industry, persuaded voters to defeat a "dangerous" ballot initiative for stricter environmental controls in California in 1972, many environmentalists despaired of ever obtaining success through the ballot box. These political failures by no means prove that the situation is hopeless however—just that bringing about political change is a much bigger and tougher job than most people realize. And there have been minor political successes against the establishment that should not be overlooked either, such as Lyndon Johnson's withdrawal from the 1968 presidential race in the face of McCarthy's surprising strength or George McGovern's victory over the old guard at the 1972 Democratic Convention.

There are a number of avenues open for political reform. The rich wield so much political power in the United States largely by default on the part of a citizenry that is apathetic and poorly informed. Part of the solution to these problems lies in education, as discussed above. The communications media could do a much more systematic job of reporting, at any given time, what legislative measures are under consideration at local, state and federal levels, interpreting what these measures would mean in practice, and telling the public who is supporting them, who is opposing them, and why. Groups such as Common Cause, the Sierra Club, and Zero Population Growth already do a very creditable job of this sort of reporting on measures related to their particular interests.

A key ingredient of political reform is *accountability.* Elected politicians and appointed bureaucrats in federal and state agencies must be held accountable to the public for their actions. They are, after all, paid with your money. Accountability requires public awareness of what decisions are being made (this has been especially lacking in the case of regulatory agencies), and it requires a regular, orderly process in which the responsible officials explain their actions to the public. An example of the trend toward *decreased* accountability at the highest level of government in the United States is that Richard Nixon in his first term as President held far fewer press conferences than any of his four immediate predecessors did in a corresponding period of time. One could also get the impression that the reporters privileged to attend such conferences know that they will not be called upon if they persist in asking questions the President finds embarrassing. Perhaps presidential press conferences should be held by law at prescribed intervals, with no topics ruled out in advance. Questioners should be chosen at random from representatives of the communications media, not by presidential preference. Such reforms are needed in other branches and at other levels of government as well.

Another means of fostering accountability might be to establish by law and support with government funds a number of groups of professional "adversaries," or critics of government. The sole responsibility of these groups would be to investigate critically the performance of government officials and agencies and to report to the public, much as Ralph Nader and his co-workers have done with private support. It would be reasonable to appropriate five percent of the budget of every government agency to support the group of professional critics reviewing that agency's performance. Similar proposals have been made with respect to critical examination of specific scientific and technical programs, under the term "adversary science."[4] (Thus, for example, 5 percent of the AEC's expenditures for research on breeder reactors would go to support a group of technically competent critics who would seek out and publicize the shortcomings of this program.)

Better information and accountability are part of the remedy for the low degree of public involvement in the workings of the American government; and the apathy that has served as an obstacle in the past will presumably diminish as economic and environmental problems continue to worsen. Once the public is informed and aroused, many steps are possible to increase the responsiveness of government and to reduce the disproportionate influence of the wealthy minority. One is to reform the processes of political contributions and campaign spending so that politicians need not pay for their victories with later favors. Another is to pay Congressmen higher salaries — say, $100,000 per year — but require them to divest themselves completely of all stock, partnerships in law firms, and other potential conflicts of interest during their terms

---

[4]"Public Science: A Proposal for the Societal Evaluation of Technology," Don Geesaman and Dean Abrahamson, *The Bulletin of the Atomic Scientists,* 1973. In press.

of office. A third constructive step would be to break the stranglehold of the seniority system on Congress.

The International Scene

At the international level, individual action to improve the situation is almost impossible, and even governments are severely limited in their influence by the lack of agreed-upon goals and effective mechanisms for action. Yet the tasks are enormous. Worldwide population limitation must be accompanied by other major changes if present trends are to be reversed and the already awesome global burden of human misery is to be kept from increasing.

The most urgent of the needed changes is a series of moves to close rapidly the widening gap between the rich and poor nations. The first logical step in such a process is the conversion of all DC economies, capitalist and socialist, from the cowboy variety to the spaceman variety. Many of the "developed" countries are actually "overdeveloped"—they have carried the process of development (industrialization) too far. They have created wasteful industrial plants capable of supplying manufactured goods for their citizenry far beyond any reasonable "need," with great damage to indispensable biological systems and to the detriment of less tangible ingredients of the quality of life. Therefore the conversion of the DC economies to the spaceman mode has been described as a process of "de-development."

During the course of de-development, excess productive capacity in the rich nations should be used to help provide necessities for the UDCs. In fact, a massive direct transfer of wealth from the DCs to the UDCs will be necessary; the gap is now so wide that no plan that does not include straightforward redistribution can hope to reduce it to acceptable size quickly enough to be meaningful to those now suffering in poverty. Such a transfer of wealth could not be accomplished simply by sending money, which would all too often end up in the pockets of the least needy; it would require careful programs of technical assistance, transfers of specific kinds of materials and goods tailored to the needs of the recipient countries, and injections of capital into projects with economic leverage—those which, once started, can sustain themselves, grow, and perhaps generate others. An obvious early focus for such aid must be nutrition, to break the vicious circle of malnutrition, apathy, and low productivity.

In proposing direct massive transfers of wealth from the DCs to the UDCs, we reject the notion that mere continued growth in the world technological and economic apparatus as it presently operates will be sufficient to cure the problem of poverty. This bankrupt view boils down to the belief that we, the rich, cannot give the poor many crumbs until our own loaf, already more than ample, gets even bigger. It is wrong both because of the agonizing slowness with which the poor's standard of living rises under existing inequities, and because of the enormous ecological impact of letting the already affluent get much more so.

Fortunately, the need for redistribution of wealth and resources is recognized by some prominent individuals both in the West and in the Soviet Union (it is, of course, widely recognized in the "Third World"). Two scientists, Lord C. P. Snow of Great Britain and Andrei D. Sakharov of the USSR, have made rather similar proposals about redistribution. Sakharov, "father of the Russian hydrogen bomb" and one of the youngest men ever elected to the Soviet Academy of Sciences, expressed his views in an extraordinary document entitled, "Progress, Coexistence, and Intellectual Freedom,"[5] which has not been published in the USSR. Among his many proposals is that, after the United States and the USSR have "overcome their alienation," they should collaborate in a massive attempt to save the UDCs. This attempt would be financed by a contribution to the effort on the part of the DCs of some 20 percent of their national income over a 15-year period. Lord Snow, an eminent physicist and novelist, supports the suggestion of Academician Sakharov. He recommended that the rich nations devote 20 percent of their GNP for 10–15 years to the task of population control and development of the poor countries. By the scale of the effort, and by its no-strings-attached nature (a substantial portion might be channeled through international agencies under control of the UDCs themselves), the people of the "other world" might be convinced that the developed countries *do* care. Though there is much suffering today in the UDCs and more is unavoidable, a substantial lowering of DC–UDC tensions could occur if the UDCs felt that a serious attempt to help was being made. Moreover, the joint DC effort could help to bring about that community of feeling that psychologists regard as so essential to the abolition of war.

Redefining Development.   A large-scale effort on the part of the DCs will not suffice, however, unless there are basic changes in the value systems related to development. If industrialization of the entire world according to the pattern of today's DCs is neither possible nor desirable, new standards of value will have to be established that will permit access to the basic human needs of adequate food, shelter, clothing, education, and medical care for *all* human beings, regardless of the economic value of their productivity. If we can learn to recognize and attempt to correct our own errors, then perhaps the UDCs will see their way clear to establishing new goals: development within environmental limitations and with careful attention to the *quality* of life.

In short, the DCs must not only give unprecedented aid to the UDCs, they must help the UDCs to avoid the mistakes made in the past by the DCs. Something like this message must come across: "By making the fundamental error of basing our standard of progress on expansion of the GNP (i.e., throughput), we have created a vast industrial complex and great mental, moral, and aesthetic poverty. Our cities are less livable each year, our air often unsafe to

[5]*Progress, Coexistence, and Intellectual Freedom*, Andrei D. Sakharov, W. W. Norton and Co., New York, 1968.

breathe, and our people increasingly regimented. We require far too large a slice of the world's resources to maintain our way of life. We, in short, are not developed, we are *overdeveloped*. We now realize that our current patterns of consumption and exploitation cannot and should not be sustained. While we are correcting our mistakes and de-developing, we want to help you to develop *wisely*—not in our image but in whatever way is most appropriate for your culture."

What wise development might mean in practice would, of course, differ from area to area. Certainly, ecologically sound agricultural development, rather than industrialization, should receive priority virtually everywhere. In general the DCs would, where needed, supply medical services, educational facilities and teachers, and technical assistance in population control and ecological planning. Roadways, electrification, and communications adequate to the demands of an agrarian society would be an almost universal need, as would help in developing improved local systems of agriculture. In all of these endeavors, the most efficient means of meeting the needs should be the first consideration: how to make the limited resources do the most good. Roads can be built without the sort of heavy machine equipment used in DCs. In fact, the simpler techniques of several decades ago would probably be more efficient in poor countries and would provide employment for unskilled labor. The same is true of electrification and communications; a single power supply or telephone for each village, with its use being shared communally, makes more sense than attempting to provide electricity to each home. Transportation should not be designed along DC lines. Buses, whether imported or locally manufactured, make far more sense than cars where only a fraction of the population can afford the latter. A suitable truck should be provided for UDC farmers, low-powered, economical, and sturdy. Several owners of small farms might own such a truck communally, or the government might provide for the transport of agricultural produce to market on a pickup-and-delivery basis.

Farm machinery need not be highly mechanized to be efficient; Japan and Taiwan have developed very efficient agricultural systems without mechanization. Economist Bruce F. Johnston[6] has written that "simple, inexpensive farm equipment that is well suited to local manufacture in small- and medium-scale rural workshops" would be far more beneficial to the economies of UDCs and more practical than the use of heavy machinery. Not the least benefit of such a system would be its dependence upon abundant farm labor.

Education is an obvious area for aid, but setting up systems that mimic those of the DCs should be avoided. Education must be tailored to the needs of the local culture, not designed to destroy it. One of the great tragedies of Latin America is the university system which has evolved there. This system produces many attorneys, philosophers, poets, and "pure" scientists but not the

---

[6]"Unemployment and Underemployment," Bruce F. Johnston, in *Are Our Descendants Doomed?*, Harrison Brown and Edward Hutchings, Jr., eds., Viking, New York, 1972.

agriculturalists, ecologists, and public-health experts whom the area so desperately needs. Education for Eskimos or Bushmen should be designed to produce first-class Eskimos or Bushmen, not caricatures of Americans or Russians; although the option to acquire technical or academic educations should remain open to those who may desire them. These special educations could be available to children of affluent classes at their own expense and to the poor through scholarship programs.

Above all, the standard for aid and development should not be to make a nation or area "self-sufficient" in terms of today's economic standards. Just as some areas within Western countries today are maintained at economic expense because they supply other values, so in the future some parts of the world will have to be maintained at economic expense because they supply other values: natural beauty, biological or cultural diversity, or lightly exploited ecological systems to perform the indispensable life-support functions of the biosphere. Similarly, while some states in the United States are largely agricultural, others are heavily industrialized. There is no reason why UDCs could not be developed differentially. Some might have considerable industry and others be limited almost entirely to agricultural production. Such disparate economic entities could perhaps be loosely federated in economic associations similar to (but perhaps more diversified than) the Common Market.

We have only hinted at the complexity of problems in wise development. What is actually required is nothing less than a transformation of human society. For, if these programs can have any chance for success, mankind will finally have to start treating the entire globe as a single entity and all human problems as part of the same complex fabric. In many cases, parochial national interests will have to be submerged for the common interest of all people. Some degree of sovereignty will have to be sacrificed if rational control over the planet's resources and the maintenance of the quality of the oceans and atmosphere are to be achieved. A new generation of human beings must emerge who act in accordance with the realization that the self-interest of each person is inextricably intertwined with the interests of mankind.

BIBLIOGRAPHY

Boulding, Kenneth E., 1971. Environment and Economics, in *Environment*, edited by William W. Murdoch, Sinauer Associates, Stamford, Connecticut.

Daly, Herman, 1973. *Toward a Steady-State Economy*. W. H. Freeman and Company, San Francisco.

Goldsmith, Edward, ed., 1972. *Blueprint for Survival*. Houghton Mifflin, Boston. An outline of a possible approach to the future.

Heller, Alfred, ed., 1972. *The California Tomorrow Plan*. William Kaufmann, Inc. Los Altos, California.

Illich, Ivan, 1971. *Deschooling Society.* Harper and Row, New York. A call for radical reform of education.

Mishan, Ezra, 1970. *Technology and Growth: The Price We Pay.* Praeger, New York.

Myrdal, Gunnar, 1970. *The Challenge of World Poverty.* Pantheon, New York.

Platt, John, 1969. "What We Must Do," *Science,* vol. 166, pp. 1115–1121, 16 May. Reprinted in *Global Ecology,* John P. Holdren and Paul R. Ehrlich, eds. Harcourt Brace Jovanovich, New York, 1971.

The conference hall for the official proceedings of the U.N. Conference on the Human Environment in Stockholm, June 1972. A start was made here for worldwide international cooperation in protecting the environment. (Courtesy of the United Nations.)

TEN

Synthesis and Recommendations

Summary

To recapitulate, we would outline the present world situation as follows:

1. Considering present technology and patterns of human behavior, our planet is grossly overpopulated. Between 2 and 3 billion people are not being properly cared for *now*. Under such circumstances, the contention of some that many more people can be easily and properly cared for in the near future is preposterous. When *every human being* has abundant and varied food, adequate clothing and shelter, first-rate medical care, ample educational opportunity, and freedom from war and tyranny, then perhaps consideration of whether more people can be given first-class accommodation on Spaceship Earth will be appropriate.

2. The large absolute number of people and the rate of population growth are themselves major hindrances to fulfilling the above-named needs of all of mankind.

3. The limits of human capability to produce food by conventional means have very nearly been reached. Problems of supply and distribution already have resulted in roughly half of humanity being undernourished or malnourished. As many as 10–20 million people are starving to death annually.

4. Attempts to increase food production further will tend to accelerate the deterioration of our environment, which in turn may eventually *reduce* the capacity of the Earth to produce food. It is not clear whether environmental decay has now gone so far as to be essentially irreversible; it is possible that

the capacity of the planet to support human beings has been permanently impaired.

5. There is good reason to believe that population growth increases the probability of a lethal worldwide plague and of a thermonuclear war. Either could provide a catastrophic "death-rate solution" to the population problem; each is potentially capable of destroying civilization and even of driving *Homo sapiens* to extinction.

6. Perhaps more likely than extinction is the possibility that man will survive only to endure an existence barely recognizable as human — malnourished, beset by chronic disease, physically and emotionally impoverished, surrounded by the devastation wrought by an industrial civilization that could not cope with the results of its own biological and social folly.

7. There are no simple answers to these threats, no technological panaceas for the complex of problems comprising the population-food-environment crisis. Of course, technology, properly applied in such areas as pollution abatement, communications, and fertility control, can provide valuable assistance. But the essential solutions entail dramatic and rapid changes in human *attitudes*, especially those relating to reproductive behavior, economic growth, technology, the environment, and resolution of conflicts.

Recommendations: A Positive Program

Although our conclusions are necessarily rather pessimistic, we wish to emphasize our belief that the problems can be solved. Whether they *will* be solved is another question. A general course of action that we feel will have some chance of ameliorating the results of the current crisis is outlined below. Many of the suggestions will seem "unrealistic," and indeed that is how we view them. But the world has been allowed to run downhill for so long that only idealistic and very far-reaching programs offer any hope for the future.

1. Population control is absolutely essential if the problems now facing mankind are to be solved. *It is not, however, a panacea.* If population growth were halted immediately, virtually all other human problems — poverty, racial tensions, urban blight, environmental decay, warfare — would remain. On the other hand, direct attacks on these problems will ultimately fail if the human population continues to grow. The situation is best summarized in the statement: "Whatever your cause, it's a lost cause without population control."

2. Political pressure must be applied immediately to induce the United States government to assume its responsibility to halt the growth of the American population. Once growth is halted, the government should undertake to influence the birth rate so that the population is reduced to an optimum size and maintained there. It is essential that a grassroots political movement be

generated to convince our legislators and the executive branch of the government that they must act promptly. The program should be based on what politicians understand best—votes. Presidents, Congressmen, Senators, and other elected officials who do not deal effectively with the crisis must be defeated at the polls, and more intelligent and responsible candidates must be elected. It is unfortunate that at the time of the greatest crisis the United States and the world have ever faced, many Americans, especially the young, have given up hope that the government can be modernized and changed in direction through the functioning of the elective process. Their despair may have some foundation, but we see no choice but to launch a prolonged and determined attempt to wrest control of the political system from the special interests which now run it and to turn it over to the people.

3. A massive campaign must be launched to restore a high-quality environment in North America and to *de-develop the United States*. De-development means bringing our economic system (especially patterns of consumption) into line with the realities of ecology and the global resource situation. Resources and energy must be diverted from frivolous and wasteful uses in overdeveloped countries to filling the genuine needs of underdeveloped countries. This effort must be largely political, especially with regard to our overexploitation of world resources, but the campaign should be strongly supplemented by legal and boycott action against polluters and others whose activities damage the environment. The need for de-development presents our economists with a major challenge. They must design a stable, low-consumption economy in which there is a much more equitable distribution of wealth than in the present one. Redistribution of wealth both within and among nations is absolutely essential, if a decent life is to be provided for every human being.

4. Once the United States has clearly started on the path of cleaning up its own mess, it can then turn its attention to the problems of the de-development of the other DCs, population control, and ecologically feasible development of the UDCs. It must use every peaceful means at its disposal to persuade the Soviet Union and other DCs to join the effort, in line with the general proposals of Lord Snow and Academician Sakharov.

5. Perhaps the major necessary ingredient that has been missing from a solution to the problems of both the United States and the rest of the world is a goal, a vision of the kind of Spaceship Earth that ought to be and the kind of crew that should man her. Society has always had its visionaries who talked of love, beauty, peace, and plenty. But somehow the "practical" men have always been there to praise smog as a sign of progress, to preach "just" wars, and to restrict love while giving hate free rein. It must be one of the greatest ironies of the history of the human species that the only salvation for the practical men now lies in what they think of as the dreams of idealists. The question now is: can the self-proclaimed "realists" be persuaded to face reality in time?

Appendix

1972 Population Data

The following data are reproduced from the 1972 World Population Data Sheet of the Population Reference Bureau. Notes, which are indicated by superscript numbers, appear at the end of the table.

Region or Country[1]	Population Estimates Mid-1972 (millions)[2]	Annual Births per 1,000 Population[7]	Annual Deaths per 1,000 Population[3]	Annual Rate of Population Growth (percent)[4]	Number of Years to Double Population[5]	Population Projections to 1985 (millions)[6]	Annual Deaths to Infants under One Year of Age per 1,000 Live Births[3]	Population under 15 Years (percent)[7]	Population over 64 Years (percent)[7]	Percent of Population in Cities[8] of 100,000+[9]	Per Capita Gross National Product (US $)[10]
WORLD	**3,782**[11]	**33**	**13**	**2.0**	**35**	**4,933**	—	**37**	**5**	**23**	—
AFRICA	**364**	**47**	**21**	**2.6**	**27**	**530**	—	**44**	**3**	**11**	—
Northern Africa	**92**	**47**	**17**	**3.0**	**23**	**140**	—	**45**	**3**	**21**	—
Algeria	15.0	50	17	3.3	21	23.9	86	47	L	14	260
Egypt	35.9	44	16	2.8	25	52.3	118	43	L	31	160
Libya	2.0	46	16	3.1	23	3.1	—	44	5	26	1,510
Morocco[12]	16.8	50	16	3.4	21	26.2	149	46	L	24	190
Sudan	16.8	49	18	3.1	23	26.0	121	47	—	3	110
Tunisia	5.4	42	16	2.6	27	8.3	120	46	L	22	230
Western Africa	**107**	**49**	**24**	**2.5**	**28**	**155**	—	**45**	**2**	**7**	—
Cape Verde Islands[13]	0.3	39	14	2.5	28	0.3	121	42	L	N.A.	120
Dahomey	2.8	51	26	2.6	27	4.1	149	46	L	6	P
Gambia	0.4	42	23	1.9	37	0.5	125	38	L	N.A.	110
Ghana[12]	9.6	47	18	2.9	24	14.9	122	45	L	18	190
Guinea	4.1	47	25	2.3	30	5.7	216	44	7	6	P
Ivory Coast	4.5	46	23	2.4	29	6.4	138	43	L	12	240
Liberia	1.2	50	23	2.7	26	1.6	137	37	L	N.A.	200
Mali	5.3	50	27	2.3	30	7.6	190	49	L	5	P
Mauritania	1.2	44	23	2.1	33	1.7	137	—	—	N.A.	140

Region or Country[1]	Population Estimates Mid-1972 (millions)[2]	Annual Births per 1,000 Population[7]	Annual Deaths per 1,000 Population[3]	Annual Rate of Population Growth (percent)[4]	Number of Years to Double Population[5]	Population Projections to 1985 (millions)[6]	Annual Deaths to Infants under One Year of Age per 1,000 Live Births[3]	Population under 15 Years (percent)[7]	Population over 64 Years (percent)[7]	Percent of Population in Cities[8] of 100,000+[9]	Per Capita Gross National Product (US $)[10]
Niger	4.1	52	23	2.9	24	6.2	148	45	L	N.A.	P
Nigeria	58.0	50	25	2.6	27	84.7	—	43	L	7	P
Portuguese Guinea[13]	0.6	41	30	1.1	63	0.7	—	37	L	N.A.	260
Senegal	4.1	46	22	2.4	29	5.8	—	42	L	15	200
Sierra Leone	2.8	45	22	2.3	30	3.9	136	37	5	7	170
Togo[12]	2.0	51	26	2.5	28	2.8	163	48	L	10	100
Upper Volta	5.6	49	29	2.0	35	7.7	182	42	L	N.A.	P
Eastern Africa	**103**	**47**	**22**	**2.5**	**28**	**149**	—	**44**	**3**	**5**	**—**
Burundi	3.8	48	25	2.3	30	5.3	150	47	L	N.A.	P
Comoro Islands[13]	0.3	—	—	—	—	0.4	—	44	L	N.A.	130
Ethiopia	26.2	46	25	2.1	33	35.7	—	44	L	3	P
Kenya[12]	11.6	48	18	3.0	23	17.9	—	46	L	7	130
Malagasy Republic	7.3	46	25	2.1	33	10.8	102	46	L	6	110
Malawi	4.7	49	25	2.5	28	6.8	119	44	L	4	P
Mauritius	0.9	27	8	1.9	37	1.2	58	42	L	17	230
Mozambique[13]	8.1	43	23	2.1	33	11.1	—	42	L	4	210
Reunion[13]	0.5	35	9	2.7	26	0.7	58	46	L	N.A.	660
Rhodesia	5.4	48	14	3.4	21	8.6	122	48	L	14	240
Rwanda	3.8	52	23	2.9	24	5.7	124	—	—	N.A.	P
Somalia	2.9	46	24	2.2	32	4.2	190	—	—	7	P
Tanzania	14.0	47	22	2.6	27	20.3	162	44	L	3	P
Uganda[12]	9.1	43	18	2.6	27	13.1	160	41	L	4	110
Zambia[12]	4.6	50	21	2.9	24	7.0	159	45	L	11	290
Middle Africa	**38**	**44**	**24**	**2.1**	**33**	**52**	—	**42**	**3**	**6**	**—**
Angola[13]	5.9	50	30	2.1	33	8.1	192	42	L	6	210
Cameroon	6.0	43	23	2.0	35	8.4	137	39	L	6	150
Central African Republic	1.6	46	25	2.1	33	2.2	163	42	L	11	130
Chad	3.9	48	25	2.3	30	5.5	160	46	L	N.A.	P
Congo (People's Rep. of)	1.0	44	23	2.1	33	1.4	148	42	L	21	220
Equatorial Guinea	0.3	35	22	1.4	50	0.4	—	35	L	N.A.	290
Gabon	0.5	33	25	0.8	87	0.6	184	36	7	N.A.	320
Zaire (Dem. Rep. Congo)	18.3	44	23	2.1	33	25.8	115	42	L	7	P
Southern Africa	**24**	**41**	**18**	**2.4**	**29**	**34**	—	**40**	**4**	**29**	**—**
Botswana	0.7	44	23	2.2	32	0.9	175	43	L	N.A.	P

Region or Country[1]	Population Estimates Mid-1972 (millions)[2]	Annual Births per 1,000 Population[7]	Annual Deaths per 1,000 Population[3]	Annual Rate of Population Growth (percent)[4]	Number of Years to Double Population[5]	Population Projections to 1985 (millions)[6]	Annual Deaths to Infants under One Year of Age per 1,000 Live Births[3]	Population under 15 Years (percent)[7]	Population over 64 Years (percent)[7]	Percent of Population in Cities[8] of 100,000+[9]	Per Capita Gross National Product (US $)[10]
Lesotho	1.1	39	21	1.8	39	1.4	181	43	5	N.A.	P
South Africa[12]	21.1	41	17	2.4	29	29.7	138	40	L	32	} 710
Namibia (Southwest Africa)	0.7	44	25	2.0	35	0.9	—	40	5	N.A.	
Swaziland	0.4	52	24	2.8	25	0.7	168	47	L	N.A.	180
ASIA	**2,154**	**37**	**14**	**2.3**	**30**	**2,874**	**—**	**40**	**4**	**16**	**—**
Southwest Asia	**82**	**44**	**16**	**2.8**	**25**	**121**	**—**	**43**	**4**	**22**	**—**
Bahrain	0.2	50	19	3.1	23	0.3	—	—	L	N.A.	420
Cyprus	0.6	23	8	0.9	77	0.7	26	33	7	18	970
Gaza[13]	0.5	44	8	3.6	19	0.8	—	50	L	N.A.	—
Iraq	10.4	49	15	3.4	21	16.7	104	48	5	31	310
Israel	3.0	27	7	2.4	29	4.0	23	33	7	55	1,570
Jordan	2.5	48	16	3.3	21	3.9	115	47	L	20	280
Kuwait[14]	0.8	43	7	8.2	9	2.4	39	38	L	59	3,320
Lebanon	3.0	—	—	—	—	4.3	—	—	—	33	580
Oman	0.7	˙50	19	3.1	23	1.1	—	—	—	N.A.	210
Qatar	0.1	50	19	3.1	23	0.1	—	—	L	N.A.	1,550
Saudi Arabia	8.2	50	23	2.8	25	12.2	—	—	—	14	380
Syria	6.6	48	15	3.3	21	10.5	—	47	L	31	260
Turkey	37.6	40	15	2.5	28	52.8	119	42	L	18	350
United Arab Emirates	0.2	50	19	3.1	23	0.2	—	32	L	N.A.	1,590
Yemen Arab Republic	6.1	50	23	2.8	25	9.1	—	—	—	N.A.	P
Yemen, People's Republic of	1.4	50	21	2.9	24	2.0	—	—	—	28	120
Middle South Asia	**806**	**44**	**17**	**2.6**	**27**	**1,137**	**—**	**43**	**3**	**11**	**—**
Afghanistan	17.9	51	27	2.4	29	25.0	—	—	—	4	P
Bhutan	0.9	—	—	2.2	32	1.2	—	—	—	N.A.	P
Ceylon	13.2	31	8	2.3	30	17.7	48	41	L	11	190
India[12]	584.8	42	17	2.5	28	807.6	139	42	L	10	110
Iran	30.2	45	17	2.8	25	45.0	—	46	L	23	350
Maldive Islands	0.1	46	23	2.3	31	0.1	—	44	L	N.A.	P
Nepal	11.8	45	23	2.2	32	15.8	—	40	L	4	P
Pakistan[15]	146.6	51	18	3.3	21	224.2	142	45	L	10	110
Sikkim	0.2	48	29	1.9	37	0.3	—	40	L	N.A.	P
Southeast Asia	**304**	**43**	**15**	**2.8**	**25**	**434**	**—**	**44**	**3**	**12**	**—**

Region or Country[1]	Population Estimates Mid-1972 (millions)[2]	Annual Births per 1,000 Population[7]	Annual Deaths per 1,000 Population[3]	Annual Rate of Population Growth (percent)[4]	Number of Years to Double Population[5]	Population Projections to 1985 (millions)[6]	Annual Deaths to Infants under One Year of Age per 1,000 Live Births[3]	Population under 15 Years (percent)[7]	Population over 64 Years (percent)[7]	Percent of Population in Cities[8] of 100,000+[9]	Per Capita Gross National Product (US $)[10]
Burma	29.1	40	17	2.3	30	39.2	—	40	L	7	P
Indonesia	128.7	47	19	2.9	24	183.8	125	44	L	12	} 100
Irian, West[13]	0.9	—	—	—	—	1.3	—	—	—	N.A.	
Khmer Republic (Cambodia)	7.6	45	16	3.0	23	11.3	127	44	L	10	130
Laos	3.1	42	17	2.5	28	4.4	—	—	—	7	110
Malaysia[12]	11.4	37	8	2.8	25	16.4	—	44	L	17	340
Philippines[12]	40.8	45	12	3.3	21	64.0	67	47	L	16	210
Portuguese Timor[13]	0.6	43	25	1.8	39	0.8	—	—	—	N.A.	P
Singapore	2.2	23	5	2.2	32	3.0	21	39	L	100	800
Thailand[12]	38.6	43	10	3.3	21	57.7	—	43	L	8	160
Vietnam (Dem. Republic of)	22.0	—	—	—	—	28.2	—	—	—	11	P
Vietnam (Republic of)	18.7	—	—	—	—	23.9	—	—	—	13	140
East Asia	**962**	**29**	**12**	**1.7**	**41**	**1,182**	**—**	**35**	**4**	**20**	**—**
China (People's Republic of)	786.1	30	13	1.7	41	964.6	—	—	—	14	P
China (Republic of)	14.7	28	5	2.3	30	19.4	18	43	L	38	300
Hong Kong[12, 13]	4.4	20	5	2.4	29	6.0	19	38	L	100	850
Japan	106.0	19	7	1.2	58	121.3	13	24	7	55	1,430
Ryukyu Islands[12, 16]	1.0	22	5	1.7	41	1.3	—	34	6	30	700
Korea (Dem. People's Rep. of)	14.7	39	11	2.8	25	20.7	—	—	—	17	280
Korea (Republic of)	33.7	31	11	2.0	35	45.9	—	40	L	33	210
Macau[13]	0.3	—	—	—	—	0.4	—	39	5	100	150
Mongolia	1.4	42	11	3.1	23	2.0	—	31	6	27	460
NORTHERN AMERICA	**231**	**17**	**9**	**1.1**	**63**	**274**	**—**	**29**	**9**	**57**	**—**
Canada	22.2	17.5	7.3	1.7	41	27.3	19.3	30	8	49	2,650
United States[17]	209.2	17.3	9.3	1.0	70	246.3	19.2	29	10	58	4,240
LATIN AMERICA	**300**	**38**	**10**	**2.8**	**25**	**435**	**—**	**42**	**4**	**31**	**—**
Middle America	**72**	**43**	**11**	**3.2**	**22**	**112**	**—**	**46**	**3**	**20**	**—**
Costa Rica	1.9	34	7	2.7	26	3.2	67	48	L	25	510
El Salvador	3.7	40	10	3.0	23	5.9	67	45	L	14	290
Guatemala	5.4	43	17	2.6	27	7.9	92	46	L	15	350
Honduras	2.9	49	17	3.2	22	4.6	—	47	L	10	260
Mexico[12]	54.3	43	10	3.3	21	84.4	69	46	L	21	580

Region or Country[1]	Population Estimates Mid-1972 (millions)[2]	Annual Births per 1,000 Population[7]	Annual Deaths per 1,000 Population[3]	Annual Rate of Population Growth (percent)[4]	Number of Years to Double Population[5]	Population Projections to 1985 (millions)[6]	Annual Deaths to Infants under One Year of Age per 1,000 Live Births[3]	Population under 15 Years (percent)[7]	Population over 64 Years (percent)[7]	Percent of Population in Cities[8] of 100,000+[9]	Per Capita Gross National Product (US $)[10]
Nicaragua	2.2	46	17	2.9	24	3.3	—	48	L	18	380
Panama	1.6	38	9	2.9	24	2.5	41	44	L	30	660
Caribbean[18]	**27**	**33**	**11**	**2.2**	**32**	**36**	**—**	**40**	**4**	**21**	**—**
Barbados	0.3	21	8	0.8	87	0.3	42	36	7	N.A.	500
Cuba	8.7	27	8	1.9	37	11.0	48	31	6	31	280
Dominican Republic[12]	4.6	49	15	3.4	21	7.3	64	47	L	18	280
Guadeloupe[13]	0.4	30	8	2.2	32	0.5	45	43	5	N.A.	540
Haiti	5.5	44	20	2.4	29	7.9	—	38	L	8	P
Jamaica[12]	2.1	33	8	2.1	33	2.6	39	46	L	28	550
Martinique[13]	0.4	27	8	1.6	44	0.5	35	43	5	N.A.	690
Puerto Rico[13]	2.9	25	7	1.4	50	3.4	26	37	7	33	1,410
Trinidad & Tobago[12]	1.1	23	7	1.1	63	1.3	37	42	L	N.A.	890
Tropical South America	**160**	**40**	**10**	**3.0**	**23**	**236**	**—**	**43**	**3**	**32**	**—**
Bolivia	4.9	44	19	2.4	29	6.8	—	42	L	15	160
Brazil	98.4	38	10	2.8	25	142.6	—	43	L	34	270
Colombia	22.9	44	11	3.4	21	35.6	76	47	L	35	290
Ecuador	6.5	45	11	3.4	21	10.1	91	48	L	21	240
Guyana	0.8	36	8	2.8	25	1.1	40	45	L	27	340
Peru	14.5	42	11	3.1	23	21.6	72	45	L	22	330
Surinam[13]	0.4	41	7	3.2	22	0.6	30	46	L	34	560
Venezuela	11.5	41	8	3.4	21	17.4	47	47	L	37	1,000
Temperate South America	**41**	**25**	**9**	**1.7**	**41**	**51**	**—**	**32**	**7**	**52**	**—**
Argentina[12]	25.0	22	9	1.5	47	29.6	58	30	7	61	1,060
Chile[12]	10.2	28	9	1.9	37	13.6	92	39	5	37	510
Paraguay	2.6	45	11	3.4	21	4.1	67	46	L	19	240
Uruguay	3.0	21	9	1.2	58	3.4	49	28	8	53	560
EUROPE	**469**	**16**	**10**	**0.7**	**99**	**515**	**—**	**25**	**12**	**38**	**—**
Northern Europe	**82**	**16**	**11**	**0.5**	**139**	**90**	**—**	**24**	**13**	**58**	**—**
Denmark	5.0	14.4	9.8	0.5	139	5.5	14.8	24	12	38	2,310
Finland	4.8	13.7	9.5	0.4	174	5.0	12.5	26	8	24	1,980
Iceland	0.2	19.5	7.1	1.2	58	0.3	13.3	33	9	N.A.	1,850
Ireland	3.0	21.8	11.5	0.7	99	3.5	19.2	31	11	31	1,110
Norway	4.0	16.6	9.8	0.7	99	4.5	13.8	25	13	26	2,160
Sweden	8.2	13.7	9.9	0.4	174	8.8	11.7	21	13	33	2,920
United Kingdom	56.6	16.2	11.7	0.5	139	61.8	18.4	24	13	71	1,890

Region or Country[1]	Population Estimates Mid-1972 (millions)[2]	Annual Births per 1,000 Population[7]	Annual Deaths per 1,000 Population[3]	Annual Rate of Population Growth (percent)[4]	Number of Years to Double Population[5]	Population Projections to 1985 (millions)[6]	Annual Deaths to Infants under One Year of Age per 1,000 Live Births[3]	Population under 15 Years (percent)[7]	Population over 64 Years (percent)[7]	Percent of Population in Cities[8] of 100,000+[9]	Per Capita Gross National Product (US $)[10]
Western Europe	**151**	**15**	**11**	**0.5**	**139**	**163**	**—**	**24**	**13**	**45**	**—**
Austria	7.5	15.2	13.4	0.2	347	8.0	25.9	24	14	36	1,470
Belgium	9.8	14.7	12.3	0.2	347	10.4	20.5	24	13	28	2,010
France	51.9	16.7	10.6	0.7	99	57.6	15.1	25	13	40	2,460
Germany (Federal Republic of)	59.2	13.3	11.7	0.2	347	62.3	23.6	25	12	54	2,190
Berlin, West[13]	2.1	9.5	19.0	−1.0	—	1.9	25.8	15	21	100	—
Luxembourg	0.4	13.2	12.3	0.1	693	0.4	24.6	22	12	N.A.	2,420
Netherlands	13.3	18.4	8.4	1.0	70	15.3	12.7	27	10	45	1,760
Switzerland	6.4	15.8	9.1	1.0	70	7.4	15.1	23	11	33	2,700
Eastern Europe	**106**	**17**	**10**	**0.7**	**99**	**116**	**—**	**24**	**11**	**24**	**—**
Bulgaria	8.7	16.3	9.1	0.7	99	9.4	27.3	23	9	21	860
Czechoslovakia	14.9	15.8	11.4	0.5	139	16.2	22.1	24	11	16	1,370
Germany (Dem. Republic of)	16.3	13.9	14.1	0.0	—	16.9	18.8	24	15	23	1,570
Berlin, East[13]	1.1	14.5	16.4	−0.2	—	1.0	20.3	22	16	100	—
Hungary	10.4	14.7	11.7	0.3	231	11.0	35.9	21	11	24	1,100
Poland	33.7	16.8	8.2	0.9	77	38.2	33.2	28	8	31	940
Romania	20.8	21.1	9.5	1.2	58	23.3	49.4	26	8	22	860
Southern Europe	**131**	**18**	**9**	**0.9**	**77**	**146**	**—**	**26**	**10**	**30**	**—**
Albania	2.3	35.3	7.5	2.8	25	3.3	86.8	—	—	10	430
Greece	9.0	16.3	8.3	0.8	87	9.7	29.3	25	10	34	840
Italy	54.5	16.8	9.7	0.7	99	60.0	29.2	24	10	29	1,400
Malta[14]	0.3	16.3	9.4	−0.7	—	0.3	27.9	28	9	N.A.	710
Portugal	9.7	18.0	9.7	0.8	87	10.7	58.0	29	9	24	510
Spain	33.9	19.6	8.5	1.0	70	38.1	27.9	28	9	33	820
Yugoslavia	21.0	17.8	9.0	0.9	77	23.8	55.2	28	7	28	580
USSR	**248**	**17.4**	**8.2**	**0.9**	**77**	**286.9**	**24.4**	**28**	**8**	**31**	**1,200**
OCEANIA[18]	**20**	**25**	**10**	**2.0**	**35**	**27**	**—**	**32**	**7**	**49**	**—**
Australia	13.0	20.5	9.0	1.9	37	17.0	17.9	29	8	65	2,300
Fiji	0.6	30	5	1.8	39	0.8	22	45	L	N.A.	390
New Zealand	3.0	22.1	8.8	1.7	41	3.8	16.7	32	8	46	2,230
Papua- New Guinea[13]	2.5	—	—	—	—	3.6	—	43	L	N.A.	210

WORLD AND REGIONAL POPULATION (Millions)

	WORLD	ASIA	EUROPE	USSR	AFRICA	NORTHERN AMERICA	LATIN AMERICA	OCEANIA
Mid-1972	3782	2154	469	248	364	231	300	20
UN Medium Estimate, 2000	6494	3777	568	330	818	333	652	35

Footnotes

[1]The table lists all UN members, and all geopolitical entities with a population larger than 200,000.

[2]Estimates from United Nations. *Total Population Estimates for World, Regions and Countries, Each Year, 1950–1985*, Population Division Working Paper No. 34, October 1970.

[3]Latest available year. Except for Northern American rates, estimates are essentially those available as of January 1972 in *UN Population and Vital Statistics Report, Series A, Vol. XXIV, No. 1*, with adjustments as deemed necessary in view of deficiency of registration in some countries.

[4]Annual rate of population growth (composed of the rate of natural increase modified by the net rate of in- or out-migration) is derived from the latest available published estimates by the United Nations, except where substantiated changes have occurred in birth rates, death rates or migration streams.

[5]Assuming no change in growth rate.

[6]Estimates from United Nations, *Total Population Estimates for World, Regions and Countries, Each Year, 1950–1985*, Population Division Working Paper No. 34, October 1970.

[7]Latest available year. Derived from *UN World Population Prospects, 1965–1985, As Assessed in 1968*, Population Working Paper No. 30, December 1969 and *UN Demographic Yearbook, 1970*.

[8]Definition: Cities—Urbanized areas, metropolitan areas and urban agglomerations as per Kingsley Davis (see footnote 9).

[9]Estimates for 1970. Data from Kingsley Davis, *World Urbanization 1950–1970, Volume I: Basic Data for Cities, Countries, and Regions* (Population Monograph Series No. 4), Berkeley, University of California, 1969.

[10]1969 data supplied by the International Bank for Reconstruction and Development.

[11]Total reflects UN adjustments for discrepancies in international migration data.

[12]In these countries, the UN estimates show a variation of more than 3 percent from recent census figures. Because of uncertainty as to the completeness or accuracy of census data, the UN estimates are used.

[13]Nonsovereign country.

[14]Kuwait has a natural rate of increase of +3.6 and Malta has a natural rate of increase of +0.7. Their growth rate differs markedly from their rate of increase because their small base population is strongly affected by migration.

[15]Pakistan (West) 1972 estimated population 66.9 million.
  Bangladesh 1972 estimated population 79.6 million.

[16]Reverted to Japan 5/15/72.

[17]US figures are based on National Center for Health Statistics, *Monthly Vital Statistics Rates*, Vol. 20, No. 12, 2/28/72, and Bureau of the Census, *Current Population Reports*, Series P-25 No. 476, February 1972, Series D.

[18]Regional population totals take into account small areas not listed in the table.

Key to Abbreviations

L = Estimated to be less than 5 percent.
P = Estimated to be less than US $100.
N.A. = Not applicable: country has no urban community over 100,000.
— = Unavailable or unreliable.

General Notes

SOURCE: *Population Reference Bureau. By Permission.*

Due to rounding to the nearest 100,000, increases in population amounting to less than that number do not appear on the *Data Sheet.*

The completeness and accuracy of data in many developing countries are subject to deficiencies of varying degree. In some cases, the data shown are estimates prepared by the United Nations.

Index

In this index 48f means separate references on pp. 48 and 49; 48ff means separate references on pp. 48, 49, and 50; 48–50 means a continuous discussion. *Passim,* meaning "here and there," is used for a cluster of references in close but not consecutive sequence (for example, 13, 14, 16, 17, 20 would be written as 13–20 *passim.*)

Abidjan, Ivory Coast, growth rate of, 43
Abortion, 230–238 *passim,* 241, 247, 256; laws on, 34, 234–235, 237, 249, 252
Abstention, as birth control, 230; periodic, 230–231
Accountability and political reform, 270
Accra, Ghana, growth rate in, 43
Acetylcholine, 169
Adversary science, 270
Advertising, control of, 265
Affluence: and environment, 8, 12–13; in U.S., 13, 213–215; and consumption, 208–211
Afghanistan: family planning in, 240; population data for, 283
Africa: population growth and structure in, 19, 22–26, 42f, 227; population data for, 46ff, 281–283, 287; food production in, 71, 86ff, 90, 94; North, 94, 281; forests of, 111; and high birth rate, 253. *See also by country*
Age composition of populations, 29–36, 247, 281–287
Agriculture, 7f, 80–90, 216–217; and ecosystem modification, 4f, 81, 159, 163–164; livestock, 4, 15, 53f, 80, 84–87, 104f, 128, 176, 188; yields, 8, 14f, 81ff, 85, 93–96, 164, 173, 218; monocultures, 8, 164, 172, 218; irrigation, 14, 80, 90–93, 108f, 218; and photosynthesis, 15; technology and mechanization of, 15, 26, 80, 82–83, 95, 164, 212f, 273; Green Revolution, 15, 93–96, 106, 187; history of, 19, 23, 25f, 41, 80, 162; and urbanization, 41; and burning of

Agriculture *(continued)*
   wastes, 60, 198; slash-and-burn, 80,
      82; and pollution, 96, 128, 131f, 137,
      184–187, 189, 198; and labor, 184;
      and climate, 198, 200. *See also*
      Fertilizers; Pesticides
Agriculture, Department of (U.S.), 172f
Agricultural revolution, 7, 22–24, 40, 80
Aid and development, 271–274, 279
Air conditioning, 59, 210
Air pollution, 61, 114–127, 136, 146,
      219–220; smog, 83, 111, 114–125,
      passim, 195, 217; by particulate
      matter, 116ff, 122, 132, 194, 199,
      220; control of, 123, 125, 263. *See
      also* Atmosphere
Airplanes: SSTs, 144f, pollution by, 194,
      199; fit, 199, 264
Alaska: petroleum in, 55; forests of, 110;
      abortion in, 234
Albania: growth rate of, 245; population
      data for, 286
Albedo, 197–199
Aldrin, 132, 135, 168, 180f
Alfalfa, 86, 154, 178
Algae: sewage-cultured, 105; blue-green,
      154; in soil, 179; blooms of, 185–186
Algeria: family planning in, 240; popula-
      tion data for, 281
Aluminum, 63, 215f
Aluminum oxide, 162
Alvik, Norway, 118f
Amazon Basin, 91, 111, 163
American Indians, and birth control, 248
Ammonia, 4, 155, 193
Anderson, J.M., 134
Anemia, iron-deficiency, 76
Angkor Wat, 162f
Animals, 12, 153; domestic, 4, 15, 53f,
      80, 84–87, 104f, 128, 176, 188; and
      food chains, 77–80; and pollution,
      181, 189, 193. *See also by name*
Anions; defined, 187
Annelida, 179
Antarctica, 52, 98, 107, 136, 170
Antibiotics, 5
Ants, leaf cutting, 2
Aphids, 174
Aquifers, subsurface, 108f
Arctic, the, 198
Argentina 54; food supply in, 74; child
      mortality rates in, 75; population
      data for, 285
Arizona, 174; air quality laws, 123
Army Corps of Engineers, 129, 187
Arsenate, 139
Arsenic, as pollutant, 139
Arsenite, 139
Arthropoda, 179

Asama, Mount, 199
Asbestos, 120f
Ash, pollution by, 118, 128, 199
Asia: resources of, 13, 66; Southeast, 13,
      23, 66, 85, 91, 111, 283–284; popula-
      tion growth and structure of, 24–28,
      40, 43; population data for, 46ff,
      283–284, 287; South, 46f, 94; East,
      46f, 94, 284; food supply of, 70f,
      73–74, 85, 91, 94; child mortality
      in, 75f; arable land in, 90; West, 94;
      forests of, 110f, Northern, 110;
      eutrophication in, 187; abortion in,
      234. *See also by country*
Asthma, 120
Aswan High Dam, 93
Atlanta, Georgia, smog in, 118
Atlantic Ocean, 103, 190
Atmosphere, 4; thermal inversion of,
      122; pollution of, 185, 193–200. *See
      also* Air pollution
Atomic Energy Commission (AEC), 141ff,
      270
Australia, 65, 116, 227; immigration
      laws in, 40; population data for, 75,
      286; arable land in, 90; and recycled
      sewage, 189
Australopithecus, 22–23
Austria: food supply in, 74; child mor-
      tality rates in, 75; family planning
      in, 242; population data for, 286
Automobiles, 131, 204, 207; use of water,
      108; internal combustion engine,
      118, 124ff, 187, 219; and pollution,
      118, 122–127, 193, 213ff; per capita,
      210; and lead, 213ff; control of, 262–
      263, 265, 268–269
Azodrin, 169, 174–176
Azusa, California, 124

Bacteria, 78, 153; and infection, 25;
      nitrogen-fixing, 86, 154f; and food
      loss, 96, 105; and nitrites, 128, 154f;
      in soil, 179, 181, 183f; and
      herbicides, 183; and oil, 192
Baikal, Lake, 187
Bangladesh, 201; family planning in, 240;
      population of, 287
Barbados: family planning in, 240; pop-
      ulation data for, 285
Barents Sea, 102f
Barley, 85
Bauxite mines, 53
Beans, 86
Beef, 87
Belgium: death rate in, 31; food supply
      in, 74; family planning in, 239; pop-
      ulation data for, 286

Benzene hexachloride (BHC), 132, 168, 173–174, 180
Beriberi, 76
Bethlehem Steel, and water pollution, 185
Biochemical cycles, 152–156. *See also by name*
Biocides, 172, 183, 193. *See also* Pesticides
Biological pest control, 80, 170, 177–178
Biomass, defined, 80
Biosphere, defined, 6
Birds: as pests, 105; DDT concentration in, 166, 170–172; and herbicides, 183; and oil spills, 190ff
Birth control, 31, 229–233; abortion, 34, 230–238 *passim*, 241, 247, 249, 252, 256; sterilization, 231, 233–234, 238, 241ff, 252, 254, 256; clinics, 234, 239, 241f, 245, 248, 253; future, 237–239; and race, 248. *See also* family planning
Birth defects, 143, 183, 201
Birth rates, 20–22, 48, 281–287; history of, 22f, 25–27; and population structure, 30–33, 36; crude, 32, 36; and population limitation, 235, 244–246, 249
Blacks, and birth control, 248
Blake, Judith, 255
Blood: and carbon monoxide, 117–120 *passim*, and nitrogen oxides, 120
Blumer, Max, 192
Bodega Head, California, 141
Bolivia: family planning in, 240; population data for, 285
Boll weevil, 174
Bollworm, 174–175
Borgstrom, Georg, 89, 109, 161, 172–173
Borlaug, Norman, 96
Botanical pesticides, 177
Botswana: family planning in, 240; population data for, 282
Bottle deposits, 131
Boulding, Kenneth, 260–261
Brain: and culture, 23; and protein deficiency, 77; and DDT, 134
Brazil, 53, 73f, 111; laterization in, 163; family planning in, 240; population data for, 285
Breeder reactors, 60, 142
Bronchitis, 117–121
Building construction, 84, 115, 148, 159, 215f
Bulgaria: child mortality rates in, 75; population data for, 286
Bureau of Reclamation, 187
Burma: family planning in, 240; population data for, 284

Cabrillo, Juan Rodriguez, 122
Cadmium, pollution by, 116, 138–139, 190, 192
Caffeine, 143–144
Calcium: deficiency, 76; in soil, 162; and DDT, 170
Calcutta, growth rate of, 44f
California, 52, 68, 83–84, 110, 128; air quality laws, 123; pesticide use in, 169, 171, 174–178; abortion laws, 235
California Tomorrow Plan, The, 125–126
Calories of food, 71–74, 85; and fossil fuels, 83; family planning in, 240; population data for, 284
Cambodia, 162f; family planning in, 240; population data for, 284
Canada, 2, 65, 74, 99, 137; population growth in, 26; population data for, 75, 284; family planning in, 242
Cancer, 170, 190, 201; and air pollution, 120f, 217, 220; and chlorinated hydrocarbons, 133–135; and radiation, 140
Cañete Valley, Peru, 173–174
Capital, and UDCs, 95
Capybara, herding of, 105
Carbamates, 177, 181
Carbon: cycle, 4, 152–154, 193; organic, 184–185, 187; radioactive, 198
Carbon dioxide: and climate, 4, 15, 165, 194, 197–199, 220; and carbon cycle, 78, 152f
Carbon monoxide, 115–120 *passim*, 124f, 217, 219
Carcinogens, *See* Cancer
Carnivores, 6–7, 77–81
Cassava, 86
Cattle, 53, 80, 86–87, 105; and screwworm program, 176; manure, 188. *See also* Livestock
Caustic soda, 137
Census, Bureau of (U.S.), 247, 249
Central America: child mortality rates in, 75; Incaparina, 104–105; population data for, 284–285. *See also by country*
Central Valley of California, 128, 178
Cereal grains, 84–86. *See also by name*
Cervical cap, 230
Ceylon: population growth in, 26f, 31; malaria in, 27; steel use in, 65; food supply in, 74, 94; population data for, 75, 283; family planning in, 240, 244
Chattanooga, Tennessee, 120
Chemical energy, 54
Chicago, 43, 83, 116, 188
Chickens, 86–87

Children: number of, 10–11, 36–37, 228–229, 242, 245, 254–255; labor of, 32; mortality rates for 35, 73–76, 248; first born, 229; day care for, 249, 255

Chile: food supply in, 74; child mortality rates in, 75; family planning in, 240, 242; population data for, 285

China, People's Republic of: food production in, 86f, 97; and nuclear weapons, 140; abortion in, 234; family planning in, 240f; population data for, 284

China: population growth in, 24, 40; floods in, 109, 112. *See also* China, People's Republic of; Taiwan

Chlordane, 132, 168, 180

Chlorinated hydrocarbons, 132–135, 165–181 *passim*, 190, 192. *See also* DDT

Chlorine, 127, 137

Cholera, 28

Cholinesterase inhibition, 169

Chromium, 64f, 139, 190

Cigarette smoking, 120f

Cirrhosis of liver, 120, 134f

Cities: development of, 8, 40–46, 52, 83, 146; renewal projects in, 43, 147; pollution in, 118–126, 131, 145–148, 194–195; population of, 207–208, 281–287; new, 250; zoning of, 250–251

Clams, 186

Clark, Colin, 48

Cleveland, and water pollution, 185

Climate, 61, 109, 193–197; global, 197–200

Climax community, 7

Closing Circle, The, 213n

Clothes dryers: in use per capita, 210

Clothing expenditure, 210–211

Clouds, 197ff

Clover, 86, 154

Coal, 118, 152f, 195, 212; mining of, 50, 61, 124, 128; consumption of, 55, 57, 63f

Coastlines, 52–53, 61

Cobalt, 63

Cod, 103

Codling moth, 169

Coffee plantations, 53

Coitus interruptus, 230, 232, 239

Colds, and air pollution, 120

Columbia: soybeans in, 54; steel consumption in, 65; food supply in, 74; family planning in, 240, 242; education in, 258; population data for, 285

Colorado Environmental Commission, 251

Common Cause, 269

Common Market, 274

Commoner, Barry, 213n

Commons, use of, 99

Communication, 261, 278

Community, defined, 6–7

Complexity, ecological, 6–7, 83, 156–159, 163–164

Condom, 230, 232, 239, 241

Congress, 251–252, 268

Coniferous forests, 110, 159

Conservationists, 112, 187

Consumer durables, 210

Consumption, 15, 205–221 *passim*

Contraceptive methods, 230–239, 242–245, 247, 252, 266. *See also by name*

Copper, 53, 63, 65f, 215f

Coral reefs, 154, 160f, 165

Corn, 84ff, 94f, 104f

Cornwallis Island, 2

Costa Rica: death rate in, 31; child mortality rates in, 75; family planning in, 240; population data for, 284

Cotton, 65, 173–176, 178, 215f

Cowboy economy, 260–264, 271

Creams, as contraceptives, 230, 232

Crime rates, urban, 146

Crops, 5, 7f, 178, 217; and agricultural practice, 80, 83, 84–87; loss of, 105, 200f; and air pollution, 115; mentioned, 159, 163. *See also by name*

Crowding, and crime, 146

Crusaders, 39

Crustacea, and herbicides, 183

Cryogenic technology, 63

Cuba: family planning in, 240; population data for, 285

Culture, evolution of, 22–24

Cyclamate, 134

Cyclohexylamine, 144

Czechoslovakia: child mortality rates in, 75; family planning in, 242; population data for, 286

DCs, 13f, 128, 221; population growth and structure in, 27f, 30–32, 42–44, 47f; resource consumption in, 53, 55, 62–63, 65–66, 262; food supply and production in, 71, 76, 87–89, 95; forests in, 110–111; and population limitation, 226, 239–241, 245f, 254, 271–273; and wealth redistribution, 271–274, 279. *See also by country*

DDD, 134, 181

DDE, 134, 168

DDT, 12, 115, 173, 177f, 180f; and malaria, 27, 167; toxicity of, 132–135, 157; as mutagen, 144; concentration of, 157, 165–172; in ocean, 189f, 218

DNA, 140, 155

2,4-D, 181, 183
Dahomey: family planning in, 240; population data for, 281
Daly, Herman, 264
Dams, 58, 92, 159
Davis, Kinglsey, 45, 254
Death rates, 20–22, 49, 147, 281–287; history of, 22–28; and population sturcture, 30–33, 35f; crude, 32, 36; and population limitation, 225, 229, 245f
Decay and decomposer organisms, 6, 78, 153, 155, 193
De-development, 279
Defoliants, 159, 162; in Vietnam, 181–183
Deforestation, 109, 159, 162, 181–183, 193–194
Delaware, zoning policies of, 250
Demographers, defined, 20
Demographic projections, 46–49, 281–287
Demographic transition, the, 25–26, 28, 239, 246
Denmark: birth rates in, 25; food supply in, 74; soil of, 179; population density of, 228; population data for, 285
Density of population, 37–39, 51f, 227–228
Denver, population limit for, 251
Dependents in populations, 30–32
Depletion quotas on resources, 264–265
Depression, the, 30, 48, 255
Desalination of salt water, 14, 92f, 108
Desert, 2
Detergents: and arsenic, 139; phosphates in, 186, 213; and oil spills, 192
Detroit: and radiation exposure, 142; and water pollution, 185
Developed countries. *See* DCs
Development and aid, 272–274, 279
Diaphragm, as contraceptive, 230, 232
Diarrhea, 75
Diazinon, 169
2,5-Dichlorophenol, 183
Dieldrin, 132, 134f, 168, 180f
Diesels, 126
Digestive processes, 77
Dilan, 180
Diminishing returns, law of, 216
Diseases, 75, 130, 177, 201; deficiency, 76; respiratory, 115, 118–121; stress-related, 145. *See* also *by name*
Dispersion of population, 29–30, 37–40
Disruptions of ecosystems, 6, 16, 150–203
Distribution of population, 29–30, 37–40, 201, 250–251

Domestic animals, 4, 15, 53f, 80, 84–87, 176, 188; feed for, 86, 104f; nitrite poisoning of, 128. *See* also *by name*
Dominican Republic: family planning in, 240, 244; population data for, 285
Donora, Pennsylvania, smog disaster in, 120
Dose response relations, 217f
Doubling time of populations, 9, 20–22, 29, 46, 281–287
Douching, 230, 232
Droughts, 88
Ducks, 86
Dumont, Rene, 74–75
Dumps and dumping, 130f; in ocean, 193
Dung, as fuel, 55
Dust, 199. *See* also Particulate pollution
Dwarfing, and malnutrition, 76
Dysentery, 128

Eagles, 170f
Earth, 4; carrying capacity of, 50–67, 226f; crust of, 63, 69, 153; climate of, 193f, 197–200. *See* also World
Earthquakes, 201f
Earthworms, 179ff
East Pakistan, Ganges Delta of, 201
Ecological pest management. *See* Integrated pest control
Ecological succession, defined, 7
Ecological systems: disruptions of, 6, 16, 150–203; complexity and stability of, 6–7, 83, 156–159, 163–164
Ecology, terminology of, 6–8
Economics, 260–268, 271
Ecosphere, defined, 6
Ecosystems. *See* Ecological systems
Ecuador: child mortality rates in, 75; fishing in, 99; family planning in, 240; population data for, 285
Education, 258, 261, 266–268, 273; sex, 252, 267
Effluents. *See* Pollution
Egypt: growth rate in 28–29; Aswan High Dam, 93; ancient, 230; family planning in, 240; population data for, 281
El Salvador: family planning in, 240; population data for, 284
Eland, herding of, 105
Electric motors, 126, 219
Electric power, 57ff, 141, 194–197; and pollution, 14, 61, 123f, 128, 131, 215, 220
Electricity, production of, 58–61, 92, 212
Emphysema, 117–121 *passim*
Employment, 265–266. *See* also Labor
Endrin, 168, 180

Energy, 54–62, 194, 197; and food chains, 7, 77–81, 166f; consumption of, 14, 15n, 65, 207, 209, 211, 216–217, 264, 279; and Laws of Thermodynamics, 54, 61, 78–80, 166f, 194

England: child mortality rates in, 75; air pollution in, 121; and recycled sewage, 189; climate of 199; family planning in, 230; birth control in, 231; abortion in, 234

Enke, Stephen, 247

Environment, 141, 202, 260–266; man and, 4–8; time lags of, 11–12; degradation of, 12–13, 206f, 219; impact of, 207, 212–221; *passim*, 250

Environmental Protection Agency, (EPA), 125, 129

Erie, Lake, 185–186

Erosion, 6, 115, 161–162, 218

Eskimos, 23, 170

Estrogens, 238

Estuaries, 52f, 137, 166, 186, 190, 218

Ethiopia: family planning in, 240; population data for, 282

Ethylene, 193

Euclid, Ohio, and water pollution, 185

Euphrates river, 41

Europe: population growth and structure in, 24–26, 30, 39–40, 245; population data for, 46ff, 285–287; resource use in, 65, 86, 90, 109f, 112; child mortality in, 75; and pollution, 131, 183, 187; abortion in, 234; family planning in, 239, 241. *See also by country*

Eutrophication, 185–187, 193, 217

Evaporation, 107f

Evolution, defined, 7

Excretion of animals, 155

FAO, 48, 71ff, 96

FDA, 132f, 138

Families: size of, 10–11, 36–37, 228–229, 242, 245, 254–255; replacement rate for, 247; future of, 253, 256, 265

Family planning, 34, 48, 230, 239–247, 251–254

Family Planning Services and Population Research Act, 251f

Famines, 71, 88, 164, 200

Far East, food production in 87f. *See also by country*

Farms and farming, 41; modernization of, 15, 26, 273; animals on, 4, 15, 53f, 80, 84–87, 104f, 128, 176, 188; roads for, 90; runoff from, 128, 184–187; use of insecticides on, 132; of marginal land, 216–217. *See also* Agriculture

Fats, 85f; concentration of chlorinated hydrocarbons in, 132, 134–135, 168f

Federal Water Pollution Control Agency, 185

Fermi fast-breeder reactor, 142

Fertility: rates, 33–36, 47, 245, 247; compulsory control of, 254, 256

Fertilizers, 65, 155, 212f; and food production, 15, 68, 80, 83, 86, 93–95; pollution by, 128, 164, 184ff, 187; recycled sewage as, 187–188

Fetus, 235–236

Fiji: family planning in, 240; population data for, 286

Filter-feeders, 166

Finland: food supply in, 74; population data for, 285

Fire-ant program, 176

Fires, 115, 159, 261

Fish: as food, 5, 13, 53, 78–79, 85, 89, 93; yields, 97–99, 102–104, 217; and pollution, 127, 133f, 134f, 160f, 168, 183, 189, 218. *See also by name*

Fissionable materials, 264. *See also by name*

Floods and flooding, 6, 109, 111, 159, 201

Florida, 171, 251

Fluorides, pollution by, 132

Foams, as contraceptives, 230, 232

Fog, 195

Food: production of, 4f, 14, 23, 44, 77–96, 277–278; chains, 6–7, 77–81, 138, 153, 156, 166–167, 184, 189f, 192; webs, 6–7, 156–159; supply of, 68–77, 105–106, 200–201, 210–212, 216; from sea, 97–107; novel sources of, 104–105. *See also* Agriculture

Food and Agricultural Organization of the U.N., 48, 71ff, 96

Forage crops, 86, 107

Ford Motor Company: and water pollution, 185

Forests, 106, 109–112, 115, 266; tropical, 2, 82, 89, 91f, 111–112, 159, 162, 181–183; temperate, 81, 110f, 159, 162, 183; destruction of, 109, 159, 162, 181–183, 193–194; clear-cutting of, 110f; soil of, 162, 179

Formaldehyde, 144

Formosa, death rates in, 28

Fossil fuels, 216, 264; and agriculture, 83, 106; pollution by, 125, 137, 165; production of, 152–154, 193; and climate, 194f, 198, 220. *See also* Coal; Natural gas; Oil

Fossilized animals, 155

Four Corners Power Plant, 123f

France: steel consumption in, 65; food
supply in, 74; child mortality rates
in, 75; waste disposal in, 131; and
nuclear weapons, 140; family
planning in, 239, 242; population
data for, 286
Freedman, Jonathan, 146
Frejka, Thomas, 36
Freshwater, 107; pollution of, 137, 183,
185–186, 189f, 196
Frontier attitudes, 39–40
Fruit flies, and caffeine, 144
Fuels. *See* Fossil fuels
Fungi, 137, 153, 185; in soil, 179, 180f,
183
Fusion power plants, 61

GNP, 14, 208–210, 214–215, 260, 272,
281–287
Gambia: family planning in, 240; popula-
tion data for, 281
Ganges Delta, East Pakistan, 201
Ganges Plain, 109
Garbage, 131; burning of, 60, 219
Gas. *See* Natural gas
Gas turbines, 126
Gasoline, 14, 118, 136–137, 220
Geese, 86
General Motors, 262
Genetic defects, and radiation, 139
Genetic variability of population, 158,
167
Genocide, 248
Geological Survey, U.S., 139
Geothermal energy, 58–59
Germany: Nazi, 40, 169; population data
for, 286. *See also* West Germany
Ghana: urbanization in, 43; family plan-
ning in, 240, 242; population data
for, 281
Ghettoes, 145ff
Glaciers, 23, 107
Goats, 86–87
Goods, 206, 209–211, 216
Government: and ecology, 201–202, 206;
and population control, 229, 239,
278–279
Grains, 71, 80, 91, 104f; high-yield, 8, 81,
85, 93–96, 218. *See also* by name
Graphite, 193
Grasshopper, herbicide secretion by, 183
Great Britain: food supply in, 91, 98–99;
air pollution in, 119ff; chlorinated
hydrocarbons in, 171; family plan-
ning in, 242. *See also* United
Kingdom
Greece: food supply in, 74; child mor-
tality rates in, 75; ancient, 109, 135,
230; population data for, 286

Green plants. *See* plants; photosynthesis
Green Revolution, 15, 93–96, 106, 187
Greenhouse effect, 197–199
Greenland, 107; fishing in, 103; ice cap,
136
Gross National Product. *See* GNP
Groundnut. *See* Peanut
Groundwater supplies, 109, 165, 187;
pollution of, 128, 130, 139
Growth rate of populations, 19–29
passim, 225, 244–247, 281–287
Guano, 155f
Guatemala: child mortality rates in, 75;
family planning in, 240; population
data for, 284

Haddam, 129
Haddock, 103
Haiti: forest of, 111; family planning in,
240; population data for, 285
Hanford, Washington, 142
Hardin, Garrett, 99
Hawaii: coral reef destruction in, 160f,
165; abortion in, 235
Health, 115, 117–122 *passim*, 127, 201;
insurance, 252; care, 266
Health, Education, and Welfare, Depart-
ment of (U.S.), 252
Hearing loss, 144–145
Heart, 117, 168
Heat, 15–16, 54; pollution by, 61, 62,
115, 128, 194–199, 220f; and climate,
165, 197–199
Heating: of space, 59, 196, 211; of water,
59, 211
Heliothis virescens, 174
Helium, 63
Hemoglobin, and carbon monoxide, 117
Hepatitis, infectious, 127f
Heptachlor, 180
Herbicides, 128, 165, 181–184
Herbivores, 6f, 77–81, 166f
Heredity, 155
Herring industry, 98–99, 103
Heyerdahl, Thor, 190
Highway systems, 8
High-yield crops, 8, 15, 81ff, 85, 93–96,
164, 173, 218
Homo sapiens, 23, 278. *See also* Humans
Honduras: forests in, 111; family plan-
ning in, 240; population data for, 284
Hong Kong: death rates in, 28, 31; food
production in, 89; family planning
in, 240, 244; population data for, 284
Hormonal insecticides, 178
Hormonal system, and birth control, 224,
231, 233
Housing, 84, 147f; per capita expenditure
for, 210–211

Housing and Urban Development Act, 251
Hubbert, M. King, 55, 57
Huffaker, Carl, 178
Human Environment, U.N. Conference on, 276
Humans, 271–274, 277–279; population growth and structure of, 2–49, 281–287; and environment, 4–8, 114–148, 150–203, 260–266; resource consumption by, 50–67, 106–112, 260–266; and food, 68–106, 156–159; population limitation of, 224–257; social and political systems of, 266–271
Humphrey, Hubert, 269
Humus, 184–185, 187f
Hunger, 70–77, 88, 96, 201
Hydrocarbons, 57, 116–125 *passim*, 219f
Hydroelectric energy, 55, 57f
Hydrofluoric acid, 193
Hydrogen peroxide, 144
Hydrogen sulfide, 4
Hydrologic cycle, 4, 57, 69, 107–108. *See also* Water
Hypertension, 145

IRRI, 85, 95
IUD, 231–232, 242
Iata, Brazil, 163
Ice caps, 107, 136
Iceland: and geothermal energy, 58; fishing in, 98, 103; volcanic activity in, 199; growth rate of, 245; population data for, 285
Illinois, nitrate pollution in, 128
Immigration 20f, 40, 251f
Incaparina, 104–105
Income: per capita, 65; taxes on, 254–255, 268
India, 65, 160f, 170; population growth and structure in, 24, 28, 40, 44f; food supply in, 73f, 86, 88f, 94–95, 105, 109; population data for, 76, 283; abortion in, 234; family planning in, 240ff, 244, 256
Indonesia: steel consumption in, 65; oil in, 66; rice in, 94; volcanic activity in, 199; family planning in, 240; population data for, 284
Industrial Revolution, 25, 216–217
Industries and industrialization, 8, 15, 25f; use of water, 108; pollution by, 125, 128, 131, 137, 186
Infanticide, 230
Infants, 74–76, 128; mortality rates of, 35, 75–76, 235, 248, 281–287
Infectious diseases, 25, 28, 278. *See also by name*

Infrared radiation, 197f
Insecticides: pollution by, 128, 132, 144, 166–178, 180, 183, 189; hormonal, 178. *See also* Pesticides
Insects: and food supply, 80, 83, 96, 105, 172–173; control of, 132, 144, 166–178, 189; resistance to pesticides, 167f
Insurance and insurance companies, 142, 252
Institute of Nutrition for Central America and Panama (INCAP), 104
Integrated pest control, 174, 177–178, 184, 207
Internal combustion engine, 116, 124ff, 187, 219
International Maize and Wheat Improvement Center (CIMMYT), 95
International Rice Research Institute (IRRI), 85, 95
Intrauterine device, 231–232, 242
Ionizing radiation, 139f
Iran: family planning in, 240; population data for, 283
Iraq: family planning in, 240; population data for, 283
Ireland: food supply in, 74; potato famine in, 164; family planning in, 239; population data for, 285
Iron, 63, 65f, 131
Iron oxide, in soil, 162
Irrigation, 14, 80, 90–93, 108f, 218; with sea water, 93
Isaacson, Peter A., 156, 170
Isodrin, 168, 180
Israel: food supply in, 74; DDT in, 170; population data for, 283
Itai-itai, 138
Italy: and geothermal energy, 58; food supply in, 74; child mortality rates in, 75; deforestation in, 109; water pollution in, 187; family planning in 239, 241f; population data for, 286
Ivory Coast: urbanization of, 43; population data for, 281

Jamaica: death rates in, 28; bauxite mines in, 53; family planning in, 240; population data for, 285
Japan, 65, 112, 199; food supply in, 13, 74, 95, 99, 102, 273; population structure in, 28, 31–32, 39f; population data for, 75, 284; pollution in, 138–139; abortion in, 234; family planning in, 242
Jellies, as contraceptives, 230, 232
Jet airplanes, 199, 264; SSTs, 144f
Johnson, Lyndon B., 269
Johnston, Bruce F., 273

Jordan: family planning in, 240; population data for, 283

Kaneohe Bay, Oahu, Hawaii, 160f
Kazakhstan, 91
Kenya: family planning in 240; population data for, 282
Keyfitz, Nathan, 35, 44
Khmer civilization, 162f
Khmer Republic: family planning in, 240; population data for, 284
Khrushchev, Nikita S., 91
Knipling, E. F., 176
Korea, Republic of: death rates in, 28; population data for, 284
Krakatoa, 199
Kwashiorkor, 76

LSD, 143
Labor, 265–266; child, 32; agricultural, 184
Labrador, fishing in, 103
Lactation, as contraceptive method, 232
Lagos, Nigeria, growth rate of, 43
Lakes, pollution of, 185–187, 193, 196
Land, 51–54; exploitation of, 4f, 7f, 218; arable, 52, 83, 89–92. *See also* Agriculture
Landfill, sanitary, 131
Landsberg, Helmut E., 197
Laos: rubber in, 53; family planning in, 240; population data for, 284
Laterization of soil, 162–163
Latin America: population growth and structure in, 24ff, 29, 42f, 227; population data for, 46f, 75f, 284–285, 287; food supply and production in, 71, 73–74, 86–90, 94, 104–105; abortion in, 234; education in, 273–274. *See also by country.*
Lead, 63, 65f, 115, 220; pollution by, 132, 135–137, 139, 190, 212–250
Lead arsenate, 173
Lebanon: family planning in, 240; population data for, 283
Legal system, 143, 188, 234–235, 239, 254–255
Legislation, 251–252
Legumes, 86, 154
Libya: food supply in, 74; population data for, 281
Life expectancy: primitive, 23; and radiation, 140
Lima, Peru, Rimac district, 42
Limestone, 152–154
Lindane, 132, 168
Litter, 115
Liver: cirrhosis of, 120, 134f; and chlorinated hydrocarbons, 134f, 168

Livestock, 4, 15, 53f, 80, 176, 188; as food, 85–87; feed for, 86, 104f
Logging, 111f, 115, 159
London, smog disaster, 117
Long Island, 139; estuary, 156–158, 166 170
Los Angeles, 43, 83, 136, 148; air pollution in, 111, 117–125 *passim*, 219; thermal pollution in, 195; zoning in, 251
Los Angeles County Air Pollution Control District (APCD), 122, 125
Lovering, T. S., 62
Lucerne, 86
Lumbering, 54, 110ff, 115, 159f
Lundberg, Ferdinand, 268
Lungs, and air pollution, 115, 117–121 *passim*, 217
Lusaka, Zambia, growth rate of, 43
Luxembourg: food supply in, 74; population data for, 286
Lygus bug, 174
Lysine, 104

M.I.T. Study of Critical Environmental Problems, 139, 194
Mahogany, 111
Maine, Gulf of, 103
Maize. *See* Corn
Malaria, 27f, 167
Malathion, 169
Malaya, death rates in, 28
Malaysia: family planning in, 240, 244; population data for, 284
Mali: family planning in, 240; population data for, 281
Malnutrition, 70, 73–77, 201
Man: primitive, 22–23, 40; modern, 23, 278. *See also* Humans
Manganese, 63ff
Mangrove forests, 182f
Manhattan, population density in, 39
Manure, 60, 184, 186, 188
Marasmus, 76
Marriage, 247, 255
Marshes, 53, 150, 170, 218
Mass transit, 264
Massachusetts, oil spill, 190, 192
Mauritius: age composition of population of, 30–31; food supply in, 74; child mortality rates in, 75; family planning in, 240; population data for, 282
McCarthy, Eugene, 269
McCloskey, Paul, 269
McGovern, George, 269
McNeil, Mary, 162–163
Meat, 85, 87, 107
Medical practice, 25, 140, 230, 261, 273

Mediterranean Sea, 93, 187
Megalopolis, 197
Mendota, Lake, Wisconsin, 193, 219
Mental illness, 146
Mercury, 63, 165; pollution by, 115f,
    132, 137–139, 190, 192, 220
Metals, 14f, 62–66, 69; precious, 63;
    heavy, 115, 135–139, 190. *See also*
    by name
Methylmercury, 137–138, 190
Mexico, 95; population growth in, 26–27;
    steel use in, 65; food supply in, 74,
    89, 95; population data in, 75, 284;
    family planning in, 240
Middle Ages: deforestation in, 109; birth
    control in, 230
Middle East, 23; oil in, 13, 66. *See also*
    by country
Migration, 20, 25, 39
Mildews, 105
Military, the: expenditures of, 13; and
    abortion, 252
Milk, 87, 107; human, 132
Milk, human, and DDT, 132
Millet, 85
Minamata City, Japan, 138
Minerals, 13, 62–67, 106, 216; as
    nutrients, 76, 86. *See also by name*
Mines, and waste disposal, 131
Minimata disease, 138
Missouri, nitrate pollution in, 128
Mites, 169, 179, 181; European red, 169
Molds, 105
Molybdenum, 63
Momentum of population growth, 10–12
Monocultures, 8, 164, 172, 218
Monuron, 181
Morgan, Karl Z., 140
Morning-after pill, 238
Morocco: family planning in, 240, 244;
    population data for, 281
Mosquitoes, 27, 167, 170, 177–178
Moths, 169, 174
Motor vehicles, pollution control
    devices, 123, 126. *See also*
    Automobiles
Mountains, 52, 196; volcanoes, 115, 199f
Mussels, and oil spills, 192
Mutagens, 143–144, 201
Mutations, 127, 140
Mysore State, 94

Nader, Ralph, 270
Nairobi, Kenya, population of, 42–43
National Academy of Sciences/National
    Research Council: Committee on
    Resources and Man, 142
National Forests, 111f
Natural gas, 55, 57, 152f

Natural selection, 7
Near East, food production in, 88. *See*
    also by country
Negroes, and birth control, 248
Nepal: family planning in, 240;
    population data for, 283
Nerve gas, 169
Nervous system: and chlorinated
    hydrocarbons, 134, 168; and
    mercury, 138; and noise, 144; and
    organophosphates, 168
Netherlands, the: food supply in, 74, 95;
    population density of, 228; family
    planning in, 239; population data
    for, 286
Netherlands Fallacy, 228
New Jersey, nitrogen pollution in, 193
New Mexico, 123
New York City: population density in,
    39, 43; air pollution in, 116; slums
    of, 145
New York state, abortion in, 235, 237
New Zealand: and geothermal energy, 58;
    food supply in, 74, 98; arable land
    in, 90; population data for, 286
Newfoundland, fishing in, 103
Newsprint consumption, 65
Nicaragua: family planning in, 240;
    population data for, 285
Niche, defined, 158
Nickel, 13, 63ff, 139
Nicotine, 167–168
Nigeria: urbanization in 43; and peanuts,
    54; family planning in, 240;
    population data for, 282
Nile delta, 93
Nitrates, 4, 128, 154f, 165, 184–188
Nitrites, 128, 55, 165
Nitrogen: cycle, 4, 152, 154–155, 165,
    180, 184; fertilizer, 65, 184–185, 213;
    fixing bacteria, 86, 154f; in soils,
    184–185; pollution, 184–185, 193f
Nitrogen dioxide, 120
Nitrogen mustards, 144
Nitrogen oxides, 116–125 *passim*, 193,
    213, 220
Nitrous acid, 144
Nixon, Richard M., 112, 252, 269f
Noise pollution, 115, 144–145
North America: population growth in,
    24f, 227; population data for, 46ff,
    75, 284, 287; resources of, 90, 109f;
    and mercury, 190. *See also* Canada;
    United States of America
North Carolina, soil of, 179
North Korea, family planning in, 240
North Pole, 116, 200
North Sea, 103
North Vietnam, family planning in, 240

Norway, 25, 116f; food supply in, 74, 98f; family planning in, 242; population data for, 285
Notestein, Frank, 48
Nova Scotia, forests of, 110
Nuclear power, 14, 55, 60–61, 140–143, 195; reactors, 14, 60, 129, 140–143, 195; weapons, 140
Nutrition, 70–77, 201
Nylon, 215f

Oats, 85
Ocean, 4f, 8, 107, 190; desalination of, 14, 92f, 108; minerals from, 67; food from, 96–104; pollution of, 98, 115, 137, 183, 186, 189–193, 195; smog over, 118; deep-sea sediments, 154ff; life in, 183, 189, 195; currents of, 196
Ocean perch, 103
Oceania: population growth in, 25; population data for, 46f, 75, 286f. *See also by country*
Oil, 13, 15, 55–57, 64ff, 152f; shales, 55n, 57; spills, 61, 128, 190–192, 218; pollution by, 115, 118, 122, 190–192; industry, 128, 174–177
Oilseed, 89, 104
Old Testament, 230
Oral contraceptive pills, 224, 231f, 239
Orange groves, 84
Oregon, zoning policies of, 251
Organophosphates, 144, 168f, 174–175, 177, 181
Orientals in U.S., 248
Overgrazing, 115, 160f, 218
Oxidants, 116, 124
Oxidation, defined, 153
Oxygen, 184ff; in atmosphere, 4, 193–194; and photosynthesis, 78, 153, 193
Oysters, 102, 166, 186, 192
Ozone, 4, 116, 124, 193

PCBs, 132, 165, 170–171, 192
Pakistan: steel consumption in, 65; food supply in, 73f; agriculture in, 92, 94f; family planning in, 240ff, 244; population data for, 283
Panama: food production in, 89, 104; family planning in, 240; population data for, 285
Panama, Isthmus of, 2
Paper and pulp industry, 65, 111f, 118f, 137
Paraguay: food supply in, 74; population data for, 285
Parasites, 75f
Parathion, 169
Parks, urban, 266

Particulate pollution, 118ff, 122, 132, 194, 199, 220
Pasadena, California, 124
Patterson, Clair C., 136
Peanuts, 54, 86
Peas, 86
Peat bogs, oxidation of, 198
Pelican, brown, 170f
Pennsylvania, 131
Peptic ulcer, 145
Peregrine falcon, 170–172
Personal options, 261–262
Peru: urbanization in, 42; food supply in, 74, 89, 99; child mortality rates in, 75; pest-control program in, 173–174; family planning in, 240; population data for, 285
Pest control, 173–178; integrated, 174, 177–178, 184, 207. *See also* Pesticides
Pesticides, 207, 212f; and Green Revolution, 93–96; pollution by, 128, 132–135, 139, 144, 165–178, 180, 183, 189; spraying, 176; mentioned, 14, 83. *See also by name*
Peterson, M. R., 134
Petrel, Bermuda, 170
Petroleum. *See* Oil
Philadelphia, 83
Philippines: death rates in, 28; food supply in, 74, 105; child mortality rates in, 75; IRRI, 85, 95; rice, 85, 94; family planning in, 240; population data for, 284
Phosdrin, 169
Phosphates, 65, 155f, 184, 186f, 193, 213
Phosphorus, 86, 162, 180; cycle, 4, 152, 155–156
Photosynthesis, 15, 77–80, 83, 152f; defined, 6; and pollution, 181, 183f, 189f
Phytoplankton, 184, 189f, 192; farming, 102
Picloram, 181, 183
Pigs, 86–87
Pill, the, 224, 231f, 239
Pindar, 107
Plague, worldwide, 278
Plaice, 103
Plankton, 97
Planned Parenthood, 239, 241
Plants, 107, 125, 184, 193–194; green, 6, 77–80, 151, 153, 189; breeding of, 80, 84; chemical defenses of, 167–168, 172, 181, 183. *See also* Agriculture; Photosynthesis
Plastics, 57, 212, 216
Platinum, 63
Plutonium, 143

Pneumonia, 120
Polar desert, 2
Police, 261
Political system, 268–269; reform of, 269–271, 278–279
Pollution, 12, 150, 212–213; control of, 14, 123, 125, 219–221, 263f, 266, 278; of air, 61, 83, 111–127 *passim*, 132, 136, 146, 194, 199, 219–220, 263; of water, 61, 98, 108, 111, 115, 127–130, 132, 137, 184–196 *passim*, 217, 219f; by wastes, 61, 115, 127–132 *passim*, 139–143, 165 185–188, 193, 217; by radiation, 61, 115, 128, 139–143, 165; by heat, 61–62, 115, 128, 194–199, 220f; and agriculture, 96, 128, 131f, 137, 184–187, 189, 198; by heavy metals, 115, 135–139, 190; by noise, 115, 144–145; and cities, 118–126, 131, 145–148, 194–197; by pesticides, 128, 132–135, 139, 144, 165–178, 180, 183, 189; by fertilizers, 128, 164, 184ff, 187; and chemical mutagens, 143–144; and soil, 178–181, 185, 187; of atmosphere, 185, 193–200
Polychlorinated biphenyls. *See* PCBs
Population, 4–16 *passim*, 205–221, 277f; growth rates of, 19–29 *passim*, 225, 244–247, 281–287; birth rates of, 20–23, 25–27, 30–33, 36, 48, 235, 244–246, 249, 281–287; death rates of, 20–36 *passim*, 49, 147, 225, 229, 245f, 281–287; history of, 22–29; age composition of, 29–36, 247, 281–287; structure of, 29–46; distribution and dispersion of, 29–30, 37–40, 201, 250–251; zero growth of, 36, 225, 247, 251–253; density of, 37–39, 51f, 227–228; data and projections for, 46–49, 281–287; genetic variability in, 158, 167; limitation of, 224–257, 259
Population Growth and the American Future, Commission on, 237, 251f
Population Reference Bureau: 1972 *World Population Data Sheet*, 29, 281–287
Pork, 87
Port Angeles, Washington, 118f
Portugal: food supply in, 74; child mortality rates in, 75; family planning in, 239; population data for, 286
Potash, 65
Potassium, 152, 162
Potatoes, 85, 164
Poultry, 86–87

Poverty, 13, 88, 146–147, 247f
Precipitation, 91, 107f, 185, 195
Pregnancy, 73f, 231
President's Science Advisory Committee Panel on the World Food Supply, 70f, 73, 76, 89, 106, 173
Presscake, 86, 89
Price-Anderson Act, 142
Primogeniture, 39
Progestin, as contraceptive, 237
Prostaglandins, 238
Protein, 89, 104, 154; deficiency, 70, 76–77; requirements, 72f; supplies, 74, 81, 85f; from sea, 99, 102
Protestants, and abortion, 235
Protozoa in soil, 179
Public Health Service (U.S.), 122, 129, 139, 185, 190
Puerto Rico, 43; death rates in, 28; family planning in, 240; population data for, 285
Pulmonary embolism, 231
Pyrethrins, 167–168
Pyrethrum, 177

RNA, 155
Racial minorities, 248, 265; in cities, 145ff
Rad, defined, 139
Radiation pollution, 115, 139–143. *See also* Radioactive substances
Radioactive substances: pollution by, 61, 128, 139–143, 165; storage of, 141f
Rainfall. *See* Precipitation
Rangeland, 53
Rats, and food loss, 105f
Recreation, 111, 261
Recycling, 131–132, 263f, 266
Redwood forest, 110
Refrigerators, in use, per capita, 210
Refuse, 60, 131, 219
Refuse Act of 1899, 129
Religion, 266–267
Replacement reproduction, 10, 35–37
Republic Steel, and water pollution, 185
Resources, 260–266, 279; consumption of, 11, 13, 206–207, 216, 221; renewable, 68–112, 226f. *See also by name*
Resources in America's Future, 108
Respiration, cellular, 152f
Respiratory diseases, 115, 116–121
Restaurants, spraying in, 132
Retirement, 265
Rhine River, pollution in, 187
Rhodesia: family planning in, 240; population data for, 282
Rhythm system, of birth control, 230–232, 239

Rice, 84–86, 88, 91, 105, 107; and
    beri-beri, 76; high-yield, 85,
    93ff, 164
Rickets, 76
Rioting, urban, 145
Risebrough, Robert W., 132
Rivers, 108, 127, 186, 196f
Riverside County, California, smog in,
    117
Rock music, 144f
Rocks, minerals in, 62, 67
Roman Catholic Church and birth
    control, 230–231, 235, 237, 239, 245
Roman civilization, 109, 135
Rosier, Bernard, 75
Rotenone, 177
Rubber, 53, 65f, 182f
Rudd, Robert L., 173
Rumania: fishing in, 98; growth rate of,
    245; population data for, 286
Runoff, 108–109; agricultural, 128,
    184–187
Rural areas, 43f, 146, 195. *See also*
    Agriculture
Rye, 85
Ryther, J. H., 97

SSTs, 144f
Sahara Desert, 130, 159–160
St. Louis, Missouri, 120, 147
Sakharov, Andrei D., 272, 279
Salinization of land, 92
Salpingectomy, 233f, 242
San Andreas Fault, 201f
San Bernardino, California, smog in, 117
San Francisco, 131, 141
San Francisco Bay, 52, 190f
San Francisco Bay Area, 150, 201f
San Pedro Bay, 122
San Rafael, California, 52
Sandstone, 162
Santa Barbara, oil leak, 190
Sardine fishery, 93
Saskatchewan River, mercury
    concentration in, 137
Saudi Arabia: family planning in, 240;
    population data for, 283
Scale, cottony cushion, 177
Scandinavia, family planning in, 239.
    See also by country
Schistosomiasis, 93
Science, 189
Scotland, DDT in, 170
Screwworm, 176–177
Sea. *See* Ocean
Sea cucumbers, 161
Seals, DDT in, 170
Seattle, sewage treatment in, 219
Seaweed culture, 102

Senegal: family planning in, 240;
    population data for, 282
Services, availability of, 261
Sewage: pollution by, 115, 127, 185–188,
    217; treatment of, 127, 187, 219f; in
    cities, 146; recycled, 188–189; oil in,
    192
Sex determination, 255
Sex education, 252, 267
Sex ratio of population, 29f, 37
Shantytowns, 42
Sheep, 54, 86–87. *See also* Livestock
Shell Chemical Co., 174–176
Shellfish, 102, 127, 192. *See also by
    name*
Shetland Islands, 98–99
Shrimp, 89
Sierra Club, the, 269
Silt, pollution by, 115, 160f, 165
Simazin, 181
Simrad Echo, 98
Signapore: death rate in, 31; family
    planning in, 240, 244; population
    data for, 284
Single-cell protein (SCP), 104
Skaptar, Mount, 199
Slash-and-burn agriculture, 80, 82
Sludge, 188–189
Slums, 42f, 145
Smallpox, 28; vaccination, 24
Smelters, 131
Smith, Ray F., 173
Smog, 114–125 *passim,* 195; and plants,
    83, 111, 217
Smokestack emission laws, 125
Snow, C. P., 272, 279
Social sciences, 267–268
Social system, 266–268
Socioeconomic measures, and population
    control, 254–257
Sodium nitrite, 144
Soil: erosion, 6, 109, 111; tropical, 89,
    91, 162–163; salt in, 92; abuses of,
    159–163; pollutants in, 178–181,
    183–185, 187; microorganisms in,
    178–181, 193
Solar energy, 4, 6, 16, 57, 152f; and
    heat, 59–60; and food chains, 77–80;
    and climate, 83, 196–198
Solid wastes, 14, 130–132, 219
Sonic booms, 144f
Sorghum, 85, 94
South Africa: food supply in, 74; family
    planning in, 240; population data
    for, 283
South America: child mortality rates in,
    75; arable land in, 90; population
    density in, 227; population data for,
    285. *See also by country*

South Korea, family planning in, 240, 242ff
South Vietnam, family planning in, 240
Soybeans, 54, 86, 89
Space heating, 59, 196, 211
Spaceman economy, 260–264, 271
Spaceship Earth, concept of, 260, 277, 279
Spain: food supply in, 74; child mortality rates in, 75; family planning in, 239; population data for, 286
Sparrowhawks, 171f
Species, 7, 156, 158; extinction of, 8, 218
Sperm, frozen, 233
Spices, 172
Spokane, Washington, 250f
Stability, ecological, 6–7, 83, 156–159, 163–164
Starvation, 74–77, 88, 96
Staten Island, New York, 121
Steam engines, 126
Steel, 65f, 116, 131, 209
Steinbach, Alan, 134
Steppe, 52
Sterilization, 231, 233–234, 252, 256; reversible, 233, 238; in UDCs, 241ff, 254
Steroid contraception 224, 231f, 237
Strip-mining, 111, 124, 128, 188, 266
Suburbs, 43–44, 146f
Sudan: family planning in, 240; population data for, 281
Sugar, 85f
Sugar beet, 86
Sugar cane, 86, 105
Sulfur, 4, 152, 180
Sulfur dioxide, 115, 120ff, 193, 217
Sulfur oxides, 116f, 124, 219
Sumbawa, 199
Supersonic transports, 144f
Suppositories, as contraceptives, 232
Surinam: food supply in, 74; population data for, 285
Sweden, 25, 27, 183; steel in, 65; food supply in, 74; population data for, 75, 285; abortion in, 234, 236
Sweet potatoes, 86
Sweezy, Alan, 255
Switzerland: steel consumption in, 65; food supply in, 74; population data for, 285
Swordfish, mercury concentration in, 138
Sydney, Australia, 118
Synergisms, 121, 217–218
Synthetic fiber industry, 215f
Syria: food supply in, 74; child mortality rates in 75; family planning in, 240; population data for, 283

2, 4, 5-T, 181, 183
Tepp, 169
Taiwan: death rates in, 28; food supply in, 74; child mortality rates in, 74; family planning in, 240, 242ff; agriculture in, 273; population data for, 284
Tambora, Mount, 199
Tanganyika. *See* Tanzania
Tantalum, 63
Tanzania: groundnut project in, 91; family planning in, 240; population data for, 282
Taxes: on autos, 126; and waste disposal, 131, 264; and population control, 252, 254f; income, 254–255, 268
Technology, 13–15, 80–81, 205–207, 211–221 *passim*, 226
Teenagers: hearing loss in, 144f; and crime rates, 146
Temperate Zone, 85, 87, 89, 91; forests of, 81, 110f, 162, 183
Tetraethyl lead, 136
Thai Desert, 160
Thailand: child mortality rates in, 75; family planning in, 240, 242; population data for, 284
Thermal inversion, 122
Thermal pollution, 61–62, 115, 128, 194–199, 220f
Thermodynamics, Laws of, 54, 61, 78–80, 166f, 194
Thermonuclear fusion 14, 60–61
Thermonuclear war, 278
Thiamine, 76
Threshold effects, 217
Thromboembolism, 231
Throughput, 209–210, 260–262, 264–265
Tibet, 40
Tidal energy, 57f
Tidal wave, 201
Tigris river, 41
Time, 48
Tin, 13, 63, 65f
Tissue, human, and chlorinated hydrocarbons, 132, 134–135, 168f
Tobacco leafworm, 174
Tobago: child mortality rates in, 75; family planning in 240, 244; population data for, 285
Tokyo: population density in, 39; growth rate of, 44–45; smog in, 114, 118
Toledo, Ohio, and water pollution, 185
Toxaphene, 168, 173f, 180
Trains, 264
Transpiration, in plants, 107f, 159
Transportation, 211, 264, 266, 273; integrated systems of, 126; in cities, 146f, 148

Trash-fired power plants, 131
Trees, 180, 217. *See also* Forests
Trinidad: death rate in, 31; child
    mortality rates in, 75; family
    planning in, 240, 244; population
    data for, 285
Trout: effect of DDT on, 134
Tropics, 87, 89, 91–92; forests of, 2, 82,
    89, 91f, 111–112, 159, 162, 181–183;
    soil of, 89, 91, 162–163
Tubal ligation, 233f, 242
Tubers, 85
Tuna, 99; mercury in, 138
Tungsten, 63f
Tunisia: family planning in, 240;
    population data for, 281
Turkey: food supply in, 74; arable land
    in, 91; erosion in, 161; family
    planning in, 240, 242, 244;
    population data for, 283
Turkeys, 86
2–5 Dichlorophenol, 183
2, 4-D, 181, 183
2, 4, 5-T, 181, 183

UDCs, 13f, 221; population growth and
    structure in, 27–33, 35, 42–44, 47f;
    resource consumption in, 55, 58, 60,
    62–63, 65–66, 262f; food supply and
    production in, 70f, 73, 76–77, 87–90,
    93–95; and population limitation,
    226–227, 234, 237, 240–246, 253;
    aid to, 271–274; and wealth
    redistribution, 271–274, 279. *See
    also by country*
Uganda: family planning in, 240;
    population data for, 282
Ultraviolet radiation, 4
Underdeveloped countries,
    See UDCs
Undernutrition, 70, 73, 75n, 76f
Unemployment, 265–266
Union of Soviet Socialist Republics,
    population growth in, 25, 40;
    population projections for, 46f, 286f;
    resource use in, 65, 90f, 110–111;
    and fishing, 98f, 102; nuclear
    weapons of, 140; water pollution in,
    187, abortion in, 234; family
    planning in, 241; and UDCs, 272
United Arab Republic: food supply in,
    74; child mortality rates in, 75;
    population data for, 283
United Kingdom: population data for,
    30–31, 75, 285; steel consumption in,
    65; food supply in, 74, 91, 98–99;
    pollution in, 119ff, 140, 170f, 199;
    family planning in, 230, 242; birth
    control in, 231, 234

United Nations: population projections
    of, 46–48; FAO, 48, 71ff, 96;
    Conference on the Human
    Environment, 276
United States of America, 213–215, 218,
    260–271; resource use in, 13, 50,
    50–66 *passim*, 108–112; population
    growth and structure in, 21, 26, 31–44
    passim, 207–208, 214, 228,
    246–252, 278–279; food supply and
    production in, 70–71, 75, 83–89
    passim, 99; population data for, 75f,
    284; pollution in, 116–122, 127–132,
    136–142 *passim*, 170, 172–177,
    183, 184–189; 195–197, 199, 204,
    220; affluence in, 208–211; family
    planning in, 230, 239, 241f, 245;
    birth control in, 233–239
University of California, 175–176
University of California at Los Angeles,
    117
Upper Volta: family planning in, 240;
    population data for, 282
Uranium, 60, 128, 143
Urban II, Pope, 39
Urbanization, 8, 40–46, 52, 83. *See also*
    Cities
Utah, sterilization laws in, 233

Van den Bosch, Robert, 176, 178
Vanadium, 63
Vasectomy, 233f, 242f
Vedalia beetles, 177
Vegetables, 85, 107
Venezuela: food supply in, 74; child
    mortality rates in, 75; family
    planning in, 240; population data
    for, 285
Vietnam, 181–183; population data for,
    284
Vital rates, 35. *See also* Death rates;
    Fertility rates
Vitamins, 76, 86
Vogt, William, 172
Volcanoes, 115, 199f

Wales, child mortality rates in, 75
Wankel engines, 126
Washington, Lake, 219
Washington, state of, abortion in, 235
Wastes: disposal of, 5, 8, 78, 141f, 146;
    solid, 14, 130–132, 219; radioactive,
    61, 128, 139–143, 165; pollution by,
    61, 115, 127–132 *passim*, 139–143,
    165, 185–188, 193, 217; sewage, 115,
    127, 146, 185–189, 192, 217, 219f;
    treatment of, 127, 129, 187, 219f
Water: cycle, 4, 57, 69, 107–108; and
    agriculture, 14, 80, 90–95, 108f, 218;

Water (*continued*)
estuarine, 52f, 137, 166, 186, 190,
218; as resource, 69, 106–109; and
photosynthesis, 78; projects, 92–93,
108; fresh, 107, 183, 185–186, 189f,
196; runoff, 108–109, 128, 184–187;
groundwater supply, 109, 128, 130,
139, 165, 187; and carbon cycle, 153;
and climate, 194, 197; consumption
of, 209, 216. *See also* Ocean; Water,
pollution of, 108, 111, 127–130; from
coal mining, 61; of ocean, 98, 115,
137, 183, 186, 189–193, 195; by
sewage, 115, 127, 185–188, 217, 219f;
by heavy metals, 115, 137, 139; and
agriculture, 128, 132, 184–187; by
pesticides, 132; of freshwater, 137,
183, 185–186, 189f, 196; by
nitrogen and phosphates, 185–187;
by heat, 195
Water buffalo, 86–87
Water hyacinths, 105
Water Pollution Control Act (1972), 130
Watt, K. E. F., 173
Wayne County, Michigan, and water
pollution, 185
Wealth, 13, 221; redistribution of,
271–272, 279
Weather system, 80, 196, 198f. *See also*
Climate
Welfare, 227, 248
West Germany: food supply in, 74;
child mortality rates in, 75
West Pakistan: agriculture in, 92;
population of, 287
Western Hemisphere, 23f, 39–40
Western Samoa, family planning
in, 240
Whale fisheries, 98, 100–101
Wheat, 82, 84ff, 88, 104, 107;
high-yield, 85, 93–96, 164
Wheat-rust fungus, 85
Wind currents, 196
Wind energy, 57
Winnipeg, Canada, 120

Wisconsin: nitrate pollution in, 128;
water pollution in, 193, 219
Withdrawal: as birth control method,
230, 232, 239
Women's rights, 230, 251, 255; liberation
movement, 34, 249–250
Wood, consumption of, 216; lumber, 54,
110ff, 115, 159f; as fuel, 55; as
cattle feed, 105
Woods Hole Oceanographic Institution,
97, 190
Woodwell, George M., 156, 170
Wool, 215
Work week, length of, 266
World: population of, 10f, 15, 19–29
passim, 46–49, 287; resource
consumption of, 55, 62, 64; food
production and supply of, 70, 72f,
271–274
Wurster, Charles F., 156, 170, 189

X-rays, 139f

Yams, 86
Yeast, in soil, 179
Yellow fever, 28
Yemen: family planning in, 240;
population data for, 283
Yields, maximum sustainable, 70
Youth: in population, 10; and
employment, 265f
Yugoslavia: food supply in, 74; child
mortality rates in, 75; population
data for, 286

Zaire: family planning in, 240;
population data for, 282
Zambia: urbanization, 43; copper mines
in, 53; population data for, 282
Zero growth of population, 36, 225,
247, 251–253
Zero Population Growth, 250, 269
Zinc, 63, 66
Zoning, 126, 250–251